TRENDS IN DYSLEXIA RESEARCH

TRENDS IN DYSLEXIA RESEARCH

HENRY D. TOBIAS
EDITOR

Nova Biomedical Books
New York

Editorial Production Manager: Donna Dennis
Senior Production Editor: Susan Boriotti
Production Editors: Marius Andronie, Rusudan Razmadze and Keti Datunashvili
Office Manager: Annette Hellinger
Graphics: Magdalena Nuñez
Editorial Production: Maya Columbus, Vladimir Klestov, Lorna Loperfido and Joanne Overton
Circulation: Ave Maria Gonzalez, Vera Popovic, Luis Aviles, Alexandra Columbus, Raymond Davis, Cathy DeGregory, Melissa Diaz, Marlene Nuñez and Jeannie Pappas

Library of Congress Cataloging-in-Publication Data
Trends in dyslexia research / Henry D. Tobias, editor.
p. cm.
Includes bibliographical references and index.
ISBN 1- 59454-219-8(hardcover)
1. Dyslexia
[DNLM: 1. Dyslexia. WL 340.6 T792 2004] I. Tobias, Henry D.
RC394.W6T74 2004
616.85'53--dc22 2004023371

An imprint of Nova Science Publishers, Inc.
400 Oser Ave, Suite 1600
Hauppauge, New York 11788-3619
Tele. 631-231-7269 Fax 631-231-8175
e-mail: Novascience@earthlink.net
Web Site: http://www.novapublishers.com

Printed in the United States of America

CONTENTS

PREFACE

Dyslexia is a brain-based type of learning disability that specifically impairs a person's ability to read. Although the disorder varies from person to person, common characteristics among people with dyslexia are difficulty with phonological processing (the manipulation of sounds) and/or rapid visual-verbal responding. The syndrome of dyslexia does not imply low intelligence or poor educational potential, and is independent of race and social background. Although dyslexia seems to be more prevalent among males than females, the exact ratio is unknown: the most commonly quoted figures are between 3:1 and 5:1. The evidence suggests that in at least two-thirds of cases, dyslexia has a genetic cause, but in some cases birth difficulties may play a role.

Dyslexia may overlap with related conditions such as dyspraxia, attention deficit disorder (with or without hyperactivity) and dysphasia. In childhood, its effects can be mis-attributed to emotional or behavioral disorders. By adulthood, many dyslexics will have developed sophisticated compensating strategies that may mask their difficulties. This new book presents state-of-the-art research in this dynamic field.

In the process of learning how to read and to write, one uses the sensory systems of audition, vision, and optomotor control. While the sense organs may be completely intact, neural information processing and saccade control within the various brain structures may exhibit developmental deficits, which impede the learning process and contribute to problems encountered in dyslexia. Chapter I describes the age development, developmental deficits and training in large groups of control and dyslexic children (age 7 to 17 years). Five tasks of low level auditory discrimination, three of dynamic vision, one of subitizing, and two of saccade control have been administred. Normal development is assessed and compared with that of the dyslexics. The analysis reveals systematic specific deficits in all domains, but only certain precentages of dyslexics are affected depending on age and task. Specific and individual daily procedures have been used to improve those deficits diagnosed earlier. The success rates are presented for the different domains. Advantages in acquiring reading and spelling skills due to the training have been assessed and are presented quantitatively.

Learning to read requires appropriate auditory-phonological and visual-spatial skills. According to the dual-route model, written words can be processed either by a sub-lexical route (analytic procedure), based on grapheme-phoneme correspondences, or by lexical route (global procedure), based on lexical units. However, the sub-lexical and the lexical routes are not independent components of written word recognition. They appear to be reciprocally related with an early role of the sub-lexical route on reading acquisition. Chapter II considers crucial aspects of selective spatial attention in learning to read by the sub-lexical route. First, Andrea Facoetti will briefly review the recent literature on reading acquisition and on the crucial issue of visual and auditory selective attention in reading and dyslexia. Secondly, she will present new empirical evidence of a specific deficit of visual attention in dyslexic children. In particular, Facoetti will report and discuss the results of recent studies related to (a) attention focusing during word reading and letter identification; and (b) the time course of attentional focusing in the left andright visual hemifields. Finally, she will discuss the different behavioral pattern in dyslexic children compared to normally reading children in relation to new studies on the neural basis of reading.

Neuropsychological studies on reading difficulties have raised controversy about whether dyslexics and poor readers (PR) are qualitatively different groups or if they suffer from the same deficiency at different degrees. The aim of the study presented in chapter III was to examine neurophysiological evidence of reading problems by auditory Event-Related Brain Potentials (ERP) and to report new findings on visual ERP recordings from the same sample and discussing them with the works on dyslexics reported in the literature. Gender differences between PR girls and boys in auditory and visual information processing is also discussed. ERP results are compatible with the view that dyslexics and poor readers would be different subgroups of reading-disabled children, as the two groups show different abnormalities in ERP components. In the literature, the main finding reported in dyslexics is an amplitude reduction and, more consistently, a delayed latency of P300 (a component related to the updating of working memory) respect to controls. In the present study, PR displayed higher P300 amplitude than controls to visual stimuli, while for the auditory stimuli PR showed the same amplitude of P300 as controls. Interestingly, in PR an early component (P200) probably related to attention showed significantly greater amplitude in PR than in the control group to both visual and auditory stimuli. For auditory stimuli, these differences were particularly marked in PR girls. In addition, N200 (a component related to stimuli categorization) amplitude was greater in the control than in the PR group for the auditory and visual stimuli. The reported results pointed out that the ERP of dyslexics in oddball tasks have smaller amplitude and delayed latency of P300 with respect to normal readers, showing that their deficiencies are located in those stages associated to stimuli evaluation and memory processing, while the PR group seem to allocate attention resources to both relevant and irrelevant stimuli during early and late stages of the information processing, although these resources could be higher for the early stages, especially during auditory processing.

There are various perceptual dysfunctions that are related to and that might be underlying the reading difficulties in developmental dyslexia. One possible underlying factor might be the malfunctioning of the phonological system or even a more general deficit in the auditory system. Recently a brain response called the mismatch negativity (MMN) has been successfully applied to investigate auditory impairments in dyslexia. It is a brain response elicited by a discriminable change in any repetitive aspect of auditory stimulation even in the absence of attention. Teija Kujala in chapter IV focuses on MMN and its relationship to dyslexia.The fact that the MMN reflects the accuracy of auditory discrimination and that it can be obtained even from unattentive subjects makes it especially attractive for studying various central auditory-system dysfunctions both in adults and children. Several recent studies showed that the MMN enables one to determine which aspects of auditory information are deficiently processed in dyslexia. Furthermore, the MMN amplitude change was recently shown to indicate cortical plastic changes resulting from successful dyslexia remediation.

Poor readers have a low performance in reading tasks but possess better reading skills than children with dyslexia. Many factors have been proposed to explain such reading disability. Among the main factors, a low verbal working memory capacity has been claimed as one of the most important. In the first part of chapter V, Juan Silva-Pereyra and Maritza Rivera-Gaxiola analyzed how the low capacity of the verbal working memory in the poor readers has an effect on the semantic and syntactic processing during sentence reading. This low capacity seems to be a consequence from a general-purpose mechanism of the working memory. In the second part of chapter V, the semantic processing was analyzed. The semantic processing underachievement that has been observed in poor readers is not a semantic deficit *per se*, but the late reflection of an early word codification problem. Poor readers seem to use less efficient and more demanding strategies to process words. These strategies consume extra attentional resources and seem to be slow, with the subject storing and accommodating new difficult information into a memory model before the next word arrives. The most invasive deficit that poor readers face when reading seems to takes place very early, probably at the first encounter with the processing of graphemes. In this way a chain reaction of general slowness is triggered. In the last part of this chapter Silva-Pereyra and Rivera-Gaxiola analyzed the early processing deficiencies in the poor readers, such as visual stimulus evaluation. They have a deficit to classify and memorize stimuli independently of the modality of the stimulus (verbal and non-verbal).

Bilingual aphasia has given rise to much research interest since the beginnings of aphasia studies. Despite this early interest, and despite the fact that bilinguals are not an exceptional population, clinical aphasia assessment and rehabilitation is carried out mostly in one language only. Many factors in fact challenge the management of bilingual or polyglot aphasic patients; these are related to clinicians' competence, to type of bilingualism in terms of skills and use, to language properties and to effects of treatment. In the chapter VI, Marina Laganaro and Mary Overton Venet will focus on some aspects of acquired bilingual alexia by means of a single-case study of a Spanish-English bilingual speaker. Before discussing their studies, they will introduce some aspects of bilingualism and alexia.

Chapter VII describes the main clinical features associated with learning disability in a group of 778 school age children studied in a Neuropsychological Clinic in Mexico City. The study was carried out retrospectively, using data abstracted from clinical records of subjects seen between 1995 and 1996. Children were mainly from low and middle socioeconomic strata and between 6 and 12 years in age. The following data were collected: age, gender, diagnosis, school grade, food intake, maternal complications during pregnancy, perinatal and postnatal neurological risk factors, and neurological signs and handedness. Subjects with learning disability had a mean age of 102.9 months and were predominantly male (male-female ratio 2:1). Among the study group, 49.1% of the children were diagnosed with non-language related learning disability, and 75.1% were from the first three school grades. 27.6% showed evidence of malnutrition, a previous history of language disorder (49.2%), and a high frequency of perinatal risk factors. Neurological soft signs were also found. Thus, this study shows that gender, food intake, and genetic and neurological variables may be associated with learning disability in school children from Mexico City.

Yasuhisa Sakurai in chapter VIII discusses three types of alexia in occipital and occipitotemporal gyrus lesions. Different alexia syndromes from retrorolandic lesions in Japanese patients have been reported. Lesion-to-symptom analysis and previous imaging studies reveal that there are three types of alexia, i.e. pure alexia for Kanji (Japanese morphograms) and Kana (Japanese phonetic writing) from a fusiform gyrus lesion (ventromedial type), pure alexia for Kana from a posterior occipital gyri lesion (posterior type), and alexia with agraphia for Kanji from a posterior inferior temporal cortex lesion. Quantitative examination with Kanji words, Kana words and Kana nonwords showed that Kana nonword reading was impaired in all three types, suggesting that widespread areas in the affected occipital and occipitotemporal cortices are recruited in reading Kana characters (corresponding to European syllables). In ventromedial type pure alexia, whole-word reading, together with letter identification, is primarily impaired because of disconnection between early visual analysis and word-form images that are stored in the posterior inferior temporal cortex, whereas in posterior type pure alexia, letter identification is cardinally impaired. Another type of alexia, alexia with agraphia for Kanji from a posterior inferior temporal cortex lesion, results from deficient whole-word images of words per se, and thus should be designated "orthographic alexia with agraphia." To account for these impairments, a weighted dual-route hypothesis for reading was proposed, in which areas concerned with reading show changes in weight of involvement according to how many times a word is recognized.

A growing body of evidence suggests that developmental dyslexia might arise from impaired information processing, which is based on neural deficiencies. During the last 15 years, research on the neurobiological basis of dyslexia has dealt mainly with 3 different issues of interest: The first one concerns abnormal morphological findings like unusual asymmetries of the temporal plana and deviations of the corpus callosum and cerebellum. The second one concentrates on the analysis of abnormal activation patterns of the left hemispherical frontal and temporal lobe, namely, of the angular gyrus and the Broca's area. Researchers assume that these unusual patterns are connected with phonological deficits. The third one refers to global impairments of subcortical systems that might play a major role in the development of dyslexia. An aberration of magno-cells of the geniculate nucleus is supposed to affect rapid information processing, which results in phonemic discrimination and awareness difficulties. In summary, the evidence for a relation between unusual asymmetries of the temporal plana and dyslexia seems to be very modest at best. A decision between the second and the third approach is beyond the scope of the available empirical data. It still remains unclear whether the information processing deficit is restricted to phonology only, or if there is a general deficit of rapid information processing. In chapter IX Wolfgang Lenhard, Alexandra Lenhard, and Erwin Breitenbach review the current findings and areas of future research concerning the neurobiological basis of developmental dyslexia.

In: Trends in Dyslexia Research
Editor: Henry D. Tobias, pp. 1-33
ISBN 1-59454-219-8

Chapter I

AUDITORY, VISUAL, AND OPTOMOTOR DEVELOPMENT, DEFICITS, AND TRAINING IN DYSLEXIA

Burkhart Fischer and Klaus Hartnegg
Center of Neurosciences, Optomotor Laboratory,
University of Freiburg

ABSTRACT

In the process of learning how to read and to write, one uses the sensory systems of audition, vision, and optomotor control. While the sense organs may be completely intact, neural information processing and saccade control within the various brain structures may exhibit developmental deficits, which impede the learning process and contribute to problems encountered in dyslexia.

This chapter describes the age development, developmental deficits and training in large groups of control and dyslexic children (age 7 to 17 years). Five tasks of low level auditory discrimination, three of dynamic vision, one of subitizing, and two of saccade control have been administred. Normal development is assessed and compared with that of the dyslexics.

The analysis reveals systematic specific deficits in all domains, but only certain precentages of dyslexics are affected depending on age and task.

Specific and individual daily procedures have been used to improve those deficits diagnosed earlier. The success rates are presented for the different domains.

Advantages in acquiring reading and spelling skills due to the training have been assessed and are presented quantitatively.

INTRODUCTION

We do not hear by our ears nor do we see by our eyes. Complex neural processing in the brain is needed before conscious perception is completed and can be reported verbally. Most basic sensory and motor functions develop during the years after birth and may be partly completed by the age of 6 years.

When children enter school at this age the brain has to learn new complex skills and control of coordinated brain activity. Errors in sensory processing which were tolerated before become very important, because if they happen too often, they may impede the process of learning. The acquiring of reading and spelling skills may be especially more difficult for children with deficits in the development of sensory and optomotor functions, as compared with children of the same age with normally developed functions.

This chapter concentrates on auditory, visual, and saccadic eye movement functions that do not require any cognitive nor language processing. The tasks to probe these functions are relatively easy for normally developed adult subjects, but -- as will be seen below -- cause difficulties for children and even more difficulties for dyslexic children between the ages of 7 and 17 years.

The chapter is divided into 3 sections presenting: (i) normal development and its comparison with that of dyslexics of the same age, (ii) the effects of daily practice of those functions that were diagnosed as significantly below the level of the age-matched controls, and (iii) the transfer of these training procedures to spelling and reading.

In any case, mean values and confidence intervals or median values are presented graphically. Where necessary the results of statistical analysis are given.

It is concluded that large proportions of dyslexics have difficulties in one or many of these sensory and optomotor domains, that daily practice helps to improve these functions, and that successful training results in a significant advantage for the dyslexics to learn how to write and to read.

1. Normal Development and Deficits in Dyslexia

The knowledge of normal development is a necessary prerequisite for any diagnosis because as a function depends on age, one needs to know the mean values and standard errors of several age groups. A single subject can then be compared with the data of an age-matched control group.

This section presents the data of large numbers of control subjects and dyslexics between the ages of 7 and 17 years performing standardized tasks under exactly the same conditions.

The different tasks have several aspects in common:

- none of the tasks require language skills nor any other cognitive skill.
- all tasks require a discrimination in a two- or four-alternative-forced-choice-design with the exception of the saccade tasks, which require different types of saccades in one of two horizontal directions.
- during the task performance, no feedback was given as to whether the response was correct or not.
- before each session the tasks were explained and the children were made familiar with the specific task requirements by allowing several trials before the start of the test session.

- failure in one or the other task cannot be explained by low intelligence levels because either their IQ was measured or the child could do one task perfectly well but failed in others with very similar requirements.
- from each task several variables were extracted for which the mean values and standard deviations or the medians were calculated.

1.1. Low Level Auditory Discrimination

The spoken language contains many physical acoustical characteristics that can be used to identify a word. Among them are basic features such as sudden changes in intensity and frequency and short temporal gaps (Buunen and van Valkenburg, 1979), when sound production is briefly interrupted. Moreover, rapidly changing acoustical signals arrive at our ears such that perfect temporal ordering is very important for successful identification of words or their parts (Mc Anally and Stein, 1996); (Merzenich et al. 1996). The signals which arrive at both ears then send information to the auditory brain centers. Incorrect temporal side order between the right and left ear signals may impede word recognition. In a review of speech perception these aspects and others have been discussed (Fitch et al. 1997) and experimental data have been published which show the importance of temporal order in children with reading disabilities (Tallal, 1980).

1.1.1. Methods

Five discrimination tasks were designed to probe the following:

1. intensity discrimination
2. frequency discrimination
3. gap detection
4. temporal order
5. side order

Fig. 1 shows 5 pairs of diagrams that explains the tasks in more detail. In all cases, one hears two different sounds one after the other with a pause of 300ms. The two sounds are very different in the beginning of the test (start value) and become progressively more similar from one trial to the next. After each pair, one has to indicate by key press which of the two was "louder" or "higher" or "contained the gap" and so on. There was no time constraint on the speed of the responses.

This procedure was followed in each task until the subject began to guess and the sequence of responses turned into random sequences of 50% probability (the guess rate) and the threshold was assigned to the subject. Each test lasted about 6 minutes. Test-retest reliability was estimated by the correlation of a first versus a second test result in 31 subjects. Highly significant correlations were found in all 5 tasks.

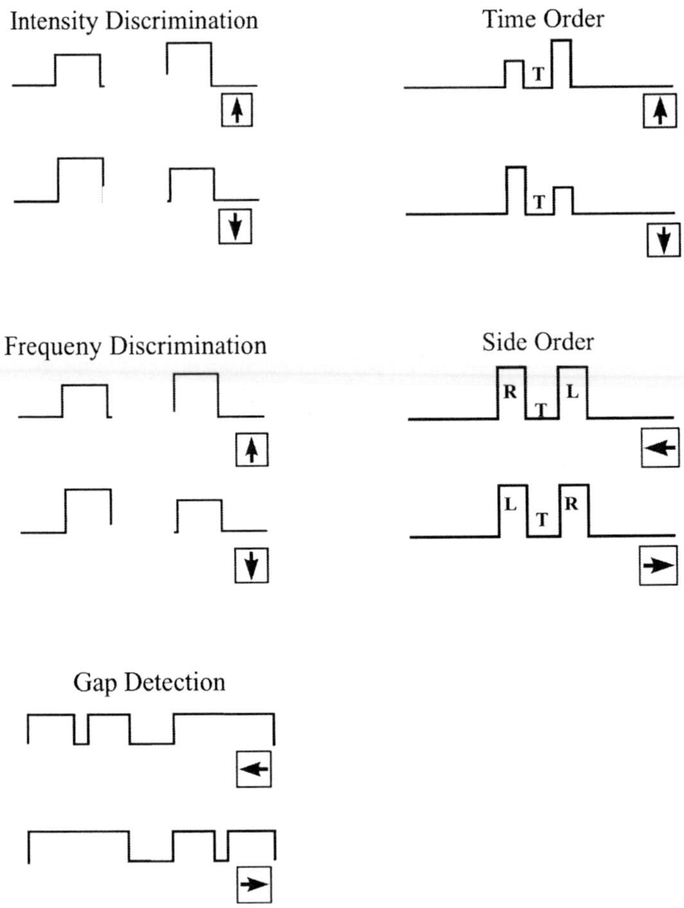

Figure 1. Schematic drawing of the 5 auditory discrimination tasks. In each task, 2 different stimuli are presented one after the other in random order. They can differ in intensity, frequency, or containing a temporal gap. The time order and side order tasks are illustrated at the right side. All tasks are two-alternative-forced-choice tasks. Details are described in the text.

1.1.2. Subjects

Control children (N=401) were recruited from German Grammar schools. They had to pass a standardized spelling test to make sure their skills were within the normal range. Dyslexic children (N=250) were recruited from the "Blicklabor" of the University of Freiburg. They performed below age standards in spelling and/or reading tests (percentiles of DRT below 25), but had normal intelligence as tested by the Kaufmann-ABC test battery or by the HAWIK test. All participants were between 7 and 17 years old and were classified into 4 age groups as follows: 7-8, 9-10, 11-13, and 14-17y.

1.1.3. Results

Low performance: The first observation was that quite a number of children were unable to do one or another task even at its easiest level (start level) and no threshold value could be assigned. These subjects were called low performers (LP) for the particular task. All subjects understood the tasks. There was no correlation between IQ (measured by the HAWIK test in a separate group of 80 children) and test auditory result. They performed some of the tasks quite well but failed in others. None of the control children and only 15 (6%) of the dyslexics failed all 5 tasks.

We first counted the number of tasks that were unsolved for each subject and calculated the mean value for each age group. The corresponding age curves are shown in Fig. 2 for both groups of controls and dyslexics. First, one sees that the normal development goes on until the age of 17 years or even longer as the number of unsolved tasks keeps decreasing. Second, it is evident that the dyslexics failed in more tasks as compared with the controls in any age group. ANOVA results indicated highly significant effects of age and group, but no interaction of (group x age).

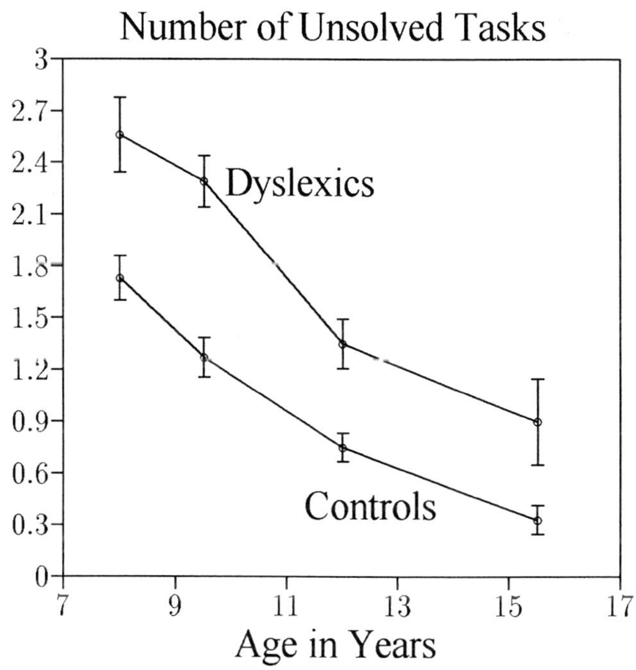

Figure 2. The figure shows the mean of the number of unsolved tasks as a function of age for both groups of subjects. N=401 controls. N=250 dyslexics.

The percent number of LP subjects was also counted for each task and group and plotted as a function of age in Fig. 3. As expected from the previous figure, LP subjects are less frequent as age increases and among the controls they fall below 10% in all tasks at the age of 17 years. Among the dyslexics many more LP subjects are found at all ages. One sees also, that most subjects have considerable problems with the frequency discrimination and time order judgement.

Threshold values: For those children and tasks where a threshold value could be assigned, we also calculated the median values. Fig. 4 shows the pairs of age curves for each of the 5 tasks. Detailed inspection of the curves shows that differences in auditory discrimination depend on both task and age. Most importantly, the median values can be very close, as in the intensity domain, or quite different in all age groups, as in the side order domain. For gap detection, large differences were obtained for the younger children but not for the older.

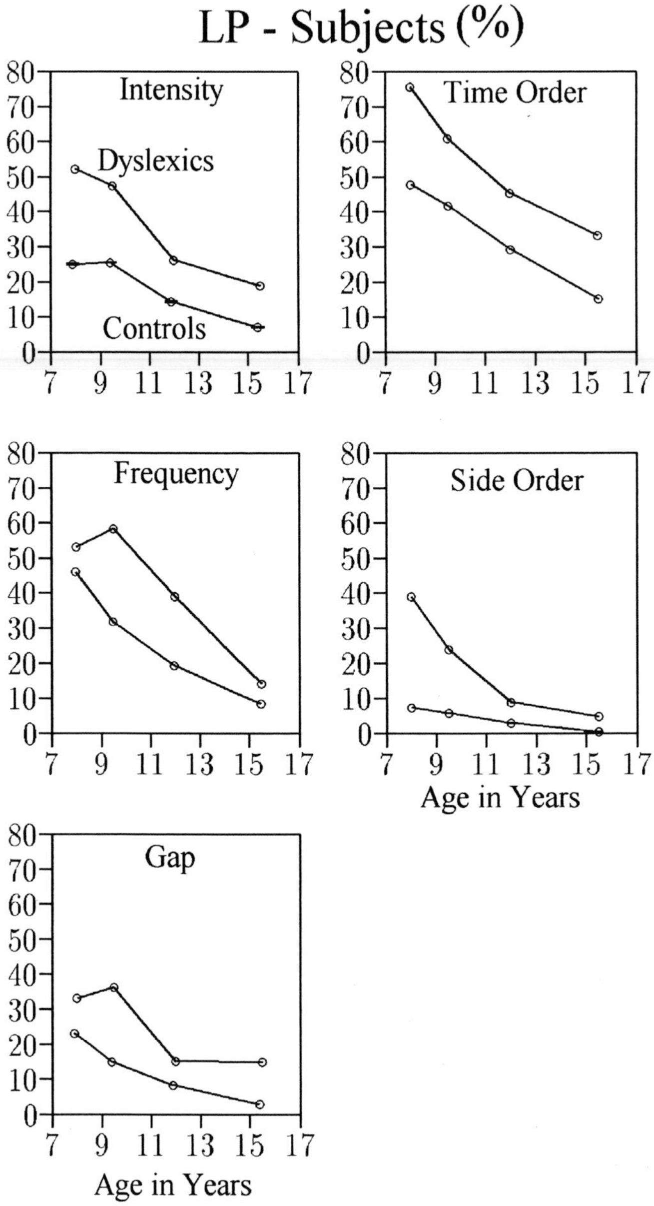

Figure 3. The figure shows the percentage of subjects who could not perform the tasks above chance level as a function of age. As in the upper left graph, all curves obtained from the dyslexics fall above those of the controls.

If one tries to calculate the percent number of subjects performing below the 16 percentile in each domain and age group, numbers below 16% were found only occasionally. In other words, once the LP subjects were eliminated, the differences in low level auditory discrimination were no longer very striking. This might explain why controversial results were found in earlier studies. If the auditory discrimination tasks are too easy, ceiling effects may prevent findings of significant differences, especially if the effects of age in the data are disregarded in the analysis.

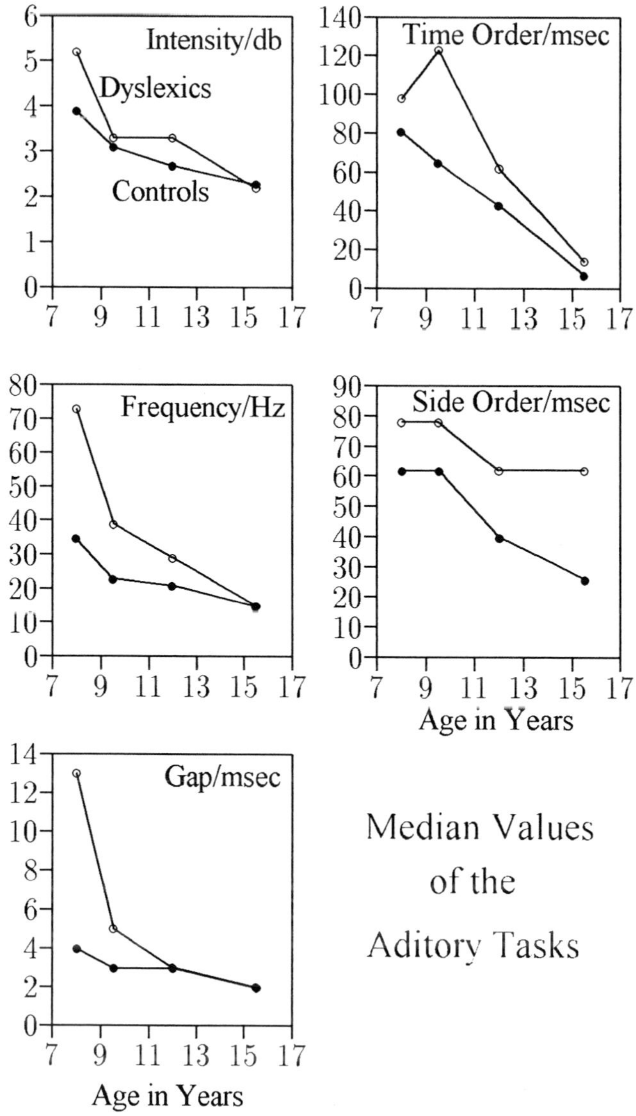

Figure 4. The median values for each task are shown as a function of age for both groups of subjects. Open circles indicate the data of the dyslexics, filled circles those of the controls.

1.1.3. Discussion

These data show, that in order to really know whether or not a dyslexic child has auditory problems, one has to use more than one test (even the 5 tests described here may not be enough). If a dyslexic child has deficits in phonological awareness or any other language related auditory domain, one has to keep in mind that these problems may be the consequence of low level auditory processing deficits, such as reported here.

We will see below that improvements of low level processing also transfers to phonological skills and specific spelling skills.

1.2. Dynamic Vision

The functional part of vision that is concerned with temporal rather than spatial processing is called dynamic vision. The best known example of a dynamic subfunction of vision is motion perception. We know that it is the magnocellular part of the visual system which is concerned with temporal processing: large cells in the retina project to the magnocellular layers of the lateral geniculate body and there are separate cortical projection for the magno- versus the parvocellular system. It is known that the magno-system feeds into the dorsal route to the parietal cortex and further on to the frontal lobe, from where important information is forwarded to the optomotor system directly or indirectly via the basal ganglia, the substantia nigra, and the superior colliculus. For review see (Fischer, 1987).

In order to test the temporal aspects of vision, one needs tests with temporally changing stimuli. One possibility is to use moving stimuli which challenges the magnocellular system. For example, some have used a Landoldt-ring, which becomes visible in a random dot pattern only when the background is moving (Schrauf et al. 2000). We have decided to use an orientation detection test in the form of a four-alternative-forced-choice design.

1.2.1. Methods

Fixation task: Fig. 5 shows a temporal sequence of frames presented to the subject on a small 4x7cm LCD-display. The stimulus looks like a small capital letter T, which could take one of the four main orientations: up, down, left, or right. Changes occurred in random order, each after 170 ms. A sequence lasted between 1 and 2 s. After the end of each sequence (trial) the subject was instructed to press one of the four keys corresponding to the last orientation perceived. In order to catch the last orientation, the subject needed to maintain fixation on the middle of the display.

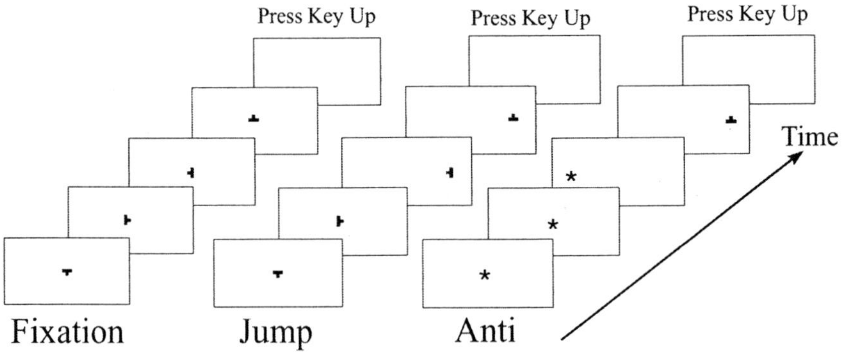

Figure 5. The methods for testing dynamic vision are illustrated by the temporal sequences of frames. The fixation task (left), the jump task (middle), and the anti task are shown separately. In each version the visual task is always to report the last orientation of the stimulus at the end of a trial. Details in the text.

Jump-task: In addition to the simple fixation test, there were two other variations. In the first, called the jump task, the rotating stimuli were suddenly displaced from the middle of the display to the left or right and continued rotation a few times until the trial was terminated and a response key had to be pressed. Unpredictably, in 20% of the trials the stimuli remained rotating in the center without a jump. The best strategy for solving this task was to make saccades to the locus of the actual rotation where the last stimulus will occur.

Anti-task: In this version, a strong distracting stimulus was presented at one side of the display while the key stimulus was presented at the opposite side. The subjects were instructed to detect the correct orientation of the test stimuli by generating a saccade in the direction opposite the distractor; therefore, this task is called the anti-task. The time between distractor onset and stimuli presentation was 220ms allowing for the typical reaction time of antisaccades. Unpredictably, in 20% of the trials the stimuli remained rotating in the center and no distractor was presented.

For each kind of task and trial type (fixation, jump, j-center, anti, a-center), the rate of correct responses was determined in percent corrected by the 25% chances of correct guesses. Therefore, there were 5 variables from the 3 tasks. Each of the 3 tests consisted of 100 trials and lasted about 5 min. There was neither time constraint on key presses nor feed back.

Subjects were recruited as described above. Altogether, 140 controls and 504 dyslexic children in the ages from 7 to 17 years contributed to the results described below.

More details of the methods have been published elsewhere (Fischer et al. 2000).

1.2.2. Results

Fig. 6 presents the 5 pairs of age curves characterizing the development of dynamic vision in the control and the dyslexic subjects. Children at the beginning of school age are already rather good in solving the fixation task. Some improvement can be seen for the subsequent years. The children had more difficulties with the jump and the anti task, because, as we will see below, saccade and antisaccade control is still far from its adult level at this young age.

In all graphs the curves from the dyslexics fell below those of the controls indicating that the dyslexics performed systematically below the level of the controls at all ages.

Percent number of impaired dyslexics: From the rank order we estimated how many dyslexics performed below the 16 percentile of the controls. The result was: 46% failed the criterion in 2 or more of the 5 variables.

1.2.3. Discussion

The present data show the development of dynamic vision as tested by an orientation discrimination task. Interestingly, the use Landoldt-rings seen by motion contrast reveals almost exactly the same age curves (Schrauf et al. 2000) showing that the development lasts beyond the age of 7 years.

The fact, that dynamic vision may be impaired in dyslexic subjects does not come as a real surprise, because earlier studies of dsylexic subjects have shown that the magnocellular system responsible for dynamic vision may not be fully developed at the level of the lateral geniculate body (Galaburda, 1993) or at higher cortical levels of the analysis of motion (Breitmeyer, 1993); (Livingstone et al. 1991); (Eden et al. 1998); (Stein and Talcott, 1999); (Lovegrove, 1993). Since it is the magnocellular system which sends information to the parietal region and further on to the frontal system, one expects that cortical saccade control may also be impaired in dyslexia while subcortical control by the brain stem structures and the eye muscles are intact.

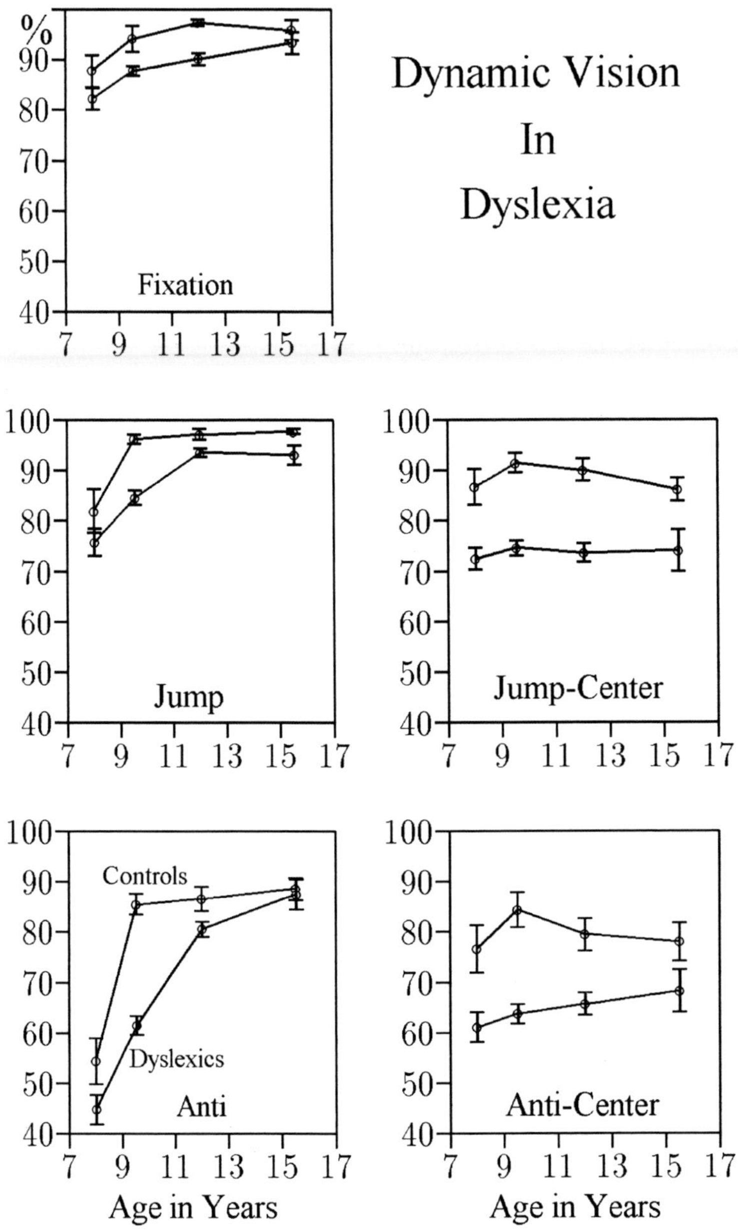

Figure 6. The figure shows the age curves for the 5 variables determined from the 3 tasks of dynamic vision. The upper curves are obtained from the contols, the lower from the dyslexics. N=140 controls. N=504 dyslexics.

We will see below that indeed dyslexics exhibit deficits in cortical saccade control especially in the frontal component.

1.3. Subitizing

When trying to learn basic mathematical operations on numbers one should have an idea of how many items a number means such that this number can be treated as an entity to which another number (entity) can be added. It is not enough to know the names of the numbers and the digits without knowing the association of how many items a number means.

Children with difficulties in learning such basic mathematical operations often have to use their fingers when trying to add the number 3 to the number 4. They may have failed to develop the association of the names of the numbers and the digits with the number itself.

It has been argued, that the development of the sense of numbers relies on a basic visual capacity, which is called "subitizing". Subitizing is a special visual capacity of being able to tell the number of stimuli at once even if they were presented only very briefly (Kaufman et al. 1949). "Briefly" means, the presentation time is too short to use saccadic eye movements for scanning the stimuli and counting them. These relationships are well explained in a book (Dehaene, 1999). It is well known that small numbers are enumerated differently than large numbers (Trick and Pylyshyn, 1994). These facts have been related to visual spatial attention (Trick and Pylyshyn, 1993).

(We are using the word "subitizing" also for item numbers above 3 or 4, when the correct responses begin to take more time for each additional item presented, because all items were presented simultaneously. See below for the data.)

A standardized test of the quality of visual subitizing was needed to really test the hypothesis. The result was that about two thirds of the children with dyscalculia exhibited deficits in visual subitizing regardless of whether numbers below four or above 4 were used in the test.

Here we report the results obtained from dyslexic children with exactly the same test for subitizing. The test was applied, because the number of characters in a word seen extrafoveally (to the right) may effect reading.

1.3.1. Methods

The task: The methods of a test of visual subitizing are illustrated by Fig. 7. The figure shows a sequence of frames presented one after another. A trial begins with the presentation of a small cross in the center or a display. The subjects were instructed to fixate on the dot. After some random time a number of small circles (items) randomly selected between 1 and 9 are presented. The presentation time was set to 100 ms, because this is the shortest reaction time for the optomotor reflex, the express saccade (Fischer and Ramsperger, 1984). Thus, the subjects were unable to make any saccade in an attempt to count the number of circles by saccades. Each item number was presented 20 times with the exception of item number 1, which was presented only 10 times. Thus each test session consisted of 170 trials.

The subjects were required to press the digit key corresponding to the number of circles they have seen. The reaction time of the key press and the digit of the response key were stored in the test instrument. From these raw data 4 variables were calculated: the basic reaction time for item numbers 1 and 2 (T1). The mean percent number of correct responses for item numbers 4-8 (PM), the mean time per item numbers 4-8 (TM), and the effective recognition speed defined as $ERS = PM/TM$. We also calculated the percentage of correct responses for item numbers 2 to 4, which characterizes the capacity of subitizing small numbers.

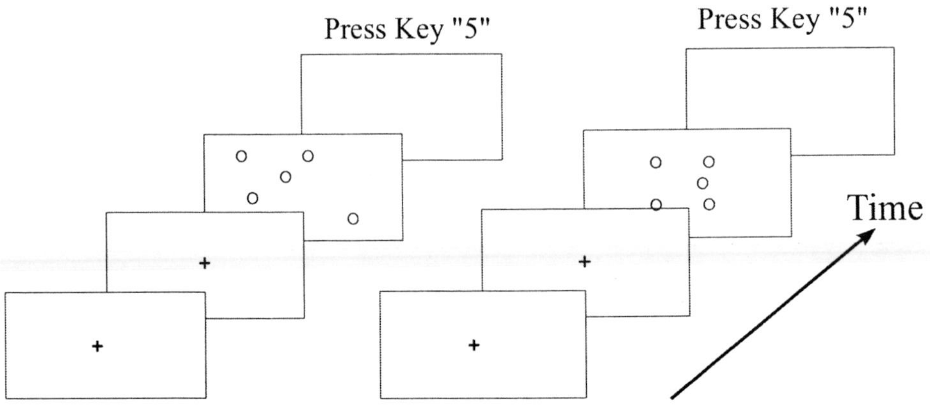

Figure 7. The methods for testing visual subitizing are illustrated by the sequences of frames. In half of the trials the items were loosely ordered (left side), in the others half were closely ordered (right side). Both types of trials were randomly separated.

To understand the definition and the meaning of these variables, Fig. 8 shows two count-curves. The figures on the left is the percent number of correct responses, while the figure on the right is the reaction time of the correct responses as a function of the number of items presented. Each data point represents the mean across the trials in the session averaged for 179 adult control subjects in the age range of 20 to 30 years.

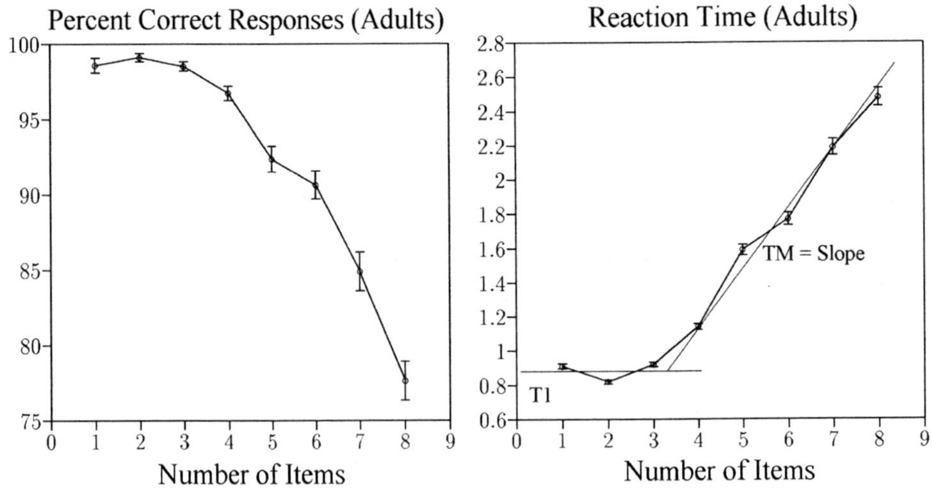

Figure 8. Count curves obtained from adult subjects. The left side shows the percent number of correct responses, the right side shows the reaction time as a function of the number of items presented.

One can see that, as expected, almost all responses are correct (above 98%) for item numbers up to 3. In agreement with the idea of subitizing the reaction times are about the same for item numbers up to 3. For item numbers above 3 the reaction times increase linearly indicating that on average each additional item needs a constant extra processing time. This time is given by the slope TM of the regression line. In other words: even though the items were presented simultaneously (for 100 ms), the recognition of the correct number of more than 3 items contains some kind of internal counting probably on the basis of visual memory.

The analysis of the 4 variables defined above shows that only two of them were statistically independent: the basic reaction time T1, and the effective recognition time ERS. The latter correlated highly with PM and TM by definition. Therefore the count curves of reaction time differ from subject to subject mainly by their vertical position (T1) and by the slope of the linear part (TM). In addition, each subject reached a certain number of correct responses (PM).

With these definitions we characterize the individual performance of the subitizing test by the variables T1 and ERS and also report on the variables PM and TM to see, whether ERS was influenced by speed, correct responses, or by both.

Control and dyslexic subjects were recruited from German schools as described above. Altogether, 219 controls and 120 dyslexic children in the age range of 7 to 17 years contributed to the results described below.

1.3.2. Results

Fig. 9 shows on the right side the age curves for the basic reaction time. First, one sees that a long lasting development takes place. Second, even the 17 year old control subjects took about 0.9 sec to press key 1 or 2. This reaction time is drastically longer than a simple reaction time obtained in a task where one has to press a button upon the occurrence of any visual stimulus. Typical simple reaction times of adults are in the order of 0.4 sec. This means that the task of subitizing needs an extra time of at least 0.5 sec even on its simplest trials where only 1 or 2 stimuli were presented.

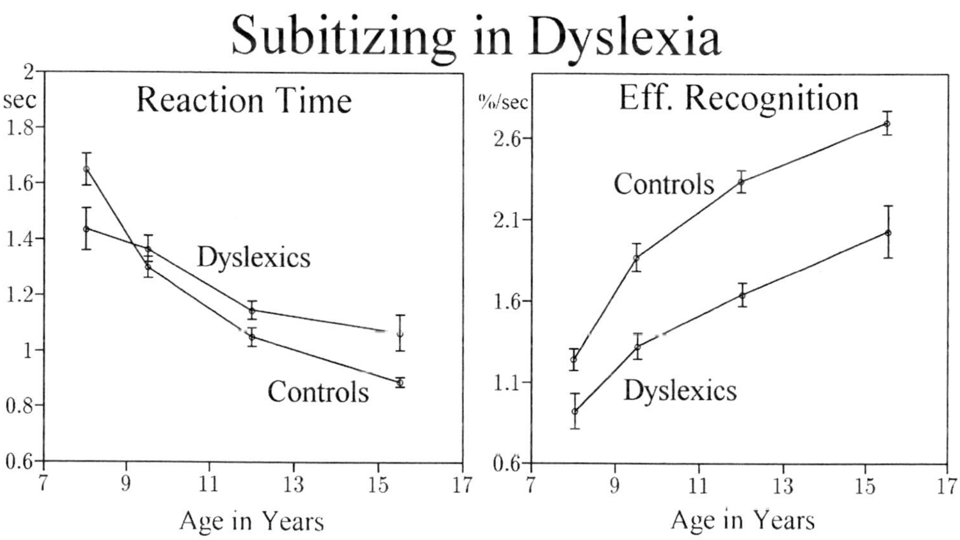

Figure 9. The basic reaction time (left) and the effective recognition speed (right) are shown as a function of age for both groups of subjects. N=219 controls. N=120 dyslexics.

While the two youngest age groups of dyslexics did not react significantly slower than the controls the two older groups showed slower reaction times. Obviously the dyslexics took longer than the controls to make sure that there were not three or more items presented.

The development of the basic reaction time and the effective recognition speed is shown by the two age curves of Fig. 9. These variables also clearly differentiate the groups across the whole age range considered. Of course, the value of ERS is determined both by the percent of correct responses and by the time per stimulus. Therefore, one wants to know, whether the deficit is due to one or the other variables or to both.

Fig. 10 shows the two variables as a function of age for both groups. In general, both aspects contribute to the deficits due to the effective recognition speed. In practice, this means that one has to look at all four variables if one wants to determine what the problem really is for each child.

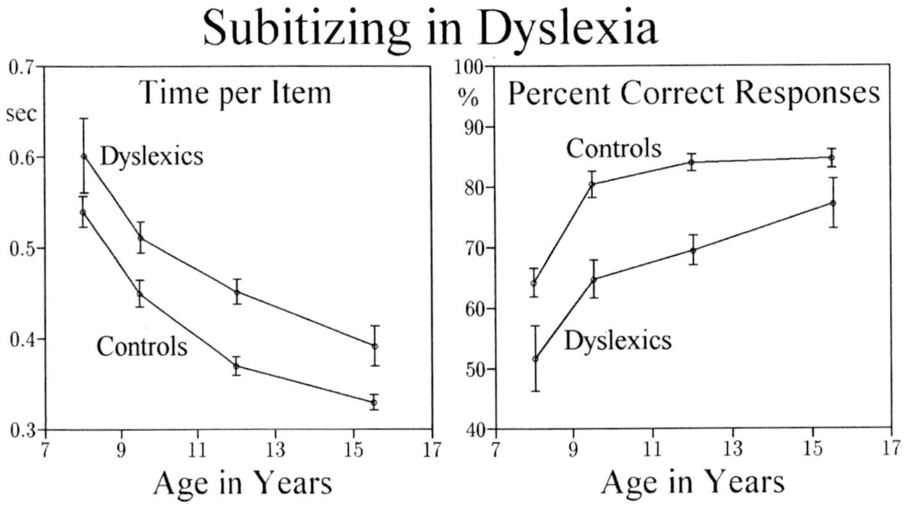

Figure 10. The time per item (left) and the percentage of correct responses (right) are shown as a function of age for both groups of subjects.

Finally we show that subitizing of small item numbers (2-4) is more difficult for dyslexics than for controls of the same age. Fig. 11 shows the pair of age curves using the variable percent correct responses divided by the corresponding reaction time. (Note that the reaction time for small item numbers is about the same). The figure shows that the development of the two groups starts at about the same point but is clearly faster for the controls than for the dyslexics.

As in the previous sections we counted the number of dyslexic subjects performing below one standard deviation of the mean of the controls. This number increased from 30% in the youngest group to about 60% in the oldest group.

Similarly, we found that the percentage of dyslexics performing below the 16 percentile limit of the controls using the variable for 2 to 4 items was only 30% to 50% depending on age.

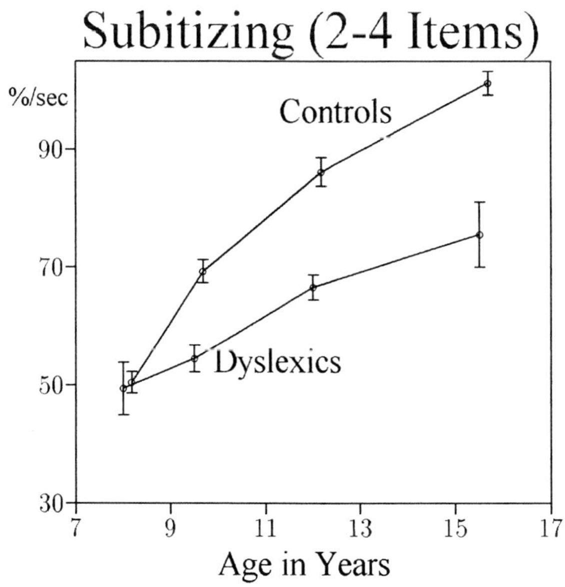

Figure 11. Subitizing of 2 to 4 items is shown as a function of age. The variable shown is the mean percentage of correct responses divided by the mean reaction time.

1.3.3. Discussion

Subitizing is a capacity of parafoveal vision, because the stimuli were presented in the neighborhood of the fixation mark on the display. The question arises, why this capacity should be important during reading or during the process of learning how to read. When trying to read words consisting of different numbers of letters it may be an advantage to recognize this number easily from parafoveal information during a given fixation of a word. Also, for programming the next saccade it may be important to take into account the number of letters to the right of the fixated part of the word. Interestingly, during normal reading one rarely makes saccades larger than 5 or 6 letters. This is about the number of items where subitizing is no longer possible without extra time.

1.4. Saccade Control

It has been discussed for a long time whether dyslexics have normal saccadic eye movements. Looking at their eye movements when they try to read there is no doubt, that the pattern appears even chaotic sometimes, because of many regressive saccades in the same line or because of saccades to another line. It was unclear though whether such patterns were the result of poor reading skills or the poor reading skills were the consequence of poor saccade control.

First of all, the logic might not be as simple as that. Second, often eye movements and control of saccades was confused. while the movements of the eye ball may be normal their cortical control may be impaired. And third, saccades are subjected to the influence of many factors reaching from the physical structure of the text, nature of the words and language, to psychological factors.

In using non-reading saccade tasks, different and controversial results were found reaching from "saccades are normal" (Olson et al. 1983) to "eye movements hold the key to dyslexia" (Pavlidis, 1981). The neurophysiological and psychophysical analysis of saccade control in normal adult human subjects and patients as well as in monkeys have brought more insight into the complex control system, which has helped to design special saccade tasks for diagnostic purposes. For review see (Fischer and Weber, 1993). In particular, the use of antisaccades has attracted neurobiologists as well as clinicians (Everling and Fischer, 1998).

In brief, one has to differentiate between at least three components of saccade control:

1. Fixation as an active process preventing the eyes from movements, especially from generating saccades during periods of information uptake from the retinal surface. This is a parietal function (Mountcastle et al. 1981) and it is supported by the fixation cells in the rostral part of the superior colliculus (Munoz and Wurtz, 1993).
2. Reflexive saccades that bring the fovea to a suddenly appearing stimulus. The reflex can be seen in isolation as an express saccade which occurs when the fixation system is disengaged and a new stimulus is presented in the periphery (Fischer and Ramsperger, 1984). Express saccades are mediated through the superior colliculus and do not need the frontal eye fields (Schiller et al. 1979). Usually, the prosaccades are made to peripheral targets and have longer reaction times, because the fixation system is engaged most of the time and the disengagement takes time (Mayfrank et al. 1986).
3. Voluntary saccades are saccades that a subject generates due to conscious voluntary decision. The ability to generate voluntary saccades can be tested by the antisaccade task, in which the subjects are instructed to look to the opposite side of a suddenly presented stimulus (Hallet, 1978); (Fischer and Weber, 1992). These saccades rely on an intact frontal brain, because we know that patients with frontal lesions are impaired on the antisaccade task (Guitton et al. 1985).

The use of a prosaccade task and an antisaccade task under special conditions allows for analyzation of the state of the saccade control system. These standardized methods were published some years ago (Fischer et al. 1997). The first application of these methods showed that the different components of saccade control have different time courses of development with the voluntary component developing until adult age (Fischer et al. 1997).

Applying these methods to dyslexic subjects has clarified the main controversy in the question of saccade control in dyslexia (Biscaldi et al. 2000). Here we give a short overview of the main results.

1.4.1. Methods

Overlap prosaccade task: The methods are illustrated in Fig. 12. Two sequences of frames are shown; the overlap task is shown at the left. The subjects see a central fixation spot for a second. Then a stimulus is presented randomly at 4 deg to the right or left side. The subject is required to make a saccade to this stimulus. From each trial the reaction time of the first saccade is determined and the mean value is calculated separately for the to sides. A session consisted of 200 trials.

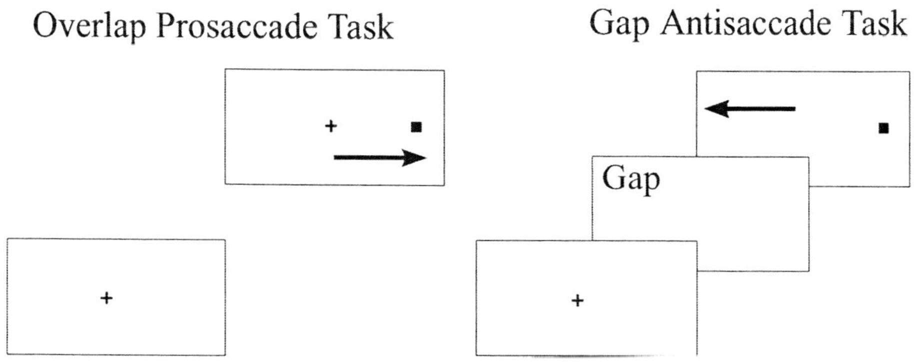

Figure 12. The figure shows the temporal and spatial arrangements of the overlap prosaccade saccade and the gap antisaccade task. For details see text.

Gap antisaccade task: The second task requires antisaccades. Each trial starts with the presentation of the fixation spot, which is turned off 800ms later and 200ms before the new stimulus is presented; again randomly at the right or left side. But this time the subject is required to generate a saccade to the opposite side (antisaccade). For as easy as this task sounds to be able to do, it is as equally difficult to follow the procedure. From each trial the time of occurrence of the first two saccades was determined together with the direction and size. From each session several variables were calculated: the mean reaction time of the correct antisaccades, the error rate, the mean reaction time of the errors, the correction time, and the rate of corrections. A session consisted of 200 trials.

Procedure: The prosaccade task was always performed before the antisaccade task. No feedback was given. The subjects were placed in a dark room with their heads fixed by a chin rest.

Eye movement recording: The eye movements were recorded either by the Iris Scalar System or by ExpressEye (Hartnegg and Fischer, 2002). Both instruments use infrared light corneal reflection and give a temporal resolution of 1ms and a spatial resolution of better than 0.2 deg. The data were stored and analyzed by a special computer program. Details of saccade identification and definition of corrective saccades have been described earlier (Fischer et al. 1997).

Subjects were recruited as described above. Altogether, 117 controls and 506 dyslexic children in the age range of 7 to 17 years contributed to the results described below.

1.4.2. Results

The results of the prosaccade and the antisaccade tasks are presented by the two pairs of age curves in Fig. 13. The left pair depicts the reaction time of the prosaccades. With the exception of the youngest group, no systematic differences were found in the age development. Both groups continue to become faster with age and the lowest value for adults do not seem to be reached by the age of 17. From this result one would like to conclude that saccade control is not disturbed in dyslexia. However, this conclusion would be premature because the data obtained from the antisaccade task show a completely different development of the two groups, as can be seen at right side of the figure.

At the beginning of school age both groups are almost completely unable to follow the instruction to look to the opposite side. Their mean errors rate is 80% and there is no difference between the two groups. During the following 10 years both groups undergo a clear development, but the dyslexics cannot follow the speed of the controls such that with increasing age the developmental deficit increases.

If one looks at the reaction times of the correct antisaccades and at the correction times, the differences between the groups are not as striking. But the rate of corrective saccades following the errors also differentiates the two groups very clearly (data not shown).

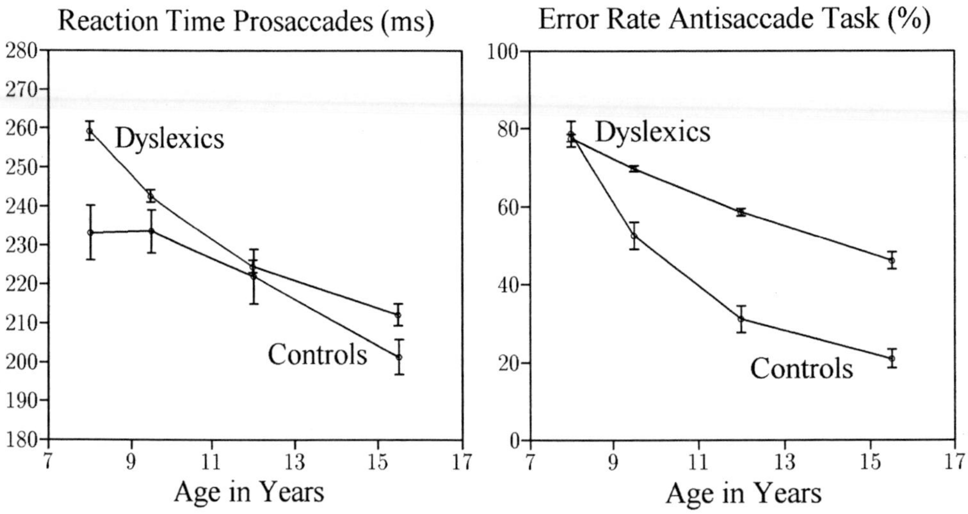

Figure 13. The reaction time of the prosaccades under overlap conditions (left) and the error rate from the antisaccade task under gap conditions (right) are shown as a function of age. N=117 controls. N=506 dyslexic subjects

This result shows that it is not the saccade control system as a whole which exhibits developmental deficits in dyslexia. The eye muscles and the brainstem mechanisms for saccade generation are usually intact and do not show any systematic deficits. It is the frontal lobe component, which runs behind indicating that the frontal control of saccades, which regulates the synchronization of the ongoing reading process and saccade generation, is not well established.

As in the previous sections it is important to count the percent of dyslexics who performed below the level of the controls. To estimate these numbers we used two variables determined from the antisaccade task. By calculating the percentage of uncorrected errors (pu) from the error rate (pe) we get the percentage of corrections (pc) we: $pu = pe \bullet (1 - pc)$. For each age group the percent of dyslexics, who reached values above one standard deviation of the mean of the controls was determined and plotted as a function of age. Fig. 14 shows that this number increases with age from 26% to 64%.

For this analysis we used 2036 dyslexics. Note that there are, by definition, also subjects among the controls, who fall beyond this criterion. These numbers are independent of age (by definition) and are close to 16% as one would have expected if the values followed a gaussian distribution exactly.

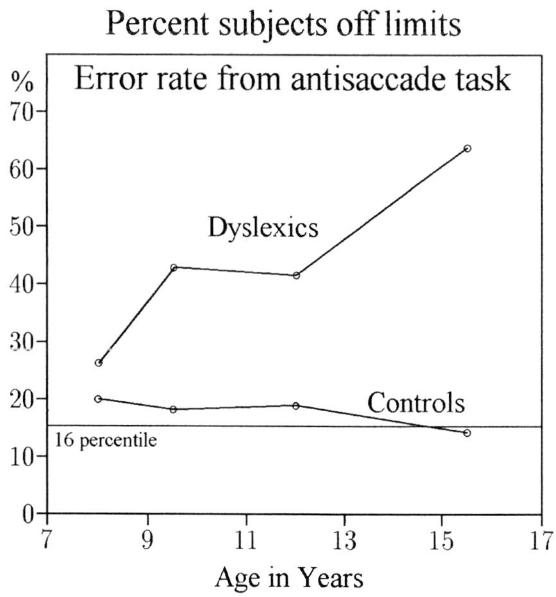

Figure 14. The percent number of control and dyslexic subjects performing more than one standard deviation above the mean is shown as a function of age. Note that for the controls these numbers are in the order of 16% and, by definition, do not depend on age.

1.4.3. Discussion

The findings on saccade control explain why there has been an ongoing controversy as to whether or not saccadic eye movements play a role in dyslexia. It all depends on (i) which of the components are tested and (ii) it must be noted, that only fractions of the dyslexic suffer from a deficit in a special component of saccade control; the frontal component. In addition, if one studies a younger group one will not find any differences, but an older group will show clear differences in the frontal component.

This makes sense, because all subjects have made millions and millions of saccadic eye movements throughout their lives. But they did not necessarily have to use their frontal control component systematically, because one can make visually guided saccades without the frontal eye fields (Schiller et al. 1980) using the collicular pathway, and for every day life this might be sufficient. Also: the dyslexics with saccade control deficits do not fail all the time to use their frontal component, the system is just not as reliable as for the control children of the same age.

Children with attention deficit hyperactivity disorder (ADHD) also exhibit deficits in antisaccade control (Klein et al. 2002). This observation has been interpreted as further support for the view that ADHD is mainly a problem of frontal or prefrontal functions (Klein et al. 2003). Under methylphenidate (Ritalin) these deficits disappear to a large extent (Klein et al. 2002).

1.5. Stability of Fixation

Saccade control is not the only eye movement system which is needed during reading. One also needs to be able to stabilize the line of sight. There are two principally different aspects of fixation stability. First, unwanted conjunctive saccades must be suppressed during fixation (simple fixation stability). Second, the angle of convergence between the two eyes should be stabilized (binocular fixation stability) by suppressing slow convergence or divergence movements.

Suppression of conjunctive saccades is mediated by a special fixation system in the parietal cortex and the superior colliculus, the activity of which inhibits the saccade neurons. Binocular stability, on the other hand, is provided by different neural systems in which activity also depends on the perception of 3D-objects, the images of which must be fused and remain fused for a period of time. Instability of this type is a dynamic problem, which, in general, cannot be solved by static prism glasses unless a small static deviation of the line of sight causes the slow drifts.

Both types of stability have been studied in dyslexic children and compared with that of control subjects of the same age.

1.5.1. Simple Stability

Fig. 15 shows the age curves for simple stability by giving the number of unwanted saccades per trial assessed during the initial fixation periods of the prosaccade trials with an overlap condition. Again, a long lasting development becomes visible with both groups starting at about the same level at age seven. With increasing age, the dyslexics run more and more behind the development of the controls. The percent of dyslexic subjects with an instability above the mean plus one standard deviation increases from about 20% for the youngest group to about 50% in the oldest group.

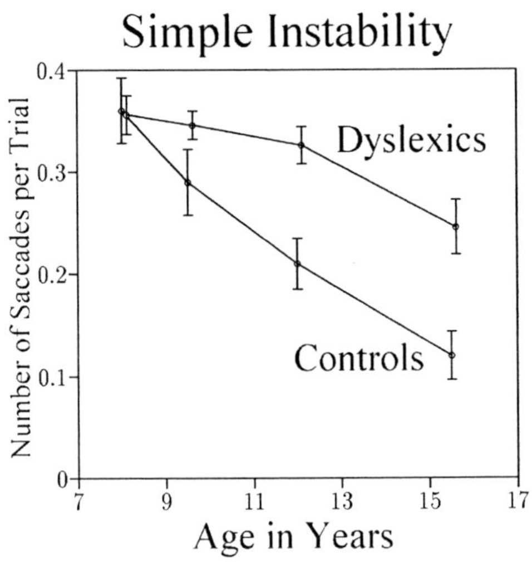

Figure 15. The simple instability of fixation measured by the number of unwanted saccades per trial from the overlap prosaccade task are shown as a function of age for both groups. N=106 controls, N=87 dyslexics.

1.5.2. Binocular Stability

To measure the binocular stability the velocity difference between the right and the left eyes was calculated as a function of time during the complete prosaccade trial with overlap conditions, i.e. when a fixation point was always visible. Periods of time, during which the absolute value of the velocity difference exceeds 3.5 deg/sec were considered as "unstable" and marked by the computer program. For each trial the total time of instability was measured by summing up the single periods. The last 20ms before and the next 30 ms after each saccade (and all blinks) were excluded from the analysis time window. The total time of instability was expressed in a percent of the time that was available for analysis in the trial under consideration. Finally, a value below 15% was tolerated as "normal", because in these trials the time of instability was correspondingly short (in the order of 150ms) and presumably did not contribute to perceptual problems. As a final measure of binocular stability, we used the percentage of trials in which this limit of 15% was exceeded.

Fig. 16 shows the result of the analysis of binocular stability for the two groups.

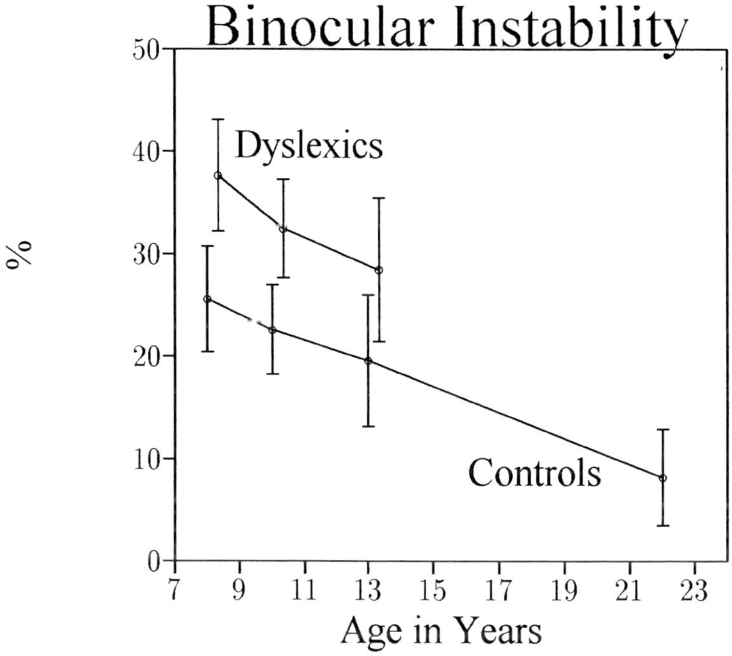

Figure 16. The binocular instability of fixation is shown as a function of age for both groups. For details see text. N=91 controls, N=68 dyslexics.

First of all, it comes as a surprise how poorly the children's eyes are stabilized with respect to both the simple and binocular aspect. In both cases the development at the age of 17 years is far from its adult level, as can be seen in Fig. 16. Averaged across age, about 25% of the dyslexics exhibited deficits in binocular stability. This number is relatively small because of the large interindividual scatter in the data.

Second, children with high simple instability do not necessarily exhibit high binocular instability and vice versa. In fact the variables did not show any significant correlation and presumably are functionally independent as pointed out above. We will see below, that a monocular training will improve the binocular stability but not the simple stability.

1.5.3. Discussion

In normally reading subjects the fixation periods are no longer than 300 to 400 msec and one may argue that it does not make much sense to test the stability during longer periods and during non-reading saccade tasks. But the idea is, that the neural systems that regulate fixation should be tested in isolation by non-reading tasks to see whether or not they function normally under these relatively simple conditions. The fact that there are systematic differences between the controls and the dyslexics, in itself is interesting enough, because one has to consider the complete process of eye movement control. At this point we can only report the experimental results, which support earlier findings on fixation stability in dyslexia (Eden et al. 1994); (Fowler, 1992).

When we discuss the effects of monocular training of saccade control we will see that the binocular stability improves but the simple stability does not. This can be regarded as an indication that the simple instability is caused by subcortical effects at the efferent part of eye movement control, presumably at the brain stem level, where saccades may be generated that were not programmed by cortical structures and that could not be prevented by central inhibition of the saccade cells by the fixation cells at the tectal level.

2. Training

In order to improve those deficits that have been encountered in a single subject daily practice of specific tasks was considered as a solution. The idea is, that the synaptic connections within the neural network be used for solving the task needs more reliability. The basic learning principle of the brain is repetition. According to Hebb (Hebb, 1949) the probability of postsynaptic impulses triggered by presynaptic impulses increases if the synapse has been used successfully before. In practice this means that a specified task always challenging the same series and/or combinations of synapses must be repeatedly performed for a period of time.

We decided to try this well known learning paradigm in the field of auditory, visual and optomotor processing by designing tasks that were given to the children for daily practice at home.

All training procedures described below have certain features in common:

- they are adaptive, because the tasks will start with a very easy version to make it possible for the child to begin the training with some success. As the child's success rate increases, each day the task becomes more difficult the next day, thereby always challenging the child at the present limits of task performance.
- the training instruments store all data of the daily training sessions to allow a post-training protocol.
- the tasks are specifically selected for each child according to the previous diagnostic results.
- the training procedures were implemented in small hand-held computers containing the program and the displays and/or providing the sounds by ear phones. These instruments were given to the children for daily practice at home. The instruments were returned to the laboratory after the training was completed and a training protocol was read out of the instrument's memory.

2.1. Training of Low Level Auditory Discrimination

The idea of training auditory perception is not new and was reviewed recently (Tallal et al. 1998).

The training tasks are essentially the same as the five diagnostic tasks described above with the exception of the starting difficulty. Those children who failed to perform a task even at its lowest level of difficulty were given verbal support to enter the training procedure. Once they have principally learned to perform the task in its easiest version the adjustment of the difficulty was left to an automatic algorithm built in the training instruments.

Altogether, 140 dyslexic children participated in the auditory training and were re-tested again, at the end. The results of pre- and post-training testing are summarized in Fig. 17. The left side shows the success rates as a percentage of the children who exceeded the 20th percentile after separate training for the five tasks. One sees that these rates are between 70 and 80% for the first three tasks but considerably lower for the time order and very low for the side order tasks.

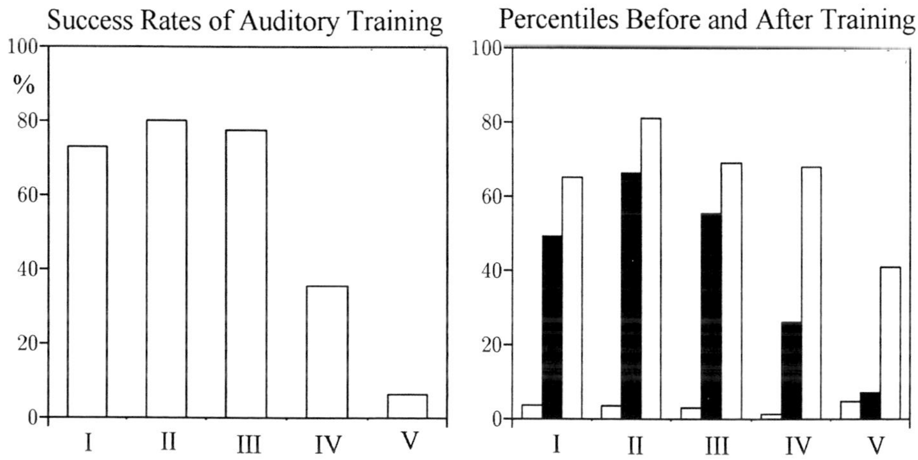

Figure 17. The effects of auditory training are shown for a group of 140 dyslexics. Left: the percentage of subjects who reached values above the 20th percentile for each of the 5 tasks. Right: the mean of the percentiles reached by the subjects before (small white columns) and after (black columns) the training. The right white columns show the mean values of those subjects who reached values above the 20th percentile.

The right side of the figure shows the mean percentiles before and after the training for all five tasks. By definition, the "before" mean values were all below 16 because all the children of the training group were selected by the criterion of having failed to reach the 16th percentile limit. After the training the total group of trained children reached the mean values indicated by the middle column. The right columns show the mean values of those children who exceeded the 20th percentile, and indicate that successful children became really good in performing the auditory tasks; if the training works, it works really well. But, unfortunately, it does not work in all cases.

2.2. Training of Subitizing

Following the idea that functions of neural systems can be improved by daily practice; this was also tried to improve visual subitizing. We knew that it was possibe to increase the limit of simultaneously enumerated numbers by 1,7 by playing action video games (Green and Bavelier, 2003), but here we wanted to try a standardized training protocol which could be used as a routine.

The task used for testing was also used for training, but at the beginning the children were given the task in a very simple form with only 1 to 3 items presented for longer times. With increasing speed of performance and with an increasing number of correct responses the task was made more and more difficult by presenting more items for shorter periods of time.

The original test task was given as the first session before the training began and again as the last session after 20 days of practice. To estimate the success of the training, the mean basic reaction time and the mean effective speed of recognition were calculated for a group of 66 subjects before and after the training. Fig. 18 shows the changes in these two variables. Actually, these data were not obtained from dyslexics but from children with difficulties in basic calculations (dyscalculia) and normal intelligence.

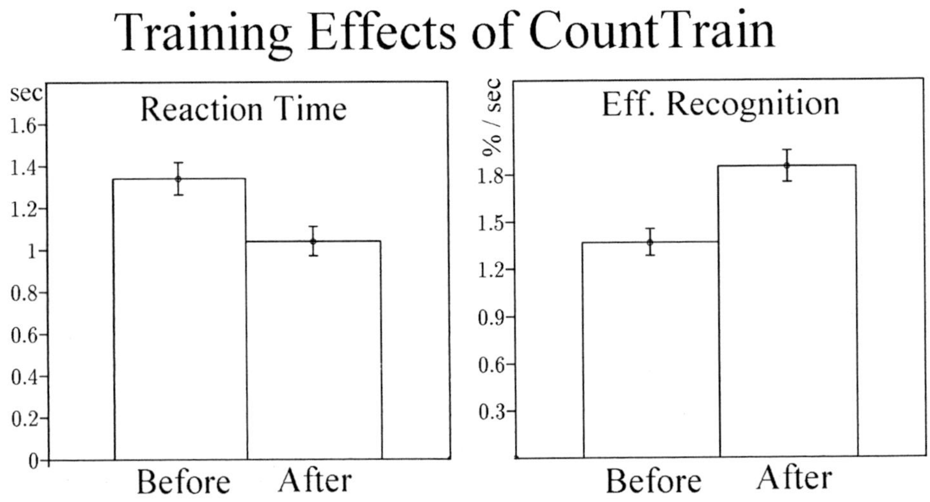

Figure 18. Effects of training of subitizing on the basic reaction time (left) and the effective recognition speed (right). N=66 subjects.

As for the other training procedures, it was also estimated how many subjects could improve their capacity of visual subitizing by counting the number of variables that were improved. Fig. 19 shows the result. If one requires that both variables improved; the success rate is in the order of 75%. Another 20% of the subjects improved in only one of the two variables.

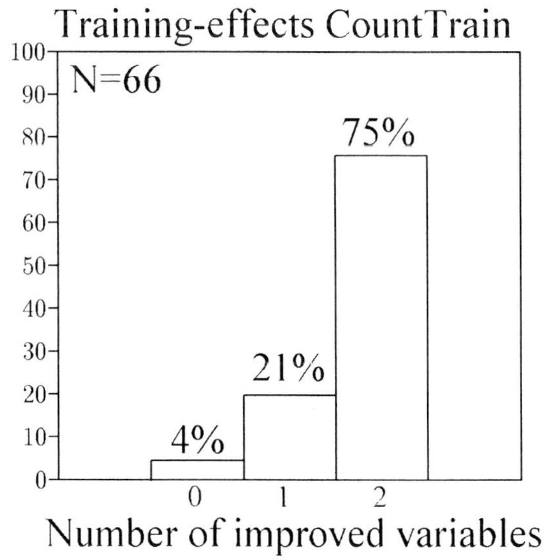

Figure 19. The percentage of subjects who improved by none, one, or both of the test variables after 3 weeks of training of subitizing.

2.3. Training of Dynamic Vision and Saccade Control

For training of dynamic vision and of the three components of saccade control we used the three versions of the test of dynamic vision described above, because the tasks require different types of eye movement control. In this way, both dynamic vision and saccade control could be improved. The training was prescribed individually for each dyslexic child on the basis of the diagnostic results obtained from the analysis of the eye movements. If necessary, the three training tasks were always given in the same order: fixation, jump, and anti. Any anti-training was preceded by a fixation training to strengthen the fixation system first to make it easier for the child to do the anti-task. Jump-training was only prescribed if the prosaccade were really too long and/or too widely scattered. Usually, a jump training lasted no longer than one week, while fixation training lasted no longer than two weeks and anti-training lasted between two and four weeks, mostly three. Daily sessions of 200 trials were recommended which lasted between 8 and 15 minutes.

The difficulty of the training was adjusted by changing the speed of orientation rotation from 5 per sec to 11 per sec in four steps. The details have been described earlier (Fischer and Hartnegg, 2000).

Altogether, 178 children participated in this study.

We do not show the data of the post-training performance of the dynamic vision tests, because the overwhelming majority of the participants succeeded in reaching the highest level of difficulty within the time limits described before. There have been exceptions, though, who needed to repeat the training for several different reasons.

To see the effect of training, Fig. 20 shows the pairs of age curves for prosaccade reaction times (left side) and for the error rate from the antisaccade task (right side). The prosaccade reaction times remained about the same on average. It is important to remember at this point that the prosaccade task did not differentiate among all groups from the beginning. Therefore, this relation should not change systematically from the training. (However, if one looks at single subjects, one observes that some increased their prosaccade reaction time while others decreased it depending on what kind of training program they had, see below.) On the other hand, the performance of the antisaccade task was systematically improved after the training at all ages.

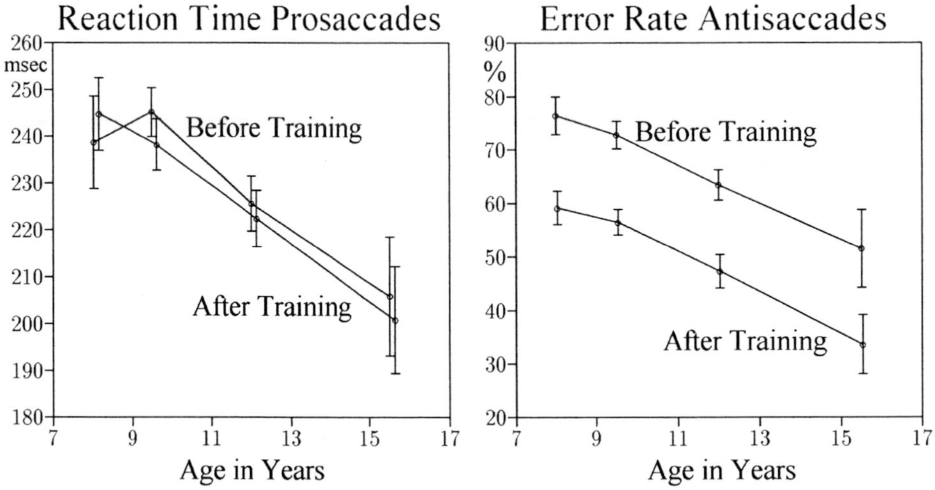

Figure 20. The figure shows the age curves before and after the saccade training. Left: Reaction time of prosaccade under overlap conditions. Right: Error rate from the antisaccade task with gap conditions. N=178 subjects.

The success rate of the optomotor training was estimated by counting the numbers of variables determined from the antisaccade task that exhibited an improvement. Using the percentage of uncorrected errors, the reaction, and the correction time as three indicators for an improvement of the performance of the antisaccade task, the success rate was 87%.

To test for the specificity of the training and to argue against placebo effects we also separately analysed the data for children who trained in the jump-task only, and others who trained in the fixation and the anti-tasks, but not the jump-task. As a result, only those components of saccade control exhibited significant changes that were part of the training; jump training decreased the reaction time of prosaccades but did not reduce the error rates or reaction times of the antisaccade task. Similarly, fixation and anti training improved the error rates but did not shorten their prosaccade reaction times.

In an attempt to improve fixation stability we followed an idea to use only one eye during the fixation and saccade training (Stein and Fowler, 1985). The result was that binocular stability improved considerably. We re-tested 24 dyslexic children with problems in binocular stability. All of them profited from the monocular training. The mean improvement was 70% of the start value with a standard deviation of 22%. The simple fixation stability did not improve though, indicating that the source for unwanted saccades is located closer to the efferent end of the pathway of eye movement control.

3. Transfer to Spelling and Reading

One cannot expect that a relatively short sensory and/or optomotor training will result in an overall and immediate improvement of the problems encountered in dyslexia. Reading and spelling need more than these basic perceptual skills and learning them takes a long time. A dyslexic child with deficits at low levels of neural information processing has to fight more problems as compared with other children.

The main purpose of the studies reported above was to show that these auditory, visual, and optomotor problems exist in dyslexia and that they can be diagnosed by standardized test methods. It was shown that they can be solved to a large extent by specific daily practice within relatively short periods of time.

Yet, one wants to know whether a successful training has some profit for the children at school. Therefore, two more studies were conducted. One on the transfer of low level auditory training to spelling and one on the transfer of optomotor training to reading.

3.1. Transfer of Auditory Discrimination to Spelling

The hypothesis to be tested is: successful training of the auditory tasks described above transfer to spelling in a situation were the children have to write words that they hear (dictation).

A group of 41 children with deficits in spelling (tested by the DRT) and with deficits in at least one of the five auditory discrimination tasks was recruited as described above. All participants were also tested for language related phonological skills (HDLDT, Brunner et al., 1996). The total group was then divided into three groups: an experimental group (N=25), a waiting group (N=6), and a placebo group (N=10). All test scores were transformed into percentiles, thereby, accounting for age.

The waiting group went on to school like all others members of the total group. The placebo group, instead of receiving the auditory training, was given a visual training consisting of the fixation task of dynamic vision described above. This visual training had almost all circumstances in common with the auditory training including the concern of the parents and the design of the training instruments (except the ear phones). After the training periods the children were retested using the HDLDT and the DRT.

The results of a pre, post-analysis are presented graphically for both tasks and for the three groups by Fig. 21.

At the left the mean values of percentiles of the pre-post testing of the HDLDT are shown. The enormous profit of the experimental group is evident. An ANOVA with repeated measurements confirmed that the interaction term (time x group) was highly significant. A t-test showed that no significant improvements were achieved by either control group.

The right part of the figure shows the result of the DRT. The advantages in spelling were smaller as compared with the HDLDT but larger in the experimental group than in the two control groups.

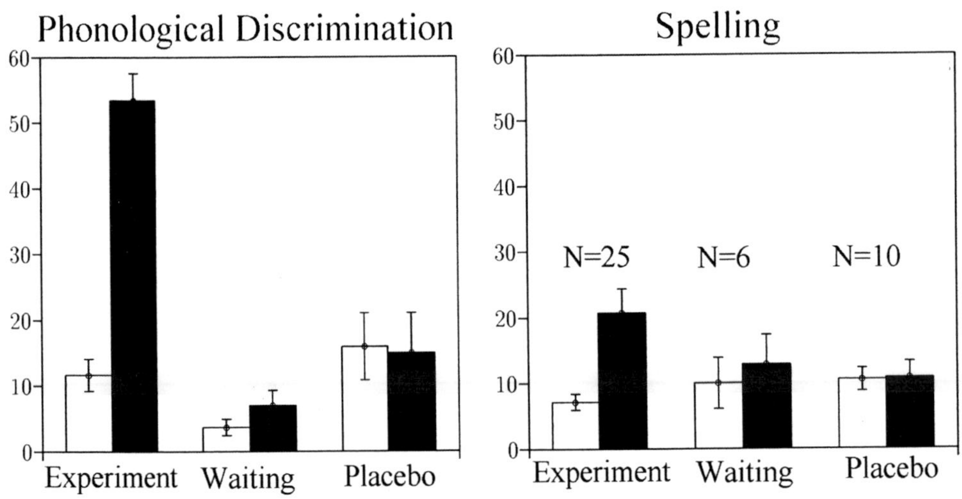

Figure 21. Mean percentiles before (white columns) and after (black columns) the training of low level auditory functions. Left: Phonological discrimination. Right: Spelling. The results are shown for the 3 groups. Significant improvements are obtained by the experimental group only.

From the above considerations one cannot expect that all types of spelling errors are affected by an improvement of low level auditory discrimination. Therefore, the three error types provided by the DRT were analysed separately. Type I errors are due to poor auditory perception, type II errors are due to failures of discriminating long from short vocals, and type III errors are due to a deficit in knowing the rules and the grammar of the German language. By definition, type III errors cannot be prevented by a perfect auditory system.

Fig. 22 shows the results of the analysis of the three error types. An ANOVA was performed for the variables separately with a result showing that the interaction (time x group) was significant only for the type I errors. The figure shows, though, that all types of errors were reduced. Therefore, a posthoc analysis of the data by t-tests was performed for the three error types. The type I errors showed a highly significant improvement (p=.0001), the type II errors were also significantly reduced (p=.01), and the type III errors failed to show any significance (p=.03). Note, that the type III errors occured relatively often when compared with the other two types of errors.

3.2. Transfer of Dynamic Vision and Saccade Control to Reading

One can hardly expect that a few weeks of training of dynamic vision and saccade control replaces the long lasting process of learning how to read. All one can hope, is (i) that in those dyslexic children who suffered only from poor saccade control reading skills, improve quickly and without further special training or (ii) that further reading lessons are more successful for trained subjects as compared to untrained dyslexics, who keep struggling with their saccade control system.

A first study of dyslexics being retested for their reading skills after the saccade training has shown that about 30% of them improved their reading skills significantly. A second study was conducted in which trained dyslexics received 6 weeks of reading together with a group of untrained children. The hypothesis was that the trained group would profit more from the reading lessons than the untrained group.

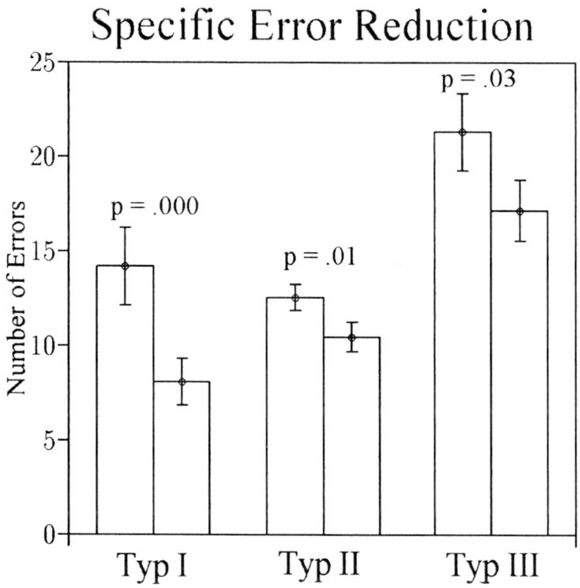

Figure 22. The analysis of specific spelling errors after auditory training shows significant reductions only for type I and type II errors. The columns indicate the number of errors before and after the training.

All members of the total group (N=18, age 8-13 years) had been diagnosed for reading, spelling, and general intelligence and were classified as dyslexics. All of them were also diagnosed with respect to their saccade control. Only those who exhibited significant deficits in the voluntary component of their saccade control system were selected as members of the total group, i.e. they failed in at least one of the 4 variables determined from the antisaccade task described above. The training and untrained groups consisted of 9 children. The two groups were matched for age. The teacher did not know who was a member of the control or the experimental group.

Pre-post test results were compared by ANOVA with repeated measurements with age as a covariate. The result indicates that both groups profited from the reading lessons. The interaction term (group x time), however, was particularly significant and showed that the effects were different in the two groups.

Fig. 23 shows the reduction of reading errors in both groups by post-hoc analysis using the two-tailed t-test of the differences of the relative error reduction given in percentages. The difference was significant at the 1% level. The experimental group reduced their errors by about 50%, while the control group showed a reduction of about only 20%.

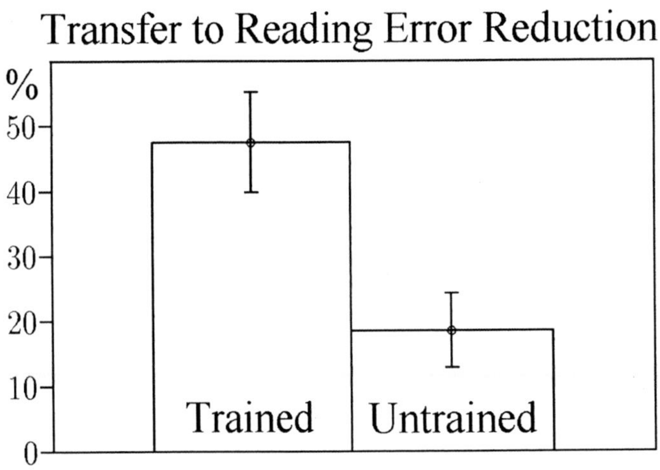

Figure 23. The effect of saccade training on reading error reduction after reading lessons. The trained group reduced the errors by about 50%, while the untrained group reduced the errors by only 20%.

We also compared the profit of the younger members of the groups separately from the profit of the older members. Despite the small number of subjects, it was quite clear that the younger children profited more from teaching lessons while the extra effect of the saccade training was relatively small. The older members, on the other hand, profited from the lessons only if they were members of the training group. This corresponds to the experience that more reading lessons do not help in older dyslexics. However, after successful saccade training they profit much more and eventually find their way to better reading competence by learning how to read by themselves or with further professional help.

Additionally, there are other problems in eye movement control: We know that binocular instability can be improved by using only one eye during the training of saccade control. We do not have our own data on the effect of this monocular training alone on reading, but from other studies one can be fairly certain that the process of learning how to read is facilitated when only one eye is used (Stein and Fowler, 1985).

CONCLUSION

The last few years of research in the field of neural processing in auditory, visual, and optomotor control functions have shown, that these functions undergo a long development lasting until adulthood. Certain proportions of dyslexics exhibit developmental deficits in one or more of these domains as has been reported earlier (Witton et al. 1998). The deficits described here can be improved to a certain extend by specific and controlled daily practice. Successful training results in specific advantages in acquiring spelling and reading skills.

While these new methods are helpful for many dyslexics they may not be the final solution in all cases of dyslexia, because other deficits that go beyond the sensory and optomotor functions may play an important role in a dyslexic child, e.g. functions of language processing itself. If possible, these deficits should be improved as well before one can expect such a dyslexic child to really improve spelling and reading skills in all respects.

But, as the present studies have shown, significant advantages can already be obtained when only the sensory and/or optomotor functions are improved.

SUPPLY OF INSTRUMENTS

The following instruments were used in the studies reported here:

- FonoFix for testing low level auditory discrimination in 5 domains
- FonoTrain for training
- FixTest for testing dynamic vision in 3 task versions
- CountFix for testing visual subitizing
- CounTrain for training
- ExpressEye for measuring and analysing saccadic eye movements by 2 tasks
- FixTrain for training of dynamic vision and saccade control by 3 tasks.

These instruments are available for use in the English and German languages. See: www.optom.de

REFERENCES

Biscaldi M, Fischer B, and Hartnegg K (2000) Voluntary saccade control in dyslexia. *Perception* 29: 509-521

Breitmeyer BG (1993) The roles of sustained and transient channels in reading and reading disabilities. In: Wright SF, Groner R (eds) *Facets of dyslexia and its remediation*. North-Holland Elsevier, Amsterdam, pp 13-32

Brunner M, Seibert A, Dierks A, Körkel B (1996) *Heidelberger Lautdifferenzierungstest.* Westra-Verlag, Heidelberg,

Buunen TJ, van Valkenburg DA (1979) Auditory detection of a single gap in noise. *J Acoustical Soc Am* 65: 534-536

Dehaene S, (1999) *Der Zahlensinn.* Birkhäuser Verlag, Basel.

Eden FG, VanMeter JW, Rumsey JM, Maisog JM, Woods RP, Zeffiro TA (1998) Abnormal processing of visual motion in dyslexia revealed by functional brain imaging. *Letters to Nature* 382: 66-69

Eden GF, Stein JF, Wood HM, and Wood FB (1994) Differences in eye movements and reading problems in dyslexic and normal children. *Vision Res* 34: 1345-1358

Everling S, Fischer B (1998) The antisaccade: a review of basic research and clinical studies. *Neuropsychologia* 36: 885-899

Fischer B (1987) The preparation of visually guided saccades. *Rev Physiol Biochem Pharmacol* 106: 1-35

Fischer B, Biscaldi M, and Gezeck S (1997) On the development of voluntary and reflexive components in human saccade generation. *Brain-Res* 754: 285-297

Fischer B, Gezeck S, and Hartnegg K (1997) The analysis of saccadic eye movements from gap and overlap paradigms. *Brain Research Protocols* 2: 47-52

Fischer B, Hartnegg K (2000) Effects of visual training on saccade control in dyslexia. *Perception* 29: 531-542

Fischer B, Hartnegg K, Mokler A (2000) Dynamic visual perception of dyslexic children. *Perception* 29: 523-530

Fischer B, and Ramsperger E (1984) Human express saccades: extremely short reaction times of goal directed eye movements. *Exp-Brain-Res* 57: 191-195

Fischer B, and Weber H (1992) Characteristics of "anti" saccades in man. *Exp-Brain-Res* 89: 415-424

Fischer B, and Weber H (1993) Express Saccades and Visual Attention. *Behav.& Brain Sciences* 16,3: 553-567

Fitch RH, Miller S, and Tallal P (1997) Neurobiology of speech perception. *Annual Review of Neuroscience* 20: 331-353

Fowler MS (1992) Binocular control in dyslexics. In: Stein JF (ed) *Vision and visual dyslexia.* Macmillan Press, pp 141-147

Galaburda AM (1993) Neuroanatomic basis of developmental dyslexia. *Neurol Clin* 11: 161-173

Green CS, Bavelier D (2003) Action video game modifies visual selective attention. *Nature* 423: 534-537

Guitton D, Buchtel HA, and Douglas RM (1985) Frontal lobe lesions in man cause difficulties in suppressing reflexive glances and in generating goal-directed saccades. *Exp-Brain-Res* 58: 455-472

Hallet PE (1978) Primary and secondary saccades to goals defined by instructions. *Vision Res* 18: 1279-1296

Hartnegg K, Fischer B (2002) A turn-key transportable eye-tracking instrument for clinical assessment. Behavior, Research Methods, Instruments, & Computers 34: 625-629

Hebb D (1949) *The oranization of behaviour: A neuropsychological theory.* Wiley, New York,

Kaufman E, Lord M, Reese T, Volkman J (1949) The discrimination of visual number. *Am J Psychol* 62: 498-525

Klein C, Fischer Jr B, Fischer B, Hartnegg K (2002) Effects of methylphenidate on saccadic responses in patients with ADHD. *Exp Brain Res* 145: 121-125

Klein C, Raschke A, Brandenbusch A (2003) Development of pro- and antisaccades in children with attention-deficit hyperactivity disorder (ADHD) and healthy controls. *Psychophysiology* 40: 17-28

Livingstone MS, Rosen GD, Drislane FW, and Galaburda AM (1991) Physiological and anatomical evidence for a magnocellular defect in developmental dyslexia. *Proc-Natl-Acad-Sci-U-S-A* 88: 7943-7947

Lovegrove W (1993) Weakness in the transient visual system: a causal factor in dyslexia? *Ann N Y Acad Sci* 682: 57-69

Mayfrank L, Mobashery M, Kimmig H, and Fischer B (1986) The role of fixation and visual attention in the occurrence of express saccades in man. *European Archives of Psychiatry & Neurological Sciences* 235: 269-275

Mc Anally KI, Stein JF (1996) Auditory temporal coding in dyslexia. *Proc R Soc Lond B Biol Sci* 263: 961-965

Merzenich MM, Jenkins WM, Johnston P, Schreiner C, Miller SL, and Tallal P (1996) Temporal processing deficits of language-learning impaired children ameliorated by training. *Science* 271: 77-81

Mountcastle VB, Andersen RA, and Motter BC (1981) The influence of attentive fixation upon the excitability of the light-sensitive neurons of the posterior parietal cortex. *J-Neurosci* 1: 1218-1225

Munoz DP, and Wurtz RH (1993) Fixation cells in monkey superior colliculus. I. Characteristics of cell discharge. *J Neurophysiol* 70: 559-575

Olson RK, Kliegl R, and Davidson BJ (1983) Dyslexic and normal readers' eye movements. *J Exp Psychol [Hum-Percept]* 9: 816-825

Pavlidis GT (1981) Do eye movements hold the key to dyslexia? *Neuropsychologia* 19: 57-64

Schiller PH, True SD, and Conway JL (1979) Effects of frontal eye field and superior colliculus ablations on eye movements. *Science* 206: 590-592

Schiller PH, True SD, and Conway JL (1980) Deficits in eye movements following frontal eye-field and superior colliculus ablations. *J-Neurophysiol* 44: 1175-1189

Schrauf M, Wist ER, and Ehrenstein WH (2000) Development of dynamic vision based on motion contrast. *Exp Brain Res* 124: 469-473

Stein J, and Fowler S (1985) Effect of monocular occlusion on visuomotor perception and reading in dyslexic children. *LANCET* 2: 69-73

Stein J, Talcott J (1999) Impaired neuronal timing in developmental dyslexia - The magnocellular hypothesis. *Dyslexia* 5: 59-77

Tallal P (1980) Auditory temporal perception, phonics, and reading disabilities in children. *Brain and Language* 9: 182-198

Tallal P, Merzenich M, Miller S, and Jenkins W (1998) Language learning impairment: integrating research and remediation. *Scandinavian Journal of Psychology* 39: 197-199

Trick LM, and Pylyshyn ZW (1993) What enumeration studies can show us about spatial attention: evidence for limited capacity preattentive processing. *J Exp Psychol Hum Percept Perform* 19: 331-351

Trick LM, and Pylyshyn ZW (1994) Why are small and large numbers enumerated differently? A limited-capacity preattentive stage in vision. *Psychol Rev* 101: 80-102

Witton C, Talcott JB, Hansen PC, Richardson AJ, Griffiths TD, Rees A, Stein JF, Green GGR (1998) Sensitivity to dynamic auditory and visual stimuli predicts nonword reading ability in both dyslexic and normal readers. *Current Biology* 8: 791-797

In: Trends in Dyslexia Research
Editor: Henry D. Tobias, pp. 35-71

ISBN 1-59454-219-8

Chapter II

READING AND SELECTIVE SPATIAL ATTENTION: EVIDENCE FROM BEHAVIORAL STUDIES IN DYSLEXIC CHILDREN*

Andrea Facoetti†
Dipartimento di Psicologia Generale, Università degli Studi di Padova, Italy
Unità di Psicologia Cognitiva, Istituto Scientifico "E. Medea" di Bosisio P, Lecco, Italy
Unità di Neuropsichiatria, Azienda Ospedaliera di Bergamo, Italy

ABSTRACT

Learning to read requires appropriate auditory-phonological and visual-spatial skills. According to the dual-route model, written words can be processed either by a sub-lexical route (analytic procedure), based on grapheme-phoneme correspondences, or by lexical route (global procedure), based on lexical units. However, the sub-lexical and the lexical routes are not independent components of written word recognition. They appear to be reciprocally related with an early role of the sub-lexical route on reading acquisition. This chapter considers crucial aspects of selective spatial attention in learning to read by the sub-lexical route. First, I will briefly review the recent literature on reading acquisition and on the crucial issue of visual and auditory selective attention in reading and dyslexia. Secondly, I will present new empirical evidence of a specific deficit of visual attention in dyslexic children. In particular, I will report and discuss the results of recent studies related to (a) attention focusing during word reading and letter identification; and (b) the time course of attentional focusing in the left andright visual hemifields. Finally, I will discuss the different behavioral pattern in dyslexic children compared to normally reading children in relation to new studies on the neural basis of reading.

* Part of this study was presented in "Right focusing deficit in dyslexic children", The 14th Annual Conference on Theoretical and Experimental Neuropsychology, Montreal, CA June 2003, to be published as an abstract in *Brain and Cognition*, 2004.

† Correspondence to: Andrea Facoetti, Dipartimento di Psicologia Generale, Via Venezia 8, 35131 Padova, Italy. Tel: +39-049-8276672, Fax: +39-049-8276600, E-mail address: andreafacoetti@unipd.it

Keywords: Reading, Development of reading, Reading disability, Phonological route, Magnocellular, Spatial attention, Attentional asymmetry, Visual and auditory selection

1. INTRODUCTION

1.1. Learning to Read and Developmental Dyslexia

According to dual-route (DR) models, skilled readers use two interactive procedures to convert print into speech (for a recent review, see Coltheart, Rastle, Perry, Langdon & Ziegler, 2001): the lexical route (i.e., orthographic procedure), that relies on whole-word recognition and retrieval of stored phonological codes and produces fast and efficient reading of familiar words, and the sub-lexical route (i.e., phonological procedure), that involves a letter-to-sound mapping of the most frequent relationships between graphemes and phonemes in a given language. These procedures allow readers to read unfamiliar words and non-words. Data from both acquired and developmental cases suggest the existence of two different subtypes of dyslexia: surface dyslexia and phonological dyslexia (e.g., Coltheart et al., 2001; Sprenger-Charolles, Colé, Lacert & Serniclaes, 2000). Surface dyslexia is characterized by impaired reading of irregular words relative to regular words and non-words, while phonological dyslexia is associated with impaired reading of unfamiliar words and non-words compared to familiar words. According to DR models, surface dyslexia would arise from damage to the lexical procedure, whereas phonological dyslexia would arise from damage to the sub-lexical procedure.

Developmental models based on the DR account assume that the two procedures are acquired serially, with beginner readers initially relying on the sub-lexical route and only later shifting to the lexical route (e.g., Frith, 1986). Other models, in contrast, propose that a single sub-lexical route is involved in learning to read both non-words and irregular words (e.g., Perfetti, 1992). Similarly, in connectionist models, non-words and irregular words are processed by a single route operating over distributed orthographic and phonological representations (e.g., Seidenberg & McClelland, 1989).

Longitudinal studies are necessary to assess the crucial and early role of the sub-lexical route in the acquisition of reading. Most longitudinal studies have shown that beginner readers use primarily the sub-lexical route for both reading aloud and silent reading. This suggests that phonological processing may gradually be replaced by lexical processing (for a recent review, see Sprenger-Charolles, Siegel, Béchennec & Serniclaes, 2003).

In addition, if the sub-lexical route plays a basic role in reading acquisition, the degree of grapheme-phoneme consistency of different languages should affect learning to read. According to consistency of the written system, less reliance on phonological processing is found in English children compared to Spanish, German or French children. Indeed, grapheme-phoneme correspondences are more consistent in Spanish, German or French as compared to English. It should be noted that Italian words could be read by using exclusively grapheme-to-phoneme conversion (i.e., the sub-lexical route), while whole-word recognition (i.e., the lexical route) seems to be less crucial, because the Italian language has a particularly transparent orthography.

Moreover, in languages with transparent orthography (i.e, German and Italian), the specific possibility to use "spelling-to-sound" correspondences via the sub-lexical route could also explain why developmental dyslexia is manifested not only by inaccurate reading but also by slow reading (for German, see Wimmer, 1993).

Finally, recent studies on dyslexia subtypes (i.e., phonological and surface dyslexia) seem to suggest the crucial role of the sub-lexical route in phonological dyslexics, demonstrating not only impaired phonological reading skills, but also impaired orthographic reading skills. Note that the "surface profile" almost disappears when dyslexic children are compared to younger children of the same reading level. Furthermore, the phonological deficits (e.g., phonemic awareness and phonological short-term memory) are severe in both types of dyslexics, since they were found even in comparison with younger reading controls. Thus, both phonological and surface dyslexics appear to suffer from a pure phonological dysfunction. It is suggested that environmental factors (e.g., limited experience with the written language and/or less incentives to overcome reading difficulties) could explain the frequently observed dissociation between phonological and surface dyslexia (for a recent review, see Sprenger-Charolles et al., 2000).

For decades researchers have been approaching reading and dyslexia not only from the standpoint of auditory and phonological contributions but also of visual contributions. Auditory and phonological mechanisms are thought to underlie sub-lexical reading, whereas visual mechanisms are thought to exclusively underlie lexical reading (e.g., Sperling, Lu, Manis & Seidenberg, 2003). However, it is widely assumed that the sub-lexical route requires a primary *graphemic parsing process* (i.e., the segmentation of a grapheme string into its constituent graphemes). Thus, it is clear that phonological assembly via the sub-lexical route involves not only appropriate phonological skills (i.e., grapheme-to-phoneme correspondences and phonological short-term memory), but also visual perceptual processing and specifically *precise and rapid selective spatial attention*.

In fact, several studies have provided evidence of phonological deficits (e.g., Bradley & Bryant, 1983; for a recent review, see Ramus, 2003), but many dyslexic children also show visual perceptual deficits (e.g., Geiger & Lettvin, 1999). In particular, phonological dyslexics have been found to have visual deficits (e.g., Borsting, Riddel, Duddeck, Kelley, Matsui & Motoyama, 1996; Cestnick & Coltheart, 1999) whereas surface dyslexics have not (e.g., Borsting et al., 1996; Cestnick & Coltheart, 1999; Spinelli, Angelelli, Deluca, Dipace, Judica & Zoccolotti, 1997), suggesting potentially unique visual perceptual contributions to non-word reading.

In addition, there is evidence that the magnocellular visual system, which plays a crucial role in selective spatial attention (e.g., Steinman, Steinman & Lehmkuhle, 1996) and in localized information processing (e.g., Omtzigt, Hendriks & Folk, 2002), is defective in dyslexics (e.g., Galaburda & Livingstone, 1993; for a review, see Stein & Walsh, 1997).

The magnocellular theory of dyslexia is an exhaustive (e.g., Stein & Walsh, 1997), albeit controversial (e.g., Skottun, 2000) view assuming that many reading disabled children are impaired specifically in the visual magnocellular pathway (e.g., Galaburda & Livingstone, 1993). The multi-modal (i.e., visual and auditory) version of the magnocellular theory of dyslexia, called "temporal processing hypothesis" (for a review, see Farmer & Klein, 1995), suggests that children with dyslexia (and also children with specific language impairments,

SLI) have specific deficits in processing rapidly presented or brief sensory stimuli within the visual and auditory domains (for a recent review, see Benasich & Tallal, 2002). Thus, the auditory temporal processing deficit that degrades the children's ability to perceive transient elements of speech is supposed to cause the phonological impairment both in developmental dyslexia and in SLI (e.g., Merzenich, Jenkins, Johnston, Schreiner, Miller & Tallal, 1996).

Recently, Cestnick and Coltheart (1999) have investigated the relationship between the sub-lexical route and deficits of the visual magnocellular system in developmental dyslexia. They measured non-word reading, irregular word reading, and performance with Ternus apparent movement displays (i.e., a visual motion detection task supposedly measuring magnocellular system function; but see Skottun, 2001) in dyslexic children and children without reading difficulties. Their results showed that performance on the Ternus task correlated with non-word reading ability but not with irregular word reading ability. Davis, Castles, McAnally and Gray (2001) partially replicated the study of Cestnick and Coltheart (1999) and confirmed the results. Davis et al. (2001) controlled general inattention and concluded that developmental phonological dyslexics, as opposed to surface dyslexics, likely have a visual perceptual deficit. Accordingly, visual perceptual performance (i.e., motion and flicker sensitivity) strongly correlated with non-word ability both in dyslexic and in normally reading adults (Talcott, Hansen, Willis-Owen, McKinnell, Richardson & Stein, 1998). Cestnick and Coltheart (1999) offered two alternative interpretations of their findings: 1) "Non-word reading requires a serial left-to-right allocation of covert attention across the letter string being read and the neural systems involved in this attentional process also play a part in responses to the Ternus display", and 2) "Poor non-word reading and abnormal Ternus performance are not directly related: perinatal/neurodevelopmental insult has affected the lateral geniculate nucleus (influencing Ternus performance) and the adjacent medial geniculate nucleus (affecting phonological ability)" (Cestnick & Coltheart, 1999, p. 231). Clearly, the two alternative interpretations are not mutually exclusive.

Cestnick (2001) also provided evidence for the second interpretation, compatible with a multi-modal temporal processing deficit. In accord with a multi-modal processing deficit, Witton, Talcott, Hansen, Richardson, Griffiths, Rees, Stein and Green (1998) showed that dyslexics are less sensitive to both specific rates of auditory frequency modulation and dynamic motion of visual stimuli. In addition, non-word reading, a unique measure of the sub-lexical route, was found to be related to these visual and auditory perceptual measures (Witton et al., 1998).

Interestingly, a recent study by Iles, Walsh and Richardson (2000) showed that only dyslexics that were impaired on a low-level psychophysical task measuring motion coherence thresholds (a magnocellular system function), also exhibited deficits in a serial visual search dependent upon higher-level processing (selective spatial attention). Note that motion thresholds correlated with non-word reading ability (Talcott et al., 1998). Thus, one could suggest a possible relationship between selective spatial attention and non-word reading. Nevertheless, more direct experimental evidence is necessary to test this hypothesis.

A recent study by Amitay, Ben-Yehudah, Banai and Ahissar (2002), investigating both visual and "auditory magnocellular" functions (i.e., flicker detection, detection of drifting gratings at low spatial frequencies, speed discrimination and detection of coherent dot motion), showed that "pure" magnocellular deficits were only present in six out of 30 dyslexic adults. In addition, disabled readers showed "impaired performance on both visual and auditory non-magnocellular tasks requiring fine frequency discriminations. The stimuli used in these tasks were neither modulated in time nor briefly presented" (Amitay et al., 2002, p. 2272). Thus, the authors concluded that dyslexics have a generally inefficient multi-modal processing of perceptual stimuli.

To explain the multi-modal perceptual deficit in dyslexics (and SLI children), Hartley and Moore (2002) presented a model based on "processing efficiency". The model suggests that the masking effects (spatial and temporal signal interference induced by "near" noise or distractor) can be better explained by a processing efficiency hypothesis rather than a temporal processing hypothesis. The processing efficiency refers to all factors, aside from temporal and spectral resolution, that affect the ability to detect visual and acoustic signals in noise (i.e., threshold signal-to-noise ratio).

I suggest that one crucial factor affecting the multi-modal processing efficiency is the *selective spatial attention* defined as the *privileged processing of information coming from a particular spatial area*. Despite the great amount of information flooding the natural scenes, we are able to focus attention on one spatial location (and/or object) and process the relevant information. Indeed, natural scenes contain a variety of different objects that cannot be all processed simultaneously. Thus, multiple stimuli compete for representation by multilevel neurons to affect motor output. It is now evident that selective spatial attention to stimuli changes neural responses to these stimuli throughout specific brain areas (for a recent review, see Corbetta & Shulman, 2002). These widespread neural changes affect many aspects of visual and auditory perceptual functions. The major effect on perceptual functions is that selective spatial attention appears to enhance the neural representation of stimuli. "This '*signal enhancement*' manifests itself in a variety of ways, including *accelerated reaction times* (RTs), *improved sensitivity* (thresholds), *reduced interactions with flanking stimuli*, and *elimination of illusory conjunctions*. Finally, attention allows decisions to be based on the selected stimulus alone and thus to disregard any distracting stimuli which may be present. Accordingly, attention is often said to *increase 'positional certainty'*" (Braun, 2002, p. 599). On the basis of these perceptual effects, selective spatial attention influences the contents of all the post-perceptual processing such as short-term memory, perceptual decisions and voluntary responses.

1.2. Visual Attention in Reading and in Developmental Dyslexia

Although spatial filtering could be achieved through two serial processes, orienting and focusing (or spatial scaling), most scientific literature considers the two processes as mutually exclusive, and associates them to two alternative models of selective spatial attention, specifically the "Spotlight model" (e.g., Posner, 1980) and the "Zoom lens model" (e.g., Eriksen & St. James, 1986). Orienting consists in moving or shifting the attended area (i.e., attentional focus) in the visual field (e.g., Posner, 1980; for a recent review, see Corbetta & Shulman, 2002), whereas focusing consists in adjusting the spatial extent of the attended area without orienting attention (e.g., Turatto, Benso, Facoetti, Galfano, Mascetti & Umiltà, 2000). It is likely that, when orienting is triggered, the two processes are simultaneously active and linked. When attention is oriented toward a visual stimulus, the final process would consist in "calibrating" the focus to the object size (e.g., Turatto et al., 2000; Castiello & Umiltà, 1990).

Some studies suggest that selective visual attention plays a basic role in word reading. Kahneman and Henik (1981) showed that color words within an attended field interfere more with color naming of a near stimulus than color words within an unattended field, suggesting that reading depends on the spatial orienting of visual attention. Accordingly, in a lexical decision task (i.e., word vs. non-word discrimination) on letter strings presented above or below fixation, the responses were faster on validly (i.e., attended location) than on invalidly (i.e., unattended location) cued conditions (McCann, Folk & Johnston, 1992).

Despite a vast literature, there is no consensus about the role of selective spatial attention in visual word processing. In fact, the early-selection theory argues that spatial attention must be focused on a word before it is identified. In contrast, the late-selection theory argues that words are processed automatically as focused attention is not required. A third possibility is that diffused vs. focused attention depends on the familiarity of the stimulus (LaBerge & Brown, 1989). Focused spatial attention might be required to process non-words and low-frequency words but not familiar words (for a recent review, see Auclair & Sieroff, 2002). Sieroff and Posner (1988) used spatial cueing to manipulate visual attention during reading. Subjects made more errors in reporting letters from the unattended side of non-words compared to words. Also, patients with neglect (left inattention caused by right parietal lesions) made more errors on the contralesional side with non-words compared to words (e.g., Sieroff, Pollatsek & Posner, 1988). Interestingly, focusing (without orienting) of visual attention showed a specific effect in non-word recognition. The size of attentional focus was controlled by presentation of large or small focusing cues and after variable delays. The subject was presented a string of five letters. The task was a simple lexical decision. Word discrimination was not affected by cue size. However, the non-word discrimination was highly affected by attentional focusing because identification was significantly slower in large compared to small cue conditions (Facoetti, Priftis, Colavito & Gianesini, 2003f).

Developmental theories assume that, at the beginning of word processing acquisition, the orthographic lexicon is not yet operating and reading mostly depends on "visual-spatial attentional and phonological processing". Thus, visual spatial attentional and/or phonological processing deficits could cause the specific impairment of the sub-lexical route, suggested to be the core of developmental dyslexia. In the sub-lexical route both focusing and orienting of visual attention are probably involved. To read a non-word, the visual system must not only focus the attention on single letters to process, inhibiting the flanked letters, but must also rapidly orient the focus of attention on the successive letter. Empirical evidence has shown that serial visual search (a task requiring both orienting and focusing of attention) correlates with reading performance (Casco, Tressoldi & Dellantonio, 1998) and that subjects with developmental dyslexia were defective on serial visual tasks (e.g., Vidyasagar & Pammer, 1999).

Of course, text reading presupposes an accurate planning and control of saccadic movements and fixations (for a recent review, see Starr & Rayner, 1997). It has been suggested that one has to orient and focus attention to the target location before a saccade can be made towards it (e.g., McPeek, Malikovic & Nakayama, 1999). Thus, when children are learning to read, they have to learn rapid focusing from left to right across the lines of text in order to allow accurate targeting of eye movements (Vidyasagar, 1999).

Brannan and Williams (1987) demonstrated that, compared to normally reading subjects, poor readers were not able to rapidly orient visual attention. In contrast, Jonkman, Licht, Bakker & Van den Broek-Sandmann (1992) investigated slower voluntary shifting of attention in dyslexics and normally reading children but without detecting any difference between the two groups. However, a series of studies has shown impaired orienting in dyslexic children, which affect only the automatic control of visual attention (e.g., Facoetti, Paganoni, Turatto, Marzola & Mascetti, 2000b).

In addition, subjects with learning disabilities made more errors than controls on the selective spatial attention task when distractor letters were adjacent to the target letter, suggesting that subjects with learning disabilities are less able to narrow the focus of visual attention (Richards, Samuels, Turnure & Ysseldyke, 1990). Accordingly, Rayner, Murphy, Henderson and Pollatsek (1989) reported the case of an adult with developmental dyslexia who performed better than controls in reporting letters shown in parafoveal vision. The authors attributed the abnormal performance to a deficit of attentional focusing present in dyslexics so that letters from words viewed parafoveally would interfere with the processing of concurrently fixed words. "In accordance with the view that ability to ignore peripheral information is related to reading skills, the severe reading disabled group showed equivalent interference from peripheral colour-words compared with the centrally placed distractor, whereas control subjects and compensated adult dyslexics presented evidence of an ability to inhibit peripherally presented items" (Everatt, McCorquodale, Smith, Culverwell, Wilks, Evans, Kay & Baker, 1999, p. 8). Again, in dyslexic vs. normally reading children, the detection of the visual onset was not either influenced by eccentricity when the stimuli were outside the attended area (Facoetti, Paganoni & Lorusso, 2000a). These data suggest a specific deficit of the attentional mechanism inhibiting laterally distracting information in dyslexic individuals.

Good and poor readers also differ in their ability to attend information inside the focus of attention and to ignore information outside the focus of attention. Good readers showed distance effect of distractor from target. The interference was larger near and dropped off as the distractor distance increased. In contrast, poor readers showed a constant distractor effect regardless of their distance form target. In addition, although poor readers were worse at both phonological and orthographic procedures, the difference was greater in the phonological task, suggesting a possible link between attentional focusing and sub-lexical route deficits (Klein & D' Entremont, 1999).

Despite this evidence, the issue of whether visual attentional focusing deficit represents a causal link to reading disorder in dyslexic children is still hotly debated (see e.g., Ramus, 2003). An important piece of evidence in favor of the attentional hypothesis is provided by our recent study showing that the dyslexics' ability to read improves following a specific training that improves their attentional focusing processes. We found that only dyslexic children trained to rapidly orient attention in the peripheral visual field, showed significant changes in attentional focusing. They could control attentional focus better as indicated by increased "costs for reorienting" (i.e., slower detection RTs to unattended vs. attended location). This treatment program also proved to be highly efficient in improving the children's reading abilities, suggesting a causal relationship between the sub-lexical route and attentional focusing (Facoetti, Lorusso, Paganoni, Umiltà & Mascetti, 2003e).

Geiger and Lettvin (1999) reported that dyslexic adults and children showed a specific disability to suppress stimuli from the periphery of the visual field, which could cause a deficit in foveal reading. Letter recognition as a function of eccentricity significantly differs between normal readers and severe dyslexics, mostly on the right visual field. In dyslexics, letters recognition was better than normal readers at 7.5°, 10° and 12.5° eccentricities, whereas letters recognition was lower at 2.5° eccentricity. The authors considered this effect a consequence of abnormal distribution of lateral masking (i.e., interference signal induced by lateral distracter stimuli) in dyslexics. In comparison to normal readers, the lateral masking in dyslexics is increased in central vision, instead of reduced in lateral vision. Letters recognition was normalized both in adults and children with dyslexia after 3-4 months of treatment consisting in increasing spatial selection in central vision and reducing peripheral vision by novel hand-eye coordination activities, and "focusing" the vision on one or two words by a window. This specific treatment also results in fast improvement in reading skills.

In a recent study Hari, Renvall and Tanskanen (2001) have searched for a core mechanism underlying the multi-modal sensory deficit in developmental dyslexia. When dyslexics were asked to make temporal order judgements, they showed a tendency to perceive the stimulus in the right visual field (RVF) as appearing first. In addition, dyslexics detected stimuli in the left visual field (LVF) significantly more slowly than normal readers, inducing the authors to suggest a left "mini-neglect" stemming from a right parietal dysfunction as a consequence of a magnocellular deficit. "Furthermore, abrupt stimuli captured attention in both visual hemifields less effectively in dyslexic adults than normal readers" (Hari et al., 2001, p. 1373). Results from a study of ours gives further support to the hypothesized left-side mini-neglect in dyslexics. Dyslexic children, compared to normal readers, exhibited a reduced flanker effect (i.e., interference effect on discrimination RTs produced by irrelevant lateral stimuli) in the LVF, suggesting a mild left inattention, and a concomitant stronger flanker effect in RVF, providing evidence for a reduced ability to "masking" distracting information on the right side (Facoetti & Turatto, 2000). The focusing of visual attention in developmental dyslexia was studied by recording RTs to the onset of a small stimulus along the horizontal axis in the two visual hemifields. In the 70% of time the target stimulus appeared inside a circle acting as focusing cue and in the 30% of time it appeared outside, allowing to study the attentional engagement both inside and outside the attended area. Dyslexic children showed an anomalous and asymmetric engagement of attention. The effect of the target eccentricity influenced RTs only when the stimulus was presented in the LVF, whereas no effect was shown when the stimulus was presented in the RVF. These results, other than to confirm a mild left inattention (e.g., Hari et al., 2001), showed that visual attention in dyslexics is completely diffused in the RVF, suggesting an attentional focusing deficit on the right side (i.e., *right over-distractibility*) (Facoetti & Molteni, 2001). Thus, it should be noted that abnormal distribution of visual perception in dyslexics (Geiger & Lettvin, 1999) is compatible with an alternative interpretation: an attentional focus excessively broad towards the right side that causes a "hyper processing" of stimulus in the RVF. Accordingly, in a recent study, Yeshurun and Carrasco (1998) observed that spatial selective attention improved performance at peripheral locations where spatial resolution was too low, but impaired performance at central locations where spatial resolution was too high.

In order to further elucidate the role of selective spatial attention in developmental dyslexia, we studied orienting and focusing of visual attention in phonological dyslexics (i.e., poor non-word readers), non-phonological dyslexics (i.e., normal non-word readers) and normally reading children, measuring target detection in cued (i.e., attended) and uncued (i.e., unattended) peripheral locations. Attentional facilitation of the target (i.e., faster RTs) at the attended location was similar in the three groups, suggesting that the focus of attention was moved normally both in phonological and non-phonological dyslexics. However, phonological dyslexics showed an asymmetrical attentional inhibition of the target (i.e., slower RTs) at the unattended location. Processing was inhibited for targets presented in the LVF but not in the RVF, suggesting a specific deficit of spatial inhibition on the right side in poor non-word readers. Given that a spatial selection mechanism operating on phoneme strings appears to be a basic component of the phonological procedure, we suggested that the right attentional inhibition deficit impairs left-to-right graphemic parsing, which would affect all subsequent processes (grapheme-phoneme conversion and phonological short-term memory). These results suggest that the sub-lexical route is specifically impaired from an attentional window excessively broad towards the right side because the letter that must be processed is not filtered from other right flanking letters. In addition, in dyslexic children the right spatial inhibition deficit correlated strongly with the non-word reading ability (Facoetti, Zorzi Cestnick, Lorusso, Paganoni, Umiltà, & Mascetti, 2004). This interpretation is strengthened by the finding that specifically improving the right visual spatial inhibition, generated beneficial effects on the dyslexic children's ability to read both non-words and words (Facoetti & Lorusso, in preparation).

1.3. Auditory Attention in Reading and Developmental Dyslexia

Although the generalities of developmental dyslexia are widely acknowledged, the precise associated neural mechanisms are poorly understood. One of the two major competing views maintains that dyslexics have normal auditory perception but have a specific deficit in coding linguistic input into phonological information. Indeed, there is much evidence that phonological processing deficits are linked to difficulties in learning to read such as: a) phonological performances predict later reading skills; b) phonological processing deficits markedly distinguish children with dyslexia from children with normal reading skills; and c) phonological training has been shown to improve the reading ability (e.g., Bradley & Bryant, 1983; for a recent review, see Ramus, 2003).

The competing view (the temporal processing deficit hypothesis) maintains that a more general auditory processing deficit characterizes dyslexia. Specifically, the difficulties in processing brief and rapid auditory cues impair the ability to accurately perceive crucial features in the speech stream, degrading the development of phonological codes (e.g., Farmer & Klein, 1995). However, recent evidence suggests that the basic deficit is not specific for auditory stimuli modulated in time or briefly presented. Instead, auditory "processing efficiency theory" (Hartley & Moore, 2002) suggests that dyslexic individuals have problems in detecting acoustic signals in noise (e.g., Amitay et al., 2002; Kujala, Myllyviita, Tervaniemi, Alho, Kallio & Naatanen, 2000). In fact, nonlinguistic auditory perceptual deficits in dyslexia involve: a) difficulties in discrimination between acoustically similar sound; b) an impaired ability to hear differences in sound frequency; c) problems in speech-sound perception (i.e., phoneme discrimination) in the presence of background noise; and d) deficits in processing rapid sound sequence (for a recent review, see Wright, Bowen & Zecker, 2000). It is suggested that all these nonlinguistic auditory perception deficits are likely related to an inability to focus auditory attention in order to discriminate properly and rapidly the features of the relevant signal sound (e.g., Vidyasagar, 1999; Hari & Renvall, 2001). Direct evidence for an auditory selective attentional deficit in dyslexics is now provided by some studies (e.g., Asbjornsen & Bryden, 1998; Renvall & Hari, 2002; Facoetti, Lorusso, Paganoni, Cattaneo, Galli, Umiltà & Mascetti, 2003d).

Hari et al. (2001) proposed that the causal link from the magnocellular deficit to reading and phonological problems involves the capture of auditory (and visual) automatic attention. "The primary cause could be sluggish attention shifting, as suggested by our previous finding that dyslexics are slower than normal readers in disengaging their attention from previous target" (Hari et al., 2001, p.1377). Accordingly, automatic capture of auditory (and visual) attention, measured using a detection task to target tone preceded (with a 100 or 250 ms cue-target delay) by spatial (left or right ear) cue tone, was slower in the dyslexic children than in the normally reading children. In normal readers, RTs were faster in the attended location compared to the unattended location (i.e., attentional facilitation) at 100 ms cue-target delay, whereas RTs were slower in the attended location compared to the unattended location (i.e., inhibition of return; for a recent review, see Klein, 2000) at 250 ms cue-target delay. In dyslexics, RTs were not faster in the attended location compared to the unattended location (no attentional facilitation) at 100 ms cue-target delay, whereas RTs were faster in the attended location compared to the unattended location (attentional facilitation) at 250 ms cue-target delay (Facoetti, Galli & Cattaneo, 2003a). In dyslexic children, the automatic capture of auditory attention also correlated strongly with the non-word ability only at shorter (100 ms) cue-target delay but not at middle (400 ms) nor at longer (550 ms) cue-target delays (Facoetti, unpublished data). It suggested that automatic capture of auditory attention could be directly linked to phonemic perception. Indeed, auditory selective attention may act to facilitate phoneme discrimination (e.g., Mondor & Bryden, 1991). Phoneme discrimination is also related to pure phonological processes involved in the sub-lexical route (i.e., grapheme-to-phoneme correspondences and phonological short-term memory).

To determine possible differences in auditory perception between dyslexics and normally reading children, we also tested the recognition of centrally localized speech stimuli in different background conditions. The results showed a larger drop of stimulus recognition in the conversation-background for dyslexics than for normal readers. However, dyslexics perceived more lateral stimuli from the background than normal readers. These results suggest a widespread auditory attention in dyslexics compared to normal readers (Geiger, Cattaneo, Galli, Pozzoli, Lorusso, Facoetti, Pesenti & Molteni, 2002). Although these data could be explained as a slowed automatic capture of auditory attention (e.g., Renvall & Hari, 2002; Facoetti et al., 2003d), further studies are necessary to elucidate the causal direction between the ability to detect signals in noise and slowed attentional capture. Nevertheless, our initial conscious perception – vision at a glance – identifying "forest before trees", is based on diffused attention (i.e., pre-attentive processing), whereas our later vision with scrutiny, incorporating into initial conscious perception detailed information, is based on serial focused attention (for a recent review, see Hochstein & Ahissar, 2002). It could be suggested that dyslexic individuals are relegated to diffused attention because of specific deficits in serial focused attention. This "diffused perception", involving both visual and auditory (also tactile, see Grant, Zangaladze, Thiagarajah & Sthian, 1999) modalities, could cause a general inefficiency processing of stimuli on any task where "vision with scrutiny" is requested (i.e., focused attention). It could be noted that the attentional focusing deficit in dyslexics may distort the development of phonological and orthographic representations that is crucial for learning to read (Hari & Renvall, 2001).

In summary: (1) at the beginning of reading acquisition, the orthographic lexicon is not yet operating, so children learn to read via sub-lexical route; (2) the first process of sub-lexical route (i.e., graphemic parsing) may be linked to visual selective attention; (3) phonemic perceptual processing, a basic skill of grapheme-to-phoneme correspondences as well as of phonological short-term memory, could be linked to auditory selective attention; (4) specific deficits of visual selective attention are shown in dyslexic children, mostly in poor non-word readers; (5) also auditory selective attention is impaired in dyslexic children; (6) both visual and auditory attention are correlated to the non-word reading ability in dyslexic children.

In the next section I will show new behavioral evidence on spatial (in the RVF) and temporal (slowed time course) attentional focusing deficits in dyslexic children.

2. EXPERIMENTS

2.1. Attentional Focusing on Words and Letters in Dyslexic Children

Dyslexic adults detected stimuli in the LVF significantly slower than normal readers, suggesting a *right parietal dysfunction* (Hari et al., 2001).

Interestingly, only phonological dyslexic children did not show a cueing effect (were not slower in uncued trials) in the RVF, resulting from a lack of spatial inhibition to unattended visual stimuli on the right side when attention was focused to the left (Facoetti et al., submitted for publication). Phonological dyslexics might have an asymmetric attentional window which is excessively broad towards the right side. Similarly, Geiger and Lettvin (1999) showed a right-side enhancement in the peripheral processing of visual information in dyslexics, as demonstrated by an increased ability in letter recognition in the RVF. Similar attentional asymmetries have been found in a "mixed" (i.e., non-selected) group of dyslexic children in studies investigating both focusing (Facoetti & Molteni, 2001) and orienting of visual attention (Facoetti, Turatto, Lorusso & Mascetti, 2001). The reduced ability to suppress distracting information in the RVF also provides empirical evidence for a *right attentional inhibition deficit* (Facoetti & Turatto, 2000).

In the present experiment we studied focusing of visual spatial attention on words and letters in dyslexic and in normally reading children. We recorded RTs to the onset of a probe visual stimulus displayed either on the left, on the center or on the right side of five-letter words during two different primary tasks, reading and middle letter discrimination tasks (blocked conditions), manipulating in this way attentional focusing engagement (i.e., diffused and focused, respectively). A preliminary report of part of this study has been presented in abstract form (Facoetti, Galli, Cattaneo & Lorusso, 2003b).

2.1.1. Participants

Twelve dyslexic children between 7 and 13 years old (mean age 10.9, ± 1.9 standard deviation, SD) were diagnosed as dyslexics based on standard exclusion criteria (American Psychiatric Association, 1994). Their performance on oral reading of a text was at least 1 SD below the norm on age-standardized Italian tests (Cornoldi, Colpo & Gruppo MT, 1981). Reading scores (speed and/or accuracy) were 2 SDs below the norm on at least one of the age-standardized Italian tests included in the battery (text reading, single word and non-word reading) (Cornoldi et al., 1981; Sartori, Job & Tressoldi, 1995).

Dyslexic participants were selected on the basis of: 1) the absence of a spoken language impairment; 2) a full scale IQ greater than 85, as measured by the Wechsler Intelligence Scale for Children-Revised (WISC-R, Wechsler, 1986); 3) normal or corrected-to-normal vision and hearing; 4) the absence of attention deficit disorder with hyperactivity (ADHD), as evaluated through DSM diagnostic criteria (American Psychiatric Association, 1994); and 5) right manual preference. Seven control children between 8 and 12 years old (mean age 10.4, ± 1.6 SD) were also selected, recommended as normal readers by their teachers. They were at or above the norm (accuracy +0.7 SD and speed +0.6 SD) on age-standardized single word Italian reading tests (Sartori et al., 1995). In addition, normally reading children were of at least average intelligence, as measured by two WISC-R (Wechsler, 1986) sub-tests (Vocabulary 10.1 standard score, ± 2.9 SD and Block design 13.1 standard score, ± 2.8 SD). The two groups of children did not differ for chronological age ($P>0.30$). All the participants' parents gave informed consent.

2.1.2. Apparatus and Procedures

Focusing engagement of visual attention was measured in a dimly lit room (1.5 cd/m^2 luminance). Participants sat in front of a monitor screen (15 inches and 0.5 cd/m^2 background luminance) with their head positioned on a headrest so that the eye-screen distance was 40 cm. Figure 1 shows the experimental setup. The fixation point (cross of 0.9° of visual angle) appearing at the center of the screen was flanked by a pre-mask array presented in the same location of the following letter string. After 500 ms a blank screen was displayed for 50 ms. Then, a letter string (Arial bold font, 0.9 x 0.7° and separated by a 1.1° distance), building a familiar word, was presented for 2000 ms. After 500 ms from letter string onset, a probe stimulus (red dot, 0.3°) was presented (in 70% of trials) peripherally either in the LVF, in the RVF (eccentricity 6°), or in the center, below (0.3°) the letter string for 25 ms. A blank screen of 2500 ms was used as an inter-trial interval. Stimuli were white (except the probe stimulus) and had a luminance of 24 cd/m^2. Participants were instructed to keep their eyes fixed on the fixation point throughout the duration of the trial. Eye movements were monitored by means of a video-camera system. Any eye movement detected was discarded but not replaced.

The probe task required the participants to respond when the red dot appeared in one of the three locations (i.e., to detect its presence anywhere on the screen). Participants were instructed to react to probe stimulus onset as quickly as possible by pressing the spacebar on the computer keyboard. Catch trials (30% of trials), in which the probe stimulus was not presented and participants did not have to respond, were intermingled with response trials.

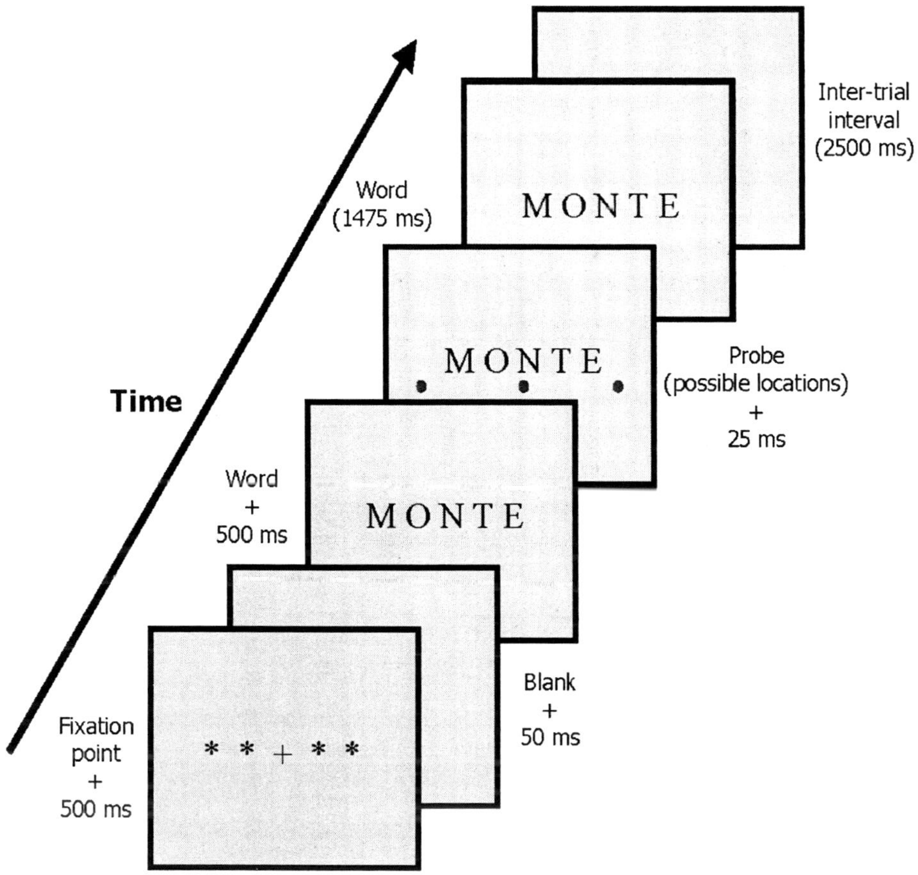

Figure 1. Schematic representation of the display used in Experiment 1 (probe task).

The aim of this study was to measure attentional focusing engagement in two different conditions – diffused attention and focused attention – by manipulating the primary task (for details, see LaBerge, 1983). In a block of trials, the primary task requires participants to read the presented word. This task measures diffused visual attention in which the attended area is widely distributed. In the other block of trials, the primary task requires participants to recognize the middle letter of the word. This task, on the contrary, measures focused visual attention in which the attended area is narrowly focused. The experimental session consisted of 160 trials divided into two blocks of 80 trials each. The block sequence was counterbalanced within participants. Trials were distributed as follows: 60 probe trials (20 for each location) and 20 catch trials.

2.1.3. Results

Primary Reading Task

Errors to probe stimulus (responses on catch trials and missed responses) were less than 4% and were not analyzed. Outliers were defined as RTs faster than 150 ms or more than 2.5 standard deviations above the mean and were excluded from the data sets before the analyses were carried out. This resulted in the removal of approximately 2% of all observations. Eye movements appeared in about 3% of total trials.

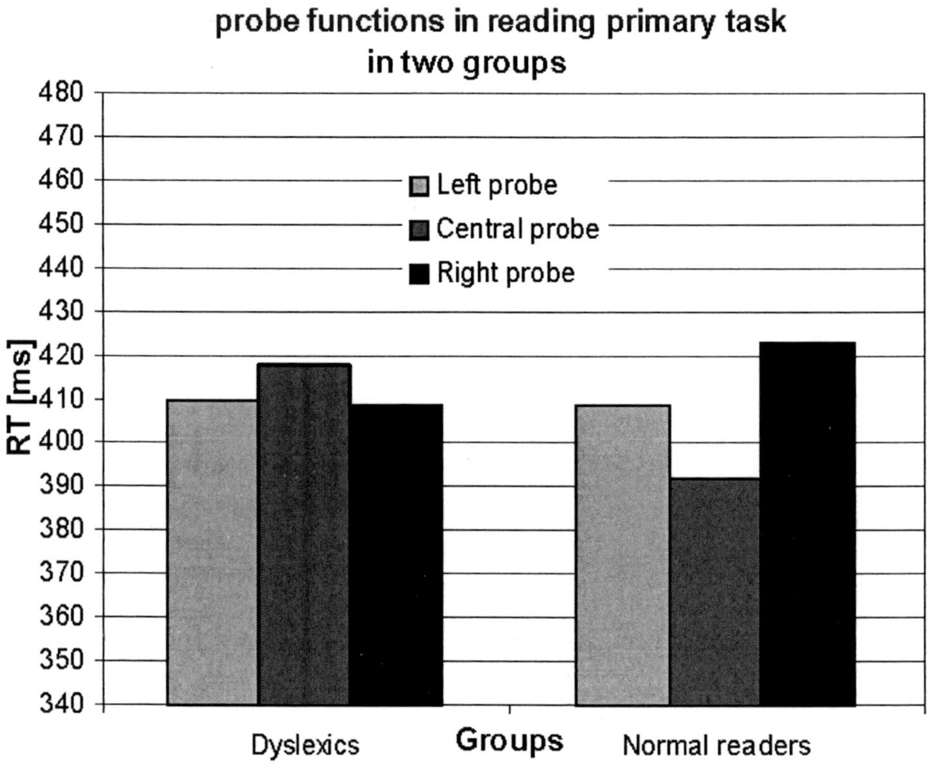

Figure 2. Mean reaction times (RTs) as a function of group (dyslexic children and normally reading children) and probe location (left, central and right) on the primary reading task. Probe location functions were not different between the two groups. Probe functions suggest a diffused attention on the word during the reading task.

Mean correct RTs were analyzed with a mixed two-way analysis of variance (ANOVA) in which the within-subjects factor was probe location (left, central or right probe stimuli), and the between-subjects factor was group (dyslexic or normally reading children). The probe location main effect was not significant ($F<1$); the group main effect was not significant ($F<1$); and finally, the two-way probe location x group interaction was not found to be significant either ($F(2,34)=1.09$, $P>0.30$).

Letter Discrimination Primary Task

Errors to probe stimulus (responses on catch trials and missed responses) were less than 5% and were not analyzed. Outliers were defined as RTs faster than 150 ms or more than 2.5

standard deviations above the mean and were excluded from the data sets before the analyses were carried out. This resulted in the removal of approximately 2% of all observations. Eye movements appeared in about 4% of total trials.

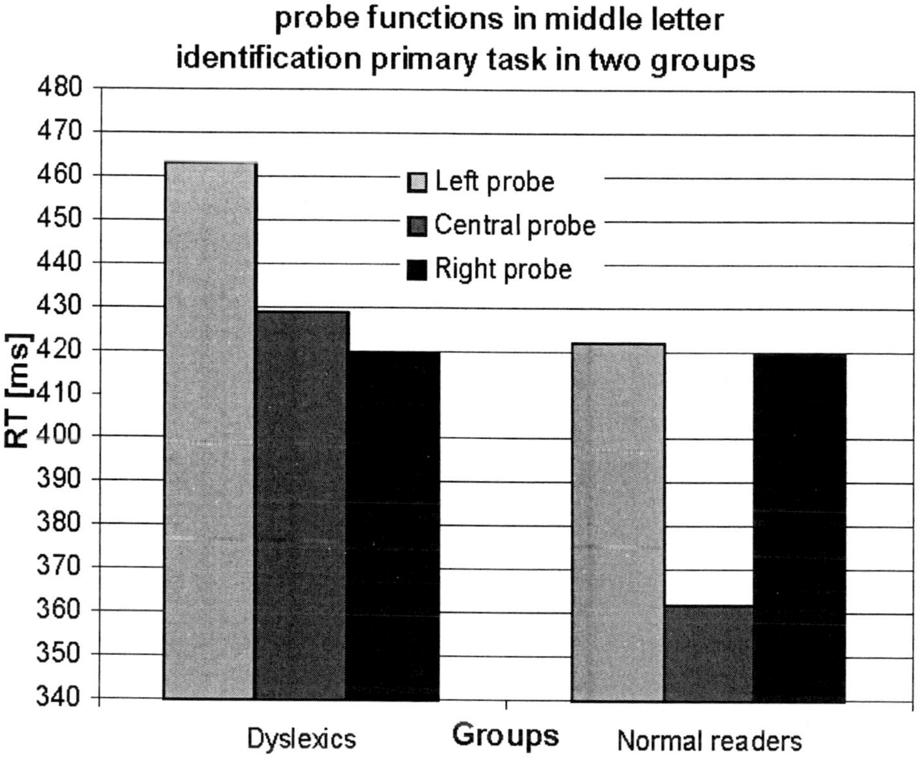

Figure 3. Mean RTs as a function of group (dyslexic children and normally reading children) and probe location (left, central and right) on the middle letter identification primary task. Probe location functions were different between two groups. In normal readers, probe function suggests a focused attention on the middle letter during the recognition task. By contrast, in dyslexics, probe function was flat on the right side, indicating a specific deficit to inhibit stimuli from the right during central overt and covert attentional focusing.

Mean correct RTs were analyzed with a mixed two-way ANOVA in which the within-subjects factor was probe location (left, central and right probe stimuli) and the between-subjects factor was group (dyslexic children and normally reading children). The probe location main effect was significant (F(2,34)=6.64, P<0.004). RTs to left probe were 442 ms, to right probe were 420 ms, whereas RTs to central probe were 396 ms. The group main effect was significant too (F(1,17)=4.49, P<0.05). RTs in normally reading children were 402 ms whereas in dyslexic children RTs were 438 ms. However, these findings should be interpreted in light of the two-way probe location x group interaction which was also significant (F(2,34)=3.46, P<0.05). Planned comparisons in normally reading children revealed that RTs - both to left probe (422 ms) and to right probe (420 ms) - were slower than RTs to the central probe (362 ms) (RTs difference 60 ms and 58 ms, respectively, Ps<0.05). In contrast, planned comparisons in dyslexic children revealed that only RTs to the left probe

(463 ms) were slower than RTs to the central probe (429 ms) (RT difference 34 ms, $P<0.05$) whereas RTs to the right probe (420 ms) were faster (RT difference –9 ms, $P>0.30$). In addition, in dyslexic children only, RTs to the left probe were significantly slower than RTs to the right probe (RT difference 43 ms, $P<0.05$). Lastly, comparisons between groups showed slower RTs in dyslexics than in normal readers at the left and central probes (RT difference: 40 ms and 67 ms respectively, $P<0.05$).

2.1.4. Discussion

The flat RT function across probe locations shown during the primary reading task seems to demonstrate a widely focused attention (as in LaBerge, 1983). In addition, this diffused attended area during the reading task did not differ significantly between dyslexic and normally reading children. It could be suggested that during single word reading diffused attention is not specifically abnormal in dyslexic individuals. The crucial perceptual deficit in dyslexia is therefore unlikely attributable to an impaired pre-attentive processing of visual stimuli (i.e., diffused attention). A recent study also showed increased crowding effects (i.e., decreased stimulus recognition in embedded vs. isolated conditions) on word identification in dyslexic children (Spinelli, De Luca, Judica & Zoccolotti, 2002). It should be noted that the crucial effect of selective spatial attention is to reduce interaction with flanking stimuli (e.g., Facoetti & Molteni, 2000; Freeman, Sagi & Driver, 2001).

In addition, the V-shaped RT function across probe locations shown during the primary letter-recognition task seems to demonstrate a narrowly focused attention (as in LaBerge, 1983). More interestingly, the two-way group x probe location interaction found in the letter detection task suggests that only in dyslexic children is there a lack of attentional inhibition to the right probe when the attentional focus was overtly and covertly focused in the central location. This attentional asymmetry, studied by a more ecological paradigm (i.e., middle letter recognition task of familiar five-letter words), seems to confirm data from other studies on attentional focus asymmetry in developmental dyslexia (e.g., Facoetti & Turatto, 2000; Hari et al., 2001; Facoetti & Molteni, 2001).

Moreover, slower RTs to the left probe than to the right probe in dyslexic children during focused attention at central letter provide new evidence to the "left mini-neglect" hypothesis (Hari et al., 2001). This result is also confirmed by the RT difference between groups (i.e., slower RTs to the left probe in dyslexics than in normal readers).

Asymmetries in visual processing in adult dyslexics have not been considered to be causally connected to the reading disorder (Hari et al., 2001; for review, see Hari & Renvall, 2001). However, our previous results in phonological dyslexics suggest a specific link between this right attentional focusing deficit and the ability to read via the sub-lexical route (Facoetti et al., submitted for publication).

It must also be noted that our results on visual attention do not rule out the alternative interpretations of a multi-modal (both auditory and visual) spatial attention deficit in developmental dyslexia (e.g., Facoetti et al., 2003d, Geiger et al., 2002) and/or of a multi-modal temporal processing deficit in phonological dyslexics (e.g., Cestnick, 2001).

2.2. Spatial and Temporal Deficits of Attentional Focusing in Dyslexic Children

Recently, we studied the time course of overt attentional focusing in dyslexic and normally reading children. A cue size procedure was used. When a stimulus is presented inside a large cue vs. a small cue, its identification time is significantly slower (i.e., cue size effect). Results showed a slower time course of attentional focusing in dyslexics vs. normal readers. In fact, in normally reading children a cue size effect (i.e., attentional focusing) was found at both cue-target delays (100 and 500 ms). In contrast, dyslexics exhibited a cue size effect at a longer cue target delay only (Facoetti, Lorusso, Paganoni, Cattaneo, Galli & Mascetti, 2003c). These results further support the hypothesis of a sluggish capture of attention in dyslexics (Hari & Renvall, 2001).

However, some studies showed an asymmetric orienting and focusing of visual attention in dyslexic individuals (e.g., Facoetti et al., 2001; Hari et al., 2001; experiment 1).

In sum, compared to normal readers, dyslexics show: 1) visual attention distributed more to the right visual stimuli than to the left visual stimuli (e.g., Facoetti & Turatto, 2000; Hari et al., 2001); 2) no evidence of slower RTs to target in the RVF when attention is focused on the LVF (e.g., Facoetti et al., 2001); and 3) a flatter identification and RT functions at increasing eccentricity from central fixation in the RVF (Geiger & Lettvin, 1999; Facoetti & Molteni, 2001).

In order to further elucidate the relationship between *temporal and spatial aspects of visual attention in dyslexia*, the present experiment studied the time course of *covert* (i.e., in peripheral vision) attentional focusing in dyslexics and normally reading children, by measuring the cue size effect to lateralized stimuli in both the LVF and the RVF. Consistent with the visual attention distribution deficit over the right side in dyslexic individuals (e.g., experiment 1; Hari et al., 2001; Facoetti et al., 2001) and in accordance with the "Sluggish Attentional Shifting" theory of dyslexia (Hari & Renvall, 2001; Facoetti et al., 2003c), our dyslexic children showed a right attentional focusing deficit and attentional focusing in the LVF only at longest cue-target delays (i.e., slower time course of attentional focusing).

2.2.1. Participants

Eleven dyslexic children (mean age 11.4, ± 2.3 SD) had been diagnosed as dyslexics based on standard exclusion criteria (American Psychiatric Association, 1994). For details about criteria, see experiment 1. Eleven control children (mean age 12.1, ± 1.8 SD) were also selected, recommended as normal readers by their teachers. The two groups of children did not differ in chronological age (P>0.30). All participants' parents gave informed consent.

2.2.2. Apparatus and Procedures

The experimental paradigm was carried out in a dimly lit room with an ambient luminance of 1.5 cd/cm^2. Participants sat in front of a monitor (15 in. and with luminance of 0.5 cd/cm^2), with their heads positioned on a headrest. The eye-screen distance was 40 cm. Figure 4 shows the experimental setup. The fixation point was a cross with a visual angle of 0.5° presented in the middle of the screen. After 500 ms, a valid pre-cue (0.5° red dot) was presented (in the LVF or in the RVF) 8° from fixation point. After an interval of 500 ms (orienting time), the focusing cue (a small or a large white circle of 2.5° or 7.5°, respectively) was presented at the same location on the screen as the orienting cue. After a variable cue-target delay (100, 500 and 900 ms), the stimulus target (0.5° white dot) was flashed at the center of the cue for 50 ms. Small and large cues in the LVF or in the RVF as well as cue-target delays were presented in random sequence. The inter-trial interval was 1500 ms. Eye movements were monitored by means of a micro-camera system. Trials where the subjects made eye movements were detected by the system and discarded.

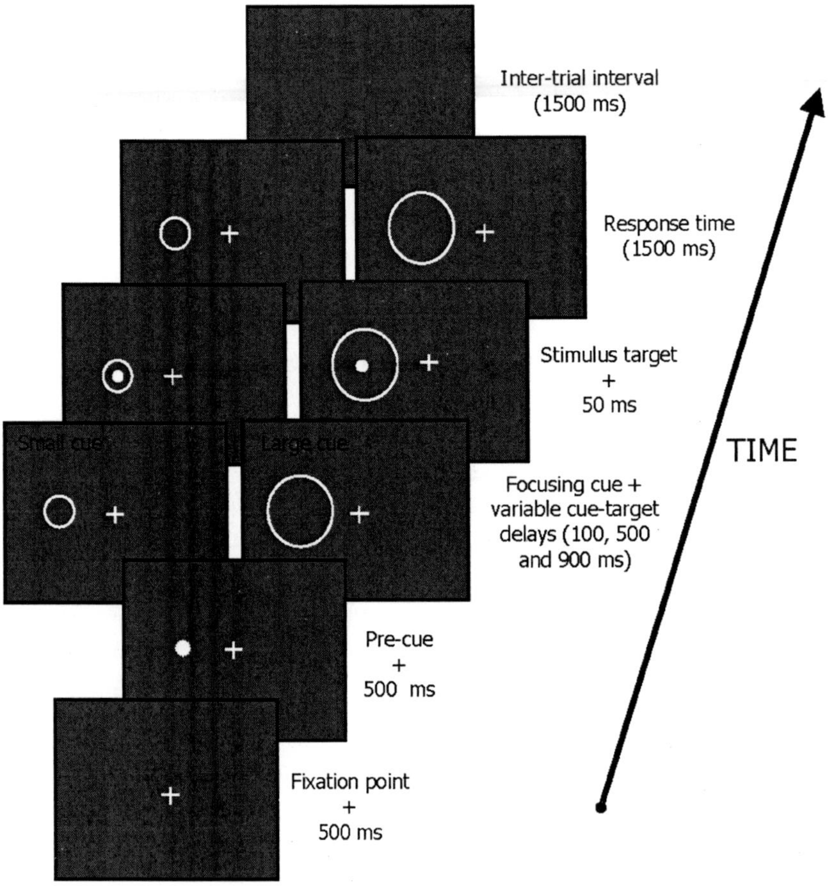

Figure 4. Schematic representation of the display used in experiment 2 (lateralized time-course of attentional focusing task).

At target onset, the participants had to press the space-bar as fast as possible and their RT was recorded by the computer. The maximum time allowed for the response was 1500 ms. Catch trials, consisting of the presentation of the focusing cue but not of the target, were interspersed with normal trials. On catch trials, the participants did not have to respond.

The experimental session consisted of 360 trials, divided into two blocks of 180 trials each distributed as follows: 90 trials in the LVF (45 trials with large cue, 15 trials for each cue-target delay; and 45 trials with small cue, 15 trials for each cue-target delay) and 90 trials were presented in the RVF with the same distribution as those in the LVF.

2.2.3. Results

Errors to target stimulus (responses to catch trials and missed responses) were less than 4% and were not analyzed. Outliers were defined as RTs faster than 150 ms or more than 2.5 standard deviations above the mean and were excluded from the data sets before the analyses were carried out. This resulted in the removal of approximately 3% of all observations. Eye movements were present in 4% of total trials.

Mean correct RTs were analyzed with a mixed four-way ANOVA in which the within-subjects factors were target location (LVF and RVF), cue size (small and large cues) and cue-target delay (100, 500 and 900 ms) and the between-subjects factor was group (dyslexic and normally reading children).

The cue size main effect was significant ($F(1,20)=11.87$, $P<0.005$), RTs in the small cue condition were 419 ms, whereas RTs in the large cue condition were 438 ms, indicating a significant cue size effect (i.e., attentional focusing). Also, the cue-target delay main effect was significant ($F(2,40)=23.07$, $P<0.0001$). A "warning effect" (RT detection decreasing when cue-target delay increases) was present (100 ms cue-target delay RTs = 470 ms, 500 ms cue-target delay RTs = 414 ms and 900 ms cue-target delay RTs = 402 ms).

The cue size x cue-target delay interaction was significant ($F(2,40)=3.41$, $P<0.05$). The cue size effect was significant at 500 and 900 ms cue-target delays (31 and 28 ms, respectively; $Ps<0.05$) but not at 100 ms cue-target delay (-1 ms, $P>0.20$).

Although the group x cue size interaction was not significant, the planned comparison showed that in normal readers the cue size effect was present (29 ms, $P<0.05$), whereas in dyslexics the cue size effect was not present (10 ms, $P>0.20$) (see figure 5).

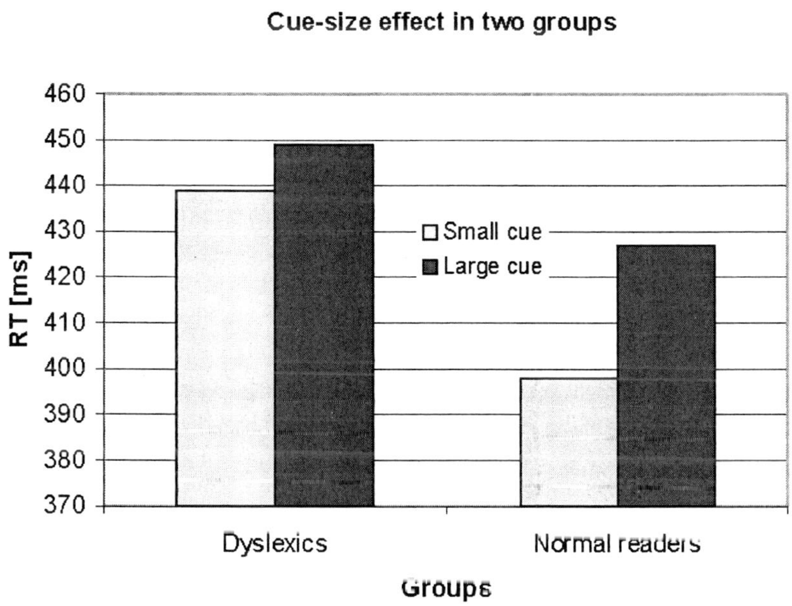

Figure 5. Mean RTs as a function of group (dyslexic children and normally reading children) and cue-size (small and large). The cue-size effect (i.e. attentional focusing) was present only in normal readers but not in dyslexics.

In addition, the group x target location x cue size interaction was significant (F(1,20)=4.5, P<0.05). The planned comparison in normal readers revealed a cue size effect in both the LVF (21 ms, P=0.06) and the RVF (35 ms, P<0.05). In contrast, the planned comparison in dyslexic children revealed a cue size effect in the LVF (27 ms, P<0.05) but not in the RVF (-5 ms, P>0.50) (see figure 6).

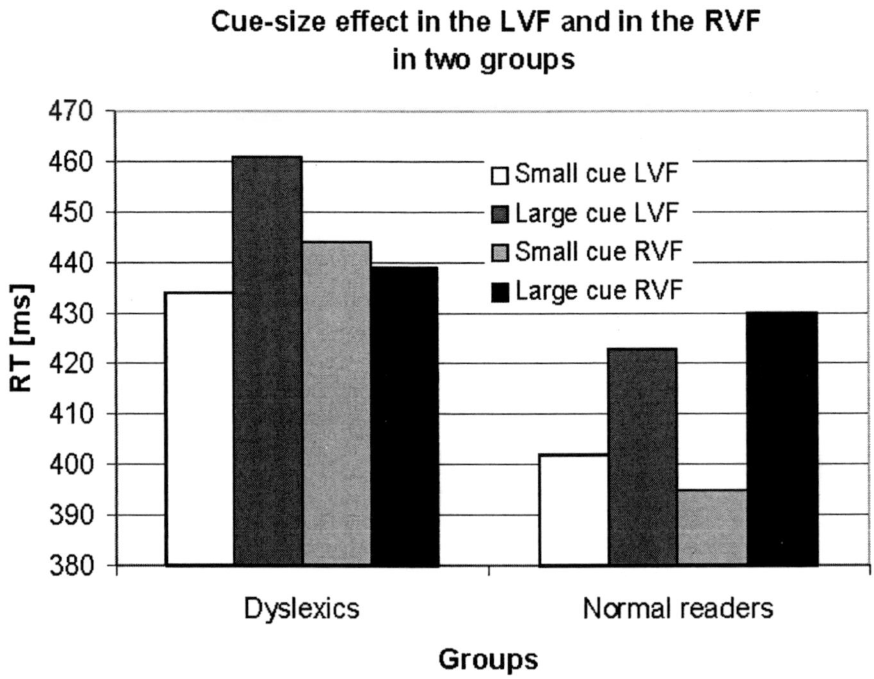

Figure 6. Mean RTs as a function of group (dyslexic children and normally reading children) and cue-size (small and large) in the LVF and in the RVF. In normal readers, the cue-size effect (i.e. attentional focusing) was present in both the LVF and the RVF. In contrast, in dyslexics, attentional focusing was present in the LVF but not in the RVF.

The group x cue-target delay interaction approached significance (F(2,40)=2.48, P=0.09). The planned comparison showed a significant RT difference between normal readers (441 ms) and dyslexics (498 ms) only at shorter cue-target delay (RT difference 43 ms, P<0.05) (see figure 7).

Although the group x cue-size x cue-target delay interaction was not significant, interestingly, the planned comparison showed that in normally reading children the cue size effect was significant both at 500 ms cue-target delay (49 ms, P<0.05) and 900 ms cue-target delay (28 ms, P=0.051), but not at the shortest (100 ms) cue-target delay (6 ms, P>0.20). In contrast, in dyslexic children a cue-size effect was present only at the longest (900 ms) cue-target delay (29 ms, P<0.05) but not at the shortest (100 ms) and middle (500 ms) cue-target delays (-8 ms and 12 ms, Ps>0.20) (see figure 8).

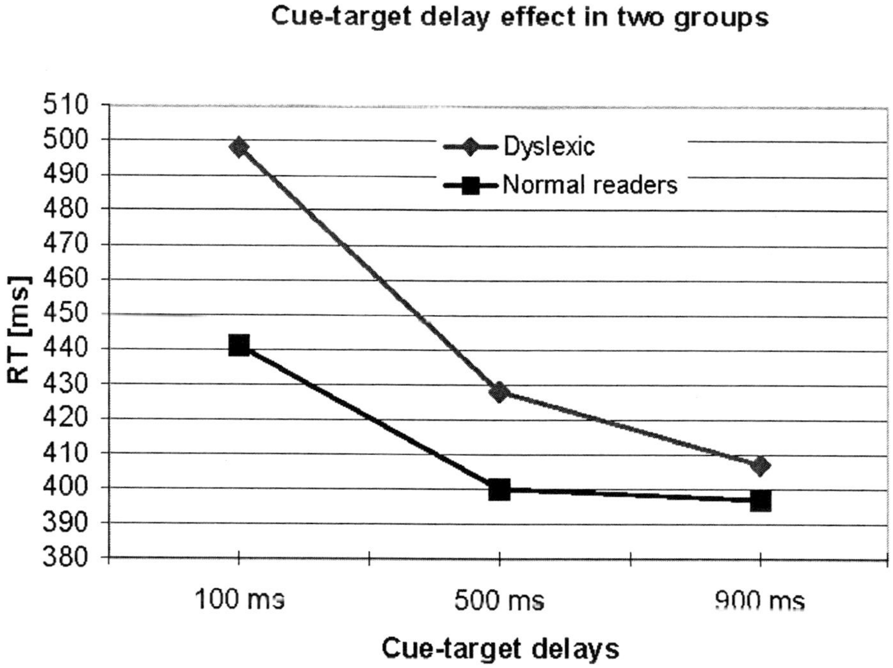

Figure 7. Mean RTs as a function of group (dyslexic children and normally reading children) and cue-target delay (100, 500 and 900 ms). RTs were slower in dyslexics than in normal readers but only at shortest cue-target delay (100 ms).

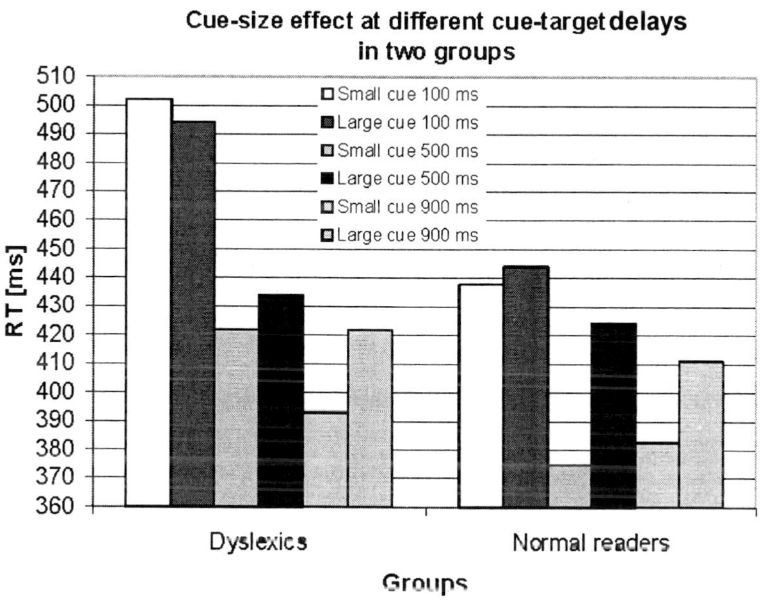

Figure 8. Mean RTs as a function of group (dyslexic children and normally reading children) and cue-size (small and large) at different cue-target delays (100, 500 and 900 ms). In normal readers, a cue-size effect (i.e. attentional focusing) was present at both 500 and 900 ms cue-target delays. In contrast, in dyslexics, attentional focusing was present only at 900 ms cue-target delay.

Finally, although the group x cue size x cue-target delay x target location interaction was not significant, planned comparisons were nonetheless carried out. Interestingly, in normally reading children, in their LVF, the cue size effect was present at 500 ms cue-target delay (46 ms, P<0.05) but not at 100 ms cue-target delay (-19 ms, P>0.20) nor at 900 ms cue-target delay (35 ms, P=0.07). Also, in the RVF, the cue size effect was present only at 500 ms cue-target delay (53 ms, P<0.05) but not at 100 ms cue-target delay (31 ms, P>0.20) nor at 900 ms cue-target delay (22 ms, P>0.20). In contrast, in the LVF of dyslexic children, the cue size effect was present at 900 ms cue-target delay (58 ms, P<0.05) but not at 100 ms cue-target delay (6 ms, P>0.20) nor at 500 ms cue-target delay (18 ms, P>0.20). In the RVF, the cue size effect was never present (at 100 ms cue-target delay 21 ms, at 500 ms cue-target delay 6 ms, and at 900 ms cue-target delay 0 ms, Ps>0.20). The planned comparison also showed that in dyslexic children at 900 ms cue-target delay, the RTs were slower in the LVF than in the RVF only in the large cue condition (RT difference 45 ms, P<0.05), not in the small cue condition (RT difference -13 ms, P>0.20) (see figures 9a and 9b).

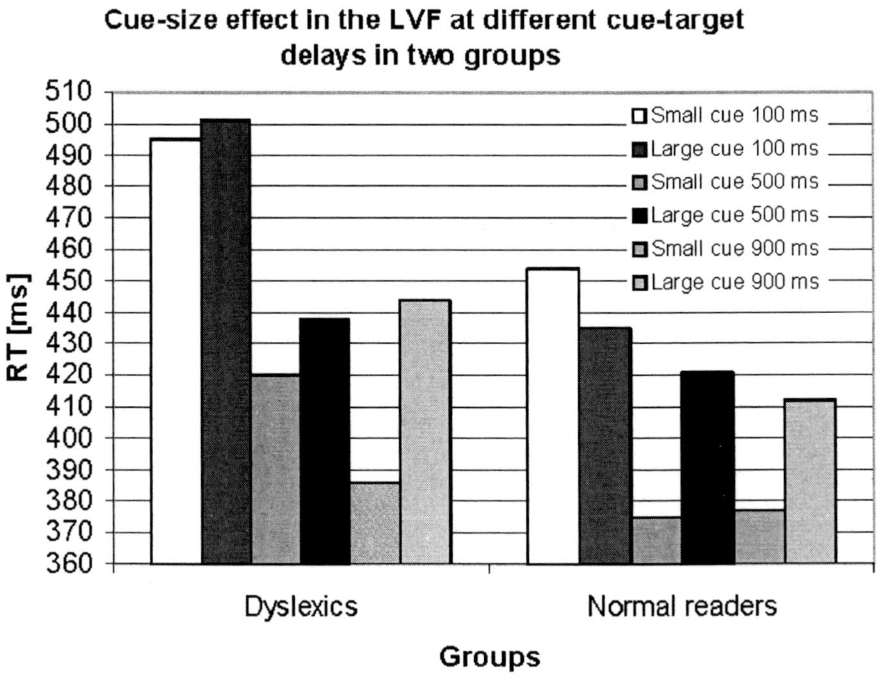

Figure 9.a. Mean RTs as a function of group (dyslexic children and normally reading children) and cue-size (small and large) at different cue-target delays (100, 500 and 900 ms) in the LVF. In normal readers, a cue-size effect (i.e. attentional focusing) was present only at 500 ms cue-target delay. In contrast, in dyslexics, attentional focusing was present only at 900 ms cue-target delay.

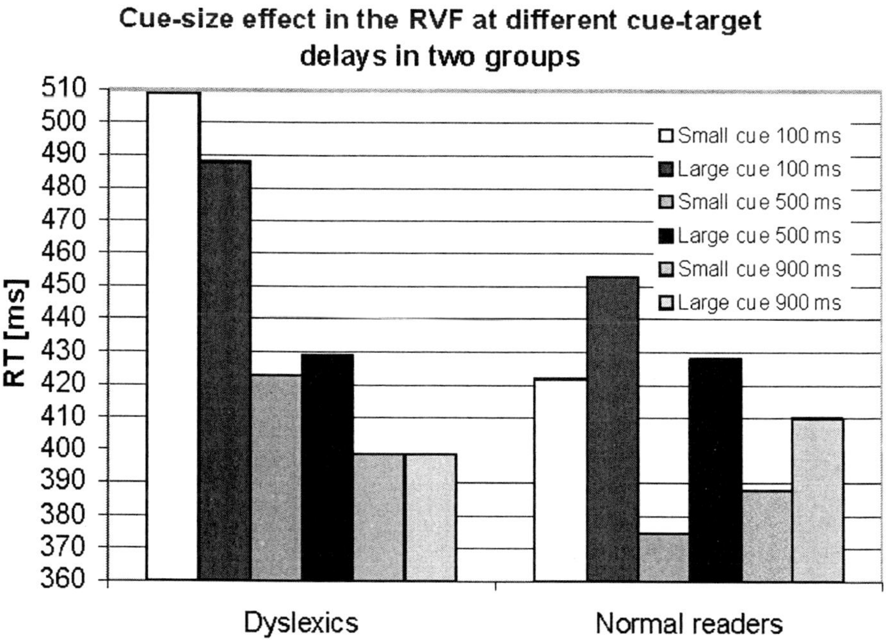

9.b. Mean RTs as a function of group (dyslexic children and normally reading children) and cue-size (small and large) at different cue-target delays (100, 500 and 900 ms) in the RVF. In normal readers, a cue-size effect (i.e. attentional focusing) was present at 500 ms cue-target delay. In contrast, in dyslexics, attentional focusing was not present at any cue-target delay.

2.2.4. Discussion

A cue size procedure was used to study the time course of covert (i.e., peripherally, outside the fovea) attentional focusing in dyslexic children. Recently, we studied the time course of overt (i.e., centrally, in the fovea) attentional focusing in dyslexic children. Our results showed that the time course of attentional focusing in dyslexics was slower than in normal readers (Facoetti et al., 2003c).

In the present study, a significant cue size x cue-target delay interaction shows that focusing was present at longer cue-target delays (500 and 900 ms) but not at the shortest delay (100 ms). This result partially confirms previous studies on covert attentional focusing in adult participants (e.g., Castiello & Umiltà, 1990; Benso, Turatto, Mascetti & Umiltà, 1998). However, these findings should be interpreted in light of group differences. Globally, attentional focusing (see figure 5) appears not to be effective in dyslexic children (no cue size effect), whereas attentional focusing is effective in normally reading children (significant cue size effect). In accord with some studies, the *attentional focusing deficit* could be the crucial impairment that hampers visual (orthographic) and auditory (phonological) perception in dyslexic individuals (e.g., Geiger & Lettvin, 1999; Brannan & Williams, 1987; Casco et al., 1998; Vidyasagar & Pammer, 1999; Facoetti et al., 2000b; Richards et al., 1990; Rayner et al., 1989; Everatt et al., 1999; Klein & D' Entremont, 1999; Facoetti et al., 2000a; Facoetti et al., 2003e; Hari et al., 2001; Hari & Renvall, 2001; Asbjornsen & Bryden, 1998; Facoetti et al., 2003d). Indeed, focusing of visual and auditory attention may directly influence perceptual processing by rapidly and intensively analyzing attended locations and reducing the interference from stimuli at unattended locations.

However, the deficit of attentional focusing in dyslexics was not absolute. In fact, the time course of covert attentional focusing was slower in dyslexics than normal readers. In the present study, in normal readers covert attentional focusing was present at middle cue-target delay, whereas in dyslexics attentional focusing was present at the longest cue-target delay only, indicating *specific attentional temporal deficit in dyslexics* (see figure 8). Accordingly, previous studies have shown that overt attentional focusing was also slower in dyslexics than normal readers (Facoetti et al 2003c).

It should be noted that the temporal deficit shown by dyslexics in the present study and in previous studies on both visual (e.g., Hari, Valta & Uutella, 1999; Facoetti et al., 2000b; Facoetti et al., 2003c) and auditory attention (e.g., Renvall & Hari, 2002; Facoetti et al., 2003d) was not precisely compatible with those originally revealed by Tallal's studies (for a recent review, see Benasich & Tallal, 2002). In fact, the auditory temporal processing deficit required to degrade the children's ability to perceive transient elements of speech should be in terms of a few tens (e.g., Merzenich et al., 1996) and not some hundreds of milliseconds as is shown in attentional studies (e.g., Renvall & Hari, 2002; Hari & Renvall, 2001; Facoetti et al., 2000b; Facoetti et al., 2003c). The attentional warning effect (see figure 7) appears to confirm a general deficit of automatic capture of visual and auditory attention in dyslexic individuals (e.g., Hari et al., 2001; Renvall & Hari, 2002; Facoetti et al., 2003c).

Note that in dyslexics a spatial deficit of attentional focusing was present specifically in the RVF (e.g., Facoetti & Molteni, 2001; Geiger et Lettvin, 1999; Facoetti & Turatto, 2000; Hari et al., 2001). In the present study, in dyslexics attentional focusing was present only in the LVF, not in the RVF (see figure 6). In the RVF in dyslexic children, not only was the gradient (e.g., Hari et al., 2001; Facoetti & Molteni, 2001), the orienting of visual attention (Facoetti et al., 2001) and the lateral masking (Geiger & Lettvin, 1999) impaired but also attentional focusing. Thus, it appears that dyslexic individuals have a *general attentional spatial selection deficit in their RVF.*

More interestingly, dyslexic children have a *spatio-temporal deficit of attentional focusing*. The time course of attentional focusing was slower in dyslexics than in normal readers (see figure 8) but this attentional temporal deficit appears to be more severe in the RVF than in the LVF. Indeed, in dyslexic children the focusing was present at the longest cue-target delay in the LVF (see figure 9a), whereas the focusing effect was never present in the RVF (see figure 9b).

Finally, only in dyslexic children, in the large cue and at the longest cue-target delay, stimuli detection was slower in the LVF than in the RVF. Interestingly, this result is in accord with the "left mini-neglect" and/or right hyper-attention in dyslexia (e.g., Hari et al., 2001; Facoetti & Turatto, 2000).

3. General Discussion: Behavioral and Neurobiological Evidence of Visual and Auditory Attentional Deficits in Developmental Dyslexia

There is large consensus that developmental dyslexia is a neurological disorder with a specific neuropsychological deficit. However, after decades of studies, there is still global disagreement over the specific neuropsychological and neurological basis of the disorder (see Stein & Walsh, 1997 or Hari & Renvall, 2001 vs. Ramus, 2003).

Dyslexia is currently considered as the specific reading impairment directly and exclusively caused by a linguistic deficit that is specific to the representation and processing of speech sounds; this is the phonological theory. At the neural level, this linguistic deficit would arise from a congenital dysfunction of left perisylvian language-dedicated cortical area. Thus, the left hemisphere dysfunction is held to be the direct cause of reading disabilities. This neurological dysfunction would be the basis of deficient phonological representation that impairs the grapheme-phoneme mapping, phonological awareness, verbal short-term memory and rapid naming (for a recent review, see Ramus, 2003). Accordingly, a recent study showed that 100% of the sampled dyslexics were affected by phonological deficits (Ramus, Rosen, Dakin, Day, Castellote, White, Frith, 2003).

I would, however, suggest that the phonological theory of dyslexia is a tautology rather than an explanation. Indeed, reading and phonology are two sides of the same coin: reading skills are improved by phoneme awareness, and phoneme awareness is improved by reading skills. However, beyond phoneme awareness, rapid naming (of colors, pictures or digits) and verbal short-term memory are also currently considered phonological deficits and are frequently present in dyslexic individuals. I would suggest that an alternative explanation about these "phonological" deficits could exist outside the phonological theory of dyslexia. The rapid naming deficit could be explained by a generally slower speed of visual (and auditory too) processing rather than a pure phonological deficit (e.g., Catts, Gilispie, Leonard, Kail & Miller, 2002). In addition, the possible relationship between processing speed and selective spatial attention is not difficult to suggest. Indeed, the crucial effect of spatial attention is to increase the speed of stimulus processing. Moreover, a direct relationship between verbal short-term memory and auditory selective attention is also possible. In fact, facilitative effects in perceptual processing of stimuli by attentional processes may also explain increased short-term memory performances.

Biological evidence from neuroimaging studies suggested that visual word identification was related to two left hemisphere posterior systems: a temporo-parietal system is associated with analytic processing of the sub-lexical route; and an occipito-temporal system constitutes a fast, late-developing word form mechanism, which underlies fluency in word recognition (i.e., the lexical route) These posterior systems appear to be functionally disrupted in developmental dyslexia (for a recent review, see Pugh, Mencl, Jenner, Katz, Frost, Lee, Shaywitz & Shaywitz, 2001). In fact, some studies on the neural basis of dyslexia have consistently shown that the visual word form area (VWFA) in the left occipito-temporal sulcus was not active in dyslexic adults (for a recent review, see McCandliss, Cohen & Dehaene, 2003). This neurological difference in VWFA as well as those more directly involved in phonological processing are probably not the cause of dyslexia but rather a simple effect of dyslexia, reflecting the absence of specialization over the course of years of successful reading experience (e.g., McCandliss & Noble, 2003). Moreover, increased neural activation on both inferior frontal and right hemisphere posterior regions in reading-disabled individuals are currently considered to be a simple compensation for the left hemisphere posterior deficits (e.g., Pugh et al., 2001).

I would suggest a relatively new causal model of developmental dyslexia (see also e.g., Bakker, 1992; Vidyasagar, 1999; Hari & Renvall, 2001) that considers the right posterior parietal cortex (PPC), specifically the temporal-parietal junction (TPJ), as the brain area originally and crucially involved in reading acquisition. Indeed, some evidence has shown that initial learning to read is predominantly mediated by the visual and spatial perceptual processing of the right hemisphere (for a review, see Bakker, 1992). Accordingly, a recent research on the development of neural mechanisms for reading revealed the *right inferior parietal area*, as a specific structure engaged by the implicit processing of words (Turkeltaub, Gareau, Flowers, Zeffiro & Eden, 2003).

Some evidence seems to suggest that the sub-lexical route is the basis of reading acquisition (for a recent review, see Sprenger-Charolles et al., 2003). Indeed, at the beginning of reading acquisition, the orthographic lexicon is not yet operating. Thus, children learn to read via the sub-lexical route. However, because the first process of sub-lexical route is currently considered to be *graphemic parsing*, that is the visual attentional segmentation of a grapheme string into its constituent graphemes, it is clear that phonological assembly also involves *precise and rapid orienting and focusing of visual attention* and not only appropriate phonological skills. In addition, phonemic perceptual processing, that is the basic skill of grapheme-to-phoneme correspondences, as well as phonological short-term memory, could instead be linked to *auditory selective attention* (see figure 10). Figure 10 shows some possible neuropsychological functions (e.g., visual and auditory perception, visual and auditory attention, phonological processes and short-term memory) involved during single non-word (or unfamiliar word) reading. After a visual perceptual (i.e., pre-attentional) processing (see figure 10 A), the decoding of letter string should require a visual spatial attentional processing (see figures 10 B and C). The attentional focus, initially oriented and focalized on the left side of the letter string by inhibitory processing of flanked letter on the right side (see figure 10 B), then requires to be rapidly oriented and finely focalized (by both enhanced processing of attended location and inhibited processing of unattended locations) to the successive letter string on the right side (see figure 10 C). Phonological processing, that is grapheme-to-phoneme conversion and the temporary storing of phoneme in short-term memory, are simultaneously activated. The final phonological process is the phonemic synthesis of all the phonemes maintained in short-term memory.

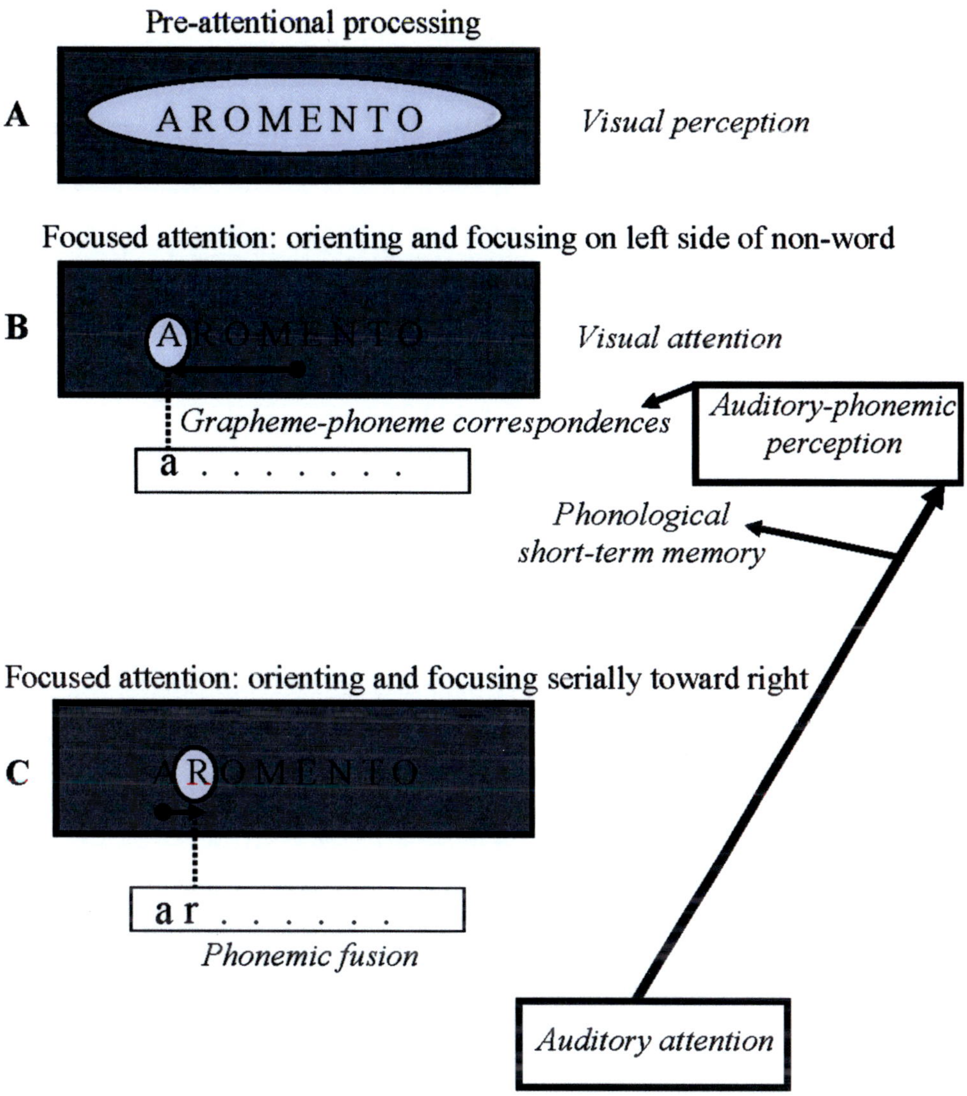

Figure 10. The role of visual and auditory attention in the sub-lexical route during reading acquisition.

Specific deficits of orienting of visual attention are shown in developmental dyslexic children and adults (e.g., Brannan & Williams, 1987; Facoetti et al., 2000b; Heiervang & Hugdahl, 2003). Globally, automatic orienting of attention was slower in dyslexics than in normal readers (Brannan & Williams, 1987; Facoetti et al., 2000b). Moreover, some studies showed that the inhibitory mechanism of automatic spatial attention (i.e., reorienting cost) was specifically impaired in dyslexic children (Facoetti et al., 2003e; Heiervang & Hugdahl, 2003). More interestingly, impairments of the mechanism that inhibits peripheral visual processing seem to be correlated to reading skills in dyslexic children. Indeed, a specific visual spatial treatment that increased the inhibitory mechanism of focusing was linked to increased reading skills in dyslexic children (Facoetti et al., 2003e).

In addition, a mild left inattention in the LVF was found in dyslexic children and adults (e.g., Facoetti & Turatto, 2000; Facoetti & Molteni, 2001; experiments 1 and 2; Hari et al., 2001). Accordingly, in dyslexic children reorienting of attention in the LVF are slowed (Facoetti et al, 2001). The alternative explanation of these results could be that dyslexic individuals have an abnormally focalized attention on the left side. In any case, the visual processing of stimuli on the left side of the letter string is impaired in dyslexics, hampering the first phase of attentional processing required for non-word reading (see figure 10 B).

Finally, and more importantly, the "filtering process" of attention in the RVF was also severely disturbed in dyslexic children (e.g., experiments 1 and 2; Geiger & Lettvin, 1999; Facoetti & Turatto, 2000; Facoetti & Molteni, 2001; Facoetti et al., 2001). An irrelevant visual stimulus in the RVF flanking the central target-stimulus was shown to be interfering more in dyslexics than in normally reading children, suggesting a right over-distractibility in dyslexics (Facoetti & Turatto, 2000). In addition, the focus of visual attention was widely diffused in the RVF in dyslexic children compared to normally reading children (e.g., Geiger & Lettvin, 1999; Facoetti & Molteni, 2001). The focusing of visual attention in dyslexic children was also abnormal in their RVF. Indeed, invalid cueing in the LVF did not slow the stimulus detection in the RVF (Facoetti et al., 2001). Interestingly, this anomalous distribution of visual attention in the RVF was specific of phonological dyslexics but not of non-phonological dyslexics. This attentional asymmetry correlated with non-word reading across dyslexic children (Facoetti et al., 2004). Furthermore, in dyslexic children an improvement of the right attentional deficit had beneficial effects on their ability to read non-words (Facoetti & Lorusso, in preparation).

In the studies presented here in detail, the results of experiment 1 confirmed attentional asymmetry in dyslexic children by using a more ecological paradigm. Indeed, only in dyslexics was the right probe stimulus during the middle letter discrimination task of five-letter words not inhibited, confirming a right attentional focusing deficit in dyslexia. Interestingly, in dyslexic children this attentional deficit was not present during the primary reading task. The results of experiment 2 do not only show a right focusing deficit but also a temporal deficit of focusing in dyslexic children. In dyslexics, compared to normal readers, the time course of attentional focusing in the LVF was slower. Also, in dyslexic children attentional focusing in the RVF was never present, not even at the longest cue-target delay. Thus, the attentional focusing in dyslexics is slowed in their LVF and severely defective in their RVF.

Note that some studies seem to show that compensated and/or non-phonological dyslexics have a more focused visual attention (e.g., Everatt et al., 1999; Facoetti et al., 2003e) mostly in their RVF (e.g., Steinman, Steinman & Garzia, 1998; Geiger et Lettvin, 1999; Facoetti et al., submitted for publication). In a study of ours, after effective reading treatment, the "reorienting cost" was greater in dyslexics than in normal readers (Facoetti et al., 2003e). These results support the notion that in dyslexic individuals a narrowed attentional focus in the RVF could increase reading skills, specifically non-word reading (Facoetti & Lorusso, in preparation). Other evidence could also suggest that in non-compensated dyslexics the attentional focus is really narrowly focalized. However, this specific attentional focusing could not be carried out immediately, only at an extended time because of the slower time course of attentional focusing (e.g., Facoetti et al., 2003c;

experiment 2). These temporal differences in attentional focusing could also explain some contradictory evidence on attentional focus in dyslexics (e.g., Juphard, Carbonnel & Valdois, 2003).

Because of the slower time course of attentional focusing in dyslexics as opposed to normal readers, visual flanking stimuli and auditory background noise could cause a "signal processing deficit". Indeed, auditory selective spatial attention is also impaired in developmental dyslexia (e.g., Asbjornsen & Bryden, 1998; Renvall & Hari, 2002). The automatic capture of auditory (and visual) attention was defective in dyslexic children (Facoetti et al., 2003d). More specifically, the time course of automatic focusing of auditory attention was slower in dyslexics than normal readers (Facoetti et al., 2003a). In addition, in dyslexic children, auditory selective attention correlated with the non-word reading ability (Facoetti, unpublished data).

What is the Neurobiological Substrate of the Attentional Focusing Deficit?

As previously suggested, a mild dysfunction of the right TPJ might underlie the focusing asymmetries shown by children and adults with dyslexia (e.g., Facoetti & Turatto, 2000; Facoetti et al., 2001; Hari et al, 2001). In support of a right TPJ impairment, Schulte-Korne, Bartling, Deimel and Remschmidt (1999), using event-related potential recordings, revealed a lower level visual processing (i.e., P200) in the right posterior region in dyslexics compared to normal readers. Again, consistent with a visual attention deficit due to right TPJ dysfunction, poor readers showed lower N100 (an early component of visual event-related potential) amplitudes in response to non-words, but not in response to words at central sites of the right hemisphere (Wimmer, Hutzler & Wiener, 2002). Interestingly, recent studies suggest that the right human inferior parietal lobe and the superior temporal gyrus make a crucial contribution to *deployment of temporal attention* (e.g., Shapiro, Hillstrom & Husian, 2002). Thus, the *right TPJ could also have an important control role in reading acquisition*, contributing to the functions of both "spatial perception" (i.e., dorsal system) and "object perception" (i.e., ventral system). Accordingly, a pure temporal deficit of visual attention was shown in dyslexic adults (Hari et al., 1999). Our present results show a right attentional focusing deficit by hyper attention in dyslexic children. This pattern is compatible with right TPJ deficit, as suggested by the finding that repetitive transcranial magnetic stimulation of the right human parietal cortex enhances visual spatial attention in the RVF (Hilgetag, Theoret & Pascual-Leone, 2001). Accordingly, patients with a right parietal damage showed a severe loss in the perception of apparent motion in their "good" RVF (Battelli, Cavanagh, Intriligator, Tramo, Hènnaf, Michèl & Barton, 2001). It is interesting to note that this bilateral motion deficit is similar to that shown by dyslexic children (e.g., Cestnick & Coltheart, 1999). This deficit is probably due to a bilateral *loss in the temporal resolution of attentional focusing* to transient events that drive the apparent motion percept. Recent studies also showed an altered activity of the right perisylvian cortex during syllable perception in dyslexic children and adults (e.g., Kujala et al., 2000; Heim, Eulitz & Elbert, 2003a; Heim, Eulitz & Elbert, 2003b). In addition, Mazzotta and Gallai (1992) found a decreased level auditory processing (i.e., P300) in the right hemisphere of phonological dyslexics. Finally, one of most specific problems in dyslexic children – the mirror visual errors – is not easily explained by left hemisphere phonological deficits. In fact, a recent study showed a highly specific disorder in discriminating mirror stimuli after a right inferior parietal lesion (Priftis, Rusconi, Umiltà & Zorzi, 2003).

Note that the spatio-temporal deficit of attention is compatible with two other possible neural impairments. First, a decreased magnocellular input to the dorsal visual stream would result in a bilateral dysfunction of the parietal lobes. This might lead to right-hemisphere symptoms because of the right lateralization of automatic selective attention (e.g., Corbetta & Shulman, 2002). Nevertheless, a recent study by Amitay et al. (2002) suggested that both visual and auditory perceptual impairments in disabled readers, although not compatible with a pure magnocellular deficit, could be explained by a parietal deficit. Accordingly, patients with bilateral parietal lesions show a significantly impaired performance on the apparent motion task in both visual fields. This indicates a bilateral temporal deficit of visual attention (Battelli et al., 2001).

Secondly, an inter-hemispheric dysfunction might also lead to the spatio-temporal attentional asymmetry shown by our dyslexic children. Mangun, Hillyard, Luck, Handy, Plager, Clark, Loftus & Gazzaniga (1994) studied the orienting of visual attention in split-brain (i.e., commissurotomized) patients. Cueing effects were obtained for targets presented in the LVF but not for those presented in the RVF (as in Facoetti et al., 2001; Facoetti et al submitted for publication). Thus, it could be suggested that the normal focusing in the RVF, achieved by attentional inhibition, is caused by an inhibitory effect of the right hemisphere on the left hemisphere via an intact corpus callosum. In accordance with the hypothesis of inter-hemispheric dysfunction in dyslexia, a recent study by Fabbro, Pesenti, Facoetti, Bonanomi, Libera and Lorusso (2001) provides evidence for a deficit of callosal transfer function in dyslexic children, specifically in the phonological subtype.

4. Conclusions

Although according to the current state of knowledge, developmental dyslexia seems characterized as a specific phonological deficit (e.g., Ramus, 2003), much evidence, both behavioral and neurobiological, now suggests a *multi-modal deficit of selective attention in dyslexic individuals*. More importantly, the multi-modal attentional deficits in dyslexics could be a cause – not only a simple consequence – of their reading problems. In addition, I suggest that, because *the reading disability is a developmental disorder*, the left perisylvian cortex deficits in dyslexic adults could be a simple effect of a *primary right TPJ dysfunction in dyslexic children* (although other neurobiological interpretations are also considered).

Acknowledgments

I wish to thank M. Molteni and M. Pezzani for access to their clinical units, S. Arrigoni, C. Cattaneo and R. Galli for help in collecting the clinical data, B. Alberti for proof-reading the manuscript, M. Piazza, K. Priftis, P. Paganoni and T. Gianesini for their helpful discussions. This work was supported by the Italian National Research Council, the Ministry of Health and the "Amici della Pediatria" Association of Bergamo General Hospital. This chapter is dedicated to Camilla.

REFERENCES

American Psychiatric Association (1994). *Diagnostic and statistical manual of mental disorders (4th Edition)*. DC author, Washington.

Amitay, S., Ben-Yehudah, G., Banai K., & Ahissar M. (2002). Disabled readers suffer from visual and auditory impairments but not from a specific magnocellular deficit. *Brain, 125*, 2272-2285.

Asbjornsen, A.E., & Bryden, M.P. (1998). Auditory attention shifts in reading disabled students: Quantification of attentional effectiveness by the Attentional Shift Index. *Neuropsychologia, 36*, 143-148.

Auclair, L., & Sieroff, E. (2002). Attentional cueing effect in the identification of words and pseudowords of different length. *The Quarterly Journal of Experimental Psychology, 55*, 445-463.

Bakker, D. (1992) Neuropsychological classification and treatment of dyslexia. *Journal of Learning Disabilities, 25*, 102-109.

Battelli, L., Cavanagh, P., Intriligator, J., Tramo, M.J., Hènnaf, M., Michèl, F., & Barton, J.J.S. (2001). Unilateral right parietal damage leads to bilateral deficit for high level motion. *Neuron, 32*, 985-995.

Benasich, A.A., & Tallal, P. (2002). Infant discrimination of rapid auditory cues predicts later language impairment. *Behavioural Brain Research, 136*, 31-49.

Benso, F., Turatto, M., Mascetti G.G., & Umiltà, C. (1998). The time course of attentional focusing. *European Journal of Cognitive Psychology, 10*, 373-388.

Borsting, E., Riddel, W.H., Dudeck, K., Kelley, C., Matsui, L., & Motoyama, J. (1996). The presence of a magnocellular deficit depends of the type of dyslexia. *Vision Research, 36*, 1047-1053.

Bradley, L., & Bryant, P.E. (1983). Categorizing sounds and learning to read: a causal connection. *Nature, 301*, 419-421.

Brannan, J., & Williams, M. (1987). Allocation of visual attention in good and poor readers. *Perception & Psychophysics, 41*, 23-28.

Braun, J. (2002). Visual attention: light enters the jungle. *Current Biology, 12*, R599-R601.

Casco, C., Tressoldi, P., & Dellantonio, A. (1998). Visual selective attention and reading efficiency are related in children. *Cortex, 34*, 531-546.

Castiello, U., & Umiltà, C. (1990). Size of the attentional focus and efficiency of processing. *Acta Psychologica, 73*, 195-209.

Catts, H.W., Gilispie, M., Leonard, L.B., Kail, R.V., & Miller, C.A. (2002). The role of speed of processing, Rapid Naming, and phonological awareness in reading achievement. *Journal of Learning Disabilities, 35*, 509-524.

Cestnick, L. (2001). Cross-modality temporal processing deficits in developmental phonological dyslexics. *Brain and Cognition, 46*, 319-325.

Cestnick, L., & Coltheart, M. (1999). The relationship between language-processing and visual-processing deficit in developmental dyslexia. *Cognition, 71*, 231-255.

Coltheart, M., Rastle, K., Perry, C., Langdon, R., & Ziegler, J. (2001). The DRC model: A model of visual word recognition and reading aloud. *Psychological Review, 108*, 204 - 258.

Corbetta, M., & Shulman, G.L. (2002). Control of goal-directed and stimulus-driven attention in the brain. *Nature Reviews Neuroscience, 3*, 201-215.

Cornoldi, C., Colpo, G., & Gruppo, M.T. (1981). *Prove di Lettura MT.* Firenze: O.S. Organizzazioni Speciali.

Davis, C., Castles, A., McAnally, K., & Gray, J. (2001). Lapses of concentration and dyslexic performance on the Ternus task. *Cognition, 81*, B21-31.

Eriksen, C.W., & St. James, J.D. (1986). Visual attention within and around the field of focal attention: A zoom lens model. *Perception and Psychophysics, 40*, 225-240.

Everatt, J., McCorquodale, B., Smith, J., Culverwell, F., Wilks, A., Evans, D., Kay M., & Baker, D. (1999). In Everatt J (Ed.) *Reading and dyslexia: visual and attentional processes*. Routledge London and New York, pp. 1-39.

Fabbro, F., Pesenti, S., Facoetti, A., Bonanomi, M., Libera, L., & Lorusso, M.L. (2001). Callosal transfer in different subtypes of developmental dyslexia. *Cortex, 37*, 65-73.

Facoetti, A., Galli R., & Cattaneo, C. (2003a). La cattura automatica dell'attenzione uditiva e visiva è rallentata nei bambini dislessici. *Riassunti delle comunicazioni del Congresso Nazionale della Sezione di Psicologia Sperimentale*, Bari.

Facoetti, A., Galli, R., Cattaneo C., & Lorusso, M.L. (2003b). Right focusing deficit in dyslexic children. *Brain and Cognition,* in press.

Facoetti A. & Lorusso M.L. (2003). Specific treatment of right attentional focusing deficit in dyslexic children. *In preparation.*

Facoetti, A., Lorusso, M.L., Paganoni, P., Cattaneo, C., Galli, R., & Mascetti, G.G. (2003c). The time course of attentional focusing in dyslexic and normally reading children. *Brain and Cognition,* in press.

Facoetti, A., Lorusso, M.L., Paganoni, P., Cattaneo, C., Galli, R., Umiltà, C., & Mascetti, G.G. (2003d). Auditory and visual automatic attention deficits in developmental dyslexia. *Cognitive Brain Research, 16*, 185-191.

Facoetti, A., Lorusso, M.L., Paganoni, P., Umiltà, C., & Mascetti, G.G. (2003e). The role of visual spatial attention in developmental dyslexia: evidence from rehabilitation study. *Cognitive Brain Research, 15*, 154-164.

Facoetti, A., & Molteni, M. (2000). Is attentional focusing an inhibitory process at distractor location? *Cognitive Brain Research, 10*, 185-188.

Facoetti, A., & Molteni, M. (2001). The gradient of visual attention in developmental dyslexia. *Neuropsychologia, 39*, 352-357.

Facoetti, A., Paganoni P., & Lorusso, M.L. (2000a). The spatial distribution of visual attention in developmental dyslexia. *Experimental Brain Research, 132*, 531-538.

Facoetti, A., Paganoni, P., Turatto, M., Marzola V., & Mascetti, G.G. (2000b). Visuospatial attention in developmental dyslexia. *Cortex, 36*, 109-123.

Facoetti, A., Priftis, K., Colavito V., & Gianesini, T. (2003f). Il fuoco dell'attenzione visiva e il riconoscimento di non-parole: Possibili implicazioni per la dislessia evolutiva.

Riassunti delle comunicazioni del Congresso Nazionale della Sezione di Psicologia Sperimentale, Bari.

Facoetti, A., & Turatto, M. (2000). Asymmetrical visual fields distribution of attention in dyslexic: a neuropsychological study. *Neuroscience Letters, 290*, 216-218.

Facoetti, A., Turatto, M., Lorusso, M.L., & Mascetti, G.G. (2001). Orienting of visual attention in dyslexia: evidence for asymmetric hemispheric control of attention. *Experimental Brain Research, 138*, 46-53.

Facoetti, A., Zorzi M., Cestnick, L., Lorusso, M.L., Paganoni, P., Umiltà, C., & Mascetti, G.G. (2004). The relationship between visuospatial attention and non-word reading in developmental dyslexia. *Submitted for publication.*

Farmer, M.E., & Klein, R.M. (1995). The evidence for a temporal processing deficit-linked to dyslexia. *Psychonomic Bulletin Review, 2*, 469-493.

Freeman, E., Sagi D., & Driver, J. (2001). Lateral interactions between targets and flankers in low-level vision depend on attention to the flankers. *Nature Neuroscience, 4*, 1032-1036.

Frith, U. (1986). A developmental framework for developmental dyslexia. *Annals of Dyslexia, 36*, 96-81.

Galaburda, A., & Livingstone, M. (1993). Evidence for a magnocellular deficit in developmental dyslexia. *Annals of the New York Academy of Sciences, 682*, 70-82.

Geiger, G., Cattaneo, C., Galli, R., Pozzoli, U., Lorusso, M.L., Facoetti, A., Pesenti S., & Molteni, M. (2002). A common generalized perceptual strategy? The evidence from dyslexics. *2nd Annual Meeting, Vision Science Society*, Sarasota, Florida, USA, B5.82.

Geiger, G., & Lettvin, J.Y. (1999). How dyslexics see and learn to read well. In Everatt J (Ed.) *Reading and dyslexia: visual and attentional processes.* Routledge London and New York, pp. 64-90.

Grant, A.C., Zangaladze, A., Thiagarajah M.C., & Sthian, K. (1999). Tactile perception in developmental dyslexia: a psychophysical study using gratings. *Neuropsychologia, 37*, 1201-1211.

Hari, R., & Renvall, H. (2001). Impaired processing of rapid stimulus sequences in dyslexia. *Trends in Cognitive Sciences, 5*, 525-532.

Hari, R., Renvall, H., & Tanskanen, T. (2001). Left minineglect in dyslexic adults. *Brain, 124*, 1373-1380.

Hari, R., Valta M., & Uutella, K. (1999). Prolonged attentional dwell time in dyslexic adults. *Neuroscience Letters, 271*, 202-204.

Hartley, D.E.H., & Moore, D.R. (2002). Auditory processing efficiency deficits in children with developmental language impairments. *Journal of Acoustic Society of America, 112*, 2962-2966.

Heiervang, E., & Hugdahl, K. (2003). Impaired visual attention in children with dyslexia. *Journal of Learning disabilities, 36*, 68-73.

Hilgetag, G.G., Theoret, H., & Pascual-Leone, A. (2001). Enhanced visual spatial attention ipsilateral to rTMS-induced 'virtual lesions' of human parietal cortex. *Nature Neuroscience, 4*, 953-957.

Heim, S., Eulitz, C, & Elbert, T. (2003a). Altered hemispheric asymmetry of auditory N100m in adults with developmental dyslexia. *NeuroReport, 14*, 501-504.

Heim, S., Eulitz C., & Elbert, T. (2003b). Altered hemispheric asymmetry of auditory P100m in dyslexia. *European Journal of Neuroscience, 17*, 1715-1722.

Hochstein, S., & Ahissar, M. (2002). View from the top: Hierarchies and reverse hierarchies in the visual system. *Neuron, 36*, 791-804.

Iles, J., Walsh, V., & Richardson, A. (2000). Visual search performance in dyslexia. *Dyslexia, 6*, 163-177.

Jonkman, I., Licht, R., Bakker, D.J., & Van den Broek-Sandmann, T.M. (1992). Shifting of attention in subtypes dyslexics children: an event-related potential study. *Developmental Neuropsychology, 8*, 243-259.

Juphard, A., Carbonnel, S., & Valdois, S. (2003). Length effect in reading and lexical decision: Evidence from skilled readers and developmental dyslexic participant. *Brain and Cognition,* in press.

Kahneman, D., & Henik, A. (1981). Perceptual organisation and attention. In M. Kubovy & B.R. Pomerants (Eds.) *Perceptual organization*. Hillsdale, N.J. Lawrence Erlbaum Associates Inc.

Klein, R.M. (2000). Inhibition of return. *Trends in Cognitive Science, 4*, 138-147.

Klein R.M., & D' Entremont, B. (1999). Filtering performance by good and poor readers. In Everatt J (Ed.), *Reading and Dyslexia: Visual and attentional Process*. Routledge, London, pp. 163-178.

Kujala, T., Myllyviita, K., Tervaniemi, M., Alho, K., Kallio J., & Naatanen, R. (2000). Basic auditory dysfunction in dyslexia as demonstrated by brain activity measurements. *Psychophysiology, 37*, 262-266.

LaBerge, D. (1983). Spatial extent of attention to letters and words. *Journal of Experimental Psychology: Human Perception and Performance, 9*, 371-379.

LaBerge, D., & Brown, V. (1989). Theory of attentional operations in shape identification. *Psychological Review, 96*, 101-124.

Mangun, G.R., Hillyard, S.A., Luck, S.J., Handy, T., Plager, R., Clark, V.P., Loftus, W., & Gazzaniga, M.S. (1994). Monitoring the visual world: hemispheric asymmetries and subcortical processes in attention. *Journal of Cognitive Neuroscience, 6*, 267-275.

Mazzotta, G., & Gallai, V. (1992). Study of the P300 event-related potential through brain mapping in phonological dyslexics. *Acta Neurologica, 14*, 173-186.

McCandliss, B.D., Cohen L., & Dehaene, S. (2003). The visual word form area: expertise for reading in the fusiform gyrus. Trends in Cognitive Science, 7, 293-299.

McCann, R., Folk C.L., & Johnston, J.C. (1992). The role of spatial attention in visual word processing. *Journal of Experimental Psychology: Perception and Performance, 18*, 1015-1029.

McPeek, R.M., Malikovic, V., & Nakayama, K. (1999). Saccades require focal attention and are facilitated by a short-term memory system. *Vision Research, 39*, 1555-1566.

Merzenich, M.M., Jenkins, W.M., Johnston, P., Schreiner, C., Miller S.L., & Tallal, P. (1996).Temporal processing deficits of language-learning impaired children ameliorated by training. *Science, 271*, 77-81.

Mondor, T.A., & Bryden, M.P. (1991). The influence of attention on the dichotic REA. *Neuropsychologia,* 29, 1179-1190.

Omtzigt, D., Hendriks, A.W., & Kolk, H.H.J. (2002). Evidence for magnocellular involvement in the identification of flanked letters. *Neuropsychologia, 40*, 1881-1890.

Perfetti, C. (1992). The representation problem in reading acquisition. In Gough P. Enri, L. & Treisman R. (Eds.), *Reading acquisition*. Hillsdale, NJ: Erlbaum, pp.107-143.

Posner, M.I. (1980). Orienting of Attention. *The Quarterly Journal of Experimental Psychology, 32*, 3-25.

Priftis, K., Rusconi, E., Umiltà, C., & Zorzi, M. (2003). Pure agnosia for mirror stimuli after right inferior parietal lesion. *Brain, 126*, 908-919.

Pugh, K. R., Mencl, W.E., Jenner, A.R., Katz, L., Frost, S.J., Lee, J.R., Shaywitz, S.E., & Shaywitz, B.A. (2001). Neurobiological studies of reading and reading disability. *Journal of Communication Disorders, 34*, 479-492.

Ramus, F. (2003). Developmental dyslexia: Specific phonological deficit or general sensorimotor dysfunction? *Current Opinion of Neurobiology, 13*, 212-218.

Ramus, F., Rosen, S., Dakin, S.C., Day, L.D., Castellote, J.M., White, S., Frith, U. (2003). Theories of developmental dyslexia: insights from a multiple case study of dyslexic adults. *Brain, 126*, 841-865.

Rayner, K., Murphy, L.A., Henderson, J.M., & Pollatsek, A. (1989). Selective attentional dyslexia. *Cognitive Neuropsycology, 6*, 357-378.

Renvall, A., & Hari, R. (2002). Auditory Cortical Responses to Speech-Like Stimuli in Dyslexic Adults. *Journal of Cognitive Neuroscience, 14*, 757-768.

Richards, G.P., Samuels, S.J., Turnure, J.E., & Ysseldyke, J.E. (1990). Sustained and selective attention in dyslexia in children with learning disabilities. *Journal of Learning Disabilities, 23*, 129-136.

Sartori, G., Job, R., & Tressoldi, P. (1995). *Batteria per la valutazione della dislessia e della disortografia evolutiva*. Firenze: O.S. Organizzazioni Speciali.

Schulte-Korne, G., Bartling, J., Deimel, W., & Remschmidt, H. (1999). Attenuated hemispheric lateralization in dyslexia: evidence of a visual processing deficit. *NeuroReport, 10*, 3697-3701.

Seidenberg, M.S., & McClelland, J.L. (1989). A distributed developmental model of word recognition and naming. *Psychological review, 96*, 523-568.

Sieroff, E., & Posner, M. (1988). Cueing spatial attention during processing of words and letters strings in normals. *Cognitive Neuropsychology, 5*, 451-472.

Shapiro, K., Hillstrom, A.P., & Husian, M. (2002). Control of visuotemporal attention by inferior parietal and superior temporal cortex. *Current Biology, 12*, 1320-1325.

Sieroff, E., Pollatsek, A., & Posner, M. (1988). Recognition of visual letter strings following injury to the posterior visual spatial attention system. *Cognitive Neuropsychology, 5*, 427-449.

Skottun, B.C. (2000). The magnocellular deficit theory of dyslexia: the evidence from contrast sensitivity. *Vision Research, 40*, 111-127.

Skottun, B.C. (2001). On the use of the Ternus test to assess magnocellular function. *Perception, 30*, 1449-1457.

Sperling, A.J., Lu, Z., Manis, F.R., & Seidenberg, M.S. (2003). Selective magnocellular deficits in dyslexia: a "phantom contour" study. *Neuropsychologia*, in press.

Spinelli, D., Angelelli, P., Deluca, M., Dipace, E., Judica, A., & Zoccolotti, P. (1997). Developmental surface dyslexia is not associated with deficits in the transient visual system. *NeuroReport, 7*, 1807-1812.

Spinelli, D., De Luca, M., Judica, A., & Zoccolotti, P. (2002). Crowding effects on word identification in Developmental Dyslexia. *Cortex, 38*, 179-200.

Sprenger-Charolles, L., Colé, P., Lacert, P., & Serniclaes, W. (2000). On subtypes of Developmental Dyslexia: evidence form processing time and accuracy scores. *Canadian Journal of Experimental Psychology, 54*, 87-103.

Sprenger-Charolles, L., Siegel, L.S, Béchennec, D., & Serniclaes, W. (2003). Development of phonological and orthographic processing in reading aloud, in silent reading, and spelling: A four-year longitudinal study. *Journal of Experimental Child Psychology,* in press.

Starr, M.S., & Rayner, K. (2001). Eye movements during reading: some current controversies. *Trends in Cognitive Sciences, 5*, 156-163.

Stein, J., & Walsh, V. (1997). To see but not to read: the magnocellular theory of dyslexia. *Trends in Neuroscience, 20*, 147-152.

Steinman, S.B., Steinman, B.A., & Garzia, R.P. (1998). Vision and Attention. II: Is Visual Attention a Mechanism Through Which a Deficient Magnocellular Pathway Might Cause Reading Disabilities?. *Optometry and Vision Science, 75*, 674-681.

Steinman, B.A., Steinman, S.B., & Lehmkuhle, S. (1996). Transient visual attention is dominated by the magnocellular stream. *Vision Research, 36*, 589-599.

Talcott, J.B., Hansen, P.C., Willis-Owen, C., McKinnell, I.W., Richardson A.J., & Stein, J.F., (1998). Visual magnocellular impairment in adult developmental dyslexics. *Neuro-Ophthalmology, 20*, 187-201.

Turkeltaub, P.E., Gareau, L., Flowers, D.L, Zeffiro, T.A., & Eden, G.F. (2003). Development of neural mechanisms for reading. *Nature Neuroscience, 6*, 767-773.

Turatto, M., Benso, F., Facoetti, A., Galfano, G., Mascetti, G.G., & Umiltà, C. (2000). Automatic voluntary focusing of Attention. *Perception and Psychophysics, 62*, 935-952.

Vidyasagar, T.R. (1999). A neural model of attentional spotlight: parietal guiding the temporal. *Brain Research Review, 30*, 66-76.

Vidyasagar, T.R., & Pammer, K. (1999). Impaired visual search in Dyslexia relates to the role of the magnocellular pathway in attention. *NeuroReport, 10*, 1283-1287.

Wechsler, D. (1986). *Scala di Intelligenza Wechsler per Bambini-Riveduta.* Firenze O.S. Organizzazioni Speciali.

Wimmer, H. (1993). Characteristics of Developmental Dyslexia in a regular writing system. *Applied Psycholinguistics, 14*, 1-33

Wimmer, H., Hutzler, F., & Wiener, C. (2002). Children with dyslexia and right parietal lobe dysfunction: event-related potentials in response to words and pseudowords. *Neuroscience Letters, 331*, 211-213.

Witton, C., Talcott, J.B., Hansen, P.C., Richardson, A.J., Griffiths, T.D., Rees, A., Stein, J.F., & Green, G.G. (1998). Sensitivity to dynamic auditory and visual stimuli predicts nonword reading ability in both dyslexic and normal readers. *Current Biology, 8*, 791-797.

Wright, B.A., Bowen, R.W., & Zecker, S.G. (2000). Nonlinguistic perceptual deficits associates with reading and language disorders. *Current Opinion in Neurobiology, 10*, 482-486.

Yeshurun, Y., & Carrasco, M. (1998). Attention improves or impairs visual performance by enhancing spatial resolution. *Nature, 396*, 72-75.

In: Trends in Dyslexia Research
Editor: Henry D. Tobias, pp. 73-98

ISBN 1-59454-219-8

Chapter III

VISUAL AND AUDITORY ERP IN POOR READERS

Jorge Bernal[1*], Mario Rodríguez[1], Guillermina Yáñez[1], Erzsebet Marosi[1], Thalía Harmony[2], Alfonso Reyes[1], Thalía Fernández[2], Juan Silva[2], Antonio Fernández-Bouzas[2], Belén Prieto[1], Lourdes Luviano[1], Héctor Rodríguez[1] and Vicente Guerrero[1]

[1] Neurociencias, FES-Iztacala. Universidad Nacional Autónoma de México.
[2] Instituto de Neurobiología, UNAM. Juriquilla, Querétaro.

ABSTRACT

Neuropsychological studies on reading difficulties have raised controversy about whether dyslexics and poor readers (PR) are qualitatively different groups or if they suffer from the same deficiency at different degrees.

The aim of the present study was to examine neurophysiological evidence of reading problems by auditory Event-Related Brain Potentials (ERP) (Bernal et al., 2000) and to report new findings on visual ERP recordings from the same sample and discussing them with the works on dyslexics reported in the literature. Gender differences between PR girls and boys in auditory and visual information processing is also discussed.

ERP results are compatible with the view that dyslexics and poor readers would be different subgroups of reading-disabled children, as the two groups show different abnormalities in ERP components. In the literature, the main finding reported in dyslexics is an amplitude reduction and, more consistently, a delayed latency of P300 (a component related to the updating of working memory) respect to controls. In the present study, PR displayed higher P300 amplitude than controls to visual stimuli, while for the auditory stimuli PR showed the same amplitude of P300 as controls (Bernal et al. 2000). Interestingly, in PR an early component (P200) probably related to attention showed

* Jorge Bernal Ph.D., Lab. de Neurometría, Proy. de Neurociencias. ENEP Iztacala. UNAM, Manuel Fernando Soto No. 68. Col. Constitución de la República. 07469. México, D.F., E-mail address: jbernal@servidor.unam.mx

significantly greater amplitude in PR than in the control group to both visual and auditory stimuli. For auditory stimuli, these differences were particularly marked in PR girls. In addition, N200 (a component related to stimuli categorization) amplitude was greater in the control than in the PR group for the auditory and visual stimuli.

The reported results pointed out that the ERP of dyslexics in oddball tasks have smaller amplitude and delayed latency of P300 with respect to normal readers, showing that their deficiencies are located in those stages associated to stimuli evaluation and memory processing, while the PR group seem to allocate attention resources to both relevant and irrelevant stimuli during early and late stages of the information processing, although these resources could be higher for the early stages, especially during auditory processing.

Regarding the gender differences, our results seem to support the observation that in reading difficulties—as in other developmental disorders—boys are more frequently affected than girls, although the dysfunction is more severe in girls. Our results also suggest that PR girls may have greater deficiencies in auditory than in visual processing.

INTRODUCTION

This chapter aims to provide new data about the attentional and memory processes of PR children studied through visual and auditory ERP. Specifically, we pointed out some electrophysiological characteristics of PR, comparing and evaluating the visual and auditory ERP of these children that were obtained using simple oddball tasks. We begin offering some basic concepts about classifications and subtypes of reading disabilities, focusing on the main characteristics of the so-called "Poor Readers" and compared them to dyslexics in some important neurobiological and electrophysiological aspects reported in the literature. We follow with a brief review on ERP and their principal endogenous components and the most important findings in ERP studies of children with reading difficulties. Finally, results about the comparison between visual and auditory ERP in PR are discussed in order to show the peculiar physiological characteristics of PR that –to our approach- made them different from dyslexics.

Definitions and Controversies in Reading Disabilities

The Diagnostic and Statistical Manual of Mental Disorders (APA, 1994) declares that a person can be diagnosed as reading disabled when his/her reading level is significantly below the expected level, given his/her age, IQ and educational level. This definition does not consider the existence of subtypes of reading problems. Nevertheless, due to the heterogeneity of subjects with this disorder, many authors felt impelled to classify reading disorder in different types. Now, the question is whether it exists as a single reading disabled group composed of subjects with different degrees of reading difficulties or there are subgroups of children with qualitatively different characteristics (Badian, 1996; Perfetti, 1985; Rayner & Pollatsek, 1989; Siegel, 1992; Stanovich, 1988).

Rayner and Pollatsek (1989) consider the existence of three groups of reading difficulties: 1) "poor readers" (PR), those who on the standardized reading tests score one or two standard deviations below the norm, but have a normal IQ; 2) "dyslexic readers", those who show a discrepancy between their IQ and their executions on reading tasks; they have a normal or above normal IQ and their scores in reading tests are two or more standard deviations below the norm, and 3) "backward readers" who have low reading performance with low general intelligence. However, other researchers only distinguish between dyslexics and poor readers (Badian, 1996; Perfetti, 1985; Stanovich, 1988), or do not distinguish subgroups at all (Mann, 1998).

In this chapter, we adopt the term reading difficulties (RD) as a general definition for all reading problems in children, and we will refer to dyslexics and poor readers as defined by the above-reviewed criterion of Rayner and Pollatsek (1989).

Differences between PR and Dyslexics

According to Perfetti (1985), the tests exploring cognitive deficiencies of the poor readers have shown that this group may have many types of cognitive problems related to reading processes. He resumed the findings on deficiencies of poor readers as compared with good readers as follows: "PR are less sensitive to orthographic structure, take longer time to name words, they are not effective in using speech codes for processing linguistic stimuli, they are deficient on tasks of phonemic awareness, they are more reliant on context, they do not use the syntactic structure with the same efficiency, they are not good when using working memory, they do not have a good recall of text and have shorter memory spans, etc".

Dyslexia is best understood as a collective term for a group of diverse reading disabilities, and no doubt, this group is the most studied of those with reading difficulties. Haberlandt (1997) resumed the problems and most important facts found in dyslexic children, assuming that not only are there many varieties of dyslexia, but also there are many theoretical models seeking to account for these subtypes. Theorists have attributed to dyslexic children specific deficiencies in visual processing, phonological processing and limitations in general language understanding and cognitive resources. Neuropsychological studies on dyslexics have described deficits in auditory and visual processes (Boder, 1973; Tallal, Miller & Fitch, 1993), in phonological processing (Torgesen, 1988), in short-term memory (Lyon, 1982; Mattis, French & Rapin, 1975), and in working memory (Swanson, 1993). Moreover, this group also shows differences in eye-fixation patterns, with high interference in the center of the their visual fields, which confuse dyslexics during recognition of letters. Their deficits in phonological decoding when they process written and spoken words reveal that they cannot adequately pronounce non-words, show difficulties to discriminate similar phonemes, tend to require a longer time to retrieve the name of a linguistic entity (whether it is a letter or a word), and are not efficient naming digits and objects shown in pictures (Haberlandt, 1997).

Olofson and Niedersoe (1999) also found that most dyslexics share a deficit in phonological decoding. Indeed, data in the literature extensively support the hypothesis about the existence of a core phonological deficit in the reading and spelling difficulties of dyslexics, resulting from higher-order dysfunction at the level of phonological awareness. Nonetheless, recent data suggest a contribution of lower-level auditory perceptual dysfunctions for those difficulties, which can be due to a comparatively slower speed of processing than normal readers in the auditory phonological system used during reading

(Breznitz & Meyler, 2003; Breznitz, 2001). This hypothesis could also be applied to the deficits observed in the processing of visual stimuli (Breznitz & Meyler, 2003).

Presently the hypothesis about the deficiencies in the phonological processing in dyslexics is extensively shared by many authors in order to explain dyslexia. Among others, Stanovich (1988) also proposed this hypothesis suggesting that poor readers also have these phonological problems, but perhaps in less severe form. Nonetheless, poor readers are different from dyslexics, as they also have a wide variety of cognitive deficits.

Whether dyslexia differs from poor reading is a hotly debated and unresolved question. We share the idea that differences between poor readers and dyslexics do exist, but other authors have declared that these differences are very subtle or are not present at all. For example, Siegel (1992) argued that the distinction between dyslexics and poor readers do not appear to be meaningful, since she did not find significant differences between groups in reading, spelling, phonological processing or in short-term memory. On the contrary, Ackerman & Dykman (1993) have shown that poor readers and dyslexics have different cognitive profiles. They have found that dyslexics have worse execution than normal readers in phonological sensitivity and speed of continuous naming or running memory span, while poor readers do not differ from the normal group in the performance of these tasks. Badian (1996) also observed significantly impaired executions in dyslexics compared to poor readers in tasks related to reading and described deficits in orthography, serial naming-speed and phonological tasks.

Badian (1996) attempted to validate the concept of dyslexia and found that at 6 or 7 years of age, dyslexics and poor readers have similar performances on reading-related tasks. However, her study provides support for the concept of dyslexia as a phonological deficit and poor reading as a developmental lag in phonological skills at ages from 8 to 10 years old.

Thus at the present, there is no agreement as to whether PR and dyslexics are qualitatively different groups or if they suffer from the same deficiency but at different degrees.

Neurobiological Studies in RD

The causes of dyslexia are not well known, however there are many studies showing that this abnormality has a neurobiological basis. Thus, it has been proposed that dyslexic subjects have deficiencies with temporal sequence processing probably due to an anatomical disorganization of some cerebral structures (Tallal et al. 1993; Galaburda & Livingstone, 1993) and several electrophysiological alterations when compared with normal subjects (Ahn, H.; Prichep, L.; John, E. R.; Baird, H.; Trepetin, M. & Kaye, H., 1980; John, Prichep, Ahn, Easton, Friedman, & Kaye, 1983; Taylor & Keenan, 1990). However, in PR there are not explicit hypotheses about the biological causes of their deficiencies in reading.

From the neurobiological point of view, at least two hypotheses have been advanced to explain the causes of dyslexia, one regarding morphological alterations in the left cerebral regions involved with speech and the second related to possible inadequate brain function especially in language areas.

In respect to the first hypothesis, there have been described microscopic alterations post mortem in male dyslexic brains (Galaburda & Kemper, 1979; Galaburda, Sherman, Rosen, Aboitiz & Geschwind, 1985; Humphreys, Kauhmann & Galaburda, 1990) which consisted in ectopias in both frontal regions and left language areas; dysplasia, and with less frequent vascular micro-malformations (ectopias means "small neuronal congregations in abnormal superficial layer localization" whereas dysplasia means "loss of characteristic architectural organization of the cortical neurons, mainly subjacent to the site of ectopias"; Habib, 2000). These results indicate that an abnormal cortical development may give rise to the cognitive deficiencies shown in subjects with developmental dyslexia. Another evidence supporting this hypothesis, was the fact that dyslexics display an absence of the normal left>right asymmetry of the planum temporale (a small part of the superior surface of the temporal lobe). In dyslexics, the planum temporale is symmetrical or presents the reverse of normal pattern. However, this description does not seem to be specific, given that the symmetrical aspect of the planum temporale is also present in 33 percent of normal brains and results that did not support the asymmetry pattern have also been reported for *in vivo* MRI studies (Habib, 2000; Robichon, Levrier, Farnarier & Habib, 2000).

Studies about relationships between neuropsychological functions and neuroanatomical and neurofunctional images in dyslexics have also given some insights about disorders in dyslexia. Robichon et al. (2000) carried out an MRI study in two groups of male adults, one dyslexic and one control matched by age, finding that compared to controls, dyslexics showed the most asymmetrical patterns in Broca's area, they also had the worst performance in the non-word reading tasks and they were leftward biased in the operculum area which correlated with a greater number of errors in a non-word dictation task. According to the authors, given that previous studies in functional neuroimaging have demonstrated that Broca's area is implicated in non-word reading (which involves segmentation and assembly procedure in reading) and that writing non-words involves cognitive operations (phoneme discrimination, phoneme segmentation, etc.) that necessarily activate the short term memory system to keep the auditory information during the task, it can be concluded that "phonological segmentation skills may relate to frontal lobe morphology while phonological memory processes may relate to parietal lobe morphology" and dyslexics showed deficiencies in both skills (Robichon et al., 2000).

In the same sense, imaging or functional imaging methods support the phonological deficit theory of dyslexia and its relation to abnormal function of the cerebral hemispheres. A PET study by Rumsey, Andreason, Zametkin, Aquino, King and Hamburger (1992) with an adult dyslexic group, showed that dyslexics did not activate the left temporoparietal region while they performed a rhyming task. The authors concluded that this finding reflects the dyslexic's phonological deficit. In another study that used rCBF, Rumsey, Horwitz, Donohue, Nace, Maisong, and Andreason (1999) found significant correlations between rCBF in the angular gyrus and reading level: a positive correlation in controls and a negative one in dyslexics, concluding that this region "is the most probable site of a functional lesion in dyslexia". Nonetheless, in a recent study using a simple repetition of words and pseudowords task, carried out with PET, McCrory, Frith, Brunswick, and Price (2000) reported some different findings since they showed that dyslexics presented decreased activation relative to controls in the right superior temporal region, right postcentral gyri and in left cerebellum irrespective of word type,

Almost all of the neurobiological studies about reading difficulties have been devoted to uncover the neurobiological bases of dyslexia while other types of reading disabilities such as those mentioned above, have received less attention. To our knowledge, only one work studied dyslexia and other reading difficulties. Dalby, Elbro and St□kilde-J□rgensen (1998) in an in vivo MRI study, compared three measures of right and left temporal lobes in groups of dyslexics, retarded readers (backwards readers according to the classification of Rayner and Pollatsek, 1989) and normal controls. The three groups solved the following tasks: phonological coding in reading (reading of non-words: the subjects indicated which word was a homophone of a real word), silent word reading (the participants selected which of four pictures correspond best to the word), passage comprehension, phonological discrimination (subjects discriminated between words that differed only by a single phoneme) and phonemic analysis (subjects found a target spoken sound in one of four illustrated words). Results showed that symmetry or right asymmetry was characteristic of the dyslexic group while in the control group and in the retarded group an opposite pattern was observed. The absence of left asymmetry was associated to deficits in phonemic analysis which may indicate that this ability is related to a leftward asymmetry in temporal lobes. The finding of asymmetry differences between dyslexics and retarded readers –although limited due to the size of the sample- is very important, since it may be interpreted as an evidence that although both groups share the same deficits in phonological characteristics, the etiology for reading difficulties could be different in at least in some groups with reading difficulties.

Electrophysiological Studies in RD

Another important source of knowledge about the neurobiological bases of reading disabilities stem from works that have used the Event-Related Brain Potentials (ERP) technique. As with neurobiological studies, most ERP studies have been focused on dyslexics, although there are some reports on PR, which fortunately will allow us to compare the results obtained from the two groups, and in doing so, to determine if the neurophysiological profiles of both groups resembled each other or if they are different. A brief introduction on ERP is given in this section.

ERP allow the study of cognitive processing with a high degree of temporal resolution (in the order of milliseconds). "ERP can be defined as patterned voltage changes on the ongoing electroencephalogram that are time locked to sensory, motor, or cognitive events. ERP arise from synchronous activities of neuronal populations engaged in information processing" (Hillyard & Picton, 1987).

ERP consist of a series of positive and negative voltage (polarity) peaks or components that appear with specific time delays related to the appearance of stimulus that elicited them. These components have been named according to whether they have positive or negative polarity and the time of appearance (latency) calculated from the stimulus presentation. In this way, the N100 or N1 is a negative peak occurring approximately 100 milliseconds after the beginning of the stimulus event; P200 is a positive component occurring approximately

200 milliseconds after the beginning of the stimulus event, etc. The early ERP components that occur with latencies <60-80 ms are determined primarily by the physical characteristics of the eliciting stimulus and are relatively insensitive to changes in the psychological state of the subject. In the literature, these responses have been named exogenous.

In contrast, many of the later ERP components are highly sensitive to changes in the psychological state of the subject, the meaning of the stimulus, and/or the information-processing demands of the task. These components have been named endogenous and they are useful for investigating the physiological bases of human perception and cognition (Hillyard & Picton 1987) and have helped us to understand the differences between normal and abnormal information processing.

Among the endogenous components are: N100, P200, N200, and P300 (see fig. 1). They have been related to different phases of information processing. These components may show changes in amplitude and/or latency depending on psychological states and experimental conditions.

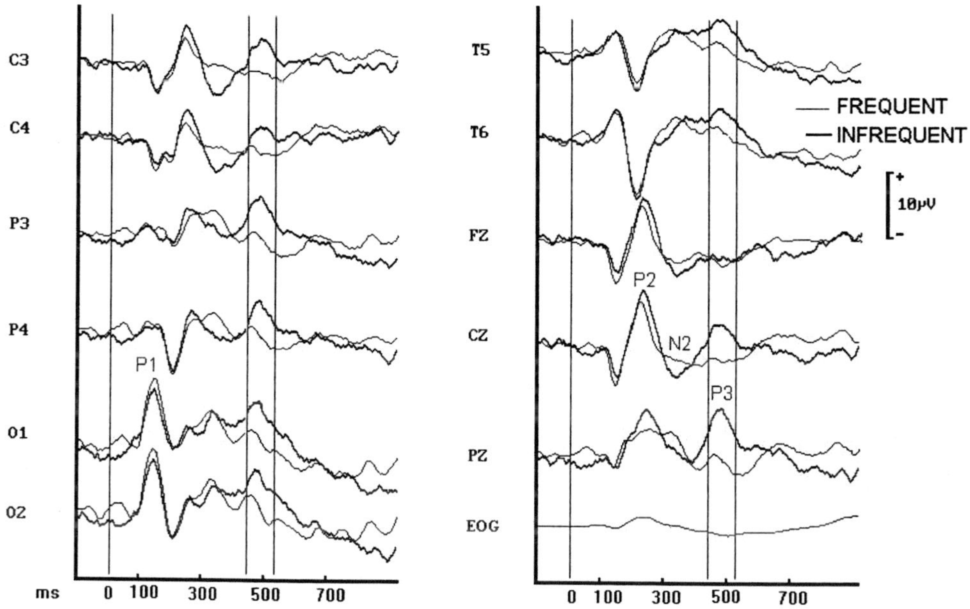

Figure 1. Visual ERP to frequent and infrequent stimuli in a control group at eleven electrode locations. Left cursor shows stimulus onset; the next two cursors show the limits of the analysis window of the P300 wave. P100 (P1) is marked at O1; P200 (P2) and N200 (N2) are marked at Cz and P300 (P3) is marked at Pz. Positivity is upwards. Calibration is 10 microvolts. EOG = electroculogram.

For instance, common findings in the ERP of RD children are lower amplitudes and longer latencies of the endogenous components compared to normal readers. The underlying physiological mechanism in low amplitudes may consist of less brain structures involved in the task or different timing in the synchronization of neural generators. A delayed latency of these components may reflect longer times for processing information related to stimulus. When, otherwise, high amplitudes and short latencies of ERP are observed, perhaps the opposite physiological mechanism occurs.

It has been observed that latencies of the P100, N200, P200 and P300 components have a direct relation with task difficulty. As task difficulty increases, so does the latency of these components. Thus, it has been suggested that the latencies of these components reflect the speed at which stimuli are evaluated and categorized (Breznitz & Meyler, 2003). For P300, Polich and Hine (1996) proposed that its latency may serve as a temporal measure of the neural activity underlying the speed of attention allocation and immediate memory operations.

N100 (N1)

It is a negative component with a fronto-central topographic distribution (Iragui, Kutas, Mitchiner & Hylliard, 1993). Some authors consider it as an exogenous component (Breznitz & Meyler, 2003) while others classified it as endogenous. N100 is related to selective attention (Elbert, 1992; Loveless, 1983; Näätänen & Picton, 1987) and may reflect an early selective process: the comparison of the attended stimulus with the model stored in memory, or some active supervising process that evaluates the arriving information or the access to memory (Loveless, 1983; Picton, 1988). Longer latencies and reduced amplitudes of N100 have been reported in children with reading difficulties (Pinkerton, Watson & McClelland, 1989) and in children with deficits in attention (Loiselle, Stamm, Maitincky & Whipple, 1980; Satterfield & Bradley, 1977). When language stimuli have been used, N100 (reported as N150 by Neville, Kutas, Chesney & Schmidt, 1986) reflected early attentional priming related to linguistic stimuli.

P200 (P2)

It is a positive wave with maximum peak at the central region (Iragui et al. 1993). As with N100, controversy exists as to whether P200 is an exogenous or endogenous component (Shibasaky & Miyasaki, 1992), or that it reflects both exogenous and endogenous processing (Dunn, Dunn, Languis, & Andrews, 1998). Polich, Ladish and Burns (1990) interpreted developmental changes of P200 as a reflection of maturation of sensory function rather than that of cognitive function. Hillyard and Picton (1987), proposed that P200 is sensitive to the physical attributes of the stimulus, however, Oken (1990) described it as an endogenous component. Johnson (1989) found that P200 amplitude is modified by the attentional demands of the tasks performed. Holcomb, Ackerman and Dykman (1986) reported higher P200 amplitude at Cz to unexpected stimuli, in the reading disabled and in children suffering from attentional deficit with or without hyperactivity as compared to controls. Bernal et al. (2000) showed that P200 could differentiate poor readers from control children in auditory ERP.

N200 (N2)

The N200 endogenous component is a negative wave whose topographic distribution depends on the sensory modality of the stimulus (Donchin, Ritter & McCallum, 1978). In auditory stimulation, the highest amplitude is observed at the vertex and in visual stimulus, at the preoccipital region (Simson, Vaughan & Ritter, 1977). This component reflects a discriminative process that responds to environmental changes in an automatic way and might participate in the orientating response (Näätänen & Michie, 1979 in Loveless, 1983). N200 can also reflect psychological processes associated in target selection (Donchin et al., 1978), or stimulus classification and discrimination (Han, Fan, Chen & Zhuo, 1999; Näätänen & Picton, 1986; Satterfield, Schell, Nicholas, Satterfield & Freese, 1990). Strong relationships have been reported between N200, task demands (Johnson, 1989; Duncan, C., Rumsey, J., Wilkniss, S., Denckla, M., Hamburger, S. & Odou-Potkin, M., 1994) and selective attention (Satterfield et al., 1990). Iragui et al. (1993) have proposed another hypothesis suggesting that N200 reflects a categorization process when decisions are made.

P300

It is a positive-going wave that occurs at 300 ms or above after the onset of a determined stimulus. Psychological processes underlying P300 have been widely studied. It has been suggested that P300 is sensible to developmental changes in the memory capacity of children (Polich et al., 1990). There is evidence that P300 reflects information processing associated to attention (Duncan et al., 1994; Holcomb, Ackerman & Dykman,1985) and memory operations (Mc Isaac & Polich, 1992). At the moment, the most accepted theoretical interpretation of P300 is that it indexes activities required for the maintenance of working memory, reflecting processes occurring when the mental model (or schema) of the environment is refreshed and updated (Donchin, Karis, Bashore & Coles, 1986). Due to its relationships in cognitive processing, P300 has been the most frequently used component in the study of neurocognitive processes.

Some Issues on ERP in Reading Difficulties

Several methodological problems have been observed in the history of ERP studies with RD children. For example, different criteria have been employed by the authors to select samples. Although, researchers are generally careful that the IQ of children must be normal or above normal, the instruments to assess the grade of reading deficits varies greatly. In some studies, the reports about the instruments used are not clearly described, in others, the criterion of selection varied from the opinion of teachers and parents for different well known tests, such as the WRAT, the Boder Test of Reading/Spelling Patterns or some other local tests. Moreover, the cut scores in the reading tests used to select the subjects also have been different. These have varied from 1 - 2.5 or more years of backwardness in reading. Despite of these differences in methods, ERP studies with RD groups had the common factor that all subjects showed problems in some degree with reading. In the next paragraphs, we will briefly review the literature on reading difficulties and ERP, indicating –whenever possible- if the children studied were dyslexics or PR.

Although the P300 endogenous component was reported by Sutton et al. in the sixties (Sutton, Braren, & John, 1965), the first ERP studies on RD children in the seventies or eighties were focused on the early components (Brying & Järvihleto, 1985; Conners, 1971; Pinkerton et al., 1989; Preston, Guthrie, Kirsch, German & Childs, 1977; Preston, Guthrie & Childs, 1974; Shields, 1973; Weber & Omenn, 1977) with the most common finding being lower amplitudes and/or longer latencies of N100, P200 and N200 components.

ERP studies of P300 have utilized visual, auditory, verbal and non-verbal stimuli. Those studies -in general- have revealed lower amplitudes and/or longer latencies of P300 and other components occurring before 300 ms in children with reading difficulties (i.e. Dainner, Klorman, Salzman, Hess, Davidson & Michael, 1981; Lovrich & Stam, 1983). Frequently, the authors have concluded that the dyslexics have deficits in the information processing.

Taylor and Keenan (1990) compared the ERP components in dyslexic children and a control sample. The authors considered a child to be dyslexic if he had a normal IQ and his scores on the reading test showed at least one year of backwardness respect to normal children, although most of the subjects in this study had more than two years of backwardness. Due to this fact, these children may be classified as dyslexics according to the criterion established by Rayner and Pollatsek (1989). Visual nonverbal and verbal stimuli were employed and presented to three age groups of children ranging from 7-12 years old. Three tasks of graded difficulties were employed: a nonalphabetic, an alphabetic, and a lexical-decision task. Dyslexics showed longer P300 and N200 latencies for language stimuli as compared to controls as well as smaller P300 amplitudes than control children, during most difficult lexical tasks. In addition, Erez and Pratt (1992) using pure tones and two nonsense monosyllables, reported decreased P300 amplitudes at midline leads in subjects with dyslexia as compared to normal ones and longer P300 latencies in response to nonsense monosyllables in dyslexics. Similar data was observed by Fawcett, Chattopadhyay, Kandler, Jarrat, Nicolson, & Proctor (1993). Barnea, Lamm, Epstein and Pratt (1994) using a paradigm similar to Sternberg's (1966), contradictorily found greater P300 amplitudes in RD children than in a control group. Smaller P300 amplitude in RD has been related to either decreased availability of attentional resources or to an inability to allocate them appropriately. Duncan et al. (1994) proposed that altered P300 is a reflection of the immaturity of the brain that impairs those cognitive processes that are necessary for successful reading.

Studies by Holcomb et al. (1985, 1986), Stelmack, Saxe, Noldy-Cullum, Cambell and Armitage (1988) and Bernal, Harmony, Rodríguez, Reyes, Yáñez, Fernández, Galán, Silva, Fernández-Bouzas, Rodríguez, Guerrero and Marosi (2000) applied the same criterion to classify the children with reading difficulties, and in our opinion the subjects of these studies are PR children. In the three studies, the children were selected if they had reading difficulties, a normal IQ and reading test scores with 1 or 2 years of backwardness, as compared to the control subjects (which is in accordance to Rayner and Pollatsek's (1989) classification criteria for poor readers). In two experiments, Holcomb et al. (1985, 1986) studied P300 to visual verbal and nonverbal stimuli and to tones and to unexpected sounds as auditory stimuli, in three clinical groups including 24 reading-disabled children and two groups with attentive problems compared with 23 control children. All subjects were 8 to 12 years old. Auditory ERP were elicited by low-probability 2000 Hz target tones and unexpected sounds presented among frequent 1000 Hz tones with an ISI of 2600 ms on an active counting task. The results showed that auditory stimuli evoked a P300 of higher amplitude in the control than in the PR group. Moreover, the authors observed for the unexpected sound a P200 of higher amplitude in the PR than in the control group. This result allows for speculation that greater P200 amplitude in PR reflects that the stimuli captured more attention from the PR subjects. For the visual stimuli, the differences between groups consisted of a greater P300 amplitude for controls as compared to PR, and smaller P300 amplitudes of PR to verbal than to nonverbal stimuli, while the controls presented a similar P300 size to both types of stimuli.

Stelmack et al. (1988) found greater P200 and no P300 differences, in a group of 7 PR compared to 10 normal readers (with mean ages of 9.2 years for the PR and 8.3 years for the control group) during a word-recognition memory task. The authors interpreted the higher P200 amplitudes of PR children during both acquisition and retrieval of words as indicative of differences at an early sensory stage of stimulus processing.

Bernal et al. (2000) studied a control group of 17 children (10 boys and 7 girls) and 15 PR children (8 boys and 7 girls), with ages 10 – 12 years old and average IQ >85. PR scored between one and two standard deviations below the scores of the normal readers, in their performance in two batteries of reading-tests in Spanish. Unlike most of the above-cited studies, this one considered gender as an independent variable. There were no differences between groups in the N100 and P300 amplitudes to infrequent or frequent stimuli. However, differences in the amplitude of the P200 and N200 components for both infrequent and frequent stimuli were observed. The PR group showed a higher P200 amplitude than the control group with a significant Group X Sex interaction, with PR girls showing greater P200 amplitudes than boys or girls of the control group. However, the control group showed significantly larger N200 amplitudes in response to the infrequent stimuli, with respect to the PR group. Likewise, Bernal et al. (2002) found that PR showed a P200 component significantly higher than P300 while in the control group there were no differences between these two components.

The authors concluded that higher P200 amplitude in PR may reflect that these children paid more attention to both kinds of stimuli compared to normal readers. Moreover, as P300 amplitudes were of the same size in PR and in controls for both frequent and infrequent stimuli, it was concluded that more attentional resources were allocated by PR in the earlier stages of processing of information, in contrast with normal subjects who displayed more attentional resources in those stages corresponding to the evaluation of stimuli and memory updating (i.e. P300). In fact, this idea seems to be shared by other authors that have reported similar findings (Stelmack et al.,1988 and Holcomb et al., 1986).

Another study by Segalowitz, Wagner and Menna (1992) compared 11 children defined as poor readers with 16 good readers (with a mean age of 15 years). They did not find differences between the two groups in P300 amplitudes or latencies to low probability target sounds of 1000 Hz presented among 1500 Hz non-target stimuli in an oddball paradigm.

Current Study: Visual ERP in Poor Readers

The present work aimed to analyze attentional and memory processes with visual ERP in PR, and to compare the results with those obtained by Bernal et al. (2000) in an auditory ERP study using an oddball task. The visual paradigm applied in the current study had the same characteristics with the auditory paradigm, and the participant subjects were the same as those studied by Bernal et al. in the cited study.

Subjects

Twenty-four right-handed children between 10 and 12 years of age (11 male and 13 female) were studied. All subjects were of middle socioeconomic class with normal pediatric and neurological examination. No subject was under medication at the time of the study. They all came from a public school. The average IQ was 117.7 (s.d. = 9.3) for the control group and 97.7 (s.d.= 14.4) for the PR group, as assessed by the Weschler Intelligence Scale for Children (Mexican revision) (WISC-RM). The control group consisted of 11 children (6 girls and 5 boys) with good academic achievement. The PR group consisted of 13 subjects (7girls and 6 boys) with low achievement in all academical subjects; 70 % of them had repeated at least one grade and attended special psychopedagogical courses, in order to cope successfully with normal educational requirements.

The division of the children in control and PR groups was based upon performance in two batteries for the assessment of reading: The Psychoeducative Battery (Ostrosky, Navarro, Canseco, Pérez & Zárate, 1984). and the Reading Disabilities Battery (Regiosa, Pérez, Manzano, & Antelo,1994).

The Psychoeducative Battery is a standardized reading test for Mexican children, which includes speed of reading and reading comprehension tests in both silent and out-loud reading.

The Reading Disabilities Battery was designed for the computerized analysis of reading. This test is called "Batería para los Trastornos de Lectura (BTL)" in Spanish and it includes 8 different subtests: word reading, reading comprehension, ordering of words into syntactically correct phrases, completion of phrases, naming, phonological categorization of pictures and words and perception of visual features.

PR scored between one and two standard deviations below the scores of the normal readers in both batteries (See Bernal et al. 2000).

Stimuli

In the present work, stimuli were geometric figures of squares and triangles (2 cm per side), that appeared on the screen of a computer for 200 ms with an interstimulus interval of 2 - 2.5 seconds. Stimuli were presented in three series that consisted of 70, 80 and 110 figures each one. In each series, the probability of presentation was of 80 % for the frequent figure (standard stimulus) and 20% for the infrequent one (target stimulus). Stimuli were presented randomly in a contrabalanced way (half of the experimental subjects of both groups had the squares as infrequent stimulus and the other half, the triangles). Stimuli were presented at the center of the monitor of the computer.

Procedure

Subjects were familiarized with the laboratory, and then seated in a comfortable chair, at 90 cm from the screen in a dark room. They were asked to count the target (infrequent) stimuli and, after each series, the children had to say the number of target stimuli counted.

At the beginning of each session, the children were taught to identify the target stimulus and rehearsed until they were able to execute the discrimination task without errors.

Recording

Nineteen Ag/AgCl electrodes were placed at Fp1, FP2, F3, F4, C3, C4, P3, P4, O1, O2, F7, F8, T3, T4, T5, T6, Fz, Cz and Pz sites of the 10-20 International System, using linked earlobes as reference. Recording and stimulation were made using a Medicid-3M computer system with amplifiers of 0.5 - 30 Hz of band range. Eye movements were monitored by bipolar electrodes attached to the right supraorbital region and outer cantus. The electrode impedance was always below 10 kohms. The sampling period was of 4 ms over a time epoch of 1024 ms with a 100 ms prestimulus baseline. EEG segments were selected visually, off-line, eliminating segments with artifacts and with EEG activity higher than 40 microvolts at any channel. Averaging was done separately for frequent and infrequent stimuli, adding the stimuli of the three series. A minimal of 15-20 clean segments were used since Taylor and Keenan (1990) have reported that 10-15 segments are enough to obtain a reliable ERP in children.

Data Analysis

Latency

The largest positive-going peak occurring after the P200-N200 complex between 280-700 ms was designated as P300 and its latency was measured at Pz in this interval, for both standard and target stimuli. Latencies of P200 and N200 components were measured in all derivations at the largest peak (also for both types of stimuli) within latency ranges of 198-258 ms and 310-410 ms respectively.

Amplitude

Mean amplitudes of P200, and N200 components relative to pre-stimulus baseline, for frequent and infrequent stimuli, were calculated at all leads within a latency window determined by examining the grand mean ERP at Cz as follows: P200 (212 - 244 ms) and N200 (324 - 356 ms in control group and 364-396 ms in PR group). For P300, this evaluation was done at Pz, within an interval of 432 -532 ms also for all leads.

Topography

Scalp topography analysis of the scaled baseline to peak amplitudes (McCarthy and Wood, 1985) of each component in frequent and infrequent conditions were done when these components and conditions were statistically different between groups. Two types of analysis were done: the topographic profile comparisons using only Fz, Cz and Pz leads and hemispheric comparisons without considering these three electrodes.

Statistical Analysis

A 4-factor ANCOVA was applied to amplitude measures of each component, for both stimulus conditions (target and standard) separately in the following way: Group (controls vs. poor readers) X Sex X Anterior-to-Posterior electrode placements: frontal (F7, F3, Fz, F4 and F8 leads), central (T3, C3, Cz, C4 and T4 leads) and parietal (T5, P3, Pz, P4, and T6 leads) X Coronal electrode placements: left lateral (F7, T3, and T5 leads), left medial (F3, C3 and P3 leads) medial (Fz, Cz and Pz leads), right medial (F4, C4 and T4 leads) and right lateral (F8, T4 and T6 leads). In these comparisons, repeated-measures ANOVA (STATISTICA), with Greenhouse-Geiser epsilon corrections were made and adjusted degrees of freedom were calculated and rounded down to the nearest whole number. If the Group main effect was significant, remaining four electrodes (Fp1, Fp2, O1 and O2) were analyzed. For latency measures, comparisons between groups were done first at Cz for P200 and N200 and at Pz for P300 with 2-factor ANCOVA (Group X Sex). If significance between groups or Group X Sex differences were found, then 4-factor ANCOVA was carried out. In any other case the analysis was finished. In all between groups comparisons (ANCOVA) IQ was employed as covariable.

As in the auditory study, the data were analyzed in order to test amplitude differences in P200, N200 and P300 components.

Behavioral tests: The responses for the Psychoeducative Battery were analyzed by Student's t-test, and those of the Reading Disabilities Battery by means of MANOVA (see Bernal et al. 2000)

ERP RESULTS

None of the groups had errors in the task of counting infrequent stimuli.

Latency

Grand average waveforms elicited by infrequent and frequent stimuli were morphologically quite similar for control and PR groups (Figures 1 and 2). P100 appeared at 100 ms in both groups, showing that the children had a good sensory response to visual stimuli; at Cz, P200 appeared at 228 ms in the control and PR groups, and it was observed at frontal (except F7 and F8), central, parietal and occipital regions. N200 was detected at the same regions as P200 as well as at postero-temporal leads; a non-significant difference between groups was observed for N200 latency (latency for controls was 340 ms and 380 ms for PR). Finally, a P300 wave can be observed with maximal amplitude at Pz, though it was clearly distinguishable at central, parietal, temporal and occipital areas. Latencies at Pz were, for control group 476 ms and for PR group 452 ms. Again, this difference was not statistically significant.

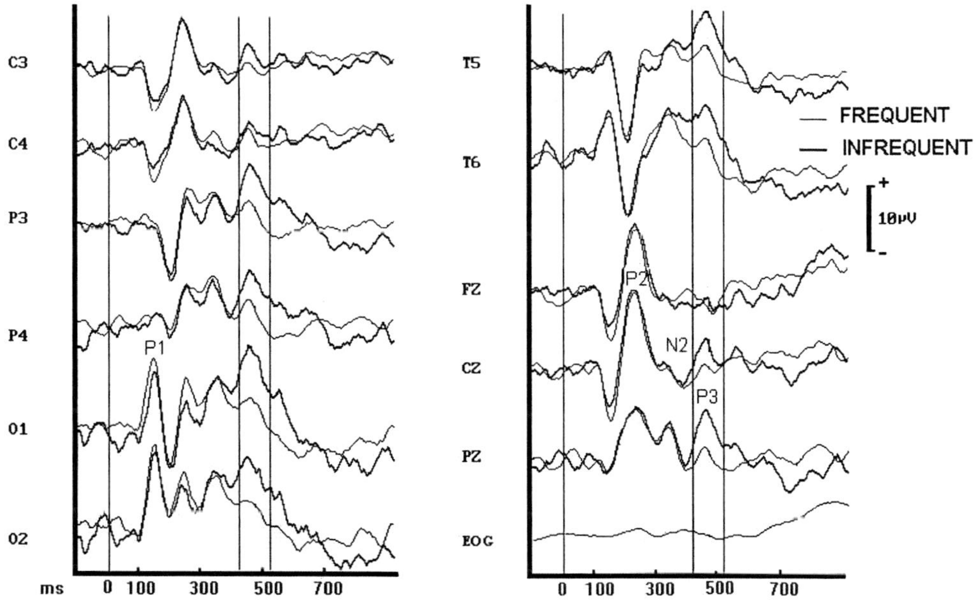

Figure 2. Visual ERP to frequent and infrequent stimuli in PR group at eleven electrode locations. Left cursor shows stimulus onset; the next two cursors show the limits of the analysis window of the P300 wave. P100 (P1) is marked at O1; P200 (P2) and N200 (N2) are marked at Cz and P300 (P3) is marked at Pz. Positivity is upwards. Calibration 10 microvolts. EOG = electroculogram.

Amplitude

Between-groups differences were observed in the amplitudes of P200, N200 and P300 components.

P200

Main effects were not significant for the frequent stimuli. Only the interaction Group X Coronal had a significant effect: ($F(2/39) = 7.52$, $p<.001$) wherein PR group showed greater amplitudes than control group (see figure 3) at midline and right medial leads ($p<.0001$ and $p<.0001$ respectively in post hoc analysis).

For infrequent stimuli, PR group also showed greater P200 amplitudes than control group as observed in the figure 4. As for the frequent stimulus, this result was significant only in the Group X Coronal interaction ($F(2/42=3.41$, $p<.037$). Thus, PR group had greater amplitudes than controls in the medial and right medial leads ($p<.04$ and $p<.008$ respectively in post hoc analysis).

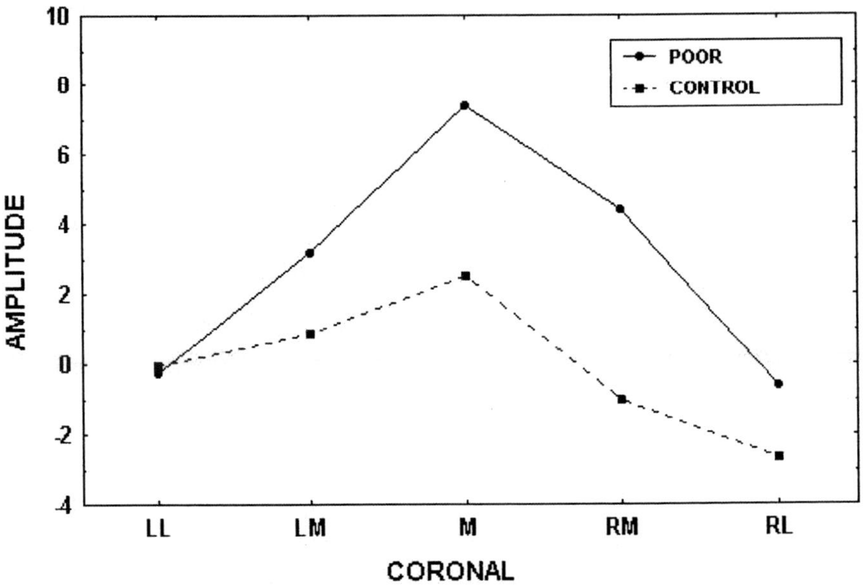

Figure 3. Topographic distribution of visual P200 mean amplitude (microvolts) to frequent stimuli at coronal regions: left lateral (LL), left medial (LM), medial (M), right medial (RM), and right lateral (RL), for control and PR groups. It can be observed that PR show higher P200 amplitude than control group at LM, M and RM regions.

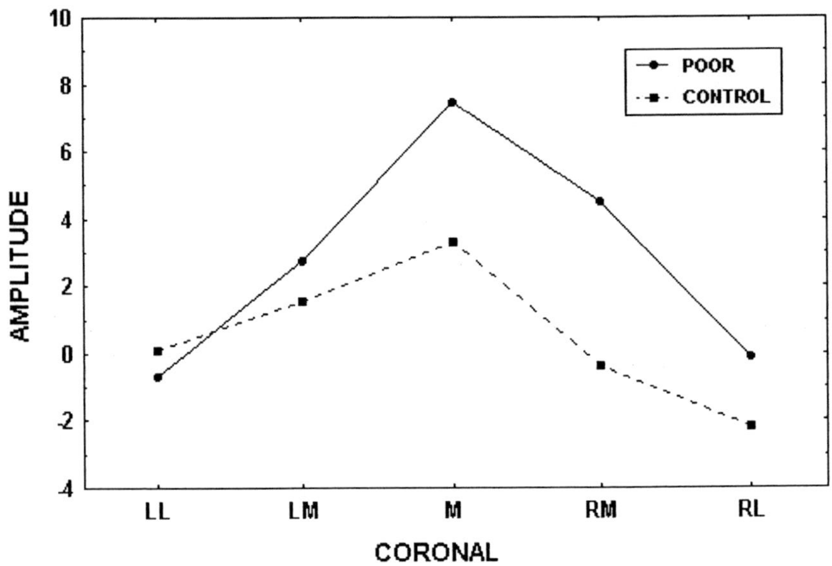

Figure 4. Topographic distribution of visual P200 mean amplitude (microvolts) to infrequent stimuli at coronal regions: left lateral (LL), left medial (LM), medial (M), right medial (RM), and right lateral (RL), for control and PR groups. It can be observed that PR show higher P200 amplitude than control group at M and RM regions.

Unlike the findings for the auditory task, the differences between-groups for visual P200 were *independent* of the sex effect.

N200

In case of the N200 component, the differences in the responses elicited by the frequent and infrequent stimuli, showed a significant main effect of Group: (F (1/18) = 6.8, p<.02 and F(1/18) =6.75 p<.02, for frequent and infrequent stimuli respectively) with the control group showing the greatest amplitudes in both cases. The Group X Coronal interaction was significant for frequent: F(4,12)= 4.83 p<.014 and for infrequent stimuli: F (4,12)=3.82 p<.013 (see figures 5 and 6). Post hoc test showed that for the frequent stimuli, control group had greater amplitudes than PR at the left medial (p<.014), right medial (p<.0001) and right lateral leads (p<.0001) and for the infrequent stimuli, controls had greater amplitudes than PR at left medial (p<.0006), medial (p<.0017), right medial (p<.00016) and right lateral leads (p<.024).

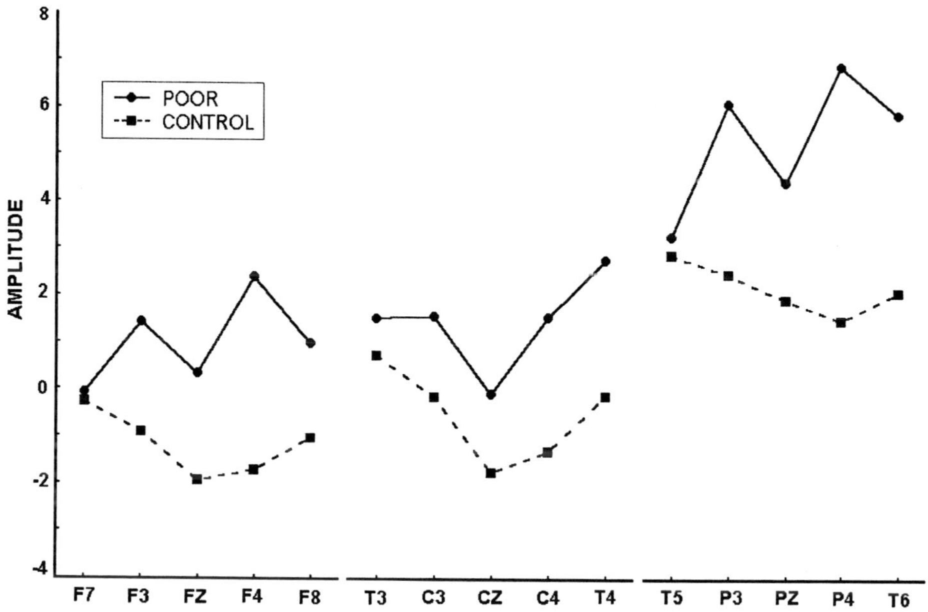

Figure 5. Topographic distribution of visual N200 mean amplitude (microvolts) to frequent stimuli at F7, F3, Fz, F4, F8, T3, C3, Cz, C4, T4, T5, P3, Pz, P4, and T6 leads for control and PR groups. It can be observed that control group shows more negative amplitudes than PR group at almost all electrode locations.

P300

PR group showed greater amplitudes than the control group in the responses to both frequent and infrequent stimuli. This effect was observed in practically every derivation (see figures 7 and 8). Main effect of Group: (F(1/18)= 9.69, p<.006 for frequent stimuli and F(1/18) = 7.86, p<.02 for infrequent stimuli.

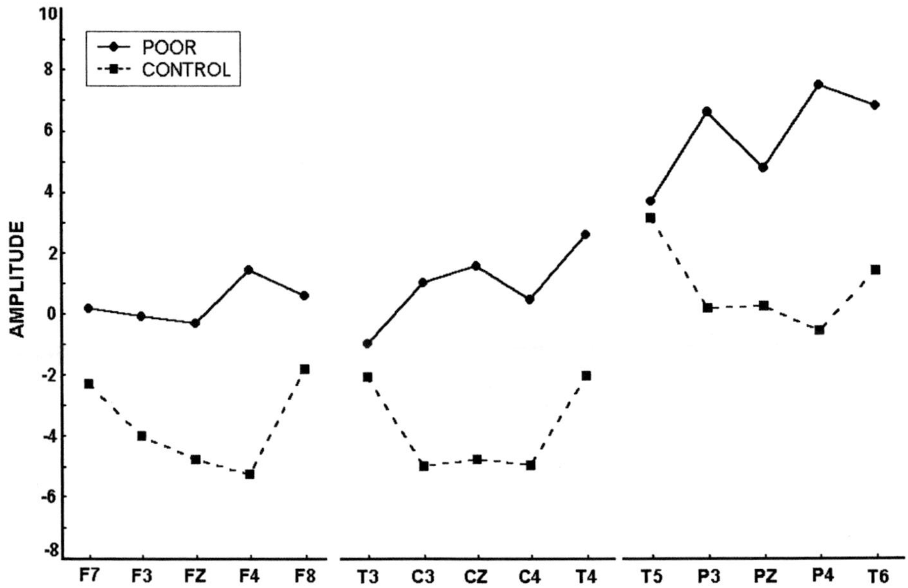

Figure 6. Topographic distribution of visual N200 mean amplitude (microvolts) to infrequent stimuli at F7, F3, Fz, F4, F8, T3, C3, Cz, C4, T4, T5, P3, Pz, P4, and T6 leads for control and PR groups. It can be observed that control group shows more negative amplitudes than PR group at almost all electrode locations.

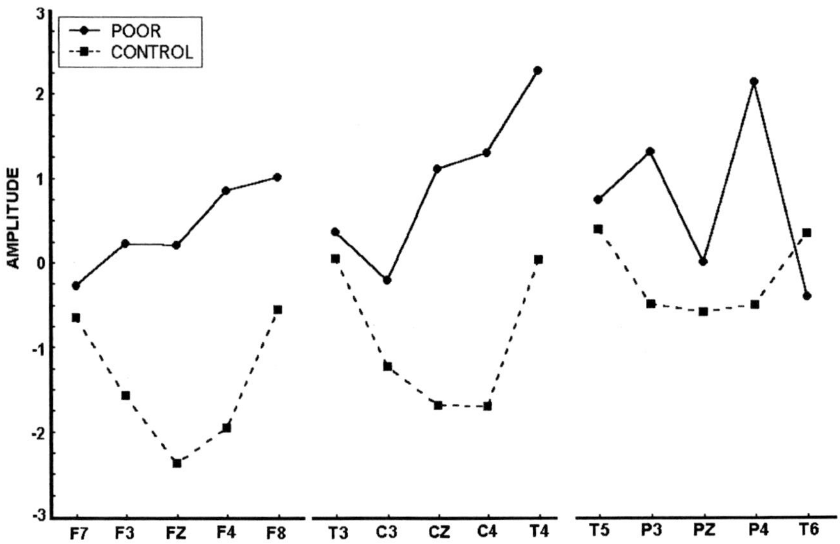

Figure 7. Topographic distribution of visual P300 mean amplitude (microvolts) to frequent stimuli at F7, F3, Fz, F4, F8, T3, C3, Cz, C4, T4, T5, P3, Pz, P4, and T6 leads for control and PR groups. It can be observed that PR group shows higher amplitudes than control group at almost all electrode locations.

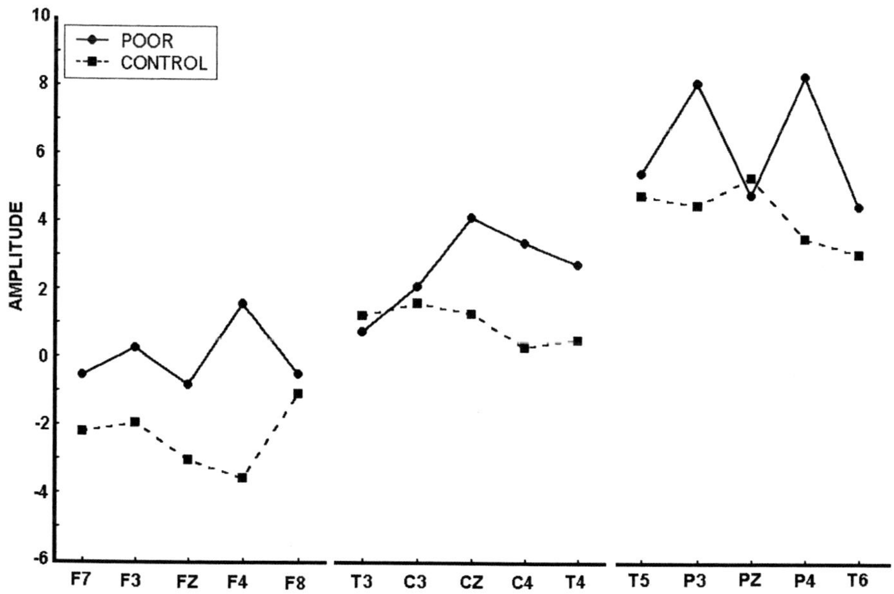

Figure 8. Topographic distribution of visual P300 mean amplitude (microvolts) to infrequent stimuli at F7, F3, Fz, F4, F8, T3, C3, Cz, C4, T4, T5, P3, Pz, P4, and T6 leads for control and PR groups. It can be observed that PR group shows higher amplitudes than control group at almost all electrode locations.

Topographic Analysis

No group differences were observed in topographic profile analysis in any components or conditions.

Discussion

As usual when ERP to auditory and visual stimuli are compared, visual P300 shows longer latency (nearly to 500 ms in both groups) than auditory P300 (nearly to 300 ms), and as it could be expected, N200 showed the same feature: visual N200 presented a latency up to 300 ms while auditory N200 latency was almost hundred milliseconds shorter.

In order to explain the reading deficiencies observed in dyslexics, Breznitz and Meyler (2003) have argued about the importance of the differences in the processing speed between visual and auditory stimuli during reading and particularly during the process of learning to read. According to the mentioned authors, the information available in the literature shows that, in order to access to the meaning of a written word it is necessary a synchronization between the phonological and orthographic information of the word. For that, the information of each sensorial modality must arrive to its specific cerebral area with a gap between them into a time threshold that let that such information could be integrated, allowing the storage of stimulus information in memory in an unified, accurate and stable form. From this model, it is obvious that as the gap increases there will be more difficulties to integrate the information of both sensorial modalities. We believe that this is more important in case of the children, mainly in the first stages of learning to read, in which children read executing the grapheme to phoneme conversion, which would suppose an accurate synchronization between auditory and visual information. However, this would not seem to be the explication for the deficiencies of PR children, since there were no latency differences between groups neither to the visual nor the auditory paradigm.

It is necessary to point out that this finding is not consistent with the results reported by Holcomb et al. (1985, 1986) wherein PR children showed delayed latency of P300 respect to controls. In dyslexics delayed latencies of P300 respect to controls have typically been reported in simple oddball tasks; this has been interpreted as a diminution in speed of information processing. Stelmack et al. (1988) and ourselves have not found delayed latencies in the ERP of PR, as Holcomb and his coworkers reported. This inconsistency in the data of ERP latencies of PR, may suggest that while in dyslexics it exists a delayed information processing, for the PR, the differences in the processing mechanisms with those of the controls, are reflected better in the amplitudes of the ERP.

Comparing the results obtained for the amplitudes of ERP in both modalities, we can observe first that the amplitude of the P200 component clearly differentiated the PR from the control group. In both sensorial modalities, PR group had greater P200 amplitudes than control group almost in all leads. However, the effect of sex in this component was evident only in the auditory ERP but not in the visual ones. Indeed, one important result reported by Bernal et al. (2000) was that PR girls showed higher P200 amplitudes -to auditory stimuli- than PR boys or that normal boys or girls in practically all the leads. The interpretation given by the authors to this fact was that the alterations in the auditory processing could be more severe in the PR girls than in PR boys. However, given that in the present study the effect of sex on visual ERP was not observed, it is possible to conclude that the severity in these alterations on girls are only valid for the auditory information. If this supposition was true, one could expect that a detailed analysis of the neuropsychological characteristics related with learning to read of the PR would give worse evaluations in PR girls than in PR boys in those tasks related to auditory processing. Unfortunately, the reported works that include girls in the samples of PR are very scarce, therefore more research is necessary to clarify this point.

Another important finding occurred with the P300 wave. Although in the auditory ERP study, no significant differences were found between PR and control groups, a notable tendency of greater P300 in PR was observed (see Bernal, Rodríguez, Yáñez & Marosi, 2002). With visual stimuli, P300 amplitude was significantly greater in the PR compared to the control group to both frequent or infrequent stimuli. In the auditory study the authors concluded that PR's higher P200 amplitude may reflect that these children paid more attention to both kinds of stimuli than normal readers and that as in P300 no significant differences were observed, it was concluded that attentional resources were allocated by PR in earlier stages of processing of information, in contrast with normal subjects who displayed more attentional resources in those stages that corresponded to the evaluation of stimuli and memory updating (i.e. P300). However, regarding the data obtained with visual ERP we can conclude that PR pay more attentional resources to both early and late stages of information processing, although in the auditory modality these resources could be more focalized in the early stages. Moreover, it is possible to conclude that PR could present deficiencies in a mechanism that direct the attentional resources allowing a better differentiation between relevant and irrelevant stimuli, preventing that same quantity of attentional resources be displayed to both types of stimuli.

Working memory is a system with limited capacity for information storage and is also occupied in the distribution of the attentional resources to incoming information; therefore this mechanism would be a prime candidate proposed to be failing in the "management of the resources of attention" in PR, which could cause a saturation of the system and consequently a deficient information processing.

It can easily be supposed the relevance that such mechanism could have in the process of reading and learning to reading in childhood, since an efficient working memory ensures that the attention concentrates in relevant aspects of the reading process. Thus, Wagner and Torgesen (1987) have proposed the main importance of working memory in the phonological processing of written language. Moreover, Just and Carpenter (1992) argued that working memory plays a central role in language comprehension, storing the intermediate and final products of a reader's or listener's computations, as she or he constructs and integrates ideas from the stream of successive words in a text or a spoken discourse. Then, it may be supposed that if a person is deficient in working memory operations related with the allocation of the attentional resources in the fundamental aspects related with reading, the execution of various fundamental processes to comprehension (such as word encoding, lexical access, syntactic and semantic analysis, etc.) would be affected due to the lost of attentional resources needed to perform those process efficiently. On the other hand, readers with an efficient management of the attentional resources could have sufficient resources available for the processing of the written information.

Interestingly, for the N200 component the results observed with auditory and visual stimuli were very similar, in both modalities N200 amplitude to infrequent stimuli was greater in the control than in the PR group and in the visual paradigm N200 to frequent stimuli was also of greater amplitude in the control than in PR group. These findings contrast with the observations made for the amplitudes of P200 and P300. However, our proposition is that perhaps these electrophysiological signs could be reflecting the more efficient mechanism of the controls to discriminate infrequent stimuli in both auditory and visual tasks, compared to PR.

Summarizing the findings about physiological differences between PR and dyslexics shown by ERP, we can say that the reported results pointed out that dyslexics' ERP in oddball tasks have smaller amplitude and delayed latency of P300 respect to normal readers, showing that their deficiencies are located in those stages associated to stimuli evaluation and memory processing. According to the results of Bernal et al. (2000, 2002) and the present findings, the peculiar characteristics of PR could be interpreted as if they allocate high quantities of attention resources to both relevant and irrelevant stimuli during early and late stages of the information processing, although these quantities could be higher for the early stages, specially during auditory processing. Furthermore, they fail to discriminate infrequent stimuli (either visual or auditory) efficiently.

Finally, we can conclude that given that the physiological differences between PR and control children are not the same than those reported between dyslexics and controls, it is suggested that the underlying mechanisms in each disorder could be distinct. This supports the idea that dyslexics and poor readers are different groups with reading deficiencies that stem from different sources.

Acknowledgements

This work was supported by projects CONACYT 42041 and DGAPA IN306902

References

Ackerman, P. T. & Dykman, R. A. (1993). Phonological processes, confrontational naming and immediate memory. *Journal of Learning Disabilities, 26*, 597-609.

Ahn, H.; Prichep, L.; John, E. R.; Baird, H.; Trepetin, M. & Kaye, H., (1980) Developmental equations reflect brain dysfunction. *Science*, 210, 1259-1262.

American Psychiatric Association. (1994). *Diagnostic and statistical manual of mental disorders* (4th ed.). Washington, DC: Author.

Badian, N. A. (1996). Dyslexia: a validation of the concept at two age levels. *Journal of Learning Disabilities, 29*, 102-112.

Barnea, A., Lamm, O., Epstein, R. & Pratt, H. (1994). Brain potentials from dyslexic children recorded during short term memory tasks. *International Journal of Neuroscience, 74*, 227-237.

Bernal, J., Harmony, T., Rodríguez, M., Reyes, A., Yáñez, G., Fernández, T., Galán, L., Silva, J., Fernández-Bouzas, A., Rodríguez. H., Guerrero, V. & Marosi, E. (2000). Auditory event-related potentials in poor readers. *International Journal of Psychophysiology, 36*, 11-23.

Bernal J., Rodríguez., M., Yáñez G., Marosi E. Reading Difficulties: Neuropsychological, electrophysiological and neuroanatomical considerations. (2002) In: Shohov, S. (Ed.) Perspectives on Cognitive Psychology. New York: Nova Science Publishers, Inc. pp.113-138.

Boder, E. (1973). Developmental dyslexia: A diagnostic approach based on three atypical reading-spelling patterns. *Developmental Medicine and Child Neurology, 15*, 663-687.

Breznitz, Z. & Meyler, A (2003). Speed of lower-level auditory and visual processing as a basic factor in dyslexia: electrophysiological evidence. Brain and *language*, 85, 166-184.

Breznitz, Z. (2001). The determinants of reading fluency: A comparison of dyslexics and average readers. In M. Wolf (Ed.), Dyslexia, Fluency and the Brain (pp. 245-276). Timonium, Maryland: York Press.

Brying, R. & Järvilehto, T. (1985). Auditory and visual evoked potentials of school boys with spelling disabilities. *Developmental Medicine and Child Neurology, 27*, 141-148.

Conners, C. K. (1971). Cortical visual evoked response in children with learning disorders. *Psychophysiology, 7*, 418-428.

Dainner, K., Klorman, R., Salzman, L., Hess, D., Davidson, P. & Michael, R. (1981). Learning-disordered children's evoked potentials during sustained attention. *Journal of Abnormal Child Psychology, 9*, 79-94.

Dalby, Elbro & St□kilde-J□rgensen (1998). Temporal lobe asymmetry and dyslexia: An in Vivo study using MRI. *Brain and Language*. 62, 51-69.

Donchin, E., Karis, D., Bashore, T. & Coles, M. G. H. (1986). Cognitive psychophysiology and human information processing. In M. G. H. Coles, E. Donchin & S. W. Porges (Eds.), *Psychophysiology: Systems, processes and applications* (pp. 244-267). New York: Guilford.

Donchin, E., Ritter, W. & McCallum, W. C. (1978). Cognitive psychophysiology: The endogenous components of the ERP. In E. Calaway, P. Tueting & S. H. Koslow (Eds.), *Event-related Brain Potentials in Man* (pp. 349-441). New York: Academic Press.

Duncan, C., Rumsey, J., Wilkniss, S., Denckla, M., Hamburger, S. & Odou-Potkin, M. (1994). Developmental dyslexia and attention dysfunction in adults: Brain potentials indices of information processing. *Psychophysiology, 31*, 386-401.

Dunn, B.R., Dunn, D.A., Languis, M., & Andrews, D. (1998). The relation of ERP components to complex memory processing. *Brain and cognition*, 36(3), 355-376.

Elbert, T. (1992). A theoretical approach to the late components of the event-related brain potentials. In A. Aersten & V. Braintenberg (Eds.), *Information Processing in the Cortex: Experiments and theory*. Berlin: Springer-Verlag.

Erez, A. & Pratt, H. (1992). Auditory event-related potentials among dyslexic and normal-reading children: 3clet and midline comparisons. *International Journal of Neuroscience, 63*, 247-264.

Fawcett, A.J., Chattopadhyay, A.K., Kandler, R.H., Jarrat, J.A., Nicolson, R. I., & Proctor, M. (1993). Event related potentials and dyslexia. In P. Tallal, A. M. Galaburda, R. R. Llinas, & C. Von Eurler (Eds.), *Annals of the New York Academy of Sciences: Vol. 682. Temporal information processing in the nervous system* (pp.342-345). New York: NY Academy of Sciences.

Galaburda, A. & Livingstone, M. (1993). Evidence for a magnocellular defect in developmental dyslexia. In P. Tallal, A. M. Galaburda, R. R. Llinás & C. von Euler (Eds.), Temporal information processing in the nervous system: Special reference to dyslexia and dysphasia. *Annals of the New York Academy of Sciences, 682*, 70-82.

Galaburda, AM. & Kemper, FL (1979). Cytoarchitectonic abnormalities in developmental dyslexia: a case study. Ann Neurol. 6, 94-100

Galaburda, AM.; Sherman, GF.; Rosen, GD.; Aboitiz, F & Geschwind, N. (1985). Developmental dyslexia: four consecutive patients with cortical anormalities. *Ann Neurol*, 18, 222-33.

Haberlandt, K. (1997). *Cognitive Psychology* (2ª. ed.). Boston: Allyn and Bacon.

Habib, M. (2000). The neurological basis of developmental dyslexia. *Brain,* 123(12), 2373-2399.

Han, S., Fan, S., Chen, L. & Zhuo, Y. (1999). Modulation of brain activities by hierarchical processing: A high-density ERP study. *Brain Topography*, 11(3), 171 183.

Hillyard S. A. & Picton T. W. (1987). Electrophysiology of human cognition. In F. Plum (Ed.), *Handbook of Physiology* (pp. 519-584). Washington, DC: American Physiological Society.

Holcomb, P. J., Ackerman, P. T & Dykman, R. A. (1985). Cognitive event-related brain potentials in children with attention and reading deficits. *Psychophysiology, 22*, 656-667.

Holcomb, P. J., Ackerman, P. T & Dykman, R. A. (1986). Auditory event-related potentials in attention and reading disabled boys. *International Journal of Psychophysiology, 3*, 263-273.

Humphreys, P.; Kauhmann, WE & Galaburda, AM (1990). Developmental dyslexia in women: neuropathological findings in three patients. *Ann Neurol.* 28, 727-38

Iragui, V. J., Kutas, M., Mitchiner, M. R. & Hillyard, S. A. (1993). Effects of aging on event-related brain potentials and reaction times in an auditory oddball task. *Psychophysiology, 30*, 10-22.

John, E.R., Prichep, L., Ahn, H., Easton, P., Friedman, J. & Kaye, H. (1983). Neurometric evaluation of cognitive dysfunctions and neurological disorders in children. *Progress in Neurobiology*, 21, 239 - 290.

Johnson, R. Jr. (1989). Developmental evidence for modality dependent P300 generators: a normative study. *Psychophysiology, 26*, 651-667.

Just, M. & Carpenter, P. (1992). A capacity theory of comprehension: individual differences in working memory. *Psychology Review, 99*, 122-149.

Loiselle, R. A., Stamm, J. S., Maitincky, S. & Whipple, S. C. (1980). Evoked potential and behavioral signs of attentive dysfunction in hyperactive boys. *Psychophysiology, 17*, 193-201.

Loveless, N. E. (1983). Event-related brain potentials and human performance. In A. Gale, & J. A. Edwards (Eds.), *Physiological Correlates of Human Behavior* (Vol. 2, pp. 79-97). London: Academic Press Inc.

Lovrich, D. & Stamm, I. (1983). Event related potential and behavioral correlates of attention in reading retardation. *Journal of Clinical Neuropsychology, 5*, 13-37.

Lyon, R. (1982). Subgroups of learning disabled readers: Clinical and empirical identification. In Myklebust H. R. (Ed.), *Progress in learning disabilities* (Vol. 5, pp. 103-133). New York: Grune and Straton.

Mann, V. (1998). Language problems: a key to early reading problems. In B. Y. L. Wong (Ed.), *Learning about learning disabilities*. San Diego: Academic Press.

Mattis, S., French, J. H. & Rapin T. (1975). Dyslexia in children and adults: Three independent neuropsychological syndromes. *Developmental Medicine and Child Neurology, 17*, 150-163.

McCarthy, G. & Wood, C.C. (1985). Scalp distributions of event-related potentials: an ambiguity associated with analysis of variance models. *Electroenceph. Clin. Neurophysiol.*, 62, 203-208.

McCrory, E., Frith, U., Brunswick, N., & Price, C. (2000). Abnormal functional activation during a simple word repetition task: a PET study of adult dislexics. *Journal of Cognitive Neuroscience,* 12(5), 753-763.

McIsaac, H. & Polich, J. (1992). Comparison of infant and adult P300 from auditory stimuli. *Journal of Experimental Child Psychology, 53*, 115-128.

Näätänen, R. & Picton, T. (1987). The N1 wave of the human electric and magnetic response to sound: A review and analysis of the component structure. *Psychophysiogy, 24*, 375-425.

Näätänen, R., & Picton, T.W. (1986). N2 and automatic versus controlled processes. Cerebral Psychophysiology: Studies in Event-Related Potentials (*EEG Suppl.* 38), 169-171.

Neville, H. J., Kutas, M., Chesney, G. & Schmidt, A. (1986). Event-related potentials during the initial processing and recognition memory of congruous and incongruous words. *Journal of Memory and Language, 25*, 75-92.

Oken, B. S. (1990). Endogenous event-related potentials. In K. H. Chiappa (Ed.), *Evoked Potentials in Clinical Medicine* (pp. 563-592). New York: Raven Press.

Olofsson, A. & Niedersoe, J. (1999). Early language development and kindergarten phonological awareness as predictors of reading problems: From 3 to 11 years of age. *Journal of Learning Disabilities, 32*, 464-472.

Ostrosky, F., Navarro, M.E., Canseco, E., Pérez, R. & Zárate, A. (1984). La Lectura y los Perfiles Cognoscitivos de una Población Escolar Mexicana. *Revista Mexicana de Psicología* 1, 53-65.

Perfetti, C. A.(1985). *Reading Ability*. New York: Oxford University Press.

Picton, T. W. (1988). The endogenous evoked potentials. In E. Basar (Ed.), *Dynamics of Sensory and Cognitive Processing by the Brain* (pp. 258-265). Berlin, Heidelberg: Springer-Verlag.

Pinkerton, F., Watson, D. R. & McClelland, R. J. (1989). A neurophysiological study of children with reading, writing, and spelling difficulties. *Developmental Medicine and Child Neurology, 31*, 569-581.

Polich, J., & Heine, M. R. D. (1996). P300 topography and modality effects from a single-stimulus paradigm. *Psychophysiology, 33(6)*, 747-752.

Polich, J., Ladish, C. & Burns, T. (1990). Normal variation of P300 in children: Age, memory span, and head size. *International Journal of Psychophysiology, 9*, 237-248.

Preston, M., Guthrie, J. & Childs, B. (1974). Visual evoked responses (VERs) in normal and disabled readers. *Psychophysiology, 11*, 452-457.

Preston, M., Guthrie, J., Kirsch, I., German, D. & Childs, B. (1977). VERs in normal and disabled adult readers. *Psychophysiology, 14*, 8-14.

Rayner, K. & Pollatsek, A. (1989). *The Psychology of Reading*. Englewood Cliffs, NJ: Prentice Hall.

Regiosa, V., Pérez, M.C., Manzano, M., & Antelo, J.M. (1994). Sistema automatizado para explorar la lectura en escolares de habla hispana. *Revista Latina de Pensamiento y Lenguaje*, 2, 141-160.

Robichon, F., Levrier, O., Farnarier, P. & Habib, M. (2000). Developmental dyslexia: atypical cortical asymetries and functional significance. *European Journal of Neurology*, 7, 35-46.

Rumsey, J., Andreason, P., Zametkin, A., Aquino, T., King, A. & Hamburger, S. (1992). Failure to activate the left temporo-parietal cortex in dyslexia. An oxygen 15 positron emission tomographic study. *Archives of Neurology,* 48,527-534.

Rumsey, J., Horwitz, B., Donohue, B., Nace, K., Maisong, J., & Andreason, P. (1999). A functional lesion in developmental dyslexia: left angular gyral blood flow predicts severity. *Brain and Language*, 70, 187-204.

Satterfield, J. H., & Bradley, B. W. (1977). Evoked potentials and brain maturation in hyperactive and normal children. *Electroencephalography and Clinical Neurophysiology, 43*, 43-51.

Satterfield, J. H., Schell, A. M., Nicholas, T. W., Satterfield, B. T. & Freese, T. E. (1990). Ontogeny of selective attention effects on Event-related potentials in attention-deficit hyperactivity disorder and normal boys. *Biological Psychiatry, 28*, 879-903.

Segalowitz, S., Wagner, J. & Menna, R. (1992). Lateral versus frontal ERP predictors of reading skill. *Brain & Cognition, 20*, 85-103.

Shibasaki, H. & Miyazaki, M. (1992). Event-Related potentials studies in infants and children. *Journal of Clinical Neurophysiology, 9*, 408-418.

Shields, D. T. (1973). Brain responses to stimuli in disorders of information processing. *Journal of Learning Disabilities, 6*, 37-41.

Siegel, L. S. (1992). An evaluation of the discrepancy definition of dislexia. *Journal of Learning Disabilities, 25*, 618-629.

Simson, R., Vaughan, H. G., Jr. & Ritter, W. (1977). The scalp topography of potentials in auditory and visual discrimination tasks. *Electroencephalography and Clinical Neurophysyology, 42*, 528-535.

Stanovich, K. E. (1988). Explaining the differences between the dyslexic and the garden-variety poor reader: the phonological core variable-difference model. *Journal of Learning Disabilities, 21*, 590-604.

Stelmack, R. M., Saxe, B. J., Noldy-Cullum, N., Cambell, K. B., & Armitage, R. (1988). Recognition memory for words and event-related potentials: A comparison of normal and disabled readers. *Journal of Clinical and Experimental Neuropsychology, 10*, 185-200.

Sternberg, S. (1966). High speed scanning in human memory. *Science, 153*, 652-654.

Sutton, S. M., Braren, J., Zubin, & E.R. John. (1965). Evoked potentials correlates of stimulus uncertainty. *Science*, 150, 1187-1188.

Swanson, H. L. (1993). Working memory in learning disability subgroups. *Journal of Experimental Child Psychology, 56*, 87-114.

Tallal, P., Miller, S. & Fitch, R. S. (1993). Neurobiological basis of speech: A case for the preeminence of temporal processing. In P. Tallal, A. M. Galaburda, R. R. Llinás & C. von Euler (Eds.), Temporal information processing in the nervous system: Special reference to dyslexia and dysphasia, *Annals of the New York Academy of Sciences, 682*, 27-47.

Taylor, M. J. & Keenan, N. K. (1990). Event-related potentials to visual and language stimuli in normal and dyslexic children. *Psychophysiology, 27*, 318-327.

Torgesen, J. K. (1988). The cognitive and behavioral characteristics of children with learning disabilities. *Journal of Learning Disabilities, 21*, 587-589.

Wagner, R. K. & Torgesen, J. K. (1987). The nature of phonological processing and its causal role in the acquisition of reading skills. *Psychological Bulletin, 101*, 192-212.

Weber, B. & Ommen, G. (1977). Auditory and visual evoked responses in children with familial reading disabilities. *Journal of Learning Disabilities, 10*, 32-37.

In: Trends in Dyslexia Research
Editor: Henry D. Tobias, pp. 99-119
ISBN 1-59454-219-8

Chapter IV

THE MISMATCH NEGATIVITY IN EVALUATING CENTRAL AUDITORY DYSFUNCTION IN DYSLEXIA

Teija Kujala
[1] Helsinki Collegium for Advanced Studies, P.O.Box 4, FIN-00014 University of Helsinki, Finland
[2] Cognitive Brain Research Unit, Department of Psychology, P.O.Box 9, FIN-00014 University of Helsinki, Finland.
E-mail: teija.m.kujala@helsinki.fi, Fax: +358-9-19124509

ABSTRACT

There are various perceptual dysfunctions that are related to and that might be underlying the reading difficulties in developmental dyslexia. One possible underlying factor might be the malfunctioning of the phonological system or even a more general deficit in the auditory system. Recently a brain response called the mismatch negativity (MMN) has been successfully applied to investigate auditory impairments in dyslexia. It is a brain response elicited by a discriminable change in any repetitive aspect of auditory stimulation even in the absence of attention. The fact that the MMN reflects the accuracy of auditory discrimination and that it can be obtained even from unattentive subjects makes it especially attractive for studying various central auditory-system dysfunctions both in adults and children. Several recent studies showed that the MMN enables one to determine which aspects of auditory information are deficiently processed in dyslexia. Furthermore, the MMN amplitude change was recently shown to indicate cortical plastic changes resulting from successful dyslexia remediation.

Key words: dyslexia, sound discrimination, auditory dysfunction, mismatch negativity (MMN)

INTRODUCTION

It is evident that various deficits may underlie dyslexia. The debate on the nature and origin of dyslexia as well as the factors underlying it has been going on for decades resulting in no clear consensus. In dyslexic individuals, perceptual problems are not confined to a single sensory system. Dysfunctions have been reported in the visual and auditory domain (for reviews, see Farmer & Klein, 1995; Stein & Walsh, 1997) as well as in the somatosensory one (Grant et al., 1999). Furthermore, impairments have been reported in processes involving the interaction of two senses, these impairments being even more severe than those within the different sensory systems (Laasonen et al., 2000). Sluggish attentional shifting is still another possible factor that might underlie reading problems (Hari & Renvall, 2001).

In the visual modality, magnetoencephalographic (MEG) measurements indicated that passive viewing of words, which normally activates the left inferior occipital region did not activate this area in dyslexic subjects, or that the activity occurred later than in control subjects (Salmelin et al., 1996). In addition, dyslexic individuals have a slowered rate of processing visual linguistic and non-linguistic stimuli (Brannan & Williams, 1988; Di Lollo, Hanson, & McIntyre, 1983; Livingstone, Rose, Drislaine, & Galaburda, 1991; Stein & Talcott, 1999; Stein & Walsh, 1997). Currently, the so-called magnocellular-system hypothesis in dyslexia has become popular, with several studies indicating impaired discrimination of visual input mediated via the magnocellular system (Stein & Talcott, 1999; Stein & Walsh, 1997). In addition, dyslexic subjects display diminished electrophysiological responses to visually-presented rapid low-contrast stimuli but normal responses to slow or high-contrast stimuli (Livingstone, Rose, Drislaine, & Galaburda, 1991). Furthermore, recent functional magnetic resonance imaging (fMRI) results indicated that dyslexic individuals have reduced activation in brain areas that predominantly receive input from the magnocellular pathway (Demp, Boynton, & Heeger, 1998).

According to several authors (Liberman & Shankweiler, 1985; Mody, Studdert-Kennedy, & Brady, 1998; Rayner, Pollatsek, & Bilsky, 1995; Schulte-Körne, Deimel, Bartling, & Remschmidt, 1998; Studdert-Kennedy & Mody, 1995), however, problems in phonological processing might be the major factor underlying the reading difficulties in most dyslexic individuals. Phoneme segmentation and awareness tasks as well as rhyming skills differentiate good and poor readers, and may serve as valid predictors of the future reading ability (see, for example, Farmer & Klein, 1995; Snowling, 2000). In particular, it has been proposed that reading-impaired have problems in discriminating phonemes involving rapid transitions (Libreman & Shankweiler, 1985; Mody, Studdert-Kennedy, & Brady, 1998; Schulte-Körne, Deimel, Bartling, & Remschmidt, 1998; Steffens, Eilers, Gross-Glenn, & Jallad, 1992), whereas according to the competing theory, dyslexic individuals might even have a more general auditory dysfunction underlying their phonological difficulties than one confined to the processing of speech sounds (Baldeweg et al., 1999; Hari & Kiesilä, 1996; Kujala et al., 2000; Laasonen et al., 2000; McGivern, Berka, Languis, & Chapman, 1991; Reed, 1989; Tallal, 1980; Wright et al., 1997). According to the latter theory, dyslexic individuals have problems in discriminating rapid temporal acoustic features typically present in speech, which would disturb the development of the veridical phonological code and thus affect correct speech perception and language development (Merzenich et al., 1996; Tallal et al., 1996).

Finally, it has been proposed that a general deficit including all sensory systems might underlie dyslexia, since the perceptual problems are often not limited to one sensory system in this disorder (Farmer & Klein, 1995; Stein & Talcott, 1999; Stein & Walsh, 1997). Moreover, the difficulties in the visual and auditory processing share many similarities so that, for example, the dysfunctions primarily relate to the discrimination of rapid stimuli. Since many cortical systems can be subdivided into the slow and fast processing systems, dyslexia might specifically relate to an impairment of the latter one.

The fact that dyslexia has a high incidence and, because of the various possible underlying causes, is difficult to remediate, there is an urgent need for better means to diagnose its subtypes as early as possible in life. The traditional way of assessment, measuring the task performance, is often problematic when used alone especially if the dysfunction should be determined in children. Thus, there is a need for such means to evaluate the deficiency involved that require a less active role from the dyslexic individual. One method that appears to be well-suited even for the very early identification of auditory-system dysfunctions is an electric brain response called the mismatch negativity (MMN).

THE MISMATCH NEGATIVITY (MMN)

Accurate information on the processing of stimuli can be obtained by recording event-related brain potentials (ERPs) that are neural responses time-locked to stimuli. With ERPs one can investigate, for example, reception and discrimination of stimuli as well as effects of attention on these processes, with milliseconds temporal resolution (see, for example, Näätänen, 1992). The MMN (Näätänen, Gaillard, & Mäntysalo, 1978) is a component of the auditory ERPs which can be elicited by any discriminable change (deviant stimulus) in some repetitive aspect (standard stimuli) in the ongoing auditory stimulation (Näätänen, 1992; Näätänen, 1991; Fig. 1). The repetitive aspects of the auditory stimulation are encoded in their sensory neural representation or memory trace. Further, if a subsequent stimulus does not fully match this representation an MMN is elicited. The duration of this sensory-memory trace can be measured with the MMN by prolonging the inter-stimulus intervals (Grau, Yago, & Polo, 1998; Mäntysalo & Näätänen, 1987; see, however, Winkler, Schröger, & Cowan, 2001). When the brain's response to the standard stimuli is subtracted from that to the deviant stimuli, the MMN can be seen approximately at 100-250 ms from stimulus-change onset. The MMN has its major generator sources in the auditory cortex but also, for example, frontal-lobe sources have also been reported (Alho, 1995; Giard et al., 1995; Hari et al., 1984; Rinne et al., 1999; Rinne et al., 2000).

In addition to simple stimulus features, such as the pitch, duration, or intensity of a sound (for a review, see Näätänen, 1992), even more complex and abstract sound changes elicit the MMN. For example, it is elicited by a phonetic change (Dehaene-Lambertz, 1997; Näätänen et al., 1997; Rinne et al., 1999; Shtyrov et al., 2000), but it also can be elicited by an order reversal of a tone pair (Saarinen et al., 1992; Tervaniemi et al., 1999), even when the tone pairs are randomly presented across a wide frequency range (Paavilainen, Jaramillo, &

Näätänen, 1998; for a review on intelligent auditory-cortex processes as reflected by the MMN, see Näätänen et al., 2001).

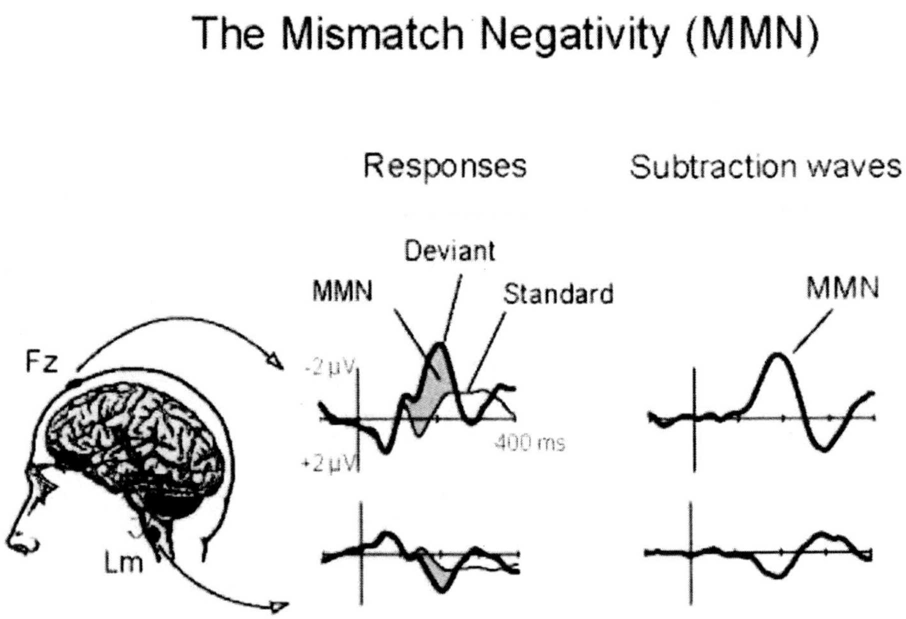

Fig. 1. The mismatch negativity (MMN) in a schematic illustration. The MMN is usually maximal at fronto-central scalp areas (Fz; the upper panel), and reverses polarity at the mastoids (the lower panel). It is elicited by occasional deviant sounds appearing among repetitive standard stimuli (the thin line represents brain response elicited by the standard stimulus and the thick line that to a deviant stimulus). The shaded area is the MMN. The MMN can be more clearly seen in subtraction waves (the response elicited by the deviant stimulus subtracted from that elicited by the standard stimulus; right column). The arrow in the auditory areas represents the activity source of the MMN (right column). The main gererator sources of the MMN are in the auditory cortices (left column).

Recent studies demonstrated that the MMN can also be used to probe the phonological system of the auditory cortex (Cheour et al., 1998; Dehaene-Lambertz, 1997; Näätänen et al., 1997; Rinne et al., 1999; Shtyrov et al., 2000). Näätänen and colleagues (1997) determined native-language phoneme representations by recording the MMN and its magnetic counterpart, MMNm. They compared vowel processing in Estonian and Finnish subjects by using vowel /e/ as the standard stimulus, and as deviant stimuli /ö/, and /o/, shared by these two languages, and /õ/ belonging to the Estonian but not Finnish language. It was found that in Estonians, the deviant /ö/, /õ/, and /o/ vowels elicited MMNs that were increasingly larger (in this order) as the physical difference between the standard and the deviant vowel grew. In Finns, however, the MMN showed an otherwise similar amplitude behavior with the exception that there was an amplitude decrement for the Estonian /õ/, which suggests that there was no representation in the long-term memory for this vowel. Source-localization with the MEG indicated that the MMNm was enhanced for the native-language phoneme in the left temporal cortex as compared to the non-native language phoneme, for which the MMNm was small in both hemispheres.

When the physical difference between the standard and deviant stimulus is made larger, then the MMN response becomes larger and earlier (Sams, Paavilainen, Alho & Näätänen, 1985; Tiitinen, May, Reinikainen, & Näätänen, 1994). Furthermore, there usually is a good correspondence between the MMN elicitation and behavioral discrimination accuracy. For example, backward-masking studies (Winkler & Näätänen, 1992) showed that if the masking stimulus is presented shortly, 20-50 ms, after the offset of each sound, then no MMN is elicited and the subjects cannot discriminate these deviant stimuli from standard sounds in a behavioral session. However, when this silent interval was prolonged to 150 ms, then the MMN was obtained and deviant stimuli were behaviorally discriminated. Furthermore, Amenedo and Escera (2000) showed a strong correlation between the MMN amplitude and behavioral discrimination for tone-duration changes. They found that the MMN amplitude predicted the psychometric function found with behavioral tests. Corroborating results were found by Kujala et al. (2001a) on the discrimination of temporal intervals. In this study, the deviant pairs differed from the standard pair in terms of the duration of the silent interval between the paired tones. An MMN was elicited by such deviant intervals that were also behaviorally discriminated, whereas a deviant interval that could not be discriminated from the standard interval elicited no MMN. Like the study of Amenedo and Escera (2000), also this study demonstrated a significant correlation between the MMN amplitude and the reaction time (RT).

There is already a large body of evidence that the MMN can serve as an index of learning-associated neural plasticity. This has been demonstrated both in learning situations occurring in laboratory as well as in natural conditions and for non-speech and speech stimuli (Kujala et al., 2001b; Kraus et al., 1995; Menning, Roberts, & Pantev, 2000; Näätänen et al., 1993; Tremblay, Kraus, & McGee, 1998; Winkler et al., 1999; Cheour et al., 2002). For example, Näätänen and colleagues (1993) determined the discrimination learning of complex spectrotemporal sound patterns which were originally difficult to discriminate from one another. They found that the MMN emerged in those subjects who learned to discriminate the difference between the patterns but not in those who failed to learn to discriminate them. Kraus et al. (1995) and Tremblay et al. (1998) obtained corroborating results by investigating the discrimination learning of speech contrasts that were initially impossible to discriminate for their subjects. They found that the MMN was elicited when the subjects had learned to discriminate the speech contrasts. Tremblay and her colleagues even found that in the course of the training, the MMN may even sometimes emerge before the subject was able to behaviorally discriminate the contrasts.

Winkler et al. (1999), in turn, used the MMN in investigtaing phoneme representations formed in natural learning conditions. They compared the processing of a Finnish phonetic contrast /e-ae/ not present in the Hungarian language (in Budapest area where the Hungarian subjects came from) in Finns and in two groups of Hungarian subjects, one not knowing Finnish and the other having a good command of Finnish. It was found that this Finnish phonetic contrast was not discriminated by Hungarians who did not know Finnish. Consistently with this, no MMN was found in these subjects. As expected, this change was discriminated by Finns in whom also an MMN was elicited. Furthermore, this contrast was discriminated by Hungarians who had a good command of Finnish and, moreover, their MMN for this contrast was very similar to the one found in the Finns. Such language-learning effects on the MMN have also been demonstrated in three- to six-year old children who acquired foreign language in a day-care center (Cheour et al., 2002). It was shown that brain's plastic changes as indexed by enhanced MMN amplitudes may take place in young children as quickly as in two months.

Importantly, the MMN can even be obtained without the subject or patient's attention to the auditory stimuli (Alho, Woods, Algazi, & Näätänen, 1992; Näätänen, 1991). It is usually measured when the subject is ignoring the sounds while being engaged in some other activity than one involving the auditory stimuli, for example, in reading a book or watching a movie. This makes it especially attractive in studying infants or patients who have problems in communicating or performing tasks. For example, the MMN has been used in studying comatose (Fischer, Morlet, & Giard, 2000; Kane, Butler, & Cummins, 1993; Morlet, Bouchet, & Fischer, 2000), aphasic (Aaltonen, Tuomainen, Laine, & Niemi, 1993; Alain, Woods, & Knight, 1998; Ilvonen et al., 2001; in press), and autistic (Kemner et al., 1995) patients, as well as children and infants (Alho et al., 1990; Cheour-Luhtanen et al., 1996; Cheour et al., 1998; Kraus et al., 1996).

As it is clear from the afore-presented, there are many features in the MMN why it is a very promising tool for clinical studies. However, the research so far has mainly demonstrated differences between clinical and healthy populations at group level. It would be important to determine whether the MMN can be used even at the individual level. Before this is possible, a lot of research should be conducted in order to determine the ways of recording and quantifying the MMN reliably. Fortunately, such research is going on and there already exist several reports on various aspects of how to improve the MMN recording and analysis (see, for example, McGee, Kraus, & Nicol, 1997; Tervaniemi et al., 1999; Schröger, 1998; Sinkkonen & Tervaniemi, 2000).

THE MMN AS AN INDEX OF AUDITORY DISCRIMINATION IN DYSLEXIA

The MMN has gained a lot of popularity during the recent years in investigations on various clinical populations. It has been used for determining auditory deficits and sensory-memory dysfunctions, as well as in determining recovery from the clinical state (see, for example, Ahveninen et al., 1999; Deouell et al., 2000; Ilvonen et al., 2001; 2003; Kujala et al., 2001b; for a review, Näätänen & Escera, 2000). According to recent studies, the MMN might also be very promising in determinig phonological and auditory dysfunctions in dyslexia. For example, Schulte-Körne et al. (1998) used the MMN to compare the discrimination of speech and non-speech stimuli in dyslexic and control adolescents. Their speech stimuli were syllables (/da/ as the standard stimulus and /ba/ as the deviant stimulus) and non-speech stimuli (sine-wave tones, 1000 Hz as the standard and 1050 Hz as the deviant stimulus). They found that the MMNs for the tone stimuli did not significantly differ between the groups, whereas the syllables elicited a smaller-amplitude MMN in dyslexic than control adolescents. The authors interpreted this result as reflecting a deficit specific to the phonological system rather than a general failure in processing auditory information in dyslexia.

Subsequent MMN studies, however, suggested that dyslexic individuals might even have problems in discriminating small pitch separations. Baldeweg and colleagues (1999) determined duration and pitch discrimination in dyslexia by the means of MMN. In Duration Condition, the standard stimulus was 200 ms long, and the deviant stimuli 160, 120, 80, and 40 ms. They found no differences between dyslexic adults and control non-dyslexic subjects in MMNs elicited by duration deviants or in the behavioral discrimination of these stimuli. In their Pitch Condition (the standard stimulus being of 1000 Hz and deviant stimuli of 1015, 1030, 1060, and 1090 Hz), all changes but the largest one elicited considerably smaller MMNs in the dyslexic than control subjects, and also were less accurately behaviorally discriminated by the dyslexic subjects. Furthermore, the MMN and discrimination performance correlated with the degree of impairment in phonological skills. Consistently, Kujala et al. (2003) found no general MMN amplitude differences between dyslexic and control subjects for a large pitch difference (500 vs. 750 Hz) whereas, however, they found a group difference in the hemispheric distribution of the MMN resulting from a diminished left-hemisphere response in the dyslexic subjects. Also other authors, unsing behavioral measures, have reported a close link between sound-frequency processing and phonological skills as well as reduced sensitivity to frequency changes of tones in dyslexia (Talcott et al., 1999; Stein & Talcott, 1999).

Csepe and Gyurkocza (in press), in turn, used consonant changes (in the place of articulation and in voicing), vowel changes, as well as tone changes in their study comparing auditory functions in dyslexia. They found diminished MMNs for all these auditory features in dyslexic as compared with control subjects. However, these differences were the most pronounced for the consonant changes. This is consistent, as well as the results of Schulte-Körne et al. (1998) discussed above, with the previous publications reporting problems in dyslexia in discriminating stimuli, both speech and non-speech sounds, that contain rapid transitions (Farmer & Klein, 1995; Reed, 1989; Tallal, 1980). The results of the afore-reviewed three studies (Schulte-Körne et al., 1998; Baldeweg et al., 1999; Csepe & Gyurkocza, in press) also suggest that dyslexic individuals generally have more difficulties in processing small than large stimulus differences, which might be one reason why dyslexic individuals have so consistently been reported to encounter problems in discriminating stop-consonants, which are separated from each other by acoustically minor sound differences.

Behavioral studies have shown that sound elements presented in rapid succession are deficiently processed by dyslexic individuals (Farmer & Klein, 1995; Reed, 1989; Tallal, 1980) and, furthermore, that masking stimuli interfere more sound detection in dyslexic than control subjects (Wright et al., 1997). Therefore, it could be expected that the correct perception of long sound patterns containing rapidly-varying acoustic features, such as words or tone patterns resembling words, might be particularly problematic for dyslexic individuals. The MMN has also been recently applied to study complex sound processing in dyslexia. It was found out that the MMN can, in fact, provide more precise information than the behavioral approaches on what failed in the perception of the complex sound, as will be described below.

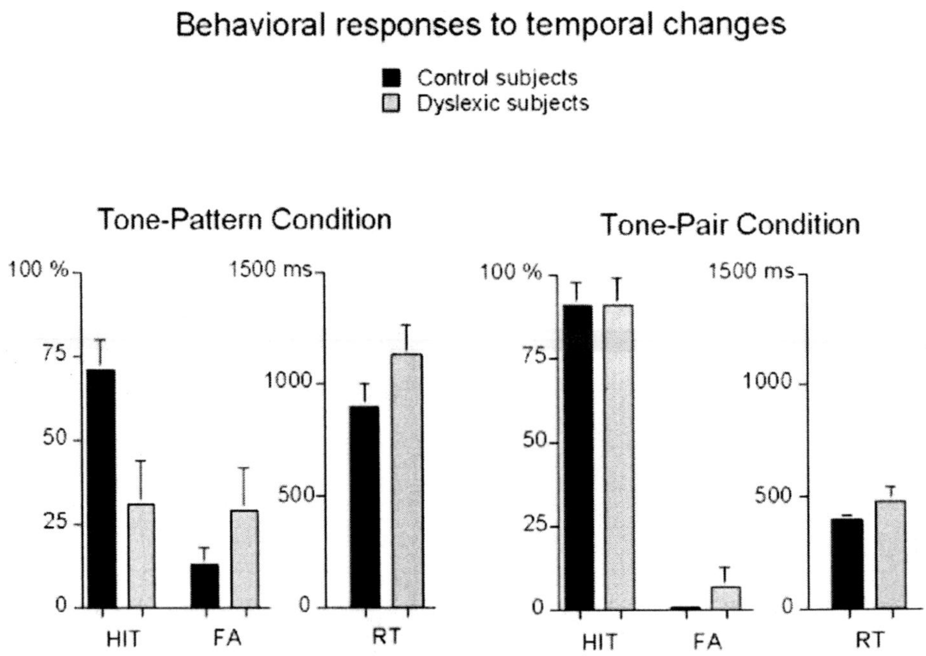

Fig. 2. Behavioral discrimination of temporal changes in tone patterns (left) and pairs (right) in dyslexic adults and control subjects. Subjects were instructed to press a response key to occasional deviant tone patterns and tone pairs (in separate blocks). The bars show the mean percentages of hit and false-alarm (FA) rates and mean reaction times (RT) (with the standard errors of the mean). The dyslexic subjects (grey bars) detected significantly less deviant tone patterns than did control subjects (black bars), whereas the groups did not significantly differ from one another in the detection of deviant tone pairs. Figure adapted from Kujala et al., 2000.

Schulte-Körne et al. (1999) compared the discrimination of sound patterns composed of tone elements with different pitches in dyslexic and control adult subjects. They found that changes in the temporal order of the pattern elements elicited MMNs that were smaller in dyslexic than control subjects. Kujala et al. (2000), in turn, used rhythmic patterns of four identical tones and simpler stimuli including two tones. In Tone-Pattern Condition involving the four tones, the deviant pattern was created by moving the third tone of the standard pattern to an earlier point of time. In the condition with the tone pairs (Tone-Pair Condition) the stimuli were created so that the first and last tones of the patterns were removed. It was found that in the behavioral session, dyslexic subjects detected a significantly smaller number of deviant tone patterns than did control subjects (Fig. 2). According to the MMN results, the dyslexic subjects failed to discriminate the difference between the standard and deviant pattern that occurred in the middle of the patterns. Namely, in control subjects the deviant tone pattern elicited two MMNs, whereas it elicited only the later one in the dyslexic subjects (Fig. 3). These two consecutive MMNs of the control subjects presumably resulted from the two differences between the deviant and standard patterns: the too early tone (the third tone presented earlier in the deviant than standard pattern) is equivalent first to an addition and then to an omission of a tone. Since only the later MMN was elicited in the dyslexic subjects, presumably their auditory system could discriminate only the change that occurred in the end of the pattern (the third tone not present in the end of the deviant pattern). This obviously affected the discrimination of the sounds at the behavioral level, since the dyslexic subjects detected less deviant patterns in the behavioral session. These results imply that the MMN might enable one to determine which segments of auditory patterns are deficiently processed. More specifically, this finding suggests that sound elements are masked or interfered by surrounding sounds of sound sequences in dyslexic individuals. This conclusion was supported by the findings from Tone-Pair Condition in this study in which the first and last tones of the patterns were removed. In this condition, there were no significant differences in the MMN (Fig. 3) or target-discrimination performance (Fig. 2) between the two groups. Presumably, in the patterns, the first and last tones interfered with the functioning of the central auditory system of the dyslexic individuals so that it could not detect the too early tone in the deviant pattern.

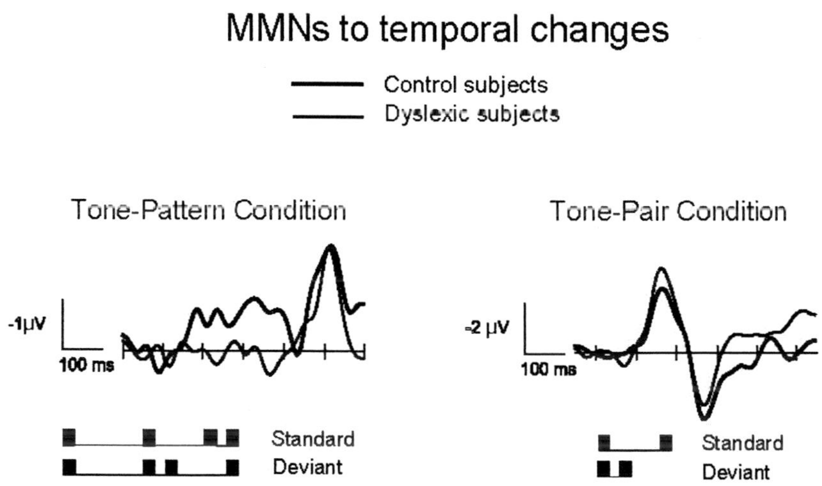

Fig. 3. The MMN indexing the discrimination of temporal changes in tone patterns (left) and pairs (right) in dyslexic and control adults (difference waves obtained by subtracting the response elicited by the standard pattern/pair from that elicited by deviant pattern/pair). Two consecutive responses were elicited by the deviant tone pattern in control subjects (thick line), whereas only the second response was present in the dyslexic subjects (thin line). In contrast, the MMNs elicited by deviant tone pairs did not significantly differ between the groups. Figure adapted from Kujala et al., 2000.

The hypothesis that the dyslexic individuals' central nervous system has an incresed vulnerability to masking effects was tested in a subsequent study in which the MMN was recorded to tone-pair (composed of 500 and 750 Hz tones) order reversals alone and to these same tone pairs with a shortly preceding or following 625-Hz tone (Kujala, Belitz, Tervaniemi, & Näätänen, 2003). It was found that the dyslexic subjects had a somewhat diminished MMN to tone-order reversals and, further, that the difference between the groups in the MMN amplitude was considerably increased when the additional sound succeded the tone pair but was not when it preceded the tone pair. These results indicate that the central auditory system of dyslexic individuals is more vulnerable to backward masking effects than that of control subjects, which has previously been suggested by behavioral studies (Wright et al., 1997).

THE MMN AS AN INDICATOR OF REMEDIATION EFFECTS IN DYSLEXIA

Since the MMN reflects neural plastic changes and the improvement of discrimination accuracy caused by training (Kraus et al., 1995; Menning, Roberts, & Pantev, 2000; Näätänen et al., 1993; Tremblay, Kraus, & McGee, 1998; Winkler et al., 1999), it holds promise in the evaluation of remediation efficacy. It is particularly suitable for this purpose in dyslexia in which the dysfunction, according to many authors, primarily involves the phonological system or the central auditory system more generally (see, for example, Baldeweg et al., 1999; Csepe & Gyurkocza, in press; Farmer & Klein, 1995; Hari & Kiesilä, 1996; Hugdahl et al., 1995; Kujala et al., 2000; Mody, Studdert-Kennedy, & Brady, 1998; Tallal, 1980).

Recently, Kujala et al. (2001b) aimed at determining the effects of a training program on the neural basis of auditory discrimination and reading skills in dyslexic children at the first grade. They also used the MMN for determining whether the trainig program caused changes in the auditory functions of the children. The training program (in which dyslexic subjects had been shown to perform worse than non-dyslexic subjects, Karma, 1999) required the matching of non-phonetic auditory and visual elements with each other. It was found that the dyslexic group that was trained with the audio-visual matching programme displayed both improved reading skills and increased discrimination accuracy (Figs. 4 and 5). After the training period, the children who had used the remediation program read more words correctly and tended to be faster in reading than the control children. In the training group, the improved auditory processing was seen in enhanced MMN amplitudes and decreased RTs to order reversals in tone pairs. Importantly, the change in the MMN amplitude correlated with the change in the reading-skill measures.

Corroborating results were obtained by Heim, Eulitz, Wienbruck, and Elbert (2000) with children having language impairment. The children were given training in syllabic speaking, writing, and reading, which resulted in improved reading, spelling, and phonological awareness. Furthermore, the MMNm responses to a syllable change (/ba/-/da/) resembled more the responses of control children after than before the training. The training effects were also observed at the behavioral level in that the language-impaired children became better in discriminating syllables along the /ba/-/da/ continuum. These results suggest that the MMN (MMNm) response can be used in evaluating the training effects in dyslexia and other language impairments.

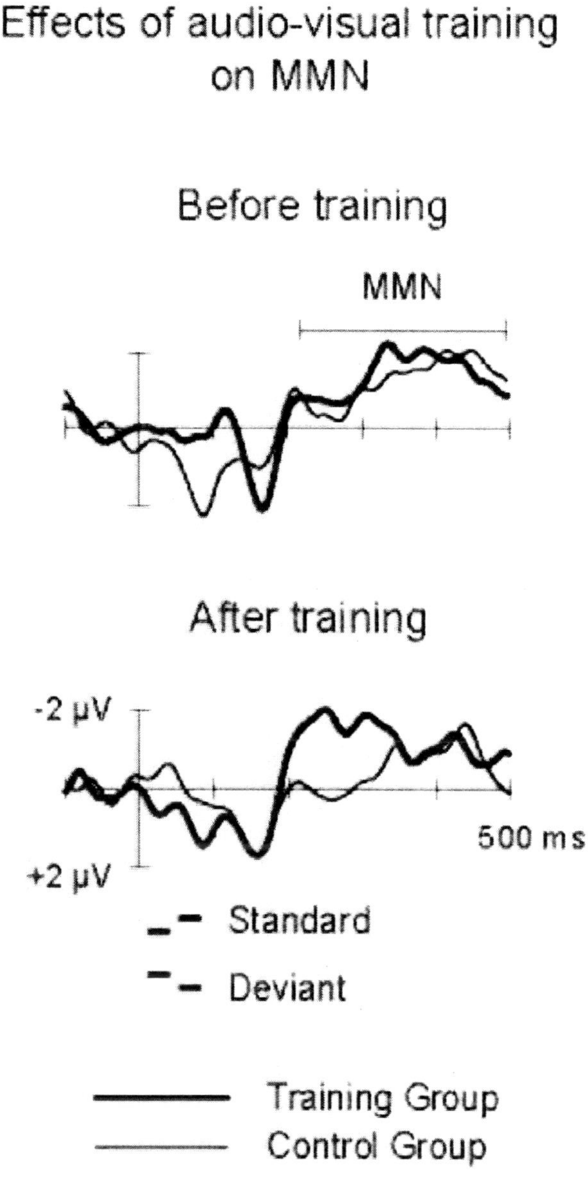

Fig. 4. The effects of audio-visual training on the MMN in dyslexic children. Before the training period, there were no significant differences in the MMN amplitudes of the training (thick line) and control (thin line) children. After the training period, the MMN of the training group had grown and was significantly larger than that in the control group. Figure adapted from Kujala et al., 2001b.

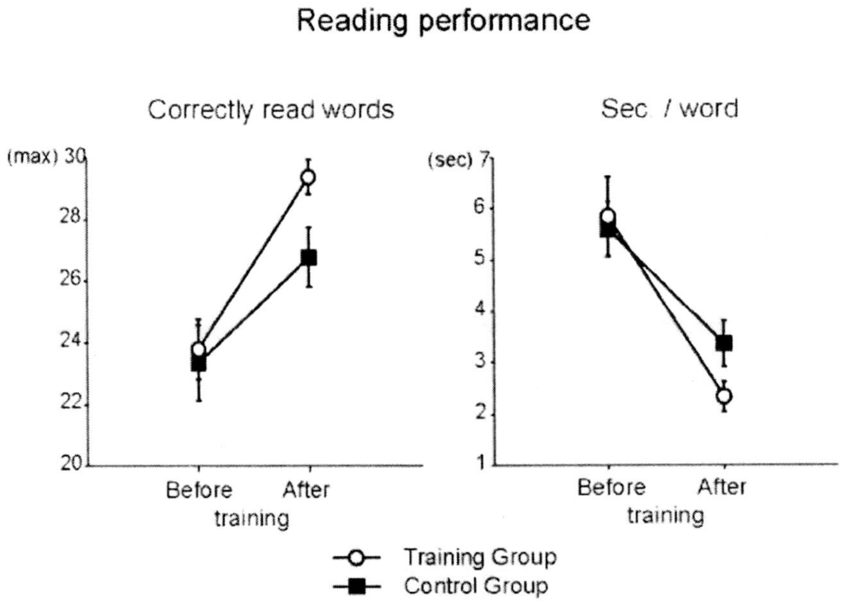

Fig. 5. The effects of audio-visual training on reading performance. The performance data of the training group is presented with white circles and that of the control group with with black squares. Before training, the groups did not differ from each other with regard to the number of correctly read words, whereas after the training, the trainig group read correctly significantly more words than did the control group. In the reading speed, no group differences were found before the training, whereas after it, the training group read nearly significantly faster than the control group. Figure adapted from Kujala et al., 2001b.

THE MMN IN EARLY DYSLEXIA IDENTIFICATION

In order to get the best training results and to prevent delays in learning the intervention for developing skills needed in reading should be given when the central nervous system has the optimal developmental stage for learning a certain skill (Pantev et al., 1998; Singer, 1995) and before the reading skill is needed. Thus, the impairments underlying reading problems in the children who are at risk for dyslexia should be identified and treated before the school-age. The MMN might be one promising tool for determining early markers of perceptual problems underlying reading impairments. Its unmatched advantage over other approaches is that it can be obtained even from small children and infants.

Since dyslexia has a strong genetic component (Pennington, 1995), it would be important to develop early markers of the disorder in infants with dyslexic close relatives. The Jyväskylä longitudinal study on dyslexia (JLD, Jyväskylä, Finland) evaluates perceptual dysfunctions in infants with a genetically increased risk for dyslexia. Furthermore, the development of these children is followed up in the project. Leppänen et al. (2002) from this project compared the MMNs of infants who were on the average six months old and either were or were not at high genetic risk for dyslexia. They reported that the central auditory processing of at-risk infants differed from that in control children. The authors used a pseudoword /ata/ as their standard stimulus. As deviant stimuli, they had two /atta/ sounds, one having a small and the other one a larger increment in the duration of the stop consonant (the silent gap corresponding the occlusion stage of the stop consonant) as compared with that in the standard stimulus. It should be noted that such contrasts are phonetically relevant in the Finnish language since they may alter the meaning of a word.

Leppänen and colleagues found several differences in the brain responses of these two groups of children. The gap-duration changes elicited MMN-type of responses which differed both in amplitude and scalp distribution between the at-risk and control children (Fig. 6). The smaller difference between the deviant and the standard stimulus elicited an MMN in the control infants but not in the at-risk infants. The larger difference elicited an MMN in both groups of infants, but the MMN was smaller in the at-risk than control group over the left hemisphere, whereas no group differences were found over the right hemisphere. These results suggest that at-risk infants are less accurate in discriminating gap durations than control infants. Furthermore, they suggest a left hemisphere dysfunction in the at-risk infants, which is consistent with several previous studies indicating functional and structural abnormalities in the left hemisphere of dyslexic individuals (Galaburda, Menard, & Rosen, 1994; Snowling, 2000; Witelson, 1977). In addition, Leppänen and colleagues (2002) found a significant correlation between the behavioral measures and the MMN. A comparison of the infants' head-turning responses and the MMN laterality to deviant stimuli indicated that a stronger left-hemisphere preponderance correlated with a better behavioral discrimination of deviant stimuli (i.e., more head turns in response to the occurrence of deviant stimuli). These results suggest that with the MMN, dysfunctions of the phonological/auditory processing in dyslexia can be determined even in infants, at least at group level.

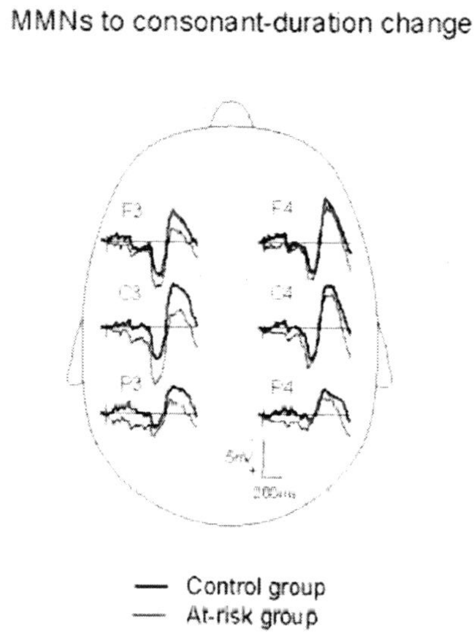

Fig. 6. The MMNs (the response elidited by the standard stimulus subtracted from that elicited by the deviant stimulus) elicited by /ata/ (standard stimulus) vs. /atta/ (deviant stimulus) pseudo-words are diminished over the left hemisphere of six months old infants who are at risk for dyslexia. The responses of the at-risk infants are presented with a thin line and that of the control infants with a thick line. Figure adapted from Leppänen et al., 2002.

CONCLUDING REMARKS

As dyslexia is a multi-dimensional disorder with sever consequences causing not only delays in educational progression but also loss of self-esteem and for some individuals even severe motivational and social problems, all new means to understand it better and to identify it early in life are urgently needed. What comes to, at least, auditory dysfunctions in dyslexia, the MMN holds a great promise in this strive. If the hypothesis that phonological or more general auditory dysfunction underlies reading impairments holds, the role of the MMN might be remarkable in dyslexia research. Many studies have shown that the MMN indexes auditory discrimination accuracy (Amenedo & Escera, 2000; Kujala et al., 2001a; Winkler & Näätänen, 2001), it can be used for determining brain's plastic changes (Kraus et al., 1995; Menning, Roberts, & Pantev, 2000; Näätänen et al., 1993; Tremblay, Kraus, & McGee, 1998; Winkler et al., 1999) also in recovery (Ilvonen et al., 2003) and remediation (Kujala et al., 2001b), and it can be used at any developmental stage, even for investigating audition in infancy (Alho et al., 1990; Cheour-Luhtanen et al., 1996; Leppänen et al., 2002). These features make the MMN attractive for investigating dyslexia and other impairments in language and auditory processing.

Evidently, the MMN can be used to probe questions such as whether dyslexia is a dysfunction specific to the phonological system or a more general auditory deficit, which has been under debate for a long time. MMN studies have so far shown that the cortical discrimination of not only speech but also non-speech sounds is affected in dyslexia (Baldeweg et al., 1999; Csepe & Gyurkocza, in press; Kujala et al., 2000; 2003; Leppänen et al., 2002; Schulte-Körne, Deimel, Bartling, & Remschmidt, 1998; 1999). This, of course, does not prove any causal relationship between dyslexia and auditory dysfunction. However, a recent study showed that a training program involving no phonetic or other linguistic material at all had a remediating effect on dyslexia (Kujala et al., 2001b). Training in which non-speech sounds and simple abstract visual symbols were used improved childrens' reading skills indicating that training brain processes not directly involving the phonological system does have beneficial effects on reading ability. Furthermore, since this training had an effect on the auditory system as indicated by the enhancement of the MMN and improved behavioral stimulus discrimination, one can deduce that the auditory system has an important role in the skills underlying the reading process. This is also supported by a recent study showing that training with speech and non-speech sounds may alleviate dyslexia (Temple et al., 2000). The MMN evidently has a close link to reading ability since in the training study of Kujala et al. (2001b) its amplitude change singificantly correlated with the change in the reading-skill scores.

In order to design and apply effective remediation programs, there should be means to precisely determine the various types of dysfunctions underlying dyslexia. This would help to specifically target the training to those aspects in perception that are affected. With the MMN, it might be possible to determine the sound features that are the most problematic for dyslexic individuals. For example, the above-reviewed study (Kujala et al., 2000) on the processing of tone patterns in dyslexia suggested that the discrimination dysfunction can in some cases be determined more precisely with the MMN than behavioral means. Another important aspect in effective remediation is to initiate it at an early developmental stage, which means that it is important to identify the existing problems at a young age. In this respect, too, the MMN holds promise, as it can be recorded in infants (Alho et al., 1990; Cheour et al., 1998; Leppänen et al., 2002) and even in premature newborn infants (Cheour-Luhtanen et al., 1996). If the auditory dysfunctions could be determined in the early infancy, as suggested by the afore-mentioned MMN findings indicating altered auditory processing in six months old infants at risk for dyslexia (Leppänen et al., 2002), a remediation program targeted on the specific central auditory processing problems of the child could be started at an early age when the central nervous system still is very plastic.

Although the MMN clearly has advantages in studying perception when compared with many other methods, there still are some difficulties in applying it to dyslexia or other clinical research. First, although some authors have claimed that they have found an MMN elicited by visual stimuli, the evidence is not yet conclusive (Alho, Woods, Algazi, & Näätänen, 1992; Berti & Schröger, 2001; Nyman et al., 1990; Tales, Newton, Troscianko, & Butler, 1999), which makes the identification of such dyslexia types that are primarily related to the dysfunction of the visual system (Brannan & Williams, 1988; Demp, Boynton, & Heeger, 1998; Di Lollo, Hanson, & McIntyre, 1983; Salmelin et al., 1996; Stein & Talcott, 1999; Stein & Walsh, 1997) problematic with the MMN. Second, the MMN signal is fairly small and therefore its extraction from the large-amplitude background EEG activity is problematic. Thus, often long data-collection sessions are required or the MMN signal obtained is not reliable enough. However, work aiming at optimizing the MMN recording and quantification methods has already been initiated (see, for example, McGee, Kraus, & Nicol, 1997; Schröger, 1998; Sinkkonen & Tervaniemi, 2000; Tervaniemi et al., 1999).

To summarize, approaches to investigate the accuracy of sound discrimination and sensory-memory functions without confounding factors such as attention or motivation is especially valuable when one wishes to identify and specify developmental deficits or learning-related problems. These dysfunctions should be detected as early as possible, so that the remediation could be started before any major learning delays occur. So far this has been problematic because of difficulties in identifying perceptual dysfunctions in infants and children by using behavioral methods. Fortunately, there are already several reports suggesting the usefulness of electrophysiological approaches in determining the central auditory processing deficits in dyslexic individuals and other clinical populations. Because the MMN can be obtained even from unattentive individuals it is particularly promising in determining perceptual functions and dysfunctions even at an early age.

ACKNOWLEDGEMENTS

This work was supported by the Academy of Finland.

REFERENCES

Aaltonen, O., Tuomainen, J., Laine, M., & Niemi, P. (1993). Cortical differences in tonal versus vowel processing as revealed by an ERP component called mismatch negativity (MMN). *Brain and Language, 44*, 139-152.

Ahveninen, J., Jääskeläinen, I. P., Pekkonen, E., Hallberg, A., Hietanen, M., Mäkelä, R., Näätänen, R., & Sillanaukee, P. (1999). Supression of mismatch negativity by backward masking predicts impaired working-memory performance in alcoholics. *Alcoholism: Clinical and Experimental Research, 23,* 1507-1514.

Alain, C., Woods, D. L., & Knight, R. T. A. (1998). Distributed cortical network for auditory sensory memory in humans. *Brain Research, 81,* 23-37.

Alho, K. (1995). Cerebral generators of mismatch negativity (MMN) and its magnetic counterpart (MMNm) elicited by sound changes. *Ear and Hearing, 16,* 38-51.

Alho, K., Sainio, K., Sajaniemi, N., Reinikainen, K., & Näätänen, R. (1990). Event-related brain potential of human newborns to pitch change of an acoustic stimulus. *Electroencephalography and Clinical Neurophysiology, 77,* 151-155.

Alho, K., Woods, D. L., Algazi, A., & Näätänen, R. (1992). Intermodal selective attention. II. Effects of attentional load on processing of auditory and visual stimuli in central space. *Electroencephalography and Clinical Neurophysiology, 82,* 356-368.

Amenedo, E. & Escera, C. (2000). The accuracy of sound duration representation in the human brain determines the accuracy of behavioural perception. *European Journal of Neuroscience, 12,* 2570-1574.

Baldeweg, T., Richardson, A., Watkins, S., Foale, C., & Gruzelier, J. (1999). Impaired auditory frequency discrimination in dyslexia detected with mismatch evoked potentials. *Annals of Neurology, 45,* 495-503.

Berti, S. & Schröger, E. (2001). A comparison of auditory and visual distraction effects: behavioral and event-related indices. *Cognitive Brain Research, 10,* 265-273.

Brannan, J.R. & Williams, M.C. (1988). Developmental versus sensory deficit effects on perceptual processing in the reading disabled. *Perception and Psychophysics, 44,* 437-444.

Cheour-Luhtanen, M., Alho, K., Sainio, K., Rinne, T., Reinikainen, K., Pohjavuori, M., Renlund, M., Aaltonen, O., Eerola, O. & Näätänen, R. (1996). The ontogenetically earliest discriminative response of the human brain. *Psychophysiol*ogy, *33,* 478-481.

Cheour, M., Ceponiene, R., Lehtokoski, A., Luuk, A., Allik, J., Alho, K., & Näätänen, R. (1998). Development of language-specific phoneme representations in the infant brain. *Nature Neurosci*ence, *1,* 351-353.

Cheour, M., Shestakova, A., Alku, P., Ceponiene, R., & Näätänen, R. (2002). Mismatch negativity shows that 3-6-year-old children can learn to discriminate non-native speech sounds within two months. *Neuroscience Letters, 325,* 187-190.

Csepe, V. & Gyurkocza, E. E. Abnormal mismatch negativity to phonetic deviations in developmental dyslexia. *Developmental Neuropsychology,* in press.

Dehaene-Lambertz, G. (1997). Electrophysiological correlates of categorical phoneme perception in adults. *NeuroReport, 8,* 919-924.

Demp, J. B., Boynton, G. M., & Heeger, D. J. (1998). Functional magnetic resonance imaging of early visual pathways in dyslexia. *The Journal of Neuroscience, 18,* 6939-6951.

Deouell, L., Bentin, S., & Soroker, N. (2000). Electrophysiological evidence for an early (pre-attentive) information processing deficit in patients with right hemisphere damage and unilateral neglect. *Brain, 123,* 353-365.

Di Lollo, V., Hanson, D., & McIntyre, J.S. (1983). Initial stages of visual information processing in dyslexia. *Journal of Experimental Psychology, 9*, 923-935.

Farmer, M.E. & Klein, R.M. (1995). The evidence for a temporal processing deficit linked to dyslexia: A review. *Psychonomic Bulletin and Review, 2*, 460-493.

Fischer, C., Morlet, D., Giard, M.-H. (2000). Mismatch negativity and N100 in comatose patients. *Audiology & Neuro-Otology, 5*, 192-197.

Galaburda, A. M., Menard, M. T., & Rosen, G. D. (1994). Evidence for aberrant auditory anatomy in developmental dyslexia. *Proceedings of National Academy of Sciences, 91*, 8010-8013.

Giard, M.H., Lavikainen, J., Reinikainen, K., Perrin, F., Bertrand, O., Pernier, J., & Näätänen, R. (1995). Separate representation of stimulus frequency, intensity, and duration in auditory sensory memory: an event-related potential and dipole-model analysis. *Journal of Cognitive Neuroscience, 7*, 133-143.

Grant, A. C., Zangaladze, A., Thiagarajah, M. C., & Sathian, K. (1999). Tactile perception in developmental dyslexia: a psychophysical study using gratings. *Neuropsychology*, *37*, 1201-1211.

Grau, C., Yago, E., & Polo, M. D. (1998) Mismatch negativity and auditory sensory memory evaluation: A new faster paradigm. *NeuroReport, 9*, 2451-2456.

Hari, R., Hämäläinen, M., Ilmoniemi, R.J., Kaukoranta, E., Reinikainen, K., Salminen, J., Alho, K., Näätänen, R., & Sams, M. (1984). Responses of the primary auditory cortex to pitch changes in a sequence of tone pips: Neuromagnetic recordings in man. *Neuroscience Letters, 50*, 127-132.

Hari, R. & Kiesilä, P. (1996). Deficit of temporal processing in dyslexic adults. *Neuroscience Letters, 205*, 138-140.

Hari, R. & Renvall, H. (2001). Impaired processing of rapid stimulus sequences in dyslexia. *Trends in Cognitive Sciences, 5*, 525-532

Heim, S., Eulitz, C., Wienbruck, C., & Elbert, T. (2000). Effects of syllabic training on literacy skills, phonological processing, and cortical organization in children with language impairment. *Society for Psychophysiological Research*, Abstracts of the Fortieth Annual Meeting, October, San Diego, CA, USA.

Hugdahl, K., Helland, T., Faerevaag, M.K., Lyssand, E.T., & Asbjoernsen, A. (1995). Absence of ear advantage on the consonant-vowel dichotic listening test in adolescent and adult dyslexics: specific auditory-phonetic dysfunction. *Journal of Clinical and Experimental Neuropsychology, 17*, 833-840.

Ilvonen, T.-M., Kujala, T., Kiesiläinen, A., Salonen, O., Kozou, H., Pekkonen, E., Roine, R. O., Kaste, M.. & Näätänen, R. (2003) Auditory discrimination after left-hemisphere stroke. A mismatch negativity study. *Stroke, 34,* 1746-1753.

Ilvonen, T.-M., Kujala, T., Tervaniemi, M., Salonen, O., Näätänen, R. & Pekkonen, E. (2001). The processing of sound duration after left hemisphere stroke: event-related and behavioral data. *Psychophysiology, 38*, 622-628.

Kane, N.M., Butler, S.R., & Cummins, B.H. (1993). Electrophysiological indicator of awakening from coma. *The Lancet, 341*, 688.

Karma, K. (1999). Auditory structuring in explaining dyslexia. In Mc Kevitt, P., Mulvihill, C., Nualláin, S. Ó., O'Riordan, C. (Eds.), *Proceedings of the 8th International Workshop on the Cognitive Science of Natural Language Processing (CSNLP-8)*, Galway, Ireland.

Kemner, C., Verbaten, M..N., Cuperus, J. M., Camfferman, G. & van Engeland, H. (1995). Auditory event-related brain potentials in autistic children and three different control groups. *Biological Psychiatry, 38,* 150-165.

Kraus, N., McGee, T. J., Carrell, T. D., King, C., & Tremblay, K. (1995). Central auditory system plasticity associated with speech discrimination learning. *Journal of Cognitive Neuroscience, 7,* 27-34.

Kraus, N., McGee, T. J., Carrell, T. D., Zecker, S. G., Nicol, T. G., & Koch, D..B. (1996). Auditory neurophysiologic responses and discrimination deficits in children with learning problems. *Science, 273,* 971-973.

Kujala, T., Belitz, S., Tervaniemi, M., & Näätänen, R. (2003). Auditory sensory memory disorder in dyslexic adults as indexed by the mismatch negativity. *European Journal of Neuroscience,* 17, 1323-1327.

Kujala, T., Kallio, J., Tervaniemi, M., & Näätänen, R. (2001a). The mismatch negativity as an index of temporal processing in audition. *Clinical Neurophysiology, 112,* 1712-1719.

Kujala, T., Karma, K., Ceponiene, R., Belitz, S., Turkkila, P., Tervaniemi, M., & Näätänen, R. (2001b). Plastic neural changes and reading improvement caused by audio-visual training in reading-impaired children. *Proceedings of the National Academy of Sciences,* 18, 10509-10514.

Kujala, T., Myllyviita, K., Tervaniemi, M., Alho, K., Kallio, J., & Näätänen, R. (2000). Basic auditory dysfunction in dyslexia as demonstrated by brain-activity measurements. *Psychophysiology, 37,* 262-266.

Laasonen, M., Tomma-Halme, J., Lahti-Nuuttila, P., Service, E., & Virsu, V. (2000) Rate on information segregation in developmentally dyslexic children. *Brain and Language, 75,* 66-81.

Leppänen, P. H. T., Pihko, E., Eklund, K. M., Guttorm, T. K., Aro, M., Richardson, U., & Lyytinen, H. (2002). Brain responses reveal speech processing differences in infants at a risk for dyslexia. *Developmental Neuropsychology, 22,* 407-423.

Liberman, I. Y. & Shankweiler, D. (1985). Phonology and the problems to learn to read and write. *Remediation and Special Education, 6,* 8-17.

Livingstone, M. S., Rosen, G. D., Drislane, F. W., & Galaburda, A. M. (1991). Physiological and anatomical evidence for a magnocellular defect in developmental dyslexia. *Proceedings of National Academy of Sciences, 88,* 7943-7947.

Mäntysalo, S. & Näätänen, R. (1987). The duration of a neuronal trace of an auditory stimulus as indicated by event-related potentials. *Biological Psychology, 24,* 183-195.

McGee, T., Kraus, N. & Nicol, T. (1997). Is it really a mismatch negativity? An assessment of methods for determining response validity in individual subjects. *Electroencephalography and Clinical Neurophysiology, 104,* 359-368.

McGivern, R. F., Berka, C., Languis, M. L. & Chapman, S. (1991). Detection of deficits in temporal pattern discrimination using the Seashore rhythm test in young children with reading impairments. *Journal of Learning Disabilities, 24,* 58-62.

Menning, H., Roberts, L., & Pantev, C. (2000). Plastic changes in the auditory cortex induced by intensive frequency discrimination training. *NeuroReport, 11*, 817-820.

Merzenich, M. M., Jenkins, W. M., Johnston, P., Schreiner, C., Miller, S. L., & Tallal, P. (1996). Temporal processing deficits of language-learning impaired children ameliorated by training. *Science, 271*, 77-81.

Mody, M., Studdert-Kennedy, M., & Brady, S. (1998). Speech perception deficits in poor readers: auditory processing or phonological coding? *Journal of Experimental Child Psychology, 64*, 199-231.

Morlet, D., Bouchet, P., & Fischer, C. (2000). Mismatch Negativity and N100 monitoring: potential clinical value and methodological advances. *Audiology & Neuro-Otology, 5*, 198-207.

Näätänen, R. (1992). Attention and brain function. Hillsdale, N.J.: Lawrence Erlbaum.

Näätänen, R. (1991). Mismatch negativity (MMN) outside strong attentional focus: A commentary on Woldorff et al. *Psychophysiol*ogy, *28*, 478-484.

Näätänen, R. & Escera, C. (2000). Mismatch negativity: clinical and other applications. *Audiology & Neuro-Otology, 5*, 105-110.

Näätänen, R., Gaillard, A. W. K., & Mäntysalo, S. (1978). Early selective-attention effect on evoked potential reinterpreted. *Acta Psychologica, 42*, 313-329.

Näätänen, R., Lehtokoski, A., Lennes, M., Cheour, M., Huotilainen, M., Iivonen, A., Vainio, M., Alku, P., Ilmoniemi, R. J., Luuk, A., Allik, J., Sinkkonen, J., & Alho, K. (1997). Language-specific phoneme representations revealed by electric and magnetic brain responses. *Nature, 385*, 432-434.

Näätänen, R., Schröger, E., Karakas, S., Tervaniemi, M., & Paavilainen, P. (1993). Development of a memory trace for a complex sound in the human brain. *NeuroReport, 4*, 503-506.

Näätänen, R., Tervaniemi, M., Sussman, E., Paavilainen, P., & Winkler, I. (2001). Primitive intelligence in the auditory cortex. *Trends in Neuroscience, 24*, 283-288.

Nyman, G., Alho, K., Laurinen, P., Paavilainen, P., Radil, T., Reinikainen, K., Sams, M., & Näätänen, R. (1990). Mismatch negativity (MMN) for sequences of auditory and visual stimuli: Evidence for a mechanism specific to the auditory modality. *Electroencephalography and Clinical Neurophysiol*ogy, *77*, 436-444.

Paavilainen, P., Jaramillo, M., & Näätänen, R. (1998). Binaural information can converge in abstract memory traces. *Psychophysiol*ogy, *35*, 483-487.

Pantev, C., Oostenveld, R., Engelien, A., Ross, B., Roberts, L. E., & Hoke, M. (1998). Increased auditory cortical representations in musicians. *Nature, 392*, 811-814.

Paulesu, E., Demonet, J.-F., Fazio, F., McCrory, E., Chanoine, V., Brunswick, N., Cappa, F. S., Cossu, G., Habib, M., Frith, C. D., & Frith, U. (2001). Dyslexia: cultural diversity and biological unity. *Science, 291*, 2165-2167.

Pennington, B. F. (1995). Genetics of learning disabilities. *Journal of Child Neurolology, 10*, 69-77

Rayner, K., Pollatsek, A., & Bilsky, A. B. (1995). Can temporal processing deficit account for dyslexia? *Psychonomic Bulletin and Review, 2*, 501-507.

Reed, M. A. (1989). Speech perception and the discrimination of brief auditory cues in reading disabled children. *Journal of Experimental Child Psychology, 48*, 270-292.

Rinne, T., Alho, K., Alku, P., Holi, M., Sinkkonen, J., Virtanen, J., Bertrand, O., & Näätänen, R. (1999). Analysis of speech sounds is left-hemisphere predominant at 100-150 ms from sound onset. *NeuroReport*, 10, 1113-1117.

Rinne, T., Alho, K., Ilmoniemi, R. J., Virtanen, J., & Näätänen, R. (2000). Separate time behaviors of the temporal and frontal MMN sources. *NeuroImage*, 12, 14-19.

Saarinen, J., Paavilainen, P., Schröger, E., Tervaniemi, M. & Näätänen, R. (1992). Representation of abstract attributes of auditory stimuli in the human brain. *NeuroReport*, 3, 1149-1151.

Salmelin, R., Service, E., Kiesilä, P., Uutela, K., & Salonen, O. (1996). Impaired visual word processing in dyslexia revealed with magnetoencephalography. *Annals of Neurology*, 40, 157-162.

Sams, M., Paavilainen, P., Alho, K., & Näätänen, R. (1985). Auditory frequency discrimination and event-related potentials. *Electroencephalography and Clinical Neurophysiology*, 62, 437-448.

Schröger, E. (1998). Measurement and interpretation of the mismatch negativity. *Behavior Research Methods, Instruments & Computers*, 30, 131-145.

Schulte-Körne, G., Deimel, W., Bartling, J., & Remschmidt, H. (1998). Auditory processing and dyslexia: evidence for a specific speech processing deficit. *NeuroReport*, 9, 337-340.

Schulte-Körne, G., Deimel, W., Bartling, J., & Remschmidt, H. (1999). Pre-attentive processing of auditory patterns in dyslexic human subjects. *Neuroscience Letters*, 276, 41-44.

Shtyrov, Y., Kujala, T., Palva, S., Ilmoniemi, R. J., & Näätänen, R. (2000). Discrimination of speech and of complex nonspeech sounds of different temporal structure in the left and right cerebral hemispheres. *NeuroImage*, 12, 657-663.

Singer, W. (1995). Development and plasticity of cortical processing architectures. *Science*, 270, 758-763.

Sinkkonen, J. & Tervaniemi, M. (2000). Towards optimal recording and analysis of the mismatch negativity. *Audiology & Neuro-Otology*, 5, 235-246.

Snowling, M. J. (2000). *Dyslexia*. 2nd Ed. Oxford: Blackwell Publishers Ltd.

Steffens, M. L., Eilers, R. E., Gross-Glenn, K., & Jallad, B. (1992). Speech perception in adult subjects with familial dyslexia. *Journal of Speech and Hearing Research*, 35, 192-200.

Stein, J. & Talcott, J. (1999). Impaired neuronal timing in developmental dyslexia - the magnocellular hypothesis. *Dyselxia*, 5, 59-77.

Stein, J. & Walsh, W. (1997). To see but not to read; the magnocellular theory of dyslexia. *Trends in Neurosciences*, 20, 147-152.

Studdert-Kennedy, M., & Mody, M. (1995). Auditory temporal perception deficits in the reading-impaired: A critical review of the evidence. *Psychonomic Bulletin and Review*, 2, 508-514.

Talcott, J. B., Witton, C., McClean, M., Hansen, P. C., Rees, A., Green, G. G. R., & Stein, J. F. (1999). Can sensitivity to auditory frequency modulation predict children's phonological and reading skills? *NeuroReprot*, *10*, 2045-2050.

Tales, A., Newton, P., Troscianko, T., & Butler, S. (1999). Mismatch negativity in the visual modality. *NeuroReport*, 10, 3363-3367.

Tallal, P. (1980). Auditory temporal perception, phonics, and reading disabilities in children. *Brain and Language*, 9, 182-198.

Tallal, P., Miller, S. L., Bedi, G., Byma, G., Wang, X., Nagarajan, S. S., Schreiner, C., Jenkins, W. M., & Merzenich, M. M. (1996). Language comprehension in language-learning impaired children improved with acoustically modified speech. *Science*, 271, 81-84.

Temple, E., Poldrack, R. A., Protopapas, A., Nagarajan, S., Salz, T., Tallal, P., Merzenich, M. M., & Gabrieli, J. D. E. (2000). Disruption of the neural response to rapid acoustic stimuli in dyslexia: Evidence from functional MRI. *Proceedings of the National Academy of Sciences, 97*, 13907-13912.

Tervaniemi, M., Lehtokoski, A., Sinkkonen, J., Virtanen, J., Ilmoniemi, R. J., & Näätänen, R. (1999). Test-retest reliability of mismatch negativity for duration, frequency and intensity changes. *Clinical Neurophysiology*, 110, 1388-1393.

Tervaniemi, M., Radil, T., Radilova, J., Kujala, T., & Näätänen R. (1999). Pre-attentive discriminability of sound order as a function of tone duration and interstimulus interval: a mismatch negativity study. *Audiology and Neuro-otology*, 4, 303-310.

Tiitinen, H., May, P., Reinikainen, K., & Näätänen, R. (1994). Attentive novelty detection in humans is governed by pre-attentive sensory memory. *Nature*, 327, 90-92.

Tremblay, K., Kraus, N., & McGee, T. (1998). The time-course of auditory perceptual learning: which comes first, the chicken or the egg. *NeuroReport*, 9, 3557-3560.

Winkler, I., Kujala, T., Tiitinen, H., Sivonen, P., Alku, P., Lehtokoski, A., Czigler, I., Csépe, V., Ilmoniemi, R. J., & Näätänen, R. (1999). Brain responses reveal the learning of foreign language phonemes. *Psychophysiology*, 36, 638-642.

Winkler, I. & Näätänen, R. (1992). Event-related potentials in auditory backward recognition masking: a new way to study the neurophysiological basis of sensory memory in humans. *Neuroscience Letters*, 140, 239-242.

Winkler, I., Schröger, E., & Cowan, N. (2001). The role of large-scale perceptual organization in the mismatch negativity event-related brain potential. *Journal of Cognitive Neuroscience*, 13, 59-71.

Witelson, S. F. (1977). Developmental dyslexia: two right hemispheres and none left. *Science*, 195, 309-311.

Wright, B. A., Lombardino, L. J., King, W. M., Puranik, C. S., Leonard, C. M., & Merzenich, M. M. (1997). Deficits in auditory temporal and spectral resolution in language-impaired children. *Nature*, 387, 176-178.

In: Trends in Dyslexia Research
Editor: Henry D. Tobias, pp. 121-149
ISBN 1-59454-219-8
© Nova Science Publishers, Inc.

Chapter V

EVENT-RELATED POTENTIALS IN POOR READERS

Juan Silva-Pereyra and Maritza Rivera-Gaxiola
Institute for Learning and Brain Sciences (I-LABS)
Department of Speech and Hearing Sciences
University of Washington, Seattle WA, USA

ABSTRACT

Poor readers have a low performance in reading tasks but possess better reading skills than children with dyslexia. Many factors have been proposed to explain such reading disability. Among the main factors, a low verbal working memory capacity has been claimed as one of the most important. In the first part of this chapter, we analyzed how the low capacity of the verbal working memory in the poor readers has an effect on the semantic and syntactic processing during sentence reading. This low capacity seems to be a consequence from a general-purpose mechanism of the working memory. In the second part, the semantic processing was analyzed. The semantic processing underachievement that has been observed in poor readers is not a semantic deficit *per se*, but the late reflection of an early word codification problem. Poor readers seem to use less efficient and more demanding strategies to process words. These strategies consume extra attentional resources and seem to be slow, with the subject storing and accommodating new difficult information into a memory model before the next word arrives. The most invasive deficit that poor readers face when reading seems to takes place very early, probably at the first encounter with the processing of graphemes. In this way a chain reaction of general slowness is triggered. In the last part of this chapter we analyzed the early processing deficiencies in the poor readers, such as visual stimulus evaluation. They have a deficit to classify and memorize stimuli independently of the modality of the stimulus (verbal and non-verbal).

INTRODUCTION

In the regular elementary school system, there are children with IQ scores that fall within the normal range but that score between one and two years below their expected reading level. Children under these circumstances have been considered poor readers (Rayner and Pollatsek 1989). Children scoring two or more years below their expected reading level are referred to as dyslexics. In other words, poor readers do not have dyslexia but a lower achievement than normal in reading skills. They otherwise comprise a very heterogeneous population that actually represents a high percentage of reading delays in every school. General-purpose mechanisms and deficiencies in specific mechanisms have been proposed to explain reading deficiencies. Among the main candidates are: a) general working memory low capacity, b) phonological rehearsal limitations, c) deficiencies in phonological skills, d) impairments to process transient auditory information, e) deficits in syntactic processing and f) semantic processing deficiencies, to mention a few. In the present chapter, we analyze and weigh the role of the factors that may be present in poor readers based on our own event-related brain potentials (ERP) studies as well as the information provided by previous behavioral and ERP reports.

Event-Related Brain Potentials

One approach to the study of reading disabled populations has been to obtain behavioral data and simultaneously record Event-Related Potentials (ERP) from electrodes placed over different regions of the scalp. ERPs are changes of voltage over time in the brain cortex elicited by the presentation of some external event, either a concrete stimulus or during a task performance. ERPs reflect the sum of the simultaneous postsynaptic activity of large groups of neurons. These voltage changes are generally small in amplitude and they are overlapped by continuous background electrical activity. In order to extract the event-related activity from the ongoing electroencephalogram (EEG), the most common procedure is to average several EEG stimulus' time-locked artifact-free segments. This procedure assumes that general brain electrical activity varies randomly across time; in other words, that the EEG is a stochastic process with zero mean whilst ERP components are constant across time.

In language studies, the use of ERPs permits one to know the exact succession of a great deal of brain electrical responses elicited by the presentation of a stimulus and make inferences about their corresponding cognitive event. Different patterns of brain electrical activity recorded during a task may reflect different cognitive processes and the differences in amplitude and latency of the ERP components across different populations may represent cognitive abilities and/or disabilities. ERP components are classified according to their polarity, the time in milliseconds of its initial or peak occurrence and its topographical distribution over the scalp. For example, the so-called N200 component is a negative (N) wave that peaks around 200 ms after the stimulus onset. In general terms, researchers have classified ERP components into two types: those that are related to the processing of physical properties of the stimuli (called exogenous), and those that are related to perception, attention, memory and other higher cognitive processes (called endogenous). In this chapter we will refer to those components related to memory and attention as "general purpose mechanisms" and those components related to language as "specific purpose mechanisms".

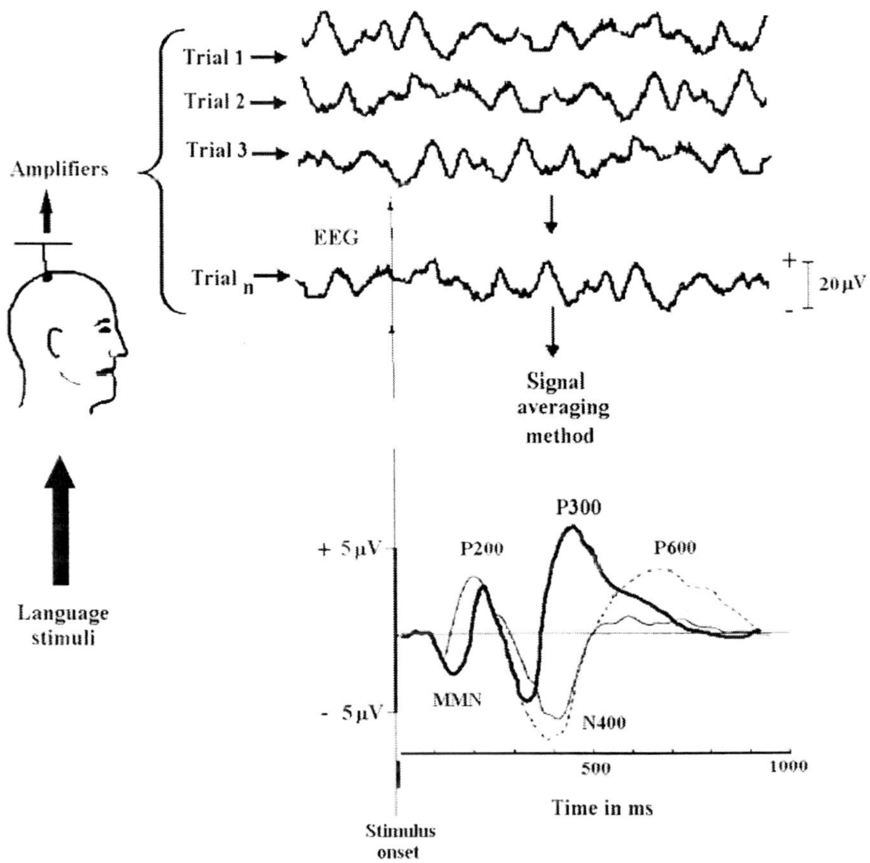

Figure 1. This figure shows idealized Event-Related brain Potentials obtained from averaging several stimuli during language studies. The ERP is not recognizable in the raw electroencephalogram (EEG) and for that reason is extracted from the EEG by averaging many presentations of the same stimulus category (i.e., phonemes, words, sentences, etc.). Mismatch Negativity (MMN), P200 and P300 are some of the endogenous ERP components related with general-purpose mechanisms that have been studied in poor readers and population with dyslexia. The MMN is elicited by auditory stimuli that are physically deviant from preceding stimuli. P200 varies in amplitude depending on the attention to the stimulus and P300 is present in oddball paradigms, where two stimuli are presented with different probabilities of occurrence. Specific purpose mechanism ERP components are the N400, the Left Anterior Negativity (LAN) and the P600. The amplitude of the N400 component is affected by the semantic relationship between the target word and the preceding context, with semantically anomalous stimuli eliciting large-amplitude N400s. The LAN and P600 components are elicited by syntactically anomalous words within a context.

General-Purpose Mechanism ERP Components

MMN

If one of the potential deficits that poor readers have is at the level of processing transient auditory information or phonological decoding, an electrophysiological measurement that could be used is the so-called Mismatch Negativity (MMN). The MMN was first described by Näätänen and collegues (Näätänen et al., 1978) and is now widely used in normal and clinical populations of all ages.The MMN has been used to evaluate central auditory dysfunction in children with reading disabilities such as dyslexia (for a review, see Kujala and, Näätänen 2001). In fact, the MMN has been widely used in both basic and clinical research and has become extremely popular due to the fact that it can be elicited even in the absence of attention. The MMN is thus a pre-attentive ERP component elicited by changes in any repetitive aspect of auditory stimulation and it reflects accuracy of auditory discrimination. It has been demonstrated that the amplitude of the MMN is diminished in subjects with dyslexia and even in infants with risk antecedents for dyslexia (Leppanen et al., 2001), suggesting that there is a very early auditory system deficit. It has been shown that the discrimination of both speech and non-speech stimuli is affected in subjects with severe reading deficits (Schulte-Koerne et al., 1998; Baldeweg et al., 1999; Csepe et al, 2001).

On the other hand, the MMN has also been used as a physical deviance discrimination marker within sentences presented via the auditory modality (Hahne et al., 2002), which then makes it an even more valuable tool that can inform us about auditory change detection under more realistic situations. Future research is awaiting the study of poor reading populations taking advantage of this component.

P200

P200 is a positive wave with peak latency around 200 ms after the stimulus onset whose typical highest peak amplitude can be seen over central recording sites. This ERP component has been related to the processing of physical attributes of the stimulus (Hillyard and Picton, 1987). Developmental changes in the P200 have been interpreted as a reflection of maturation of sensory functions (Polich et al., 1990). However, it has been reported that the P200 can also be modified by the attentional demands of different tasks (Johnson, 1989). Topographical differences in the presentation of this component suggest the use of different cognitive strategies in stimuli processing (Khan et al., 1999). An anterior P2 peak has been associated with stimulus evaluation and attentional demands (Luck and Hillyard, 1994); P2a's amplitude decreases with age (Taylor and Khan, 2000) but increases with the task's level of difficulty (Stelmack et al., 1988; Taylor and Khan, 2000). The reported decrease in latency with age is consistent with other developmental ERP studies which show that, with increasing age, children become faster or use more efficient strategies for evaluating visual stimuli, with some of the more pronounced effects being seen at anterior sites (Stauder et al., 1993; Taylor and Smith, 1995).

P300

One ERP component that has been widely and traditionally studied in neurophysiology is the so-called P300 component. The P300 wave is an endogenous positive deflection with an average peak latency at 300 ms or more after stimulus onset. The P300 is typically elicited by a rarely and randomly presented target stimulus in a detection task. One prominent interpretation of the P300 is that it represents stimulus evaluation and memory updating (Donchin and Coles, 1988; Polich and Kok, 1995). Some studies have indicated that the amplitude of a P300 is inversely related to stimulus and subjective probabilities (Donchin and Coles, 1988) and directly related to relevance within the task (Donchin et al., 1986; Donchin and Coles, 1988; Johnson, 1988; Ruchkin et al, 1990).

According to the so-called "memory updating model" (Donchin and Coles, 1986), infrequent events elicit large P300 because the immediate memory for the preceding target stimulus has decayed and is refurbished by neural events which occur upon the presentation of a new target stimulus. In contrast, frequent stimulus events, maintaining stronger representations, do not require as much updating and therefore yield smaller P300 waves. This model also considers that the amplitude of a P300 is proportional to the amount of attentional resources in terms of the processing capacity employed in a given task (Donchin and Coles, 1988; Kramer and Strayer, 1988). In fact, it has been proposed that the amplitude of the P300 indexes brain actions stemming from "tasks that are required in the maintenance of working memory" (Donchin et al., 1986 p. 256). Other studies have supported such relationship between P300 and working memory (Nielsen-Bohlman and Knight, 1994; Garcia-Larrea and Cezanne-Bert, 1998). According to Kramer et al. (1986), amplitude changes in the P300 component can be interpreted in terms of a trade-off of resources between the probe-comparison component and the memory rehearsal component of the memory search task. Memory rehearsal is conceived as a spontaneous ongoing activity that is not time-locked with the stimulus. In this way, when the memory load increases, resources from the probe comparison component of the task are re-allocated and used for memory rehearsal.

Latency of the P300 seems to reflect stimulus classification speed (Magliero et al., 1984). It has been shown that although latency is sensitive to manipulations that affect stimulus evaluation, it is independent of both response selection and execution processes (McCarthy and Donchin, 1981; Smulders et al., 1995). The neuropsychological tests that produce the strongest correlation between P300 latency and mental performance are those that assess how rapidly subjects can allocate and maintain attentional resources (Polich and Kok, 1995). According to the memory-updating model, P300 latency reflects the time used for stimulus evaluation, updating the mental model of the environment (Donchin and Coles, 1986).

Specific Purpose Mechanism ERP Components

N400

The N400 is a negative-going wave between 300 and 600 ms, peaking around 400 ms after critical stimulus onset, with a posterior, slightly right, amplitude predominant asymmetry (Kutas and Hillyard, 1980; Kutas and Van Petten, 1994). The N400 has been shown to vary systematically with the processing of semantic information (Kutas and Federmeier, 2000). It was first observed in response to a semantically anomalous word within a sentence context (Kutas and Hillyard, 1980). It has also been observed using other paradigms which involve semantic processing such as priming (Bentin et al., 1985; Brown and Hagoort, 1993; Holcomb, 1988; Silva-Pereyra et al., 1999). Although it is especially large to semantic violations, the N400 is not simply an index of anomaly, but rather a part of the brain's normal response to words. The prevalent view of the N400 is that it reflects 'contextual integration'. Visual sentence processing developmental studies (Holcomb et al., 1992; Juottonen et al., 1996) have shown that with age, the N400 effect decreases in amplitude and increases in latency. These results suggest, that as children acquire better reading skills, they rely less on semantic context for language comprehension. More specifically, the previous results appear to be consistent with Stanovich's interactive compensatory model (Stanovich, 1980) in which younger unskilled readers are said to compensate for less well developed bottom-up word recognition skills through lower reading and by engaging higher strategic processes (which rely on contextual information).

LAN and P600

ERP studies evaluating the outcomes of the presentation of sentences with syntactic anomalies show: a) an early left anterior negativity (henceforth LAN), b) a late parietally-distributed positivity (called P600), or c) a combination of both. LAN is a negative wave elicited around 300 and 500 ms over left frontal regions and has been observed in correlation with phrase-structure violations (Münte et al., 1993; Neville et al., 1991, Friederici et al, 1996), the processing of sub-categorization information (Rösler et al., 1993), agreement violations (Gunter et al., 1997), and even agreement errors in pseudoword combinations (Münte et al., 1997). Moreover, a LAN has been observed during the processing of function words when compared to open-class words (Neville et al., 1992). It has been proposed that the LAN component is automatic and independent of lexical information. It occurs in phrase structure violations and does not seem to be affected by manipulations such as the proportion of syntactic violations (Hahne and Friederici, 1999). It has been suggested that this component reflects an initial automatic process through which the subject recognizes the category of the words read in context. The LAN component has not only been found to respond to differences in grammaticality, but also to differences in working memory load, which shows up in sentences with filler-gap dependencies without any ungrammaticality (Kluender and Kutas, 1993). It is suggested that the LAN could reflect syntactic working memory (Kolk et al., 2003). However, it remains unclear as to why the interaction between syntactic complexity and grammaticality has no effect on the LAN.

The P600 component is a positive wave with a long latency, beginning around 500 ms with a duration of a few hundred milliseconds. It is presented in many syntactic violations and has a centroparietal distribution. The P600 has been found to covary with several syntactic anomalies, such as garden-path sentences, outright phrase structure violations (Osterhout and Holcomb, 1992, 1993; Neville et al., 1991), subjacency violations (Neville et al., 1991), and agreement violations (Coulson et al., 1998). Some authors suggest that the P600 is a late member of the family of the P300 component and that it is not necessarily produced by linguistic events (Coulson et al., 1998). However, Osterhout et al. (1996) found that the P600 is independent of the P300 effect. In their study, Osterhout and colleagues presented subjects with three types of sentences to read: sentences with a syntactic violation, non-anomalous sentences with the critical word of larger size, and sentences with a combination of the two variables (i.e., syntactic violation and a word in a large size). The larger size word condition produced a P300 effect that was sensitive to the manipulations of stimulus' probability. The double anomaly condition added the effects of the two components. These results suggest that P300 and P600 effects are different and independent.

It has been proposed that the P600 component evoked by syntactic violations represents a repair process while the P600 elicited by ambiguity resolution represents a reanalysis process (Friederici et al., 2002). Friederici et al. (2001) claim that the P600 is a component that reflects a mixture of subcomponents, probably including diagnosis, prosodic and syntactic reanalysis, revision and syntactic integration. Moreover, it has also been suggested that the P600 could reflect a reinterpretation process through which the subject tries to find the meaning of a sentence after having noted a grammatical error (Canseco González et al., 1997).

Working Memory Load and Sentence Processing

In the last 10 years, deficiencies in working memory have been proposed as one of the main factors in reading disabilities (Ackerman et al., 1990; Swanson, 1992; Torgesen, 1985). Working memory may be defined as the system in charge of the temporary maintenance and manipulation of information necessary for the performance of complex cognitive activities such as comprehension, learning and reasoning (Baddeley, 1998). Working memory plays a critical role in language comprehension. Listeners and readers must be able to maintain quickly and/or retrieve some representation of earlier presented words and phrases. Comprehenders must also store the theme of the text, the representation of the situation to which it refers, the major propositions from preceding sentences and a running, multilevel representation of what is currently being read (Just and Carpenter, 1992).

Baddeley's model (1998) of working memory consisted of a general attention resources system (i.e., central executive) that coordinates other storage systems (i.e., articulatory loop and spatial sketch pad). The processing resources used by the central executive to perform the functions of coordination are limited. The articulatory loop is supposed to be involved in language processing and is used mainly to maintain verbally coded information. The view of a limited capacity used for processing and maintenance also forms the basis of Just and Carpenter's (1992) theory. Instead of the multicomponent view of working memory from Baddeley and colleagues, Just and Carpenter have proposed a model with two limited working memory capacities: a spatial and a verbal working memory capacities. The verbal working memory capacity serves both storage and processing functions. The storage function is related to the maintenance of intermediate and/or final products of comprehension and the processing functions refer to syntactic parsing, thematic role assignment, comparison and integration information, for example. Just and Carpenter theorized that deficits in the storage of verbal working memory capacity will slow down normal language processing and that accuracy will deteriorate. Such low capacity is likely to occur in situations in which individual working memory capacity is low, syntactic complexity is high, or task demands are high.

Waters and Caplan (1996), on the other hand, have proposed an alternative model which consists of two separate language working memory resources, one for more automatic and one for more controlled verbal processing. The first resource is referred to as "the psycholinguistic resource pool". The processes that draw this pool are those operations that "obligatorily" (that is, automatically) follow a given sentence input, such as acoustic-phonetic conversion, lexical access, parsing, thematic role assignment and information structure. The second resource involves more general mechanisms that can be seen during controlled verbal tasks, such as verbal reasoning or the deliberate search for a piece of information in semantic memory. Syntactically complex sentences make a higher demand on this resource than syntactically simple sentences, but their demand on the resource pool for controlled verbal processing is the same.

The two theories make different predictions about the impact of additional load and span differences on syntactic processing. The single verbal resource theory (i.e., Just and Carpenter's) predicts that syntactic processing will be harder under high additional working memory load, especially for low span readers, whereas the separate resources theory (i.e., Waters and Caplan's) predicts that syntactic processing should not be affected by memory load and memory span differences. Both theories predict that syntactic complexity has a "negative" effect on the processing. Vos et al. (2001) in a study carried out with adults, evaluated how the processing of sentences with morphosyntactic violations is constrained by working memory capacity. The authors manipulated syntactic complexity, working memory load and verbal working memory span. The working memory load was manipulated by presenting participants with a set of sentences from which they should recall the last word of every sentence. How heavily the system was loaded depended on the number of sentences in the set. Individual working memory span was evaluated using Daneman and Carpenter's (1980) reading span task. Before the experimental session, subjects were also classified according with their "reading span" (i.e., they have to read a set of unrelated sentences and recall the final word of each sentence in a set. The number of sentences in a set was gradually increased). The reading span is the maximum number of recalled final-words in a particular set of sentences. The authors showed that reaction times to the processing of morphosyntactic violations were not influenced by the working memory manipulations. However, the ERP responses to the morphosyntactic violations, that is, LAN and P600, were affected by syntactic complexity, load and span. The amplitude of the LAN was related to both the combination of syntactic complexity and additional working memory load, and to individual differences in working memory span. The LAN disappeared for the high-complexity, high-load condition as well as for the low-span group. Furthermore, the onset of the P600 was delayed under a high additional working memory load and for the low-span group. Kolk et al's work (2003) also failed to support Waters and Caplan's model (1996) regarding the structure of verbal working memory. They compared ERP effects of syntactic and semantic anomalies in subject and object relative sentences. Syntactic anomalies consisted in subject-verb disagreement, while semantic anomalies referred to implausible events. Although the semantic anomalies did not elicit an N400 effect, they did elicit P600 effects as did the syntactic anomalies. Both effects showed similar centroparietal distributions. For both kinds of anomalies, the P600 effects were modulated by syntactic complexity, this being inconsistent with the theory proposed by Waters and Caplan (1996). Even if the detection of semantic anomalies draws from a separate resource pool, it is still dependent upon information provided by the parsing process.

The previously mentioned studies have manipulated three different variables within the same experiment in order to separate the possible components of verbal working memory (i.e., syntactic complexity, additional memory load and span). Manipulations of this kind are also of interest in the study of poor readers, given that it has been proposed that this population may present a low working memory capacity (Isaki 1997, de Jong 1998). It is not surprising that verbal working memory tasks consistently differentiate students with and without learning disabilities. Moreover, high correlations between working memory and achievement have been obtained (Dixon et al., 1988; Swanson et al., 1989; Swanson, 1992; 1994). In a very recent study, Avecilla-Ramirez and her colleagues (2003) investigated the effects of the working memory load capacity in a group of poor reading children as well as in normal children. The ERP experiment comprised two tasks. The first one was an acceptability judgment task in which sentences with and without syntactic and semantic violations had to be read and judged as well formed or not. The second task included reading a series of sentences, judging their acceptability and paying attention and retaining the last word of each sentence in memory. After the presentation of two or three sentences, a single word was presented that could or could not be one of the final words of the sentences recently presented. The subject had to decide whether the word belonged to the corresponding series of sentences or not. The ERP results from Avecilla-Ramirez et al's study (2003) showed a positive wave around 500 ms over central and parietal regions (P600) for syntactic violations in the acceptability judgment task in normal readers. During the working memory task, normal readers showed a decrease of the P600 effect (see top panel of figure 2). These findings are in accordance with the single resource theory, where the syntactic processing would slow down and/or deteriorate under a high additional load (Just and Carpenter, 1992). No significant P600 effects during either the acceptability judgment task or the working memory task were found in this group of poor readers (see bottom panel of figure 2). These results are also consistent with Just and Carpenter's (1992) single verbal resource theory. However, and most importantly, these results suggest that working memory in poor readers may be taxed to the maximum, even when the subjects just have to read the sentences. It is important to note here, that even the mere reading and acceptability judgment tasks are high-memory demanding in ERP protocols. Sentences are presented word by word with full sentences completed in 6 or 7 seconds (in order to avoid large eye movements), which subsequently makes integration of very simple sentences a complex task.

Avecilla-Ramirez et al. (2003) reported no LAN effects in their grand averages for any task and type of population (normal and poor readers). Although it has been proposed that LAN effect can reflect an automatic mechanism of morphosyntactic error detection (Friederici et al., 1995), it remains unclear the specific syntactic mechanisms that elicit it, given that various studies have failed to obtain a significant effect during sentence processing (Gunter et al., 1997; Munte et al., 1997).

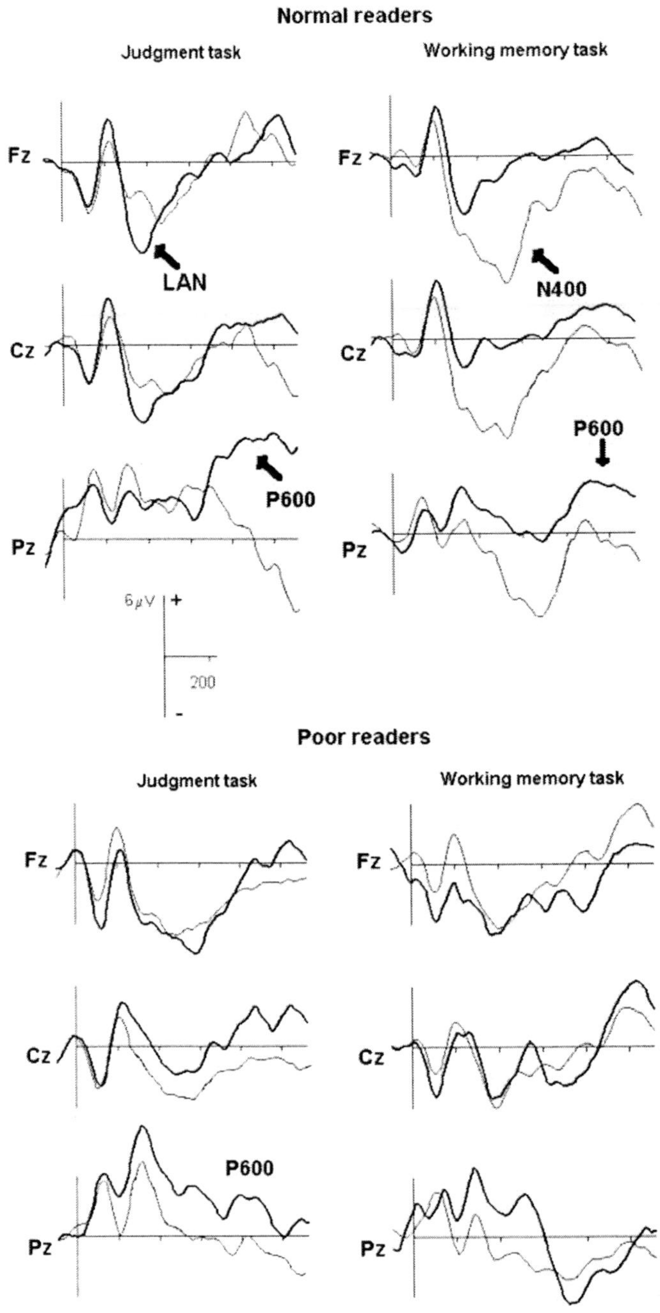

Figure 2. ERP grand averages elicited by syntactically anomalous and non-anomalous sentences from normal and poor readers during acceptability judgment and working memory tasks (from Avecilla-Ramirez et al., 2003). The P600 effect that is elicited by the syntactically anomalous condition is blocked when the working memory capacity is loaded. Poor readers do not show a P600 effect neither for acceptability judgment nor working memory tasks.

More consistent than the LAN effects is the occurrence of the N400 component. It has been argued that the N400 is modulated by the level of complexity of the task (Gunter et al., 1995). For example, the well-formedness judgment of a sentence is an easier task than a working memory task; thus, the N400 would be smaller in the first task. On the other task, while the subjects read better with age, they tend to utilize better strategies probably using other cues such as pragmatics to integrate the semantic information. Consequently the N400 effect also decreases. Under these circumstances, poor readers would have to use the semantic context of the sentence more and employ more memory resources to do the semantic integration, given that, as we mentioned previously, they have to read word by word until completing the sentence. In the Avecilla-Ramirez et al.'s (2003) study, a large N400 effect elicited by the semantically anomalous sentences regarding the normal readers was observed (see figure 3). The authors reported that during the acceptability judgment task normal readers elicited short duration N400 effect only in left frontal sites. In the working memory task, however, the N400 effect between the semantically anomalous and non-anomalous conditions was larger. In their poor readers' group, on the other hand, there were no significant differences between semantically anomalous and non-anomalous conditions in both tasks although an increase in the N400 amplitude during the working memory task was also observed.

Another important reason why working memory load and reading abilities may interact and be reflected by the N400 effect is that the subjects are required to pay attention to the final word of each sentence. They must recall them and subsequently verify if the following word presented after two or three sentences is one of the words that they were retaining in memory. This implies that the subject focus his attention to the words at end of the sentence where the semantic anomaly may or may not be. This attention to the last word generates expectancy. The N400 effect is modulated by the close probability of ending words (Kutas and Hillyard, 1980). This interpretation is supported by the results of Chwilla et al. (1995; 1998; 2000) and Silva-Pereyra et al. (1999) who claim that the N400 not only reflects an automatic but also a controlled process.

In sum, specific purpose mechanism ERP components such as P600 and N400 seem to be modulated by variations in the load of the subject's verbal working memory. Poor readers, subjects considered to have a low capacity working memory, have shown an important decrease of both ERP effects, even under very simple conditions (i.e., reading sentences).

In this way, although the results from Avecilla-Ramirez et al. (2003) support Just and Carpenter's (1992) model regarding the interaction of grammaticality, working memory load and verbal working memory capacity, poor readers also seem to display failures in a more general processor that makes possible the differentiation between poor and normal readers in verbal and non-verbal tasks, as claimed by Swanson and colleagues (Swanson, 1992; Swanson and Sachse, 2001). In other words, the fact that a specific verbal working memory may be altered in poor readers, unfortunately, does not free them from a more general disturbance.

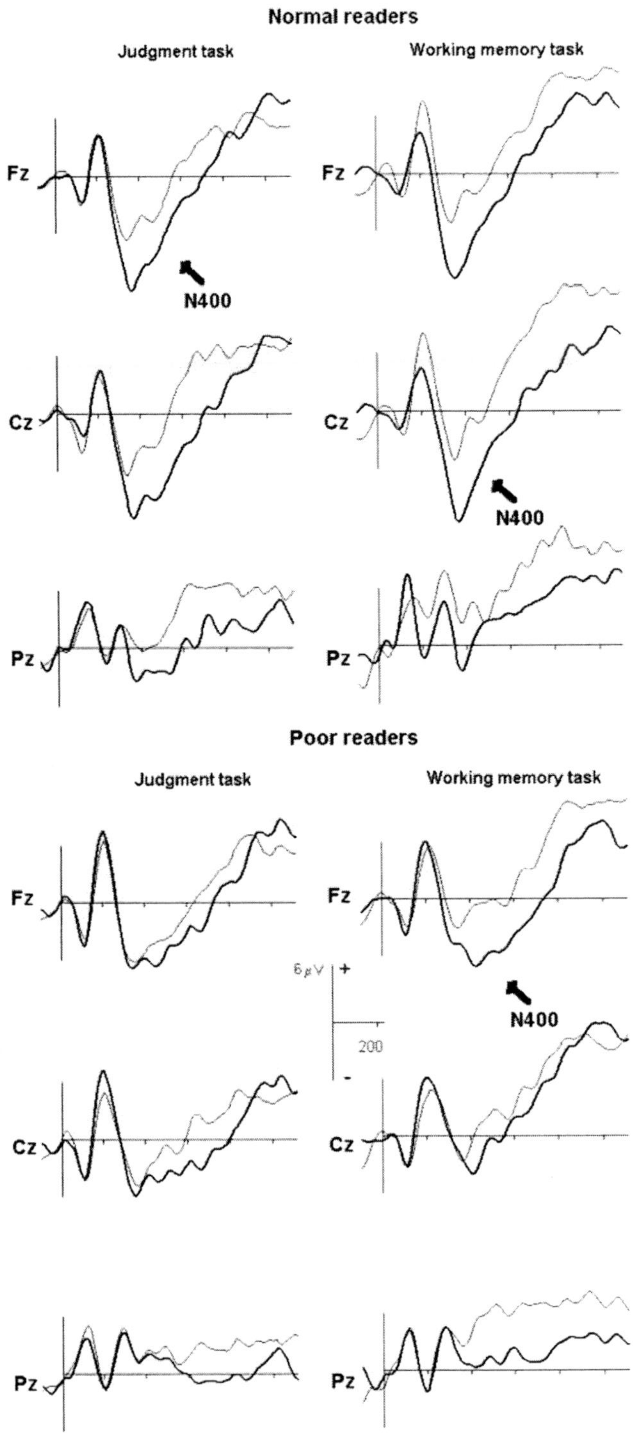

Figure 3. ERP grand averages elicited by semantically anomalous and non-anomalous sentences from normal and poor readers during acceptability judgment and working memory task (based on Avecilla-Ramirez et al., 2003). The N400 effect increases in amplitude when the capacity of the working memory is loaded as normal readers displayed. Poor readers show the same pattern as normal readers but the effect is not significant.

SEMANTIC PROCESSING

While there is abundant and convergent evidence showing that poor readers tend to be deficient in phonologically based skills (for a review see Beitchman and Young, 1997), deficits in syntactic processing (Byrne, 1981), working memory capacity (Swanson, 1992; Swanson and Sachse, 2001), and/or impairments in the time course of processing of the rapid, transient characteristics of auditory and visual input (Tallal et al., 1993), there is also evidence of a deficiency in semantically based skills (Champion 1997; Ben-Dror et al., 1995; Gillon and Dodd, 1994; Stelmack et al., 1988; Vellutino et al., 1988). Differences have been reported favoring normal readers in semantic memory as well as in semantic learning tasks using visual symbols and pair associates (Vellutino and Scanlon, 1985; Vellutino and Scanlon, 1995; Waterman and Lewandowski, 1993). In an ERP study, Stelmack et al. (1988) found larger frontal N400 amplitudes for normal readers with respect to reading disabled children during word recognition. They claimed that this effect was consistent with a more extensive semantic evaluation or memory search attributed to that component. In contrast to the previous, the N400 elicited during word-list tasks without priming has been observed having a more anterior distribution and being largest at central and frontal locations (especially the midline) (Nobre and McCarthy, 1994) in normal adults. Despite the distributional difference, the anterior N400 is thought to be closely related to the classic N400 and probably reflect similar cognitive processes. On the other hand, picture-processing paradigms also show an N400 effect that may mirror the pattern found in word-prime studies (Barret and Rugg, 1990; Holcomb and McPherson, 1994). The N400-like effect elicited by pictures is the result of both a frontally distributed N300 and a more widely distributed N450 (Barret and Rugg 1990). There is no evidence of amplitude change with age on picture processing development, however, latency decreases with increasing age (Friedman et al; 1990). Although it has been suggested that the N450 could be related with the processing of semantic relationships between non-verbal stimuli, other studies comparing picture with word semantic processing using ERPs have suggested that the semantic analysis of words and pictures may involve different, or at least partially non-overlapping neural systems (Holcomb and McPherson, 1994).

In an attempt to evaluate how poor readers between 8 and 11 years of age could access semantic information independently of stimulus kind, Silva-Pereyra et al. (2003) carried out a study consisting of two categorization tasks: figure (F) and word (W) categorization tasks. Participants were instructed to respond to animal figures (or words) in a sequence of animal/non-animal figures (or words) presentation. The authors showed that the two categorization tasks elicited three ERP components in both poor and normal readers: P2, N400 and P300 (see figure 4). An anterior P2 on frontopolar and frontal leads that was more pronounced over the left hemisphere was seen mainly during the word categorization task. Following the P2 component, a frontally negative waveform around 445 ms and a posterior negativity around 520 were clear during the figure categorization task. A dual-negative-going, anteriorly maximal but widely distributed negative peak between 350 and 560 ms in the word categorization task was evident. At posterior sites a positive-going component peaking around 750 ms was present and largest for the animal condition, which had the lowest presentation probability (and was therefore considered a P300). This P300 peak was practically absent in poor readers during the word categorization task (bottom panel of figure 4).

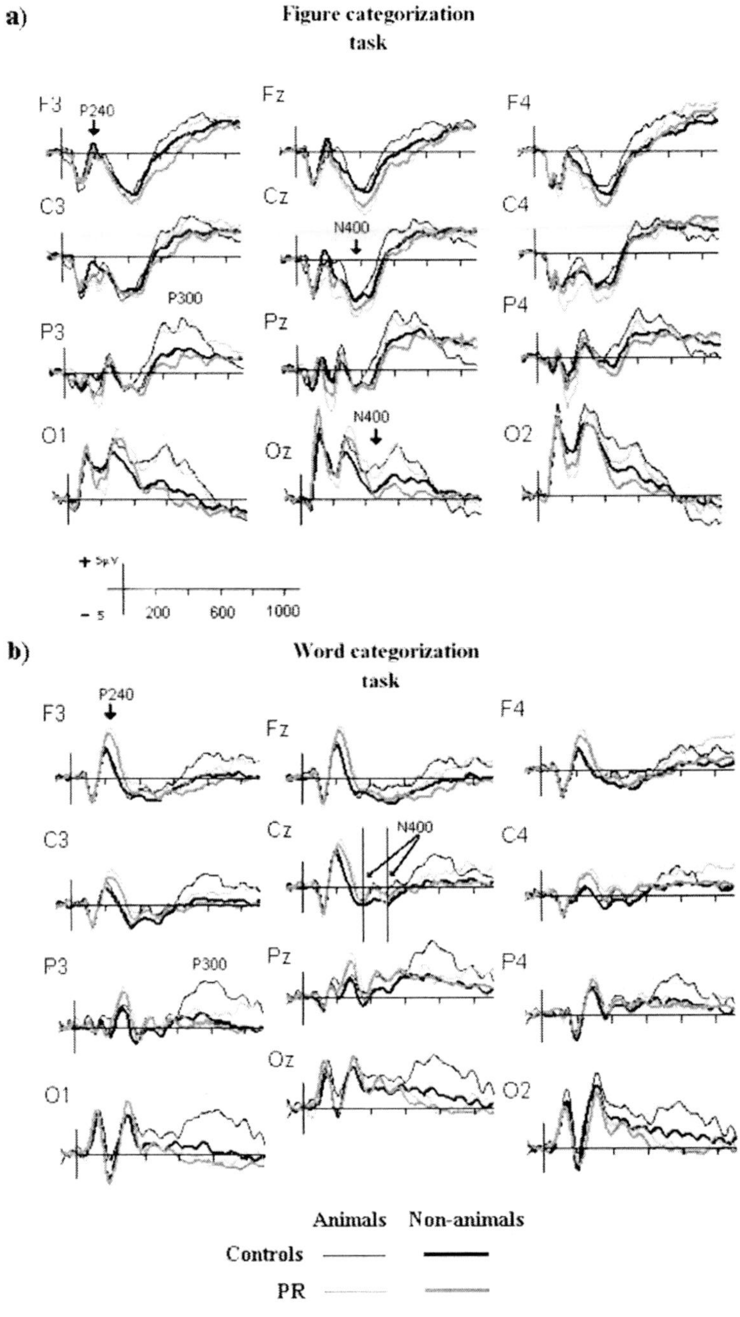

Figure 4. This figure shows: a) grand average ERPs to figures (animal and non-aminal) for poor readers and controls; and b) ERPs to words (animal and non-animal) for both groups. Larger P2 amplitudes and smaller P300 amplitude for poor readers during the word categorization task were observed. Two cursors on both N400 peaks are shown at Cz from 350 to 560ms (based on Silva-Pereyra et al., 2003).

Phonological processes such as accessing a word by first decoding the written symbols into sound representations and phonological coding to maintain information in working memory have been implicated in reading failure (Beitchman and Young, 1997; Wagner and Torgesen, 1987). Deficiencies at the phonological level interfere at least with the activation of word meaning or slow down the semantic information access (Zecker and Zinner, 1987). Poor readers could primarily activate the meanings of words using the phonological route (i.e., conversion grapheme-phoneme before access to the meaning), which could make the whole process even slower. Support for this is Silva-Pereyra's finding that poor readers presented longer reaction times and a higher percentage of errors with respect to the normal readers during the word categorization task. Good readers, on the other hand, primarily activate the meanings of words using the direct route (i.e. without the translation processing from grapheme to phoneme) (Jared et al., 1999). Silva-Pereyra et al.'s (2003) results showed that poor readers also have a larger and longer anterior P2 than controls during the word categorization task. This effect was more pronounced over the left hemisphere and on frontopolar and frontal leads as Bernal and collegues (2000) found using an odd ball paradingm. Right > Left posterior P2 hemisphere asymmetries have been related with better reading skills (Segalowitz et al 1992) and Left > Right anterior P2 asymmetries have been found in children at risk for reading difficulties (Khan et al., 1999). Although there is a controversy about distributional ERP component differences between poor and normal readers, the lateralization of semantic processing with increased age has also been reported (Holcomb et al., 1992). Silva-Pereyra et al.'s (2003) results clearly showed Left > Right P2 asymmetries in the poor readers' group and, in agreement with Khan et al. (1999) this group of population employs less mature strategies for word processing. Even the allocation of more attentional resources could be the expression of an inappropriate strategy.

The maturation of the prefrontal cortex is extremely important during cognitive development (Stauder et al., 1993) and therefore, reading. Segalowitz et al. (1992) argue that poor readers may have difficulty with attentional requirements for visual processing and metacognitive strategies associated with reading, which place a demand on the frontal system. According to Taylor and Smith (1995), the latency of the P2 component decreases with age. This developmental trend could mean that children become faster or that they have more efficient strategies to evaluate stimuli with increasing ages. Khan et al. (1999) observed longer anterior P2 latencies in a group of children at risk for reading difficulties. This observation was replicated in Silva-Pereyra et al.'s study (2003), where poor readers showed longer P2 latencies, which may mirror the use of an immature stimulus evaluation strategy and a deficit to reallocate attentional resources.

Silva-Pereyra and colleagues (2003) did not find differences between normal and poor readers regarding the N400 component during the figure categorization task. Both groups showed an anterior negativity around 445 ms and a posterior negativity around 520 ms. These two negativities have been previously observed during picture priming (Barret and Rugg, 1990) and picture list studies (Coch et al., 2002). Both normal and poor readers showed a more pronounced anterior N400 during figure categorization than during word categorization. These amplitude topographical distribution differences may reflect different cognitive components involved in figure vs. word semantic processing (Holcomb and McPherson, 1994). The point to emphasize here is that Silva-Pereyra et al.'s group of poor readers showed no differences in their performance and N400 component with respect to normal readers during the figure categorization task where access to semantic information is also necessary. Both groups showed a negative dual-peak during the word categorization task that was mainly distributed over central leads. Prior studies have shown that stimuli presented in list form tend to elicit such anteriorly distributed negativities (Nobre and McCarthy, 1994). This finding has also been previously reported by other groups (Coch et al., 2002; Dykman et al. 2000). According to Coch and collegues' explanation, the later peak may mirror a postlexical confidence. The two peaks of the N400 in both normal and poor readers may mirror the postlexical revision necessary to match or mismatch the target (Silva-Pereyra et al., 2003).

The experimental design used in Silva-Pereyra et al.'s (2003) study implied subjects making semantic category decisions with different probabilities of stimulus type in a word (or figure) list presentation. Poor readers displayed larger P300 amplitudes for animals compared to non-animals during the Figure task, as expected, but not during the Word task. The non-significant P300 effect during the Word task in poor readers was interpreted as a less efficient categorization processing of two types of stimuli. A prolonged P300 peak latency in the Word task was also found in poor readers as previous studies have shown (Silva-Pereyra et al. 2001). The decision process in this last study could have produced a large P3 in addition to a previous N400 according to the studies of Halgren (1990) Hill et al., (2002) Nielsen-Bohlman and Knight, (1994) Polich (1985) and Stelmack et al. (1988); or, according to Deacon et al., (2000) a P3 overlapping the N400, which is also sensitive to priming and manipulations of expectancy. However, other studies have shown that such overlapping is only partial (Chwilla et al., 1995; Kutas and Van Petten, 1994) or not at all affected by the P3 component (Nobre and McCarthy, 1994). Previous studies on subjects with dyslexia, reading disabled and/or subjects with attention deficit disorders have also reported an attenuation of the P300 effect (Diniz Jr et al., 1997) and attributed it to less efficient processing systems. P300 latency, on the other hand, seems to reflect stimulus classification speed (Magliero et al., 1984) and it has also been commonly interpreted as reflecting the time needed for stimulus evaluation and memory updating (Polich and Kok, 1995).

Overall, Silva-Pereyra and collaborators' results support the notion that poor readers take more time than controls to update their context model during a word categorization task because their processing system is not fast enough to read the odd trial and accommodate the new information in the previous memory model. The word categorization task used needs both word recognition and semantic processes to allow a decision on whether an item belongs to one or other semantic category. Reading comprehension requires the developing ability to read quickly, accurately and effortlessly (Adams, 1990). Freeing cognitive resources to allow for the integration of a word and their context, which then leads to understanding the meaning of a text (Stanovich, 1980; 1988), may be impaired in poor readers.

P300 and Memory

Poor readers have lower scores than controls during working memory tasks (De Jong, 1998; Isaki and Plante, 1997). Visual (Holcomb et al., 1985) and auditory (Holcomb et al.,

1986) ERP studies have shown that children with attention and reading deficits have smaller and apparently modality-independent-P300s. ERP studies have shown smaller amplitudes and longer latencies of the P300 component in poor readers (Diniz Jr et al., 1997; Holcomb et al., 1985; Ollo and squires, 1986) and in subjects with dyslexia (Taylor and Keenan, 1990). This amplitude attenuation of the P300 component was also observed in children with dyslexia using an oddball auditory paradigm to verbal and non-verbal stimuli (Erez and Pratt, 1992), during a lexical decision task (Taylor and Keenan, 1990) and during a Sternberg task (Barnea et al., 1994). Children with dyslexia also display longer P300 latencies than normal children in all non-alphabetic, alphabetic and lexical decision tasks (Taylor and Keenan, 1990). It has been reported that only adults with dyslexia who have a history of attention-deficit disorder show smaller than normal P300s (Duncan-Johnson et al., 1994). Similar results were also observed in children with learning and reading disabilities (Diniz Jr et al., 1997). Holcomb et al. (1985) found that reading disabled and control subjects could be better differentiated from one another by the amplitude of the P300 when non-target word stimuli were contrasted with nonlinguistic symbols. Symbols elicited larger P300s than words in reading disabled children, while the two kinds of stimuli elicited equivalent amplitudes in controls. Some authors have suggested that the long latencies observed in children with dyslexia and reading disabled children is due to the fact that stimulus evaluation and memory updating takes more time (Holcomb et al., 1985). Considering that, we can claim that a general-purpose mechanism may be involved in the deficiencies of the poor readers. Silva-Pereyra et al. (2001) reported a study in which a Sternberg paradigm and color discrimination tasks were used in order to explore verbal and non-verbal working memory in poor readers. In the Sternberg task, each trial started off with the presentation of a memory set with either 3 or 5 digits. Right after that, a single probe digit was displayed. Subjects had to respond if the probe was or was not in the memory set. Behaviorally, poor readers and normal readers did not differ from one another (i.e., their reaction times did not differ). However, poor readers significantly made more errors with respect to normal readers, replicating what Barnea et al. (1994) have reported. Both groups showed that RTs and the number of errors increased significantly with the increasing set size, as well as for negative with respect to positive probes as other previous Sternberg studies have reported (Barnea et al, 1994; Pelosi et al., 1995; Pratt et al., 1989). The ERP analysis of Silva-Pereyra et al.'s (2001) study showed that neither poor readers nor controls displayed the amplitude decrease expected according to the literature previously mentioned during the Sternberg task. However, a frontal positivity with a mean peak latency of 600 ms after stimulus onset was observed for poor readers when they responded to positive probes during the set 5 condition (see figure 3). The authors argued that these large positivities mirrored a failure in the typical or normal re-allocation of resources postulated by Kramer et al. (1986). Silva-Pereyra et al. (2001) argued that poor readers had to confront an increase in the memory load, but could not take resources that were being used to compare the probe; in this way, subjects were forced to attract extra resources for memory rehearsal, a process that may have been reflected as the frontal positivity. Normal readers, however, did not find the set-5 condition too demanding and did not need to re-allocate resources; therefore, their P300s remained with similar amplitudes. Taylor and Keenan (1990) have also reported a larger frontal P300 in a group of children with dyslexia, compared with normal readers, during a lexical decision task. Moreover, Taylor and Keenan

(1990) found larger amplitudes for the more difficult experimental condition, as opposed to an easy condition.

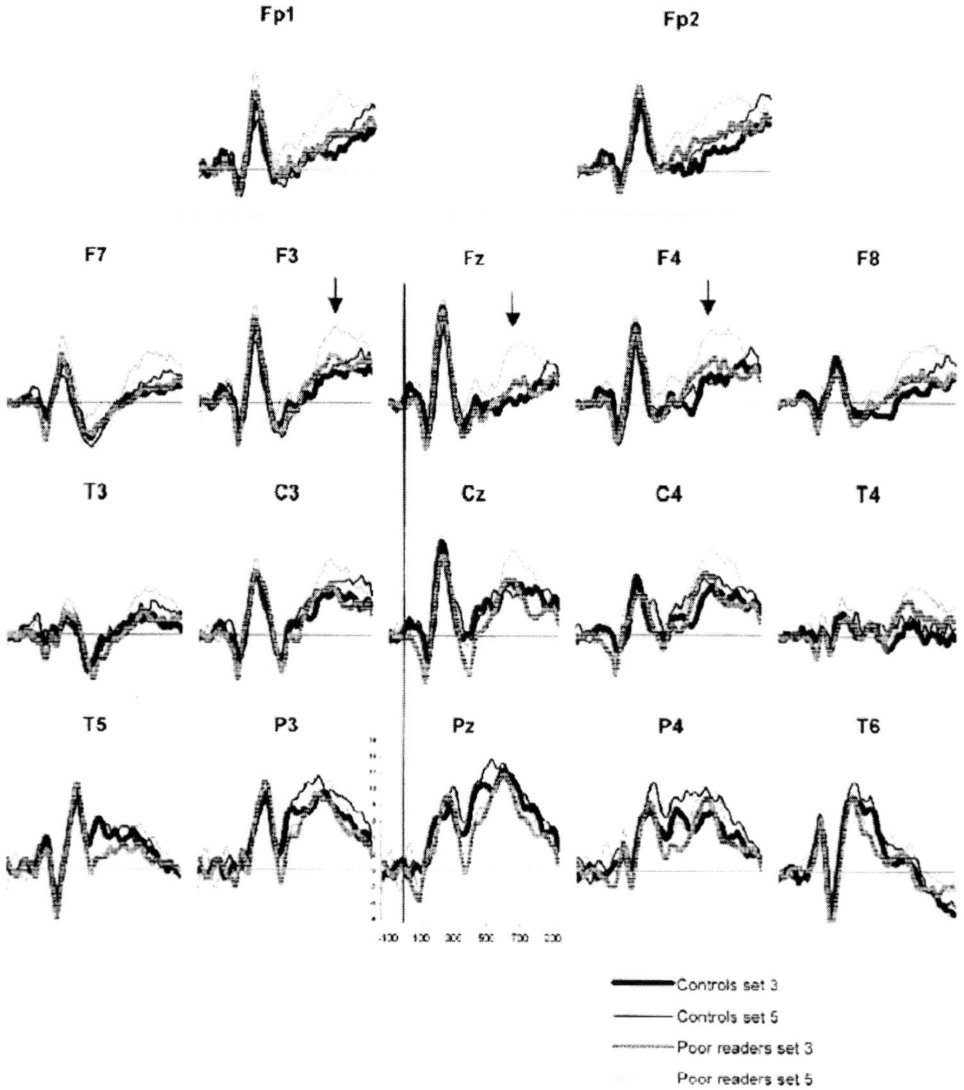

Figure 5. This figure shows grand average ERPs for set 3 and set 5 positive probes in both normal and poor readers. Larger P300 amplitudes for set 5 in poor readers rather than normal readers over frontopolar and central electrode sites have been marked with arrows (based on Silva-Pereyra et al., 2001).

According to the updating model point of view (Polich and Kok, 1995), the behavioral results from the Sternberg task carried out in Silva-Pereyra et al.'s (2001) study support the notion that poor readers have processing deficits only in the evaluation of stimuli but not in the selection of a response. Poor readers' performance is similar to that of children with dyslexia when performing a visual task (Taylor and Keenan, 1990). Both groups of population show processing or encoding impairments with visual stimuli in general (Taylor and Keenan, 1990; Neville et al., 1993). Although subjects with dyslexia may also have some difficulty with the translation of visual information into a speech code (Lovegrove, 1991), they also seem to have deficits in the classification and memory processing of visual stimuli (Holcomb et al., 1985). Poor readers have some difficulty with the translation of visual information into a linguistic code as well as with the retention of such stimuli for continuous evaluation. Lovegrove (1991) claimed that reading disabled children display large and consistent deficits in the functions of the transient visual system. The role of this system in reading is to permit the integration of information from successive fixations and to produce a good temporal resolution (Lovegrove, 1991). The enormous amount of information contained in a given text and the evaluation of a sentence or text updating and understanding may therefore be a lot more difficult for these subjects and may also be reflected as late P300s during memory tasks.

In order to evaluate whether the deficiencies in the poor readers are not exclusive to verbal stimuli, Silva-Pereyra et al. (2001) carried out a second experiment that consisted of a color discrimination task. The task was presented as a video game. Children would drive a spacecraft and he/she had to shoot violet spaceships (V) with one button and other than violet spaceships (green, red, yellow, dark and light blue) with another (O). If the response was correct, the shot spaceship exploded; otherwise, the spaceship would lose gas. The child was told to attempt to keep as much gas as possible. In this task, no significant differences in reaction times between normal and poor readers were found, but longer reaction times for V than O correct shootings were observed in both groups. A higher percent of errors was observed in poor readers with respect to normal readers.

In contrast to the results obtained during the Sternberg task and in agreement with previous studies (Holcomb et al., 1985, Taylor and Keenan, 1990), the group of poor readers from Silva-Pereyra et al.'s (2001) study displayed a smaller P300 over posterior regions and higher amplitudes over anterior areas. Some ERP studies have reported an important relationship between P300 amplitude reduction and manipulations on the difficulty of perceptual processes (Kok, 1986; Ruchkin et al., 1988). Increasing difficulty is usually accompanied by an increase in reaction time and a decrease in response accuracy, and it is assumed to affect primarily early (encoding) processing stages (Sanders, 1980). Kok (1997) also observed a decrease in P300 amplitude as a function of display load. Such effect appeared to be more prominent at posterior scalp sites, which is in agreement with Silva Pereyra et al.'s (2001) findings. Smaller P300 amplitudes in children with dyslexia with respect to controls have been usually interpreted as reflecting a less efficient and less effective processing of task-relevant stimuli (Taylor and Keenan, 1990). Poor readers not only re-allocate resources for high memory demanding tasks, but they do so differently from either normal readers or children with other types of deficits. Poor readers apparently use fewer resources over posterior regions and a higher amount over frontal areas. Perhaps these re-allocation differences are due to deficits in the early temporal evaluation of visual stimuli as was claimed by Lovegrove (1991). Silva-Pereyra et al. (2001) claim that such a deficiency could be independent of linguistic stimuli because, in their study, linguistic processing could be avoided during the color discrimination task. In other words, poor readers challenged in this task seem to be related to a more general target identification deficit.

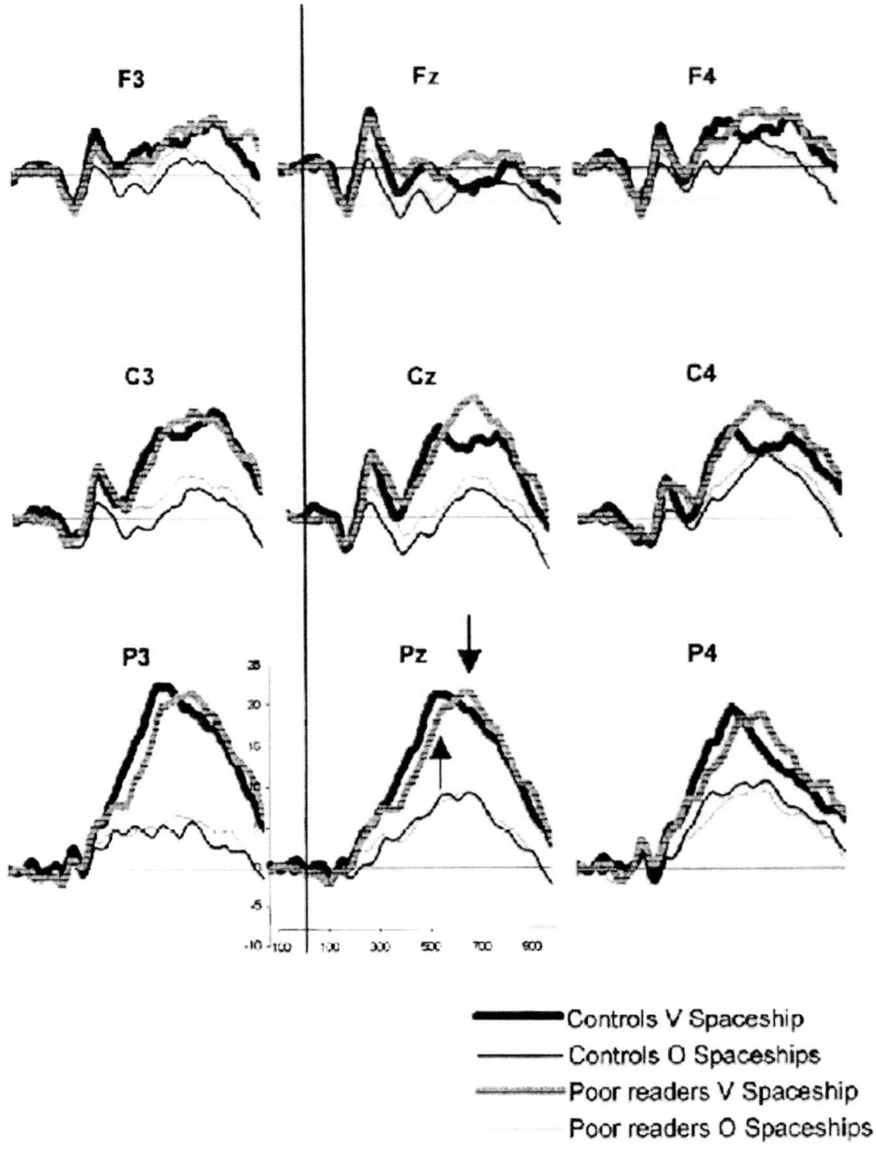

Figure 6. This figure shows grand average ERPs to both V and O spaceships of normal and poor readers. Arrows over P300s peak on Pz were marked to highlight differences in latency (based on Silva-Pereyra et al., 2001).

Longer P300 peak latencies in poor readers rather than normal readers have been found during verbal working memory tasks (Barnea et al., 1994; Silva-Pereyra et al., 2001), lexical decision tasks (Taylor and Keenan, 1990) and oddball paradigms (Iragui et al., 1993; Holcomb et al., 1986). Silva-Pereyra et al (2001) have found longer P300 latencies in poor readers during color discrimination task as is shown in figure 6, which may suggest that the time needed to identify a target stimulus is longer for these children. Prolonged latencies in poor readers with respect to controls have been observed independently of set size or probe type in the Sternberg paradigm (Diniz et al. 1997; Silva-Pereyra et al., 2001). Taking into consideration the hypothesis of a low memory capacity as one of the deficits in poor readers (Swanson et al., 1996), and given that the poor readers showed longer latencies for both set sizes in comparison with normal readers, it is possible to consider that, for these children, even 3 digits was too large a number to identify, recognize or remember.

CONCLUSION

A low verbal working memory capacity has been postulated as one of the most important factors influencing performance in poor readers. Although the single resource verbal working memory theory is still under debate, there is further evidence that points out to support an interaction between grammaticality, syntactic complexity, memory load and word span. An increase in demands of an individual's working memory seems to have an effect over specific-purpose-mechanism ERP components such as the P600 and N400. Semantic processing also seems to be affected by a highly loaded working memory. However, although poor readers may appear as underachievers in semantic tasks, it may not be because of a semantic processing deficit itself (Waterman and Lewandowski, 1994). Silva-Pereyra et al.'s (in press) study suggests that poor readers have deficiencies very early in the processing of words. Every word presented is a challenge for these children because it takes them a long time and much effort to read, although when finally read, they can immediately decide the semantic category to which the word belongs. Poor readers seem to use less efficient and more demanding strategies to process words. These strategies consume extra attentional resources and seem to be slow, with the subject storing and accommodating new difficult information into a memory model before the next trial arrives. The most invasive deficit that poor readers face when reading seems to take place very early, probably at the first encounter with the processing of graphemes. In this way a chain reaction of general slowness is triggered. The reason why "graphemes" trigger such complex and non-efficient processing remains elusive. In the same line, Silva-Pereyra et al. (2001) show that poor readers have longer P300 latencies than normal readers during both verbal and non-verbal tasks. Their results suggest that poor readers experience difficulty in the temporal processing of visual information, stimulus evaluation as well as in the retention of these visual stimuli for continuous processing. The fact that ERP latency differences were also observed during verbal and non-verbal tasks, suggests that poor readers' enconding deficiencies go beyond linguistic stimuli processing. Poor readers also displayed greater P300 amplitude over frontal regions than normal readers during the Sternberg task and smaller posterior P300 amplitude during the spaceships task. The results may reflect a higher degree of difficulty in the Sternberg task and perhaps some alteration in the re-allocation of resources in both tasks.

The great amount of skills required for reading and the possibility that poor readers do not constitute a homogeneous population makes the issue of targeting the causing factor very challenging. As explored in this chapter, both behavioral and ERP research hold promising empirical evidence that inform theory. Clinical and basic research await further support in order to be able to intervene appropriately.

REFERENCES

Ackerman, P.T., Dykman, R.A. and Garner, M.I., (1990). Counting rate, naming rate, phonological sensitive and memory span: major factors in severe dyslexia. Journal of *Learning Disabilities.* 23, 325-27.

Adams, M.J. (1990) *Beginning to read: Thinking and learning about print.* Cambridge, MIT press

Avecilla-Ramirez, G. Silva-Pereyra, J. Harmony, T. and Sanchez, L. (2003) Working memory capacity in semantic and syntactic process in poor readers. *Poster presented at the tenth Annual Meeting of Cognitive Neuroscience Society.* New York, NY.

Baddeley, A. (1992) Working Memory: The interface between Memory and Cognition. *Journal of Cognitive Neuroscience.* 4,3, 281-288.

Baddeley, A. (1998). *Human memory. Theory and practice.* Allyn & Bacon Press, USA. pp. 85-101.

Baldeweg, T., Richardson, A., Watkins, S., Foale, C. and Gruzelier, J. (1999) Impaired auditory frequency discrimination in dyslexia detected with mismatch evoked potentials. *Annals of Neurology.* 45:495-503.

Barnea, A., Lamm, O., Epstein, R. and Pratt, H. (1994). Brain potentials from dyslexics children recorded during short-term memory tasks. *International Journal of Neurosciences.* 74, 227-237.

Barret, S.E. and Rugg, M.D. (1990) Event-related potentials and the semantic matching of pictures. *Brain and Cognition.* 14: 201-212.

Beitchman, J.H. and Young, A.R. (1997). Learning Disorders with a special emphasis on reading disorders: A review of the past 10 years. *Journal of the American Academy of Child ans Adolescent Psychiatry.* 36. 1020-32.

Ben-Dror, I., Bentin, S. and Frost, R. (1995) Semantic, phonologic, and morphologic skills in reading disabled and normal children: Evidence fron perception and production of spoken *Hebrew Reading Research Quarterly.* 30: 876-893.

Bentin, S., McCarthy, G. and Wood, C.C. (1985) Event related potentials, lexical decision and semantic priming. *Electroencephalography and Clinical Neurophysiology.* 60:343-355.

Bernal, J., Harmony, T., Rodriguez, M., Reyes, A., Yanez, G., Fernandez, T., Galan, L., Silva, J., Fernandez, Bouzas, A., Rodriguez, H., Guerrero, V. and Marosi, E. (2000) Auditory event related potentials in poor readers. *International Journal of Psycho-physiology.* 36: 11-23.

Brown C, Hagoort P. (1993). The processing nature of the N400: Evidence from masked priming. *Journal of Cognitive Neuroscience.* 1993, 51: 34-44.

Byrne, B. (1981) Deficient syntactic control in poor readers: Is a weak phonetic memory code responsible? *Applied Psycholinguist.* 2: 201-212.

Canseco-González, E., Love, T., Ahrens, K., Walenski, M., Swinney, D., & Neville, H. (1997). Processing of grammatical information in jabberwocky sentences: An ERP study. Poster presented at the fourth *Annual Meeting of Cognitive Neuroscience Society*. Boston.

Champion, A. (1997) Knowledge of suffixed words: A comparison of reading disabled and nondisabled readers. *Annals of Dyslexia,* 47: 29-55.

Chwilla, D., Brown, C. and Hagoort, P. (1995) The N400 as a function of the level processing. *Psychophysiology*. 32: 274-285.

Chwilla D., Hagoort P. and Brown C. (1998) The mechanism underlying backward priming in a lexical decision task. Spreading activation versus semantic matching. *Quart Journal of Experimental Psychology*. 51A: 531-560.

Chwilla D., Kolk H. and Mulder G. (2000) Mediated priming in the lexical decision task: Evidence from event-related potentials and reaction time. *Journal of Memory and Language*. 42: 314-341.

Coch, D. Maron, L., Wolf, M. and Holcomb, P.J. (2002) Word and picture processing in children: An event related potential study. *Developmental Neuropsychology*. 22: 373-406.

Coulson, S. King, J., and Kutas, M. (1998) Expect the unexpected: Event-related brain response to morphosyntactic violations. *Language and Cognitive Processes. 13*, 21-58.

Csepe,V. and Gyurkocza E.E. (2001) Abnormal mismatch negativity to phonetic deviations in developmental dyslexia. *Developmental Neuropsychology*.

Daneman, M. andCarpenter, P.A. (1980) Individual differences in working memory and reading. *Journal of Verbal Learning and Verbal Behavior*, 19, 450-466.

De Jong, P.F. (1998) Working memory deficits of reading disabled children. *Journal of Experimental Child Psychology*. 70: 75-96.

Deacon, D., Hewitt, S., Yang, C.M. and Nagata, M. (2000) Event-related potential indices of semantic priming using masked and unmasked words: Evidence that the N400 does not reflect a post-lexical process. *Cognitive Brain Research*. 9: 137-146.

Diniz Jr, J., Mangabeira-Albernaz, P.L., Munhoz, M.S. and Fukuda, Y. (1997) Cognitive potentials in children with learning disabilities. *Acta Otolaryngological (Stockh).*, 117: 211-3.

Dixon, P., LeFevre, J. and Twillwey, L.C. (1988) Word Knowledge and working memory as predictors of reading skill. *Journal of Educational Psychology*. 80, 465-472.

Donchin, E. and Coles, M. (1988) Is the P3 component a manifestation of context updating?. *Behavioral and Brain Sciences*. 11, 355-372.

Donchin, E., Karis, D., Bashore, T.R., Coles, M. and Gratton, G. (1986) Cognitive psychophysiology and human information processing. In M.G.H. Coles, E. Donchin, S.W. Porges (Eds), *Psychophysiology: Systems, processes and applications* (pp.244-267), New York, The Guilford Press.

Dykman, R.A., Akerman, P.T., Loizou, P.C. and Casey, P.H. (2000) An event-related potential study of older children with an early history of failure to thrive. *Developmental Neuropsychology*. 18:187-212.

Erez, A. and Pratt, H. (1992) Auditory event-related potentials among dyslexic and normal-reading children 3CLT and midline comparisons. *International Journal of Neuro-sciences.* 63, 247-264.

Friederici, A. (1995) The time course of syntactic activation during language processing: A model based on neuropsychological and neurophysiological data. *Brain and Language,* 50, 259-281.

Friederici, A., Hahne, A. and Mecklinger, A. (1996) Temporal structure of syntactic parsing: Early and late event-related brain potential effects elicited by syntactic anomalies. *Journal of Experimental Psychology: Learning, Memory and Cognition*, 22, 1219-1248.

Friederici, A., Hahne, A. and Saddy, D. (2002) Distinct neurophysiological patterns reflectins aspects of syntactic complexity and syntactic repair. *Journal of Psycholinguistic Research.* 31 45-63.

Friederici, A., Mecklinger, A., Spencer, K., Steinhauer, K. and Donchin, E. (2001) Syntactic parsing preferences and their on-line revisions: a spatio-temporal analysis of event-related brain potentials. *Cognitive Brain Research.* 11, 305-323.

Friederici, A., Wang, Y., Herrmann C., Maess B. and Oertel U. (2000). Localization of Early Syntactic Processes in Frontal and Temporal Cortical Areas: A Magneto-encephalographic Study. *Human Brain Mapping*, 11, 1-11.

Friedman, D., Putnam, L. and Sutton, S. (1990) Longitudinal and cross-sectional comparisons of young children's cognitive ERPs and behavior in a picture-matching task: Preliminary findings. *International Journal of Psychophysiology* 8: 213-321.

García-Larrea, L. and Cézanne-Bert, G. (1998) P3, Positive slow wave and working memory load: a study on the functional correlates of slow wave activity. *Electroencephalography and Clinical Neurophysiology.*108, 260-273.

Gillon, G. and Dodd, B. (1994) A prospective study of relationship between phonological, semantic and syntactic skills and specific reading disability. *Reading and Writing*, 6:321-345.

Günter, T., Jackson J.L. and Mulder, G. (1995) Language, memory and aging: an electrophysiological exploration of the N400 during reading of memory-demanding sentences. *Psychophysiology*, 32(3): 215-229.

Günter, T.C., Friederici, A.D. and Hahne, A. (1999) Brain responses during sentence reading: visual input affects central processes. *NeuroReport*, 10. 3175-3178.

Günter, T., Stowe, L. and Mulder, G. (1997) When Syntax meets semantics. *Psychophysiology.* 34, 660-676.

Hahne, A. and Friederici, A. (1999) Electrophysiological evidence for two steps in syntactic analysis: Early automatic and late controlled processes. *Journal of Cognitive Neuroscience*, 11, 194-205.

Hahne, A., Schroeger, E. and Friederici AD. (2002) Segregating early physical and syntactic processes in auditory sentence comprehension. *NeuroReport.* 13(3):305-309.

Halgren E. (1990) Insights from Evoked potentials into the neuropsychological mechanisms of reading. In: Scheibel AB, Wechsler AF, editors. *Neurobiology of higher cognitive function.* Guilford Press, New York, pp.103-150.

Hill, H., Strube, M., Roesch-Ely, D. and Weisbrod, M. (2002) Automatic vs. controlled processes in semantic priming differentiation by event-related potentials. *International Journal of Psychophysiology*. 44: 197-218.

Hillyard, S.A. and Picton, T.W. (1987) Electrophysiology of cognition. In: Plum, F. (Ed) *Handbook of Physiology*, American Physiological Society. Washington, DC. pp.519-584.

Holcomb P. (1988) Automatic and attentional processing: An event-related brain potential analysis of semantic priming. *Brain and Language*. 1988, 35: 66-85.

Holcomb, P., Ackerman, P. and Dykman, R. (1985) Cognitive event-related brain potentials in children with attention and reading deficits. *Psychophysiology*. 22, 656-667.

Holcomb, P., Ackerman, P. and Dykman, R. (1986) Auditory event-related brain potentials in attention and reading disabled boys. *International Journal of Psychophysiology*. 3, 266-273.

Holcomb, P.J., Coffey, S.A, and Neville, H. (1992) Visual and auditory sentence processing: A developmental analysis using event-related brain potentials. *Developmental Neuropsychology*. 8: 203-241.

Holcomb, P.J. and McPherson, W.B. (1994) Event-related brain potentials reflect semantic priming in an object decision task *Brain and Cognition*. 24: 259-276.

Iragui, V.J., Kutas, K., Mitchiner, M.R. and Hillyard, S.A. (1993) Effects of aging on event-related brain potentials and reaction times in an auditory oddball task. *Psychophysiology* 30, 10-22.

Isaki, E. and Plante, E. (1997) Short-term and Working memory differences in language/learning disabled and normal adults. *Journal of Communication Disorders*. 30, 427-36.

Jared, D., Levy, B.A. and Rayner, K. (1999) The role of phonology in the activation of word meanings during reading: evidence from proofreading and eye movements. *Journal of Experimental Psychology: General*. 128: 219-64.

Johnson, Jr. R., (1989) Developmental evidence for modality dependent P300 generators: a normative study. *Psychophysiology*. 26, 651-667.

Johnson, R. (1988) The amplitude of the P300 component of the event-related potential: review and synthesis. In Ackles, J.R. Jennings and M.G.H. Coles (Eds) *Advances in Psychophysiology: A Research Annual,* Vol 3 (pp. 69-137). Greenwich, CT: JAI Press, Inc.

Juottonen, K., Rebonsuo, A. and Lang, H. (1996) Dissimilar age influences on two ERP waveforms (LPC and N400) reflecting semantic context effect. *Brain Research and Cognition. Brain Research*. 4: 99-107.

Just, M. and Carpenter, P. (1992) A capacity theory of comprehension: individual differences in working memory. *Psychological Review*. 99, 122-149.

Khan, S.C., Frisk, V. and Taylor, M. (1999) Neurophysiological measures of reading difficulty in very-low-birthweight children. *Psychophysiology*, 36: 76-85.

Kluneder, R. and Kutas, M. (1993) Bridging the gap: Evidence from ERPs on the processing of unbounded dependencies. *Journal of Cognitive Neuroscience*. 5 196-214.

Kok, A. (1986) Effects of degradation of visual stimuli on components of the vent-related potential (ERP) in Go/no go reaction tasks. *Biological Psychology* 23, 21-38.

Kok, A. (1997) Event-related potentials (ERP) reflections of mental resources: a review and synthesis. *Biological Psychology* 45, 19-56.

Kolk, H., Chwilla, D., Van Herten, M. And Oor P. (2003) Structure and limited capacity in verbal working memory: A study with event-related potentials. *Brain and Language*.85, 1-36.

Kramer, A.F. Schneider, W. Fisk. A.D. and Donchin, E. (1986) The effects of practice and task structure on components of the event-related brain potential. *Psychophysiology*. 23, 33-47.

Kramer, A.F. and Strayer, D.L. (1988) Assessing the development of automatic processing : An application of dual-track and event-related brain potential methodologies. *Biological Psychology* 26, 231-267.

Kujala, T. and Naatanen, R. (2001) The mismatch negativity in evaluating central auditory dysfunction in dyslexia. *Neuroscience and Biobehavioral Reviews* 25:535-543.

Kutas M. and Federmeier K. (2000) Electrophysiology reveals semantic memory use in language comprehension. *Trends in Cognitive Sciences*. 4: 463-470.

Kutas, M. and Hillyard, S. (1980) Reading senseless sentences: Brian potentials reflect semantic incongruenty. *Science* 207:203-204.

Kutas, M. and van Petten, C.K. (1994) Psycholinguistics electrified. In: Gernsbacher, M.A. (Ed.), *Handbook of psycholinguistics*. Academic Press New York, pp.83-143.

Leppanen P., Pihko E., Eklund K.M., Guttorm, T.K., Aro, M., Richardson, U. and Lyytinen, H.(2001) Brain responses reveal speech processing differences in infants at risk for dyslexia. *Developmental Neuropsychology*.

Lovegrove, W.J. (1991) Is the question of the role of visual deficits as a cause of reading disabilities a close one? Comments on Hulme. *Cognitive Neuropsychology*. 8, 435-441.

Luck, S.J. and Hillyard, S.A. (1994) Electrophysiological correlates of feature detection during visual search. *Psychophysiology*, 31: 291-308.

Magliero, A., Bashore, T.R., Coles, M. and Donchin, E., (1984) On the dependence of P300 latency on stimulus evaluation processes. *Psychophysiology* 21, 171-186.

McCarthy, G. and Donchin, E. (1981) A metric for thought: a comparison of P300 latency and reaction time. *Science* 211, 77-80.

Münte, T., Heinze, H. and Mangun, G. (1993) Dissociation of brain activity related to syntactic and semantic aspects of language. *Journal of Cognitive Neuroscience*, 5, 335-344.

Munte, T., Szentkuti, A., Wieringa, B.Matzke, M. and Johanes, S. (1997) Human brain potentials to reading syntactic errors in sentences of different complexity. *Neuroscience Letters*. 235, 105-108.

Näätänen, R., Gaillard, A.W.K. and Mäntysalo, S. (1978) Early selective attention effects on the evoked potential: a critical review and reinterpretation. *Biological Psychology* 8, 81-136.

Neville, H., Coffey, S., Holcomb, P. and Tallal, P. (1993) The neurobiology of sensory and language processing in language-impaired children. *Journal of Cognitive Neuroscience*, 5:2, 235-253.

Neville, H., Mills, D. and Lawson, D. (1992) Fractionating language: Different neural subsystems with different sensitive periods. *Cerebral Cortex, 2,* 244-258.

Neville, H., Nicol, J., Brass, A., Forters, K., & Garret, M. (1991) Syntactically based sentence processing classes: Evidence from event-related brain potentials. *Journal of Cognitive Neuroscience,* 3, 151-165.

Niclscn-Bohlman, L. and Knight, R. (1994) Electrophysiological dissociation of rapid memory mechanisms in humans. *NeuroReport,* 5: 1517-1521.

Nobre, A.C. and McCarthy, G. (1994) Language-related ERPs: scalp distributions and modulation by word type and semantic priming. *Journal of Cognitive Neuroscience*. 6: 233-255.

Ollo, C. and Squires, N. (1986). Event-related potentials in learning disabilities. In R.Q., Cracco and I. Bodis-Wollner (Eds.) *Evoked Potentials*. (Vol. 3 pp. 497 512). New York: Alan R Liss, Inc.

Osterhout, L. and Holcomb, P. (1992). Event –related brain potentials elicited by syntactic anomaly. *Journal of Memory and Language*. 31, 785-806.

Osterhout, L. and Holcomb, P. (1993) Event related potentials and syntactic anomaly: Evidence of anomaly detection during the perception of continuous speech. *Language and Cognitive Processes,* 8, 413-437.

Osterhout, L., McKinnon, R., Bersick, M and Corey V. (1996) On the language-specifityu of the brain response to syntactic anomalies: Is the syntactic positive shift a member of the P300 family? *Journal of Cognitive Neuroscience,* 8, 507-526.

Pelosi, L., Hayward, M. and Blumhardt, L. (1995) Is memory-scanning time in the Sternberg paradigm reflected in the latency of event-related potentials? *Electroencephalography and Clinical Neurophysiology*. 96, 44-55.

Polich, J. (1985) Semantic categorization and event-related potentials. *Brain and Language*. 26: 304-21.

Polich, J., Ladish, C. and Burns, T. (1990) Normal variation of P300 in children: Age, memory span, and head size. *International Journal of Psychophysiology*. 9, 237-248.

Polich, J. and Kok, A. (1995) Cognitive and biological determinants of P300: An integrative review. *Biological Psychology*. 41: 103-146.

Pratt, H., Michalewski, H., Barret, G. and Starr, A. (1989) Brain potentials in a memory-scaning task. I. Modality and task effects on potentials to the probes? *Electroencephalography and Clinical Neurophysiology*. 72, 407-421.

Rayner, K. and Pollatsek, A. (1989) *The psychology of reading*. Prentice Hall Englewood Cliffs. N.J. p. 529.

Rösler, F., Friederici, A., Pütz, P. and Hahne, A. (1993) Event-related brain potentials while encountering semantic and syntactic constraint violation. *Journal of Cognitive Neuroscience,* 5, 345-362.

Ruchkin, D., Johnson, Jr. R., Canoune, H., Ritter, W. and Hammer, M. (1990) Multiple sources of P3b associated with different types of information. *Psychophysiology*, 27, 157-176.

Ruchkin, Jonhson, Jr. R., Mahaffey, D. and Sutton, S. (1988) Towards a functional categorization of slow waves. *Psychophysiology*. 25, 339-353.

Sanders, A.F. (1980) Stage analysis of reaction processes. In G.E. Stelmach, J. Requin (Eds). *Tutorials in Motor Behavior* (pp. 331-354). Amsterdam, North Holland.

Schulte-Korne, G., Deimel, W., Bartling, J. and Remschidt H. (1998) Auditory processing and dyslexia: evidence fro a specific speech processing deficit. *NeurReport* 9:337-40.

Segalowitz, S.J., Wagner, W.J. and Menna, R. (1992) Lateral vs. Frontal ERP predictors of reading skill, *Brain and Cognition*. 20, 85-103.

Silva-Pereyra, J., Fernández, T., Díaz-Comas, L., Harmony, T., Fernández-Bouzas, A., Bernal, J., Rodríguez, M., Rivera-Gaxiola, M. and Marosi, E. (2001). Delayed P300 during color discrimination and Stenberg tasks in Poor Readers. *International Journal of Psychophysiology*. 40, 17-32.

Silva-Pereyra, J., Harmony T, Villanueva, G., Fernandez, T., Rodriguez, M., Galan, L., Diaz-Comas, L., Bernal, J., Fernandez-Bouzas, A., Marosi, E., and Reyes A. (1999) N400 and lexical decisions: Automatic or controlled processing? *Clinical Neurophysiology*. 100, 813-824.

Silva-Pereyra, J., Rivera-Gaxiola, M. Fernández, T., Díaz-Comas, L., Harmony, T., Fernández-Bouzas, A., Bernal, J., Rodríguez, M. and Marosi, E. (2003) Are poor readers semantically challenged? An event-related brain potential assessment. *International Journal of Psychophysiology,* 49(3); 187-199.

Smulders, F.T., Kok, A., Kenemans, J.L. and Bashore, T.R. (1995) The temporal selectivity of additive factors effects on the reaction process revealed in ERP component latencies. *Acta Psychologica*, 90, 97-109.

Stanovich, K.E. (1980) Toward an interactive-compensatory model of individual differences in the development of reading fluency. *Reading Research Quarterly*, 16:32-71.

Stanovich, K.E. (1988) Explaining the differences between the dyslexic and the garden-variety poor reader: the phonological-core variable-difference model. *Journal of Learning Disabilities* 21, 590-604.

Stauder, J.E.A., Molenaar, P.C.M. and van der Molen, M.W. (1993) Scalp topography of event-related brain potentialsand cognitive transition during childhood. *Child Development*. 64: 769-788.

Stelmack, R.M., Saxe, B.J., Noldy-Cullum, N., Campbell, K.B. and Armitage, R. (1988) Recognition memory for words and event-related potentials: a comparison of normal and disabled readers. *Journal of Clinical and Experimental Neuropsychology*. 10: 185-200.

Swanson, H.L. (1992). Generality and modifiability of working memory among skilled and less skilled readers. *Journal of Educational Psychology* 84, 473-488.

Swanson, H.L. and Sachse, L.C. (2001) A subgroup analysis of working memory in children with reading disabilities: Domain-general or domain specific deficiency? *Journal of Learning Disabilities*. 34:249-263.

Swanson, H.L. (1994). Short-term memory and working memory: Do both contributed to our understanding of academic achievement in children and adults with learning disabilities? *Journal of Learning Disabilities*. 27, 34-50.

Swanson, H.L., Ashbaker, M.H. and Lee, C. (1996) Learning-disabled readers' working memory as a function of processing demands. *Journal of Experimental Child Psychology*. 61, 242-275.

Swanson, H.L., Cochran, K. and Ewers, C. (1989) Working memory in skilled and less skilled readers. *Journal of Abnormal. Child. Psychology*. 17, 145-156.

Tallal, P., Miller, S. and Fich, H. (1993) Neurobiological basis of speech. A case of the preeminence of temporal processing. In: P. Tallal, A. Galaburda, R. Lllinás and C. Von Euler (Eds.), *Temporal information processing in the nervous system: special reference to dyslexia and dysphasia*. Vol., 682, Ann. N.Y. Acad. Sci., New York, pp. 27-47.

Taylor, M.J. and Keenan, N.K. (1990) Event-related potentials to visual and language stimuli in normal and dyslexic children. *Psychophysiology*, 27: 318-327.

Taylor, M.J. and Khan, S.C. (2000) Top-down modulation of early selective attention processes in children. *International Journal of Psychophysiology*. 37: 135-147.

Taylor, M.J. and Smith, M.L. (1995) Maturational changes in the ERPs to verbal and nonverbal memory tasks *J. Psychophysiology*. 9: 283-297.

Torgesen, J.K. (1985) Memory processes in reading disabled children. *Journal of Learning disabilities*. 21: 604-612.

Underwood, G. and Batt, V. (1996) *Reading and Understanding: An Introduction to the Psychology of reading*. Blackwell Publishers, UK.

Vellutino, F.R. and Scanlon, D.M. (1985) Free recall of concrete and abstract words in poor and normal readers. *Journal of Experimental Child Psychology*. 39: 363-380.

Vellutino, F.R., Scanlon, D.M. and Spearing, D. (1995) Semantic and phonological coding in poor and normal readers. *Journal of Experimental Child Psychology*. 59: 76-123.

Vellutino, F.R., Scanlon, D.M. and Tanzman, M.S. (1988) Lexical memory in poor and normal readers. *Canadian Journal of Psychology*. 42: 216-242.

Vos, S.H., Gunter, T.C. Kolk, H., and Mulder, G. (2001) Working memory constraints on syntactic processing: An electrophysiological investigation. *Psychophysiology*. 38, 41-63.

Wagner, R. and Torgesen, J.K. (1987) The nature of phonological processing and its casual role in the acquisition of reading skill. *Psychological Bulletin*. 101: 192-212.

Waterman, B. and Lewandowski, L. (1993) Phonological and semantic processing in reading-disabled and nondisabled males at two age levels. *Journal of Experimental Child Psychology*. 55: 87-103.

Waterman, B. and Lewandowski, L. (1994) Orthographic, phonologic and semantic processing in reading-disabled and nondisabled subjects. *Perceptual and Motor Skills*. 79:35-45.

Waters, G. and Caplan D. (1996) The capacity theory of sentence comprehension: Critique of Just and Carpenter (1992). *Psychological Review*. 4, 761-772.

Zecker, S.G. and Zinner, T.E. (1987) Semantic code deficit for reading disabled children on auditory lexical decision task. *Journal of Reading and Behavior*. 19: 177-189.

In: Trends in Dyslexia Research
Editor: Henry D. Tobias, pp. 151-167
ISBN 1-59454-219-8

Chapter VI

ASSESSMENT AND TREATMENT OF ACQUIRED BILINGUAL ALEXIA: A CASE STUDY OF A SPANISH-ENGLISH SPEAKER

***Marina Laganaro** *and Mary Overton Venet*†**
University Hospitals of Geneva and Faculty of Psychology
University of Geneva

ABSTRACT

This paper describes a single-subject study aimed at evaluating the characteristics of an acquired reading impairment observed in bilingual speaker. In an earlier study (Laganaro & Overton Venet, 2000), a first study was presented in which in-depth evaluation of the patient's alexic disturbance was carried out in both languages. Results showed a high degree of parallelism in the reading impairment in both languages, both from a quantitative and qualitative point of view, with traits of letter-by-letter and aphasic alexia in both languages, English and Spanish. The second part of the study addressed therapy: the patient received an intensive alternating computer-assisted home-based remediation programme using a crossover AB-BA design aimed at improving his reading: therapy A consisted of tasks aimed at inhibiting letter-by- letter reading. This was alternated with therapy B which was designed to train phonological assembly. Results showed transfer of gains between languages when common reading processes were involved and language-specific gains with the phonological tasks.

In this paper, further outcome data is presented involving the same patient, in which we report assessment in both Spanish and English one-year after conclusion of the prior study. No change was observed compared to the earlier evaluation. In a further study at 2 ½ years after prior therapy, we specifically identify which deficits co-occur in the two

* Marina Laganaro, Service de Rééducation, Hôpitaux Universitaires de Genève, Av. Beau-Séjour 26, CH-1211 Genève 14, E-mail: marina.laganaro@hcuge.ch

† Mary Overton Venet, Faculté de Psychologie et Sciences de l'Education, Université de Genève, Bvd. Pont d'Arve 40, CH-1205 Genève, E-mail: Mary.OvertonVenet@pse.unige.ch

languages, and we examine whether there has been further spontaneous improvement. Furthermore, we present a programme of experimental therapy and evaluate its contribution to further gains, replicating the assessment and therapy methodology from the earlier study. Taken together, our results only partially support the hypothesis that transfer of gains occurs in areas where two languages are structurally similar. The question of generalization of treatment from one language to another as a function of the orthographic systems of the languages and the implications of these results regarding language choice in bilingual aphasia therapy are discussed.

Keywords: alexia, bilingual, treatment, generalisation

INTRODUCTION

Bilingual aphasia has given rise to much research interest since the beginnings of aphasia studies (Pitres, 1895, see Paradis, 1983 for a compilation of early studies). Despite this early interest, and despite the fact that bilinguals are not an exceptional population, clinical aphasia assessment and rehabilitation is carried out mostly in one language only. Many factors in fact challenge the management of bilingual or polyglot aphasic patients; these are related to clinicians' competence, to type of bilingualism in terms of skills and use, to language properties and to effects of treatment (Roberts, 1998). In the present chapter, we will focus on some aspects of acquired bilingual alexia by means of a single-case study of an Spanish-English bilingual speaker. Before discussing our studies, we will introduce some aspects of bilingualism and alexia.

Bilingual Alexia

Reports by Grosjean (1982) estimate at 50% and over the number of bilingual or mutilingual speakers world-wide. Wiener et al.'s (1995) study provides empirical data on the incidence of multilingualism in a large New York out-patient department, which provides some precious information about the linguistic abilities, and amongst these, the pre-morbid reading/writing practices of the multilingual individuals who were referred for speech therapy intervention. This study provides evidence of huge disparities in competence in each language, in the real functional use of each language in every day living, and in particular indicates the existence of specialized areas of bilingual proficiency in either language, this being particularly true for reading and writing skills. It appears therefore crucial that assessment of bilingual alexia should include information on pre-morbid functionality and effective use of each language (see, for example, the questionnaire proposed by Grosjean, 2003).

Indeed, case studies show that functional use of a language at the time of a stroke, as well as other variables, including early acquisition and literacy in a language, are some of the determining factors that favourably influence recovery in cases of bilingual reading and writing disorder.

In the history of bilingual alexia, a considerable number of case studies have described patients displaying recovery patterns of different kinds. In his review, Paradis (1989) reports

8 cases of acquired reading/writing disorder in bilinguals. Five of them display differential recovery, two have parallel recovery and one has a selective recovery. Recent case descriptions also focus on similarity or difference in reading performance between the bilingual's languages. In their study, Sasanuma and Park (1993) report two cases of parallel impairment in Japanese-Korean bilingual alexics. These two languages have two distinct scriptal systems: logographic (kanji) and symbols representing phonological units (kana/hangul). Both patients displayed parallel reading impairment. Patient 2 is of particular interest, since he presented a selective impairment in the ability to recover phonology from print in both languages, whereas he was far better at reading kanju characters in both Japanese and Korean. Béland and Minouni (2001) also describe a parallel alexia in the case of a French-speaking man whose mother tongue was Lebanese Arabic. The experiments conducted on the reading impairment in each language offer insights into the parallelism of a disorder despite the radical differences between the two languages in terms of their orthographic systems, in particular script direction and degree of opacity. Their patient displayed features of a deep dylexic syndrome in both languages with semantic, visual and morphological errors in word reading, and severely impaired non-word reading. This was also the case in Arabic, a relatively transparent orthographic system, attesting to a severe impairment of the ability to recovery phonology from print in both languages. On the other hand, Kremin et al. (2000) describe a head-injured French-English bilingual speaker presenting differences in his reading skills between the two languages. Their case displayed a mixed alexia with letter-by-letter reading, together with features of a surface alexia in French, but speedier and more accurate whole-word reading and lexical access in English. Contrary to the French data in which there was a clear effect of orthographic regularity on the patient's left-to-right grapheme-phoneme conversion capacities, the patient's performance on the English word-set did not display any effect. Moreover, use of a supposed direct visuo-semantic route in English resulted in far better word reading comprehension to that observed in French. However, extrapolation from this case would appear difficult, in view of the fact that the reading data was more limited for English; the patient's L2, than for the French data. Finally, Karanth (2002) also reports two different alexic patterns in an English-Hindi bilingual patient, who presented two different alexic patterns: deep dyslexia in English and complete alexia in Hindi.

Studies showing similar impairment in two languages with different orthographic systems, as well as reports of different impairments in languages with similar orthography, challenge models of reading and organisation of the bilingual system. Among the numerous factors which are thought to account for the data on differential impairment between languages in bilingual aphasia, the question of the linguistic features of the writing system is considered important.

Alexia and Orthographic Systems

Although there is strong neuropsychological evidence for the existence of two routes in reading (an analytical or phonological assembling route and a lexical access route in which the semantic or lexical representation is addressed directly from the visual level without phonological mediation), how the two routes are used in languages with different orthographic systems is controversial. Indeed, the relationship between the orthographic form and the phonological form of a word varies across languages sharing the same alphabetic system. Some languages like Serbo-Croatian or Spanish have shallow orthography, in that the phonological form is transparently represented by the orthography (the grapheme-phoneme relationship is consistent and invariant and predicted by a small set of rules). Other languages like English or French have deep orthography with a non-transparent relationship between graphemes and phonemes.

Since the classical two routes models of reading come essentially from observations in languages with non-transparent orthography (Saffran & Martin, 1977; Beauvois & Derouesné, 1979, Patterson, Marshall & Coltheart, 1985), it has been argued that differences in the grapheme-phoneme correspondence between languages may result in different reading processing (Katz and Feldman, 1983; Katz and Frost, 1992; Ardila, 1991). In order to try to deal with these differences in the orthographic systems, Katz and Feldman (1983) postulate the orthographic depth hypothesis (ODH). In its original strong form, the ODH assumed that only the assembling process is used in languages with a completely shallow orthography, this means that there is no orthographic input lexicon in readers in languages with shallow orthography. This original hypothesis was replaced by a weaker version of ODH (Katz and Frost, 1992), in which both routes; assembled phonology and visual-orthographic coding, are always involved in reading words. The degree to which one kind of information (lexical or sublexical) predominates is a function of the degree of transparency of the orthographic system. The lexical route (addressed routine) predominates in languages with deep orthography and sublexical route (assembling) in languages with shallow orthography.

In connectionist or parallel distributed models of single word reading (Seidenberg and McClelland, 1989; Plaut et al., 1996) this controversy on the respective weights of two reading procedures has not been focused on. In these models a single system accounts for analytical and lexical processes, in that the phonological system can receive information from the orthographic lexicon (word form system) before the appropriate word form has been completely activated and the access to meaning can be phonologically mediated even for words with deep orthography. However, connectionist models that attempt to account for patterns of dyslexia observed in neuropsychological studies introduce into the model two different procedures for reading (Ans, et al. 1998).

Thus, more recent positions assume that readers of any alphabetic system use multiple procedures in reading; behavioural studies demonstrate the implication of lexical information in reading shallow orthography as in deep orthography (Tabossi and Laghi, 1992; Sebastiàn-Gallés, 1991). However, when languages with a deep orthography and languages with a shallow orthography are directly compared, differences in reading performance and in brain activity have been reported (Paulesu et al. 2000, for English and Italian) supporting the idea that differences in reading processing depend on language properties. On the other hand, there is no evidence for a correlation between the degree of transparency and degree of involvement of each procedure in reading.

Since the two languages of the bilingual alexic patient we are going to present, English and Spanish, have different degrees of orthographic transparency, we will briefly discuss the differences in their orthographic systems. English has a deep orthography. Henderson (1982) estimates that 21% of English words violate grapheme-phoneme relation rules. Spanish has a shallow orthography, as a result of which pronunciation can be inferred with a few rules. There is fixed grapheme-phoneme correspondence for most graphemes and only for very few graphemes (g and c) pronunciation variation is rule governed depending on context. There are no clear quantitative distinctions between deep and shallow orthography in Spanish and English. Gontijo et al. (2003) quantify an orthographic depth index by dividing the total number of grapheme-phoneme correspondences by the total number of graphemes in the language. This index corresponds to 2.4 for English (3.9 when calculated on the most frequent graphemes only). A partial calculation on Brazilian Portuguese, a shallow orthography language like Spanish, carried out by Gontijo et al. (2003) led to an orthographic depth index of 1.07, thus quite different from English. Despite this, as we mentioned it earlier, we cannot clearly predict the relationship between an orthographic depth index and reading processing. Moreover, the implication of each route in reading may be affected not only by orthographic characteristics, but also by other linguistic variables like word frequency and by individual variables such as skill (see Seidenberg, 1992).

Whether reading implies the same processes in different languages and whether the impairment of reading processing has the same consequences on different languages is an important issue in bilingual alexia. In fact, following the ODH discussed above, one can expect that impairment in the assembling route for example affects a language with a shallow orthography like Spanish more than a language with deep orthography like English. To our knowledge, there are only few contributions to the understanding of reading processes originating from studies on bilingual alexia. Some neuropsychologists have followed the strong ODH and claimed that reading in English and Spanish use two different cognitive operations due to their different orthographic systems (Ardila, 1991). This assumption implies that phonological dyslexia should not be observed in acquired alexia in languages with shallow orthography. However, some studies report cases of patients clearly reading with a lexical route in Spanish, (Ferreres & Miravalle, 1995; Cuetos et al, 1996; Iribarren et al. 1999) thus lending support to the universality of reading models. Among the mentioned studies, the patient who displayed deep alexia in English and a complete alexia in Hindi may be interpreted as evidence that an impairment in the assembling route results in greater impairment in reading a language with shallow than with deep orthography (Karanth, 2002). However, patients with similar deep dyslexia patterns in languages with both shallow orthography and a deep orthography have also been described (Béland and Minouni, 2001), thus a differential loss may also be interpreted as selective impairments of language specific processes or representations.

In this chapter, we present a single-subject study aimed at evaluating the characteristics of an acquired reading impairment observed in a bilingual speaker. We first report results from an earlier study (Laganaro & Overton Venet, 2001), in which in-depth evaluation of the patient's alexic disturbance and rehabilitation was carried out in both languages. We then present a new study carried out with the same patient, in which we report assessment in both Spanish and English one year and 3 years after the conclusion of the prior study, in order to analyse whether the patterns of deficits were still parallel between the two languages, and whether further spontaneous improvement had occurred. Furthermore, we present a programme of experimental therapy and evaluate its contribution to further gains, replicating the assessment and a therapy methodology from the earlier study.

STUDY 1. BILINGUAL PARALLEL ASSESSMENT AND REHABILITATION

In this section we present a parallel bilingual assessment and rehabilitation in an English-Spanish speaking alexic patient. The aim of this study was two-fold. First, we assessed whether the alexia characteristics were the same in the two languages. Secondly, we carried out two different treatment methods in each language in order to analyse whether the effects were language specific or whether they generalised across languages. Since the experiments have been published elsewhere (Laganaro and Overton, 2001), details of methodology and results are omitted here.

Case Description

OL was a fifty year-old male native speaker of Spanish (L1) with a graduate degree in English (L2); he used English professionally. According to bilingual classifications (Paradis, 1989) the patient's history indicates that he is probably a co-ordinate bilingual. OL suffered a gunshot wound in the left temporo-parieto-occipital brain region resulting in right hemianopia, conduction aphasia with alexia, agraphia and acalculia. Reading remained his major residual deficit at 8 months post-onset. In addition, there was evidence of moderate phonological disturbances in all expressive tasks and verbal short term memory was severely impaired, whereas visual-spatial span was unaffected. There was no evidence of visual agnosia.

In the first part of this study, an in-depth bilingual reading assessment was designed. Reading assessment tests (oral single word and non-word reading; lexical decision; letter naming; oral reading of a short text; text comprehension; spelled-word identification) were created in parallel in Spanish and English, that is, tests included the same number of items and items were matched within and between the two languages on lexical characteristics in terms of length and frequency.

The results indicated a parallelism in OL's bilingual alexic profile, both from a quantitative and a qualitative point of view. The type of alexia has been characterised as mixed, showing characteristics of the letter-by-letter alexia and of phonological alexia. On the one hand, there was a marked word-length effect in lexical decision in both languages and use of a grapheme-based deciphering strategy. He also had impaired letter naming. On the other hand, OL's showed a significant difficulty with oral reading of non-words in English and Spanish.

No significant differences were observed on the test scores between English and Spanish, with the exception of lexical decision reaction times. These were slower for Spanish than for English on limited and on unlimited conditions. Thus, the results provided evidence for an English-Spanish parallelism in the alexic profile, both from a quantitative and a qualitative point of view.

In the second part of the study, two types of alexia treatment were carried out successively in each language with an assessment period after each therapy period. The first therapy program (Treatment A) was created on the basis of rehabilitation methods that aim to facilitate the recovery of a whole word reading strategy and inhibit letter-by-letter reading by presenting stimuli for short time periods (Gonzalez Rothi & Moss, 1992, but see also Mahrer et al., 1998). The second treatment program (Treatment B) consisted of a task involving phonological assembly and encoding. This included silent judgement of homophony between non-words (Goodall et al., 1998) and phonological assembly inspired by phoneme-blending tasks used to treat phonological alexia (De Partz, 1986; Berndt and Mitchum, 1994). For both treatments computer-assisted programs were developed for each language. Stimuli used in the treatment tasks were different from those used in the assessment tasks.

Treatment A took place during two weeks in English, followed by treatment B, with an assessment after each period. Then the same therapy sequence was carried out in Spanish and finally, an evaluation in both languages rounded off the entire treatment and post-therapeutic assessment period. We will here only discuss the results in terms of efficacy and generalisation across languages. An improvement was observed in most assessment tasks, however not all results generalised from one language to the other. Table 1 shows the significant gains in each language for each assessment task.

Only non-word reading, time-limited lexical decision and reading speed were analysed as therapy outcome, since OL obtained high scores at pre-test (>90%) at the other assessment tasks.

Non-word oral reading benefited significantly from treatment in both languages, and gains seem to be related essentially to Treatment B (phonological assembly). Benefits on non-words reading were significant in English after English phonological assembly treatment and Spanish non-word reading improved significantly from phonological assembly treatment, both in English and in Spanish. Thus, a transfer of gains occurred from English to Spanish, but not from Spanish to English.

Table 1. Summary of gains after each language-specific treatment

Treated-Language	*Evaluated task*	Gains in each language
L2	*Non-Word oral reading*	L2 + L1
(English)	*Lexical decision*	(L2) + L1
	Reading Time	L2
L1	*Non-Word oral reading*	L1
(Spanish)	*Lexical decision*	(L1 + L2)
	Reading Time	L1

[in brackets : statistically non-significant gains]

OL's lexical decision in the limited presentation condition improved in both languages, but improvement reached a statistically significant result only for Spanish after therapy in English. OL continued to make gains in English after treatment in Spanish, although significance levels were not reached. Finally, reading time decreased in both languages from base-line to the end of the study and gains appeared to be specific to each language treatment period.

Thus, despite the fact that alexia assessment showed a parallel profile in Spanish and English, therapy- linked recovery showed both patterns, language specific benefits and transfer of gains. Transfer of gains from the treated to the untreated language was found on the lexical decision task after treatment with limited stimuli presentation time. These gains are bi-directional, that is performances improved in Spanish after treatment in English and vice-versa. However, only gains in Spanish after treatment in English reached statistical significance. Transfer of gains was also observed for non-word reading, but only from English to Spanish. Language specific gains were observed for word oral reading and for reading speeds. Gains in text reading time does not appear to be related to a specific treatment type. In fact neither therapy A, nor therapy B were predicted to speed up reading times; however, both addressed processes that are relevant to oral reading for text: a lexical reading strategy through rapid presentations in therapy A and phonological assembly in treatment B.

In summary, the bilingual alexia assessment showed that OL presented a mixed alexia, with characteristics of letter-by-letter and phonological alexia in both English and Spanish. A parallel profile in both languages emerged from all the assessed tasks at a qualitative level. In the quantitative analyses, a parallelism was observed on all scores; only lexical decision reaction times were slower for Spanish than for English on both testing conditions (limited and unlimited). Treatment carried out in each language separately showed a bi-directional transfer of gains in the lexical decision task after the training timed lexical decision and unidirectional transfer, from L2 to L1, in a phonological task (non-words reading).

Study 2: Bilingual Alexia Follow-Up

This second study started one after the end of the previous study; it was aimed at assessing long-term follow up of bilingual alexia. Moreover, we undertook a new period of language specific therapy for alexia in order to analyse whether the targeted therapy was still effective 4 years post-onset and if the same patterns of generalisation emerged.

At this later time, despite very good recovery in the oral modality, OL complained of acute difficulty with reading, especially with material subject to rapid displays (eg. ticker-tape messages on TV and road signs on the freeway).

Part 1. Bilingual Alexia Assessment

Two parallel alexia assessments were carried out in Spanish and in English with OL at one year and two and a half years after the previous study. Only the tasks in which OL was still impaired at the end of the previous study were assessed in the present study.

Method

Assessment included a lexical decision task under limited time presentation, a non-word reading task and a timed oral reading of a short text in each language.

The lexical decision task constituted of two parallel lists was administered in each language. Each list (n=96) was composed of an equal number of words - matched for length

(4-5, 7-8 graphemes) and lexical frequency (Alameda and Cuetos, 1995 for Spanish; CELEX, Baayen et al., 1993 for English) - and non-words, matched for length to the words. Half of the non-words were homophones with real words (eg. *pheat* homophone with *feet*, and *sanaoria*, homophone with *zanahoria* for Central America Spanish, where "z" is pronounced /s/) and half of the non-words were non-homophones. In each list, the previous variables were manipulated in a 2x2 orthogonal design for words (length x lexical frequency) and for non-words (length x phonological similarity with non-words). The lexical decision sub-test was carried out by means of a computer-driven assessment at an 150 msecs exposure, projected to the left visual field. Only one of the two lists for each language was assessed in April 01, while items from both lists were mixed and tested in January 03.

The same non-words from the two lists were used for a non-word-reading task. The texts in Spanish and English were short narratives, constructed using the same overall number of words; in addition, the words used in the text were matched for mean word-length. The measures on this test was the overall oral text reading time.

Results

The results of the three tasks were compared across the three testing periods, that is, the end of the first study and 1 and 3 years later.

Figure 1 shows the results for the lexical decision task. It can been observed that performances decreased in Spanish one year after the end of study 1. This result is significant at the corrected Chi square test (χ^2=4.3, p<.05). Two years later the performances were still the same as in April 2001; they were equivalent in Spanish and in English.

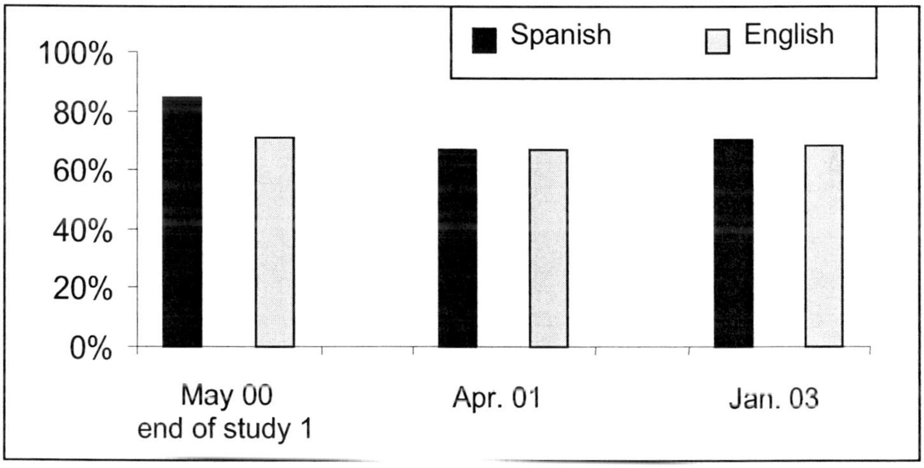

Figure 1. Percent correct in the lexical decision task in Spanish and English of the three testing periods

Remember that both lists were tested in January 2003. This permitted several comparisons across lists and item variables. Results compared across lists were similar for the two English lists and for the two Spanish lists. Moreover, none of the controlled variables (lexical frequency, length and phonological similarity for non-words) affected correct responses in Spanish or in English (all p > .3 at Fisher exact test).

Reaction times for correct answers were smaller for Spanish than for English at all testing periods (see table 2), as already observed in Study 1. These differences were significant at both new testing periods (respectively: April 01: $F(1, 134)=10.4$, $p < .01$; January 03, on two lists: $F(1, 264)=23.3$, $p < .0001$). The contribution of the manipulated variables on reaction times was analysed for results on all lists in January 03. None of the manipulated variables affected reaction times in Spanish nor in English (lexical frequency in English: $F(1, 94)=2.27$, $p=.13$, and for all other variables $F<1$).

Table 2. Lexical decision reaction times (in msec) at the three testing periods for English and Spanish

	may 00	apr.01	jan.03
Spanish	1149	1406	1852
English	1784	1842	3324

In reading aloud non-words, production was scored correct only if the target was pronounced correctly at the first attempt. We observed (see Figure 2) that performance remained stable throughout the three year period in Spanish, while an increase was observed in English. However, the changes in English did not reach significance at Chi Square analysis ($\chi^2=3.05$, $p=.08$).

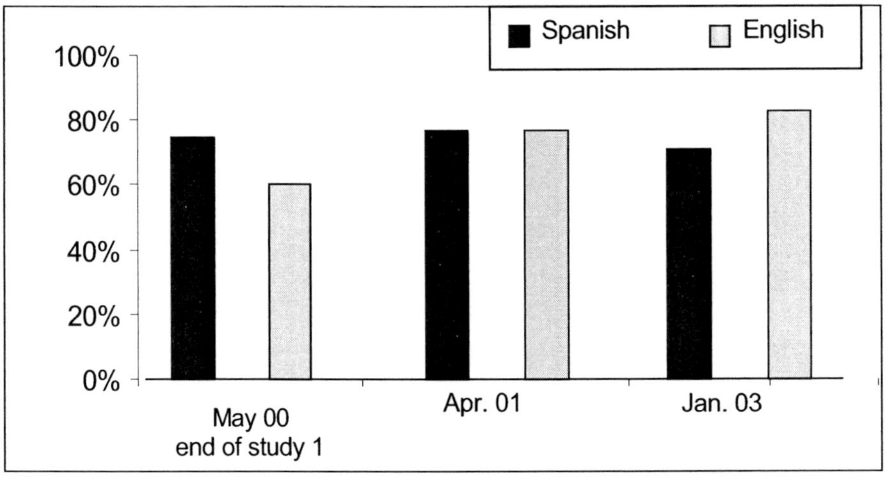

Figure 2. Performance on non-word reading task (percent correct) at each testing period

List comparisons also revealed similar results across lists for both Spanish and English and results were similar in both languages (all $\chi^2<1$). Length and phonological similarity to words affected correct responses in that performances were better on shorter words and on pseudo-homophones, however both results were only marginally significant at the Fisher test (length: $p = .07$; phonological similarity: $p=.06$).

Finally, text reading time was comparable between Spanish and English (respectively 2.2 and 2.5 seconds per word) and no changes occurred across the period.

In sum, testing at 8 months after rehabilitation carried out in the previous study showed a decrease in performance in lexical decision and a non-significant increase in reading aloud non-words in English. At this time all results were equivalent in Spanish and English. Two years later results were unchanged.

Part 2. Monolingual Treatment

In this part of the study, we replicated one of the therapy periods from the previous study in order to analyse whether therapy was still effective almost 4 years post-onset and whether its effects generalised across languages.

Method

A computer-based treatment was set up in Spanish. The last two assessments described in the previous section were used as a baseline for the therapy period; a post-therapy assessment was carried out at the end of the therapy period on the same stimuli and tasks as described in the previous section. The computer-based therapy included tasks designed to inhibit letter-by-letter reading. This included rapid left visual-field presentation of stimuli on a computer screen in judgement tasks such as lexical decision, word categorisation and word associations. The stimuli used in therapy consisted of those of assessment list 2 (lexical decision list and non-word reading list).

Two levels of difficulty were built into the task, through shortened presentation times (400 and 200 msec). OL spent 2 weeks, working for 3 weekly sessions at home on the therapy program before undergoing the post-test assessment.

Results

Performances were compared pre and post-therapy on all the testing lists and in both languages. Figure 3 shows results on the lexical decision and the non-word reading tasks before and after therapy.

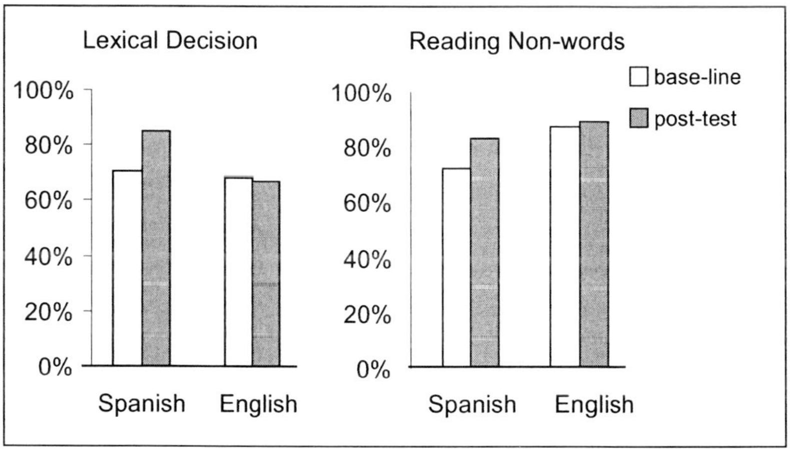

Figure 3. Correct responses (percent) on lexical decision and reading tasks for Spanish and English before and after therapy.

We observed an increase of performance in the lexical decision task in Spanish after therapy. This increase is significant at the McNemar Chi Square test on both lists, the treated one ($p<.02$) and the non-treated one ($p<.05$). Performances in English in this task do not change after the therapy in Spanish.

Moreover, reading non-words aloud improved slightly on all lists and in both languages. This increase after therapy is significant only for the treated list in Spanish (McNemar Chi Square = 4.03, $p<.05$).

In sum, benefits are observed after a period of targeted therapy on lexical decision in time-limited conditions and in reading non-words. Both results are significant only in Spanish, the treated language. Gains in the lexical decision task are not item-specific, since performance increased significantly on both lists. Interestingly, benefits are also observed on reading non-words aloud and a significant increase occurs on treated items.

Discussion

We reported a single-subject study aimed at evaluating the characteristics of an acquired reading impairment observed in a bilingual speaker. We also explored the question of the transfer of therapy benefits from one language to the other. We will first discuss the results of the parallel assessment and then those of therapy.

Bilingual Alexia Profile

The parallel Spanish and English evaluation of the patient's alexia showed a high degree of parallelism in the reading impairment overall, with traits of letter-by-letter and aphasic alexia in both languages. Performances on all tasks were identical in Spanish and English both from a qualitative and quantitative point of view, with the exception of lexical decision times, which were slower in English at all testing periods. Thus, our patient's assessment provides evidence for a parallelism between Spanish and English alexia at 8 months and 4 years post-onset. His alexia was characterised as mixed, with features of letter-by-letter alexia (impaired letter naming and slowed reading times with a length effect in reading and lexical decision) and phonological alexia features (poorer pseudo-word reading). In the literature there are some similar mixed alexia reports in monolingual patients. Friedman et al. (1993) described a patient with features of pure alexia associated with a phonological alexia and Friedman and Hadley's patient (1992) presented a word-length effect and poorer pseudo-word than word reading without aphasia or agraphia; they described him as a "letter-by-letter surface alexic". Concerning OL's phonological impairment, we observed parallel performance in English and Spanish on tasks involving phonological output (words and non-words reading and text reading time), with better word reading compared to non-words in both languages. Remember however that OL had a conduction aphasia and produced phonological paraphasias in other production tasks, thus, we can not exclude that the greater difficulty with reading non-words may be due to the phonological encoding impairment and not to phonological alexia.

Concerning bilingual pure alexia, one may expect that letter-by-letter reading affects reading to a greater extent in a language with deep orthography such as English than in a language with shallow orthography. In fact, even though the ODH predictions are based on central reading processing, a peripheral impairment such as that resulting in letter-by letter alexia results in the inhibition of lexically mediated word reading, since the word form system cannot be addressed instantly. Yet we observed that on all non-phonological tasks including lexical decision the number of errors and length effect are similar in both languages. However, a difference was observed in reaction times, with shorter latencies in Spanish in both the limited and the unlimited conditions. This difference is clearly linked to different time costs in accessing the lexico-orthographic representation and not to phonological encoding processing (no differences were observed in overt reading time in Spanish and English and non-word reading also was equivalent). Thus, it may be that longer latencies in English reflect a cost in accessing the lexicon via a letter-by-letter reading strategy in a deep orthography compared to a shallow orthography. However, shorter reaction times in Spanish than in English may also be due to the fact that Spanish is the patient's first language and our data does not permit to dissociate an effect of orthography from an effect of early language acquisition.

Therapy Issues in Bilingual Alexia

The second part of each study addressed therapy. In study 1, the patient received an intensive computer-assisted home-based remediation programme alternating tasks aimed at inhibiting letter-by-letter reading and tasks training phonological assembly. Two recovery patterns were found, a language specific recovery and a transfer of gains from one language to the other. Bi-directional, although not always significant, transfer of gains was observed in the lexical decision task after the training timed lexical decision. This task requires the same strategy in both languages, namely the inhibition of a letter-by-letter reading. Unidirectional transfer from English (L2) to Spanish (L1) was observed in a phonological task (non-words reading) and only language specific gains were observed on the other tasks. Taken together, these results support the predictions about transfer of gains into the untreated language when common processes are targeted, such as inhibiting letter-by-letter reading. On the other hand, improvements were limited to the treated language when treatment involved language–specific phonological representations, with the exception however of a gain in Spanish non-word reading after English treatment. Improvoment in reading Spanish non-words can be attributed to the fact that a therapy task specifically targeted phonological blending skills, and that these skills are common to both languages. However, subsequent treatment of the same type carried out in L1 did not result in gains in L2. Thus, it seems that improved phonological assembly alone cannot account for OL's better oral reading of non-words in Spanish.

In Study 2, a new therapy period involving lexical decision and judgement tasks with rapid item presentation was carried out in Spanish at 3 years post-onset. An increase in lexical decision performance was observed in Spanish only, on the treated and the untreated lists. Moreover, an item-specific effect on non-word reading was also observed. Thus, this second rehabilitation study shows that therapy might still be effective almost 4 years post-onset. But the transfer of gains after a rapid presentation therapy observed in study 1 has not been confirmed in this second study, where all results were language-specific. Two explanations can be suggested here. It may be that a plateau has been reached in L2 and that only L1 can further increase some years after onset. An alternative explanation concerns transfer of gains that could be harder to obtain from L1 to L2 than in the other direction as already discussed above (remember that even in Study 1 statistically significant transfer of gains were only described from English to Spanish). A second period of therapy carried out in English would have helped to disambiguate these two explanations. Unfortunately, the study was abandoned because of the patient's unavailability.

Taken together, our results only partially support the hypothesis that transfer of gains occurs in areas where two languages are structurally similar (Paradis, 1995, Sasamuna & Park, 1995). In fact, we observed transfer of gains after therapy aimed at inhibiting letter-by-letter reading, a processing that may be common to both languages. However, this transfer was only marginal from L1 to L2 in the first study and no transfer at all was observed in the second study. Moreover, unidirectional transfer from English to Spanish was observed in non-word reading. Thus, other factors play a role in the transfer of therapy gains in addition to the functional distance or similarities between languages. These factors may be linked to partially separate representations between languages, to pre-morbid performance and to language use.

Another puzzling result in the second therapy study is the improvement in non-word reading performance in Spanish after a therapy targeting lexical-semantic processing. This result is clearly linked to therapy since the effect is specific to the treated items. An explanation for this result is that some phonological information is activated in the lexical tasks we proposed. This therapy outcome is consistent with theories that postulate a participation of sublexical information in lexical tasks and the integration of the lexical and the phonological route in all reading tasks.

Conclusions

Bilingual alexia challenges clinical practice, especially when both languages are of daily use for the patient, and it challenges cognitive research in the consideration of structural differences between languages and their consequences to models of reading. Our bilingual case description showed parallel features of alexia at each treatment session in two languages with different orthographic transparency, Spanish and English. Despite these similar alexic features, a significant transfer of gains after therapy in one language only occurred from English (L2) to Spanish (L1). Our therapy results are encouraging on the one hand, in that alexia therapy is still beneficial more than three years post-onset. On the other hand, however, the lack of generalisation to L2 raises the question of language choice in therapy. In fact, today, no prediction can be made about therapy benefits on the untreated language since various variables may affect the transfer of therapy including the structural properties of languages and the subject's bilingual features. It is worth using technology and exiting multilingual data bases to construct therapy in order to target all patients' languages in treatment.

REFERENCES

Alameda, J.R. & Cuetos, F. (1995). *Diccionario de frecuencia de las unidades lingüisticas del castellano*. Vol. I and II. Universidad de Oviedo.

Ans, B., Carbonnel. S. & Valdois, S. (1998). A connectionist multiple-trace memory model for polysyllabic word reading. *Psychological Review*, 105, 678-723.

Ardila, A. (1991). Errors resembling semantic paralexias in Spanish-speaking aphasic alexics. *Brain and Language, 41,* 437-45.

Baayen, R.H., Piepenbrock, R. & Gulikers, L. (1993). *CELEX, Centre for lexical information*, Max Planck Institute for Psycholinguistics, Nijmegen.

Beauvois, M.F. & Derouesné, J. (1979). Phonological alexia, three dissociaitons. *Journal of Neurology, Neurosurgery and Psychiatry, 42*, 1115-1124.

Beland, R.& Mimouni, Z. (2001), Deep dyslexia in the two languages of an Arabic/French bilingual patient. *Cognition*, 82, 77-126.

Berndt, R.S. & Mitchum, C.C. (1994). Approaches to the rehabilitation of « phonological assembly » , elaborating the model of nonlexical reading. Riddoch MJ & Humphreys G (eds), *Cognitive Neuropsychology and Cognitive Rehabilitation.* Laurence Erlbaum, Hove.

Cuetos, F., Valle-Arroyo, F. & Suarez, M.P. (1996). A case of phonological dyslexia in spanish. *Cognitive Neuropsychology, 13*, 1-24.

De Partz, M.P. (1986). Reeducation of a deep dyslexic patient, rationale of method and results. *Cognitive Neuropsychology, 3*, 149-177.

Ferreres, A.R. & Miravalles, G. (1995). The produciton of semantic paralexias in Spanish speaking aphasics. *Brain and Language, 49*, 153-172.

Friedman, R.B. & Hadley, J.A. (1992). Letter-by-letter surface alexia.. *Cognitive Neuropsychology, 9(3)*, 185-208.

Friedman, R.B., Beerman, M., Lott, S.N., Link, K., Grafman, J. & Robinson, S. (1993) Modality specific phonological alexia. *Cognitive Neuropsychology, 10(6)*, 549-568.

Gontijo, P.F.D., Gontijo, I. & Shillcock, R. (2003). Grapheme-phoneme probabilities in British English. *Behaviour Research Methods, Instruments & Computers, 35*, 136-157.

Gonzalez Rothi, L.J. & Moss, S. (1992). Alexia without agraphia , potential for model assisted therapy. *Clinical Communication Disorders, 2*, 11-18.

Goodall, W.C. & Phillips, W.A. (1995). Three routes from print to sound , evidence from a case of acquired dyslexia. *Cognitive Neuropsychology, 12(2*), 113-147.

Grosjean, F. (1982). *Life with Two Languages: An Introduction to Bilingualism*. Cambridge, Mass: Harvard University Press

Grosjean, F. (2003). *Questionnaire for bilinguals*. Unpublished. Neuchâtel: Neuchâtel University.

Henderson, L. (1982). *Orthography and word recognition in reading*. London: Academic Press.

Iribarren, C., Jarema, G. & Lecours, R. (1999). Lexical reading in Spanish , two cases of phonological dyslexia. *Applied Psycholinguistics, 20(3),* 407-428.

Karanth, P. (2002). The search for deep dyslexia in syllabic writing systems. Journal of *Neurolinguistics, 15*, 143-155.

Katz,-Leonard; Feldman,-Laurie-B (1983). Relation between pronunciation and recognition of printed words in deep and shallow orthographies. *Journal of Experimental Psychology: Learning, Memory, and Cognition, 9*, 157-166

Katz, L. & Frost, R. (1992). The reading process is different for different orthographies: the orthographic depth hypothesis. In R. Frost and L. Katz (eds.) Orthography, phonology, morphology and meaning. Amsterdam: Elsevier Science Publishers.

Kremin, H., Chomel-Guillome, S. Ferrand, I. & Bakchine, S. (2000). Dissociation of reading strategies: letter-by-letter reading in the native language and normal reading in the learned language. A case study. *Brain and Cognition*, 2000, 43, 282-286.

Laganaro, M. & Overton Venet, M. (2001). Acquired alexia in multilingual aphasia and computer-assisted remediation in both languages , issues of generalisation and transfer. *Folia Phoniatrica et Logopedica*, 53, 135-144.

Mahrer, L.M., Clayton, M.C., Schober-Peterson, D. & Gonzalez Rothi, L.J. (1998). Rehabilitation of a case of pure alexia , exploiting residual abilities. *Journal of the international Neuropsychological Society, 4*, 636-647.

Paradis, M. (1983). *Readings on aphasia in bilinguals and polyglots*. Montréal: Didier.

Paradis, M. (1989). Bilingual and polyglot aphasia. In F. Boller & J. Frafmann (eds), *Handbook of neuropsychology*, vol. 2. Amsterdam: Elsevier.

Paradis, M. (Ed.) (1995). *Aspects of Bilingual Aphasia*. Pergamon Press.

Patterson, K., Marshall, J.C. & Coltheart M. (1985). *Surface dyslexia, Neuropsychological and Cognitive Studies of phonological reading*. Hillsdale, NJ: Erlbaum.

Paulesu, E., McCrory, E., Fazio, F., Menoncello, F., Brunswick, N., Cappa, S., Cotelli, M. Cossu, G., Corte, F., Lorusso, M. Pesenti, S., Gallagher, A., Perani, D., Price, C., Frith, C.D. and Frith, U. (2000). A cultural effect on brain function. *Nature Neuroscience, 3*, 91-96.

Pitres, A. (1895). Etude sur l'aphasie chez les polyglottes. *Revue de Médecine, 15*, 873-899. English traduction in : Paradis, M. (Ed.) (1983). Readings on aphasia in bilinguals and polyglots. Quebec : Marcel Didier.

Plaut, D., McClelland, J.L., Seidenberg, M.S. & Patterson, K. (1996). Understanding normal and impaired word reading : computational principles in quasi-regular domains. *Psychological Review, 103*, 56-115.

Roberts, P.M. (1998). Clinical research needs and issues in bilingual aphasia. *Aphasiology*, 12(2), 119-130.

Saffran, E.M. & Martin O.S.M. (1977). Reading without phonology, evidence from aphasia. Quarterly Journal of Experimental Psychology, 29, 515-525.

Sasanuma, S. and Park, H.S. (1995). Patterns of language deficits in two Korean-Japanese bilingual aphasic patients – A clinical report. In M. Paradis (Ed), Aspects of Bilingual Aphasia *(111-122). Pergamon, Elsevier Science.*

Sebastián-Gallés, N. (1991). Reading by analogy in a shallow or-thography. *Journal of Experimental Psychology: Human Perception and Performance, 17*, 471–477.

Seidenberg, M.S & McClelland, J.L. (1989). A distributed developemental model of word recognition and naming. *Psychological Review, 96*, 523-568.

Seidenberg, M.S. (1992). Beyond orthographic depth in reading: equitable division of labor. In R. Frost and L. Katz (eds.) *Orthography, phonology, morphology and meaning.* Amsterdam: Elsevier Science Publishers.

Tabossi, P. & Laghi. L. (1992). Semantic priming in the pronunciation of words in two writing systems: Italian and English. *Memory and Cognition, 20,* 302-313.

Wiener, D., Obler, L.K. & Taylor Sarno, M. (1995). Speech/language management of the bilingual aphasic in a U.S. urban rehabilitation hospital. In M. Paradis (Ed). *Aspects of Bilingual Aphasia* (37-56). Pergamon, Elsevier Science.

In: Trends in Dyslexia Research
Editor: Henry D. Tobias, pp. 169-185

ISBN 1-59454-219-8

Chapter VII

MAIN CLINICAL CHARACTERISTICS OF DEVELOPMENTAL LEARNING-DISABLED CHILDREN AT A NEUROPSYCHOLOGICAL SERVICE

Adrián Poblano[1*], *Sonia Borja*[1] *and Carmina Arteaga*[1]
[1]Laboratory of Cognitive Neurophysiology, National Center for Rehabilitation, Mexico City. Mexico

ABSTRACT

This chapter describes the main clinical features associated with learning disability in a group of 778 school age children studied in a Neuropsychological Clinic in Mexico City. The study was carried out retrospectively, using data abstracted from clinical records of subjects seen between 1995 and 1996. Children were mainly from low and middle socioeconomic strata and between 6 and 12 years in age. The following data were collected: age, gender, diagnosis, school grade, food intake, maternal complications during pregnancy, perinatal and postnatal neurological risk factors, and neurological signs and handedness. Subjects with learning disability had a mean age of 102.9 months and were predominantly male (male-female ratio 2:1). Among the study group, 49.1% of the children were diagnosed with non-language related learning disability, and 75.1% were from the first three school grades. 27.6% showed evidence of malnutrition, a previous history of language disorder (49.2%), and a high frequency of perinatal risk factors. Neurological soft signs were also found. Thus, this study shows that gender, food intake, and genetic and neurological variables may be associated with learning disability in school children from Mexico City.

---

* Correspondence to: A. Poblano, Calzada México-Xochimilco 289, Colonia Arenal Guadalupe, Delegación Tlalpan, 14389. México D.F., México. E-mail drdyslexia@starmedia.com

INTRODUCTION

The purpose of this chapter is to discuss the main clinical characteristics of learning disabilities (LDs) in children at a neuropsychological service from the point of view of professionals dedicated to identifying and treating them (Poblano et al., 2002a). It is our hope that our data may be identical to results from other clinics or at least may serve as a point of comparison. LDs in children is one of the most common developmental concerns at school age, occurring in as many as 10% of the elementary school population (Shaywitz, 1998). Although no prevalence studies of LDs have been performed in Mexico, earlier work of García-Pedroza et al. (1983) showed a 19.6% prevalence of minimal brain dysfunction in 9-year-old children from Tlalpan county in Mexico City in a search for epileptic children. There are good arguments that agree that LDs are developmental alterations separately disturbing one or several brain circuits or modules specializing in various aspects of cognitive functions.

DEFINITION

LDs are characterized by unexpected difficulty in reading for children who otherwise possess normal intelligence and have received the adequate opportunities necessary to learn these cognitive abilities (Gerson-Wolfenberger and Ruijssenaars, 1997). Children with learning disabilities frequently have difficulties in language and non-language processing abilities such as dyslexia and dysgraphy; however, this latter alteration has received less attention by researchers. Some investigators including our work group think that LDs are a heterogeneous group of alterations that conform within a wide spectrum of cognitive dysfunctions and that will gradually appear in the future as different types of new syndromes. Diagnosis of LDs is multidisciplinary, and recent advances in our knowledge of their neurobiological and cognitive influences within the framework of a dynamic neurocognitive model allow physicians, psychologists, educators, and speech therapists to approach and become involved with patients presenting a possible Learning disability (LD).

BRAIN ORGANIZATION AND FUNCTION

The relationship between brain structure and complex behavior is a central concern of cognitive neuroscience. Most researchers would agree that the processing of information hierarchically (Luria, 1975) along dedicated centers could not sustain the fast calculations required for mental activity. Instead, according to current concepts, complex behavior is likely subserved by large-scale neurocognitive networks that enable more versatile computation architectures (Mesulam, 1990).

People are smarter than existing digital computers because the brain is likely to use parallel-distributed computational stochastic strategies, which are particularly well suited for natural tasks and usually require simultaneous consideration of many factors and information and constraints (Skarda and Freeman, 1987).

The cognitive operations that produce language can be divided into components such as phonetics, syntax, and semantics. The dominance of the left hemisphere for language is now firmly established for the right-handed. The larger size of the posterior language area in the left hemisphere provides an anatomic substrate for dominance. Spoken language is commonly traced to two areas: Wernicke´s area in the temporal-parietal junction and Broca´s area in the frontal operculum. These areas and their interconnections sustain the basic process of language. Anatomic studies in dyslexic subjects has shown damage around cortical language areas by means of microscopic techniques (see latter Neuroanatomic Studies in this chapter).

Learning to Read

When a child studies reading and writing for the first time in the first year of elementary school, he or she is faced with a large number of letter shapes that do not obey shape constancy; for example, if one turns a /d/ 180° one gets a /p/. Moreover, the novice reader is faced with other difficulties: moving the order of letters in a word usually changes the meaning of that word (/mean/ can change to /name/, but /mean/ and /MEAN/ both will have the same meaning). Word order is also critical with regard to the meaning of a sentence: /She is at school./ is different from /Is she at school?/

Reading also implies analysis of syntactic and semantic information that is prominent during the advanced stages of learning to read. However, learning to read implies developmental changes in balance of perceptual and language processing. The balance changes from the right to left hemisphere during the reading process from the early to advanced stages of learning to read (Simos et al., 2002).

During the earliest stages of learning to read, children adopt a logographic strategy, in which letter order is largely ignored and phonologic factors are entirely secondary, a stage in which children may recognize words from graphic features alone. Later in their development children move into an alphabetic recognition strategy and then to an orthographic reading stage (Poblano et al., 1996a; Lovett, 1997).

Hypothesis and Clinical Spectrum of Learning Disabilities

Developmental learning disabilities are defined as specific and significant impairment in reading abilities, unexplainable by any kind of deficit in general intelligence, learning opportunity, motivation, or sensory acuity, in two systems: language and non-language components. Language and non-language systems can be conceptualized as complex and dynamic large-scale neurocognitive networks. At each module, neural systems engage in different kinds of processing such as phonetics, syntax, semantics, and discourse. In the same way, visual and somatosensory systems are engaged in analyzing different features of the visual objects or in planning or performing complex motor behavior. Thus symptoms of LDs can be of two types: language and non-language characteristics (Poblano et al., 1994).

GENETICS

LDs are both familial and inherited. A family history can highlight one of the most important risk factors that one half of children who have a parent with an LD reported to have a disorder. This fact was one of the most important risk factors found in our sample (see later, Clinical Characteristics issue). A rate among siblings of affected subjects of approximately 40% and among parents ranging from 27-49% provides an opportunity for early identification of affected siblings. Linkage studies implicate loci on chromosomes 6 and 15 in LDs (Grigorenko et al., 1997).

NEUROANATOMIC STUDIES

Neuropathology

There are three main post-mortem reports in seven brain specimens in dyslexic subjects (Galaburda and Kemper, 1979; Galaburda et al., 1985; Humphreys et al., 1990). The main findings concern lack of asymmetry in temporo-parieto-occipital areas between both cerebral hemispheres and collections of ectopic neurons around Peri-Sylvian areas mainly in the left hemisphere. These cerebral areas have long been related to language and reading processing (Henderson, 1986) and their alteration may help to explain some symptoms present in subjects with an LD. However, this collection of ectopic cells is not limited only to the left hemisphere, because the right hemisphere is also damaged, and although this fact is not emphasized by other researchers, we believe it can explain other symptoms that are non-language related in subjects with an LD.

In another article, thalamic lesions were reported in one of the studied cases, concerning a bilateral disruption of cytoarchitecture in the medial geniculate nuclei and the lateral-posterior nuclei (Galaburda and Eidelberg, 1982), the latter probably engaged in language decoding. Recently in the medial geniculate nuclei, dyslexic subjects showed no typical asymmetry and the left nuclei were significantly smaller and had fewer large neurons than the right (Galaburda et al., 1994). These last anomalies have been forgotten, but underlie dysfunction of sub-cortical brain centers engaged mainly in language processing.

Cranial Tomography

It is important to note that Cranial tomography (CT) has not been found to be useful in evaluating children with disorders of a developmental origin such as non-specific mental retardation. For example, Haslam et al. (1981) found that in CT there was proportionality more of symmetric occipital width than expected in comparison with a control sample and previously established norms. Differences in verbal or performance IQ were not related to relative cerebral size.

Magnetic Resonance Imaging (MRI)

When considering the results of studies it is important to keep in mind that, typically, the Magnetic resonance imaging (MRI) scans evaluate for obvious structural abnormalities and deviation in normal patterns of parieto-occipital asymmetry (L > R) that according to neurobiological theory correlate with unique neurolinguistic processes such as those in reading. Gross brain structure was remarkably normal in the language and learning impaired group. Semiautomatic morphometry was used to measure hemisphere volumes and cerebral asymmetries in six cerebral areas. The volume of left posterior perisylvian regions was significantly reduced in LDs. Asymmetries in inferior-anterior and superior-posterior cerebral regions were also significantly different in LDs group, suggesting that hemisphere specialization of function may be anomalous (Jernigan, et al. 1991). In another paper, authors evaluated LDs with MRI. All groups (control and dyslexic) had left-sided asymmetry for the temporal regions and right-sided asymmetry for the parietal regions. The group with dyslexia had exaggerated asymmetries, owing to a significant shift of right planar tissue from the temporal to parietal regions (Leonard, et al. 1993). They also had a higher incidence of cerebral anomalies bilaterally. MRI has been used to reveal functionally relevant variations and anomalies in cerebral structure.

Neurophysiologic Studies

There are many neurophysiologic studies that can be used in children with LDs (Poblano, 1997), but the most frequently employed have been electroencephalography and event-related potentials, and more recently functional Magnetic resonance imaging. Thus we present an overview of both of these types of studies. Later we review the other test performed on some groups of LD children, because several results differed that could help us to explain certain characteristics of LD children.

Electroencephalography (EEG)

Quantitative electroencephalography (EEG) analysis has yielded conflicting results with respect to the presence of differences between LD and control children, i.e., John et al., (1977) described an abundance of delta and theta activity during an eyes-closed condition. On the other hand, Duffy et al. (1980) described abnormal bi-frontal and left-posterior higher values of alpha power in children with an LD. Recently, Klimesch et al. (2001a, 2001b) found differences in tonic and phasic lower theta in occipital sites during pseudo-word processing tasks. Lower alpha-band children with dyslexia showed increased phasic response to words and pseudo words in the right hemisphere, but a lack of response to words in the left occipital site. Upper alpha band children with LD showed an increase in upper alpha power, whereas low beta-band children exhibited a diffuse pattern of low desynchronization for word and number stimuli. Our work team studied the relationship between EEG activity and salivary testosterone levels (Poblano et al., 2003), because according to Geschwind and Behan (1982) higher fetal testosterone value is the putative factor responsible for LDs. Even so, we found no evidence of differences in EEG or salivary testosterone levels between children with LDs and controls.

Event-Related Potentials

Event-related potentials (ERP) recorded with a variety of speech and non-speech sounds have been studied in children with LD and in control children. These studies found that ERP differ as a function of the evoking stimuli and thus reflect differences in the processing of stimuli between LD and control children. Several studies reported that ERP are sensitive to phonetic, syntactic, and semantic differences, which are important to discriminate in reading (Taylor and Keenan, 1990). Recently, it has been reported that developmental ERP predict LD at 8 years of age using neonatal brain responses (Molfese, 2000); thus, this kind of study deserves greater attention and confirmation.

Functional Magnetic Resonance Imaging MRI (fMRI)

Recently functional MRI (fMRI) has been used successfully to compare brain activation between dyslexic and normal readers with results showing language and non-language symptoms. For example, presentation of moving stimuli in dyslexics failed to produce the same task-related activation in area V5/MT, part of the magnocellular visual subsystem, than was observed in controls (Eden et al., 1996). However, other studies showed that brain activation patterns differed significantly between groups with dyslexic readers showing relative underactivation in Wernicke´s area, the angular gyrus, and striate cortex, and relative overactivation in inferior frontal gyrus. The first study emphasizes non-language impairment, while the latter supports a conclusion that impairment in dyslexia is of language-oriented in nature (Shaywitz et al. 1998).

Other Studies

In this section we include not only electrophysiological recordings, but also comment on any test with potential usefulness in a clinical examination of different neurological and cognitive functions in LD children.

- Electro-oculography. Several authors held that difficulties in learning to read is associated with abnormal eye movements (Eden, et al. 1994; Poblano, et al. 1996b; de Luca, et al. 1999). Great effort has been devoted to the analysis of eye movements in reading. Differences with respect to this typically exhibited by expert readers has been noted. Later, techniques involving measurement of the number and duration of fixations during reading allowed for quantitative comparisons between dyslexic and normal readers. Both parameters were altered in dyslexics: the number of forward saccades was higher, the fixation duration was longer, and these findings were related to damaged linguistic processing (Poblano et al., 1996b). Visual training and saccade control has been used for the treatment of dyslexic children (Fisher and

Hartnegg, 2000). Thus Electro-oculography is potentially interesting clinical test for the future in the examination of LD children, especially when it is used with complex stimuli related to reading tasks, in order to search for strategies used by LD children when coding face-read events.

- Magnetoencephalography. Recording the magnetic fields and currents of the brain suggest that in fluent reading, visual processing occurs around 100 milliseconds after seeing a word, in the posteromedial extrastriate cortex bilaterally. Afterward the first reading-specific signal is detected about 150 msec after word onset in the left inferior occipital and temporal cortex. After 200 msec, the left superior temporal cortex is engaged in semantic processing, and is disrupted in dyslexics around 200 msec after seeing a word (Salmelin, et al., 2000). However, Magnetoencephalographs devices are expensive and require complex installations, but give interesting results about reading the mechanisms disturbed in otherwise healthy children and helping EEG examinations in providing the dynamics of subcortical networks information blinded to EEG scanning.
- Positron Emission Tomography. Studies performed in dyslexic subjects showed significant difference in the medial temporal lobe, with dyslexic subjects having significantly higher absolute and relative brain metabolism along an anterior-posterior gradient than controls (Hagman, et al. 1992). Other papers report left angular gyrus functionally disconnected from extrastriate occipital and temporal lobe regions during single-word reading (Horwitz, et al. 1998). Abnormalities have a similar pattern despite cultural diversity, such as has been observed in Italian, French and English dyslexics (Paulesu, et al. 2001).
- Hand Motor Coordination. Temporal characteristics of bimanual coordination have been compared between dyslexic and control children with results suggesting that the inter-limb dynamics in dyslexics show deficits in timing precision in bimanual tasks that required integration of asynchronous responses (Wolf et al., 1990; Rousselle and Wolf 1991; Moore et al., 1995). Because dysgraphia and hand dyspraxias are common in LD children, these studies deserve more attention in the future to investigate for mild motor handicaps in writing.
- Visual Evoked Potentials. Earlier investigations in Visual evoked potentials showed a slowing of principal waves in dyslexics when compared with those of control children (Cohen and Breslin, 1984). Further studies found difficulties in tests requiring low-contrast visual information and suggested a dysfunction of the magnocellular defect in the visual pathway in dyslexic children (Livingstone et al., 1991; Lehmkuhle et al. 1993). Further studies are lacking in a comprehensive role for Visual evoked potentials, and their utility is limited in research studies to date.
- Auditory Dichotic Tests. Hearing acuity in dyslexics is untouched (Poblano, et al., 1991), but perception of complex sound such as language was found disturbed in children with LDs. Because reading disability has been related to non-right-handedness, auditory tests in search for left or right auditory preference listening such as dichotic tasks have been performed. Left-hand dyslexic and control children have higher values in recognition of visuo-spatial stimuli presented in the half-left field in relation to right-handed dyslexic and control groups (Hugdalh et al., 1989);

thus results are non-conclusive and more research is needed to determine if the auditory hemisphere preference is disturbed in dyslexic children.

- Vestibular Test. Overall, the Vestibular test produced controversial results. Rotational vestibular responses were performed at low frequencies (0.1 to 0.16 Hz), and there are no differences between dyslexic and control groups in gain, phase, and symmetry (Brown et al., 1983). Other researchers found alterations in electronystagmographic studies; the vestibulo-ocular reflex was evaluated and 27% of children with dyslexia were hyperreflexic and 8% were hyporreflexic. In the rotational test a lack of visual suppression was found in 48%, and in the caloric test there was pathology of visual suppression in 50% of cases (Jerabek and Krejcova, 1991). No clinical utility has been reported for the vestibular test at present.
- Posturography. Some studies found alteration in balance and coordination in LD children (Shumway-Cook et al. 1987; Horak et al., 1988); however these studies were carried out in motor-impaired children and LD children. Thus, we must be cautions with these results. Recently we found longer latencies in motor response in carefully selected LD children (Poblano et al., 2002), but clinical utility of posturography in LD children is still limited.

Clinical Characteristics

Although major symptoms involve educational settings, much evidence suggests that LDs reflect subtle neurologic dysfunction. Learning problems may also have an impact in social and emotional adjustments of children with LD and are of great concern to health professionals. Overall, symptoms may be of two types: linguistic and non-linguistic (Poblano et al., 2002a).

Language-Related Symptoms

Children with LD often have associated deficits in domains such as language acquisition, misspelling, and not only dysphasic delay, but also subtle impairment in perception and or articulation of speech. The reading disorder itself may appear as primary at the time when the child learns to read and becomes confused with morphologically similar letters (such as b and d), and experiences difficulty in acquiring a global logographic strategy that allows whole word recognition from graphic features alone. This latter aspect appears to be the core dysfunction in grapheme-to-phoneme conversion and is critical in learning to read (Poblano et al., 1996b). Overall, language symptoms can be divided into expression and comprehension alterations.

Non-Language Related Symptoms

Non-verbal symptoms include problems in tactile, visuo-spatial, and motor control functioning (Poblano, et al. 2002b) with associated difficulties in arithmetic, social perception, comprehension, and dealing with new information. Some authors suggest that speech and skilled movements share neural mechanisms of timing precision and serial order control; brain mechanisms for the temporal organization of language processes overlap extensively with those for skilled manual action (Ghez, et al. 1996).

Soft neurologic signs are known to be related to LDs and include signs involving fine and gross movements, asymmetries, dyskinesia, visuo-motor coordination, sensory integration, laterality, and clumsiness.

Data from Our Children´s Neuropsychological Clinic

We performed a survey of 778 patients seen for the first time at the Children's Neuropsychologic Clinic of the Institute of Communication Disorders, part of the National Center for Rehabilitation in Mexico City (Poblano, et al. 2002a) and diagnosed children with LDs during 1995-1996. Children's ages ranged from 6 to 12 years. Patients came mainly from low (86.2%) and middle (13.7%) economic strata. Male/female ratio was 2:1 (see Figure 1). Three hundred eighty two subjects were diagnosed as having LDs of non-language (visuo-somatosensory-motor) type (49.1.%), three hundred forty four (44.2%) showed language plus non-language deficit alteration, and fifty two (6.6%) fell into the language delay group (see Figure 2).

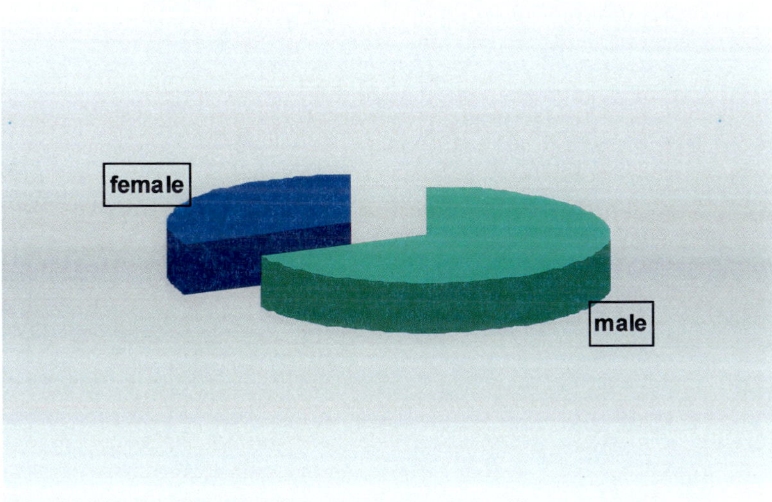

Figure 1. Male/female ratio in the sample.

Of the 778 children studied, 75.1% were in the first three school grades and the remainder were in the higher grades of elementary school. Food intake was clinically qualified as low caloric/protein intake in 27.6% of the group (215 subjects).

One or more maternal complications during pregnancy were noted in 21.4% of the sample children. The main complications of pregnancy were transvaginal bleeding (*n* = 113, 14.5%), preclampsia (*n* = 21, 2.6%), pregnancy after 35 years of age (*n* = 21, 2.6%), and hypertension (*n* = 12, 1.5%) (see Figure 3). The main risk factors in neonates were hyperbilirubinemia (*n* = 121, 15.5%), including three patients who required blood transfusions and 47 who were treated with phototherapy, asphyxia (n = 88, 11.3%) and very early preterm birth with birth-weight less than 1,500 g (n = 55, 7%) (see Figure 4).

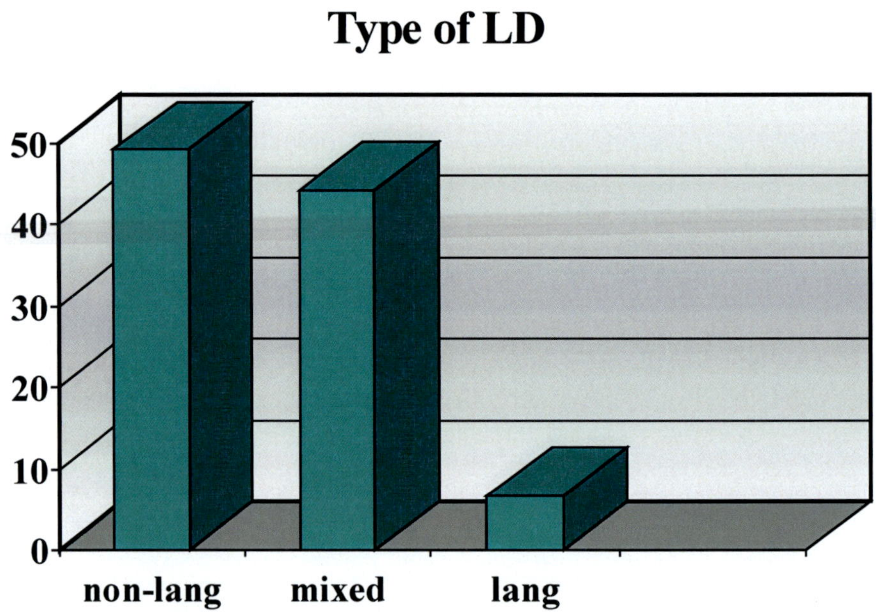

Figure 2. Type of learning disability. Non-lang = non-language type, mix = language-non-language type, lang = pure language type. Data presented as a percentage.

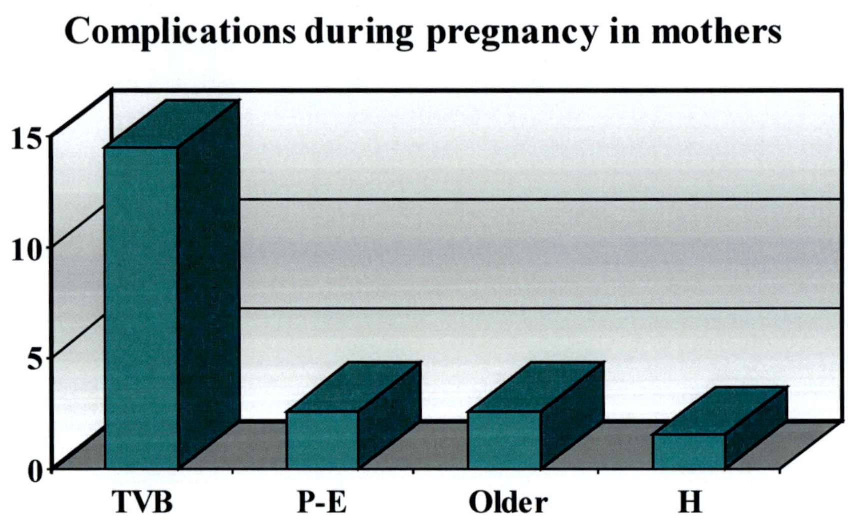

Figure 3. Complications during pregnancy in mothers. TVB = transvaginal bleeding, P-E = preclampsia, Older = pregnancy after 35 years of age, H = hypertension. Data presented as a percentage.

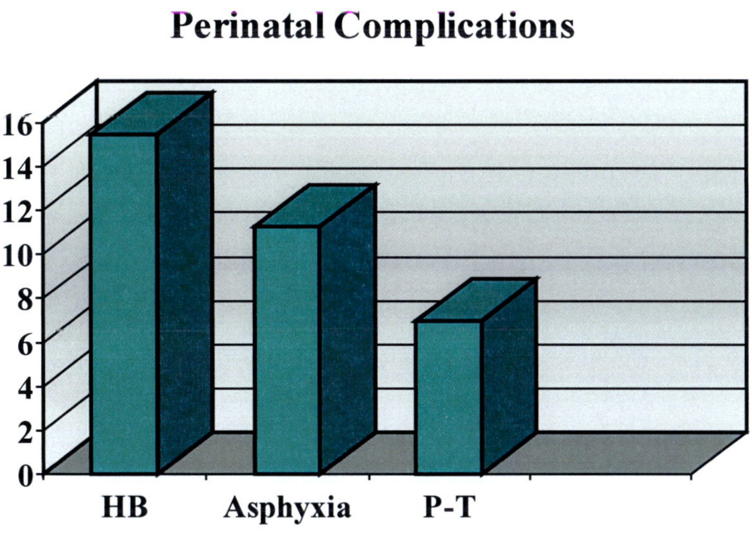

Figure 4. Perinatal complications of the LD children. HB = hyperbilirubinemia, Asphyxia = neonatal asphyxia, P-T = very preterm birth. Data presented as a percentage.

Neurologic history disclosed a delay in language development in 383 children (49.2%), mild head trauma without loss of consciousness in 162 patients (20.8%), breath-holding spells in 110 patients (14.1%), delay in motor development in 60 patients (7.7%), co-morbidity of attention deficit-hyperactivity disorder in 35 patients (4.5%), and febrile seizures in 30 patients (3.8%) (see Figure 5).

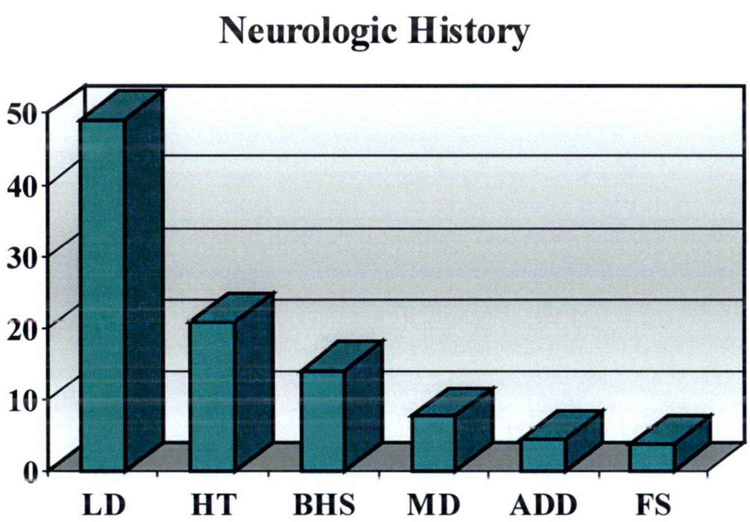

Figure 5. Neurologic history in children with LD. LD = language delay, HT = mild head trauma, BHS = breath holding spells, MD = motor delay, ADD = Attention deficit disorder, FS = febrile seizures. Data presented as a percentage.

In the neurologic examination, the most common signs were dysgraphystesias in 185 patients (23.7%), dysterognosias in 54 patients (6.9%), hand dyspraxias in 43 patients (5.5%), dysdiadochokinesia in 40 patients (5.1%), and dysmetry in 39 patients (5%) (see Figure 6). Handedness showed that 776 subjects (98.4%) were right-handed and only 12 subjects (1.5%) were left-handed.

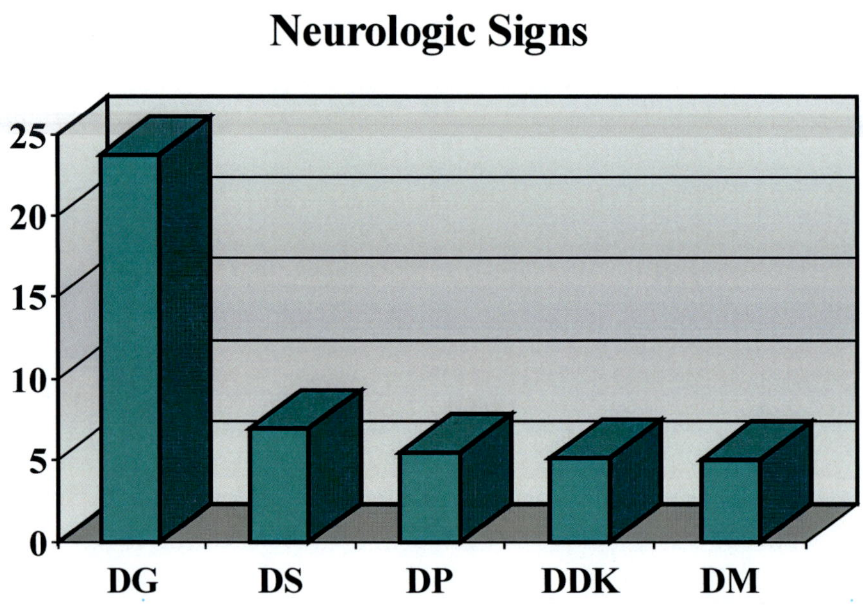

Figure 6. Neurologic signs in children with LD. DG = dysgraphy, DS = dysterognosias, DP = dyspraxia, DDK = dysdiadochokinesia, DM = dysmetry. Data presented as a percentage.

COMMENTS

In this study we included only children treated at our Neuropsychologic Clinic and not from the general elementary school population; thus our results are limited to only an urban population with access to specialized health care services in Mexico City. The study was descriptive and no correlations among variables were carried out.

Our data show that diagnosis was performed in the first three years of elementary school with interest from parents and teachers. In the future early identification may be mandatory to avoid complications derived from LDs (Ramey et al., 1999).

Gender differences in LD prevalence are under research; earlier studies showed a consistent prevalence in male children. However, this idea was biased and it is suggested that boys and girls present with a similar frequency of LDs (Shaywitz et al., 1990). In underdeveloped countries, parents have the idea that males will be the only economic support of the family; thus females with LDs do not receive the same attention.

Nearly one half of our population has non-language LDs, and nearly one half, a mixed type including language and non-language LDs. Pure language LDs are the less frequent type of LD. This result is in agreement with data from other studies that showed that language and non-language groups are present in LDs in children (Fein et al., 1988; Kinsbourne et al., 1999).

In underdeveloped countries, malnutrition is common, and a relationship among poverty, malnutrition, and academic failure is well-established (Campbell and Ramey, 1994). The main alterations correlated with malnutrition are delayed vocabulary and impaired visual perception and visual-kinesthetic and auditory-visual inter-sensory integration (Cravioto and Cravioto, 1990).

Thus data from Children's Neuropsychological Clinic in Mexico City support the hypothesis that LDs have a wide spectrum of clinical characteristics, with symptoms in at least two areas: language and non-language systems. More research is needed to attain comprehensive knowledge of LDs in the future, by means of prospective, well-designed, and meta-analysis studies and information about the challenges of rare cases.

REFERENCES

Brown, B., Haegerstrom-Portnoy, G., Yingling, C.D., Herron, J., Galin, D., Marcus, M. (1983) Dyslexic children have normal vestibular responses to rotation. *Archives of Neurology* 40: 370-373

Campbell, F.A., Ramey, C.T. (1994) Effects of early intervention on intellectual and academic achievement: a follow-up study of children from low-income families. *Child Development* 65: 684-698

Cohen, J., Breslin, P.W. (1984) Visual evoked responses in dyslexic children. *Annals of the New York Academy of Science* 425: 338-343

Cravioto, J., Cravioto, P. (1990) Some long-term psychobiologic consequences of malnutrition. *Annals of Nestlé* 48: 93-102

de Luca, M., di Pace, E., Judica, A., Spinelli, D., Zoccolotti, P. (1999) Eye movements patterns in linguistic and non-linguistic task in developmental dyslexia. *Neuropsychologia* 37: 1407-1420

Duffy., F.H., Denckla, M.B., Bartels, P.H., Sandini, G. (1980) Dyslexia: Regional differences in brain electrical activity by topographic mapping. *Annals of Neurology* 7: 412-420

Eden, G.F., Stein, J.F., Wood, H.M., Wood, F.B. (1994) Differences in eye movements and reading problems in dyslexic and normal children. *Vision Research* 34: 1345-1358

Eden, G.F, van Meter, J.W., Rumsey, J.M., Maisong, J.M., Woods, R.P., Zeffiro, T.A. (1996) Abnormal processing of visual motion in dyslexia revealed by functional brain imaging. *Nature* 382: 66-69

Fein, G., Davenport, L., Yingling, C.D., Galin, D. (1988) Verbal and nonverbal memory deficits in pure dyslexia. *Developmental Neuropsychology* 4: 181-197

Fisher, B., Hartnegg, K. (2000) Effects of visual training on saccade control in dyslexia. *Perception* 29: 531-542

Galaburda, A.M., Kemper, T.L. (1979) Cytoarchitectonic abnormalities in developmental dyslexia: a case study. *Annals of Neurology* 6: 94-100

Galaburda, A.M., Eidelberg, D. (1982) Symmetry and asymmetry in the human posterior thalamus. II. Thalamic lesions in a case of developmental dyslexia. *Archives of Neurology* 39: 333-336

Galaburda, A.M., Sherman, G.F., Rosen, G.D., Aboitiz, F., Geschwind, N. (1985) Developmental dyslexia: four consecutive patients with cortical anomalies. *Annals of Neurology* 18: 222-233

Galaburda, A.M., Menard, M.T., Rosen, G.D. (1994) Evidence for aberrant auditory anatomy in developmental dyslexia. *Proceedings of the National Academy of Science USA* 91: 8010-8013

García-Pedroza, F., Rubio-Donnadieu, F., García-Ramos, G., Escobedo-Ríos, F., González-Cortés, A. (1983) Prevalence of epilepsy in children: Tlalpan, México City, México. *Neuroepidemiology* 2: 16-23

Gerson-Wolfenberger, D.C.M., Ruijssenaars W.A.J.J.M. (1997) Definition and treatment of dyslexia: a report by the committee on dyslexia of the health council of the Netherlands. *Journal of Learning Disabilities* 30: 209-213

Geschwind, N., Behan, P. (1982) Left-handedness: association with immune disease, migraine and developmental learning disorder. *Proceedings of the National Academy of Sciences of U.S.A.* 79: 5097-5100

Ghez, C., Cooper, S., Martin, J. (1996) Kinematics and dynamic factors in the coordination of prehension movements. In: Wing, A.M., Haggard, P., Flanagan, J.R. (editors). *Hand and Brain. The Neurophysiology and Psychology of Hand Movements.* San Diego, Academic Press. pp. 187-211

Grigorenko, E.L., Wood, F.B., Meyer, M.S. (1997) Susceptibility loci for distinct components of developmental dyslexia on chromosomes 6 and 15. *American Journal of Human Genetics* 60: 27-39

Hagman, J.O., Wood, F., Buchsbaum, M.S., Tallal, P., Flowers, L., Katz, W. (1992) Cerebral brain metabolism in adult dyslexic subjects assessed with positron emission tomography during performance of an auditory task. *Archives of Neurology* 49: 734-739

Haslam, R.H.A., Dalby, J.T., Johns, R.D., Rademaker, A.W. (1981) Cerebral asymmetry in developmental dyslexia. *Archives of Neurology* 38: 679-682

Henderson, V.W. (1986) Anatomy of posterior pathways in reading: a reassessment. *Brain and Language* 29: 119-133

Horak, F.B., Shumway-Cook, A., Crowe, T.K., Black, F.O. (1988) Vestibular function and motor proficiency of children with impaired hearing, or with learning disability and motor impairments. *Developmental Medicine and Child Neurology* 30: 64-79

Horwitz, B., Rumsey, J.M., Donohue, B.C. (1998) Functional connectivity of the angular gyrus in normal reading and dyslexia. *Proceedings of the National Academy of SciencesUSA* 95: 8939-8944

Hugdahl, K., Ellertsen, B., Waaler P.E., Kløve, H. (1989) Left and right-handed dyslexic boys: an empirical test of some assumptions of the Geschwind-Behan hypothesis. *Neuropsychologia* 27: 223-231

Humphreys, P., Kaufmann, W.E., Galaburda, A.M. (1990) Developmental dyslexia in women: neuropathological findings in three patients. *Annals of Neurology* 28: 727-738

Jerabek, J., Krejcova, H. (1991) Oculomotor and vestibular findings in developmental dyslexia. *Acta Otolaryngol (Stockh)* suppl 481: 513-514

Jernigan, T.L., Hesselink, J.R., Sowell, E., Tallal, P.A. (1991) Cerebral structure on magnetic resonance imaging in language- and learning-impaired children. *Archives of Neurology* 48: 539-545

John, E.R., Karmel, B.Z., Corning, W.C., Easton, P., Brown, D., Ahn, H., John, M., Harmony, T., Prichep, L., Toro, A., Gerson, I., Barlett, F., Thatcher. R., Kaye, H., Valdes, P., Schwartz, E. (1977) Neurometrics. *Science* 196: 1393-1410

Kinsbourne, M., Tocci-Rufo D., Gamzu, E., Palmer, R.L., Berliner, A.K. (1999) Neuropsychological deficits in adults with dyslexia. *Developmental Medicine and Child Neurology* 33: 763-775

Klimesch, W., Doppelmayr, M., Wimmer, H., Schwaiger, J., Röhm, D., Gruber, W., Hutzler, F. (2001a) Theta band power changes in normal and dyslexic children. *Clinical Neurophysiology* 112: 1174-1185

Klimesch, W., Doppelmayr, M., Wimmer, H., Gruber, W., Röhm, D., Schwaiger, J., Hutzler, F. (2001b) Alpha and beta band power changes in normal and dyslexic children. *Clinical Neurophysiology* 112: 1186-1195

Lehmkuhle, S., Garzia, R.P., Turner, L., Hash, T., Baro, J.A. (1993) A defective visual pathway in children with reading disability. *New England Journal of Medicine* 328: 989-996

Leonard, C.M., Voeller, K.K.S., Lombardino, L.J., Morris, M.K., Hynd, G.W., Alexander, A.W., Andersen, H.G., Garofalakis, M., Honeyman, J.C., Mao, J., Agee, F., Staab, E.V. (1993) Anomalous cerebral structure in dyslexia revealed with magnetic resonance imaging. *Archives of Neurology* 50:461-469

Livingstone, M.S., Rosen, G.D., Drislane, F.W., Galaburda, A.M. (1991) Physiological and anatomical evidence for a magnocellular defect in developmental dyslexia. *Proceedings of the National Academy of Sciences USA* 88: 7943-7947

Lovett, M.W. (1997) Developmental reading disorders. In: Feinberg, T.E., Farah, M.J., editors. *Behavioral Neurology and Neuropsychology*. New York, McGraw-Hill. pp. 773-787

Luria, A.R. (1975) Neuropsychology: Its sources, principles, and prospects. In: Worden, F.G., Swazey, J.P., Adelman, G., editors. *The neurosciences: Paths of discovery*. Cambridge, The MIT Press. pp. 335-361

Mesulam, M.M. (1990) Large-scale neurocognitive networks and distributed processing for attention, language, and memory. *Annals of Neurology* 28: 597-613

Molfese, D.L. (2000) Predicting dyslexia at 8 years of age using neonatal brain responses. *Brain and Language* 72: 238-245

Moore, L.H., Brown, W.S., Markee, T.E., Theberge, D.C., Zvi, J. (1995) Bimanual coordination in dyslexic adults. *Neuropsychologia* 33: 781-793

Paulesu, E., Démonet, J-F., Fazio, F., McCrory, E., Chanoine, V., Brunswick, N., Cappa, S.F., Cossu, C., Habib, H., Frith, C.D., Frith, U. (2001) Dyslexia, cultural diversity and biological unity. *Science* 291: 2165-2167

Poblano, A., Druet, N., Peñaloza, Y., Jiménez, R. (1991) Brainstem and middle latency auditory evoked potentials in dislexic and control children (in Spanish). *Boletin Medico del Hospital Infantil de Mexico* 48: 434-439

Poblano, A., Druet, N., Kauffman-Janssen, B., Huipe-Valencia, H. (1994) Learning disability and attention deficit disorder in children (in Spanish). In: *Communication Disorders Medicine*. Hernández, O.F., Arroyo, C.J.A., Peñaloza, L.Y. (editors), Mexico City, Secretariat of Health. pp. 213-238

Poblano, A., Fukumoto-Okamoto L.E., Silva-Valencia, M.J., Martínez-Wbaldo, M.C. (1996a) Development of graphemes in pre-school children (in Spanish). *Pedagogia* 11: 36-41

Poblano, A., Córdova de Caballero, B., Castillo, I., Cortes, V. (1996b) Electro-oculographic recordings reveal reading deficiencies in learning disabled children. *Archives of Medical Research* 27: 509-512

Poblano, A. (1997) Neurophysiological recordings in learning disabled children (in Spanish). In: *Electrophysiological recordings for the diagnosis of communication disorders.* Hernandez, O.F., Flores, R.T., Peñaloza, L.Y. (editors), Mexico City, Secretariat of Health. pp. 286-293

Poblano, A., Valadez-Tepec, T., Arias, M.L., García-Pedroza, F. (2000) Phonological and visuo-spatial working memory alterations in dyslexic children. *Archives of Medical Research* 31: 493-496

Poblano, A., Borja, S., Elías, Y., García-Pedroza, F., Arias, M.L. (2002a) Characteristics of specific reading disability in children from a neuropsychological clinic in México City. *Salud Publica de Mexico* 44: 323-327

Poblano, A., Ishiwara, K., Arias, M.L., García-Pedroza, F., Marín, H., Trujillo, M. (2002b) Motor control alteration in posturography in learning-disabled children. *Archives of Medical Research* 33: 485-488

Poblano, A., Rothenberg, S.J., Fonseca, M.E., Cruz, M.L, Flores, T., Zarco, I. (2003) Salivary testosterone and EEG spectra of 9 to 11-year-old male children. *Developmental Neuropsychology* 23: 375-384

Ramey, C.T., Campbell, F.A., Ramey S.L. (1999) Early intervention: successful pathways to improving intellectual development. *Developmental Neuropsychology* 16: 385-392

Rousselle, C., Wolf, P.H. (1991) The dynamics of bimanual coordination in developmental dyslexia. *Neuropsychologia* 29: 907-924

Salmelin, R., Helenius, P., Service, E. (2000) Neurophysiology of fluent and impaired reading: a magnetoencephalographic approach. *Journal of Clinical Neurophysiology* 17: 163-174

Shaywitz, S.E. (1998) Dyslexia. *New England Journal of Medicine* 338: 307-312

Shaywitz, S.E., Shaywitz, B.A., Fletcher, J.M., Escobar, M.D. (1990) Prevalence of reading disability in boys and girls. Results of the Connecticut Longitudinal Study. *JAMA* 264: 998-1002

Shaywitz, S.E., Shaywitz, B.A., Pugh, K.R., Fulbright, R.K., Constable R.T., Mencl, W.E., Shankweiler D.P., Liberman, A.M., Skudlarski, P., Fletcher, J.M., Katz, L., Marchione, K.E., Lacadie, C., Gatenby, C., Gore, J. C. (1998) Functional disruption in the organization of the brain for reading in dyslexia. *Proceedings of the National Academy of Sciences USA* 95: 2636-2641

Simos, P.G., Fletcher, J.M., Foorman, B.R., Francis, D.J., Castillo, E.M., Davis, R.N., Fitzgerald, M., Mathes, P.G., Denton, C., Papanicolaou A.C., (2002) Brain activation profiles during the early stages of reading acquisition. *Journal of Child Neurology* 17: 159-163

Skarda, C.A., Freeman, W.J. (1987) How brain make chaos in order to make sense of the world. *Behavioral and Brain Sciences* 10: 161-195

Shumway-Cook, A., Horak, F., Black, F.O. (1987) A critical examination of vestibular function in motor-impaired learning-disabled children. *International Journal of Pediatric Otorhinolaryngology* 14: 21-30

Taylor, M.J., Keenan, N.K. (1990) Event-related potentials to visual and language stimuli in normal and dyslexic children. *Psychophysiology* 27: 318-327

Wolf, P.H., Michel, G.F., Ovrut, M., Drake, C. (1990) Rate and precision timing of motor coordination in developmental dyslexia. *Developmantal Psychology* 26: 349-359

In: Trends in Dyslexia Research
Editor: Henry D. Tobias, pp. 187-222
ISBN 1-59454-219-8

Chapter VIII

Three Types of Alexia in Occipital and Occipitotemporal Gyrus Lesions. A New Classification of Alexia.

Yasuhisa Sakurai *

Department of Neurology, Mitsui Memorial Hospital, Tokyo, Japan

Abstract

Different alexia syndromes from retrorolandic lesions in Japanese patients have been reported. Lesion-to-symptom analysis and previous imaging studies reveal that there are three types of alexia, i.e. pure alexia for Kanji (Japanese morphograms) and Kana (Japanese phonetic writing) from a fusiform gyrus lesion (ventromedial type), pure alexia for Kana from a posterior occipital gyri lesion (posterior type), and alexia with agraphia for Kanji from a posterior inferior temporal cortex lesion. Quantitative examination with Kanji words, Kana words and Kana nonwords showed that Kana nonword reading was impaired in all three types, suggesting that widespread areas in the affected occipital and occipitotemporal cortices are recruited in reading Kana characters (corresponding to European syllables). In ventromedial type pure alexia, whole-word reading, together with letter identification, is primarily impaired because of disconnection between early visual analysis and word-form images that are stored in the posterior inferior temporal cortex, whereas in posterior type pure alexia, letter identification is cardinally impaired. Another type of alexia, alexia with agraphia for Kanji from a posterior inferior temporal cortex lesion, results from deficient whole-word images of words per se, and thus should be designated "orthographic alexia with agraphia." To account for these impairments, a weighted dual-route hypothesis for reading was proposed, in which areas concerned with reading show changes in weight of involvement according to how many times a word is recognized.

* Address correspondence to: Yasuhisa Sakurai, M.D., Ph.D., Department of Neurology, Mitsui Memorial Hospital, 1 Kanda-Izumi-cho, Chiyoda-ku, Tokyo, 101-8643 Japan, TEL 81-3-3862-9111, FAX 81-3-5687-9765, e-mail: ysakurai-tky@umin.ac.jp

Key words: Pure alexia, Alexia with agraphia, Angular gyrus, Fusiform gyrus, Letter-by-letter reading

The mechanisms underlying recognition of letters and words and comprehension of sentences have been investigated in the fields of classic lesion-to-symptom analyses, [1] cognitive neuropsychology, [2] connectionism, [3] and functional neuroimaging. [4] In this chapter, the author describes reading impairments from focal lesions and the results of our positron emission tomography (PET) activation studies. Based on these findings, a new classification of alexia and a new hypothesis for the mechanism of reading are proposed.

I. Kanji and Kana vs Regular and Irregular Words

Let us describe briefly the relationship between Japanese and European languages. Fig. 1 shows the correspondence of European letter strings, regular nonwords (pseudowords), regular words (that obey spelling-sound rules) and irregular words to Kana (Japanese phonetic writing) nonwords, Kana words and Kanji (Japanese morphogram or ideogram) words, according to their pronunciation regularity and word-form (orthography). Phonologically, Kana symbols parallel European consonant-vowel syllables or mora in the sense that they develop one-to-one character-to-sound correspondence. Orthographically, Kana characters correspond to European letters. Kana character strings are regular, whether they are words or nonwords, since there is no pronunciation ambiguity in translating Kana characters to their corresponding sounds. Thus, Kana words are comparable to regular words, and Kana nonwords are comparable to regular nonwords (pseudowords). [5] Conversely, single Kanji characters or words correspond to mora too, but they are irregular, because there is nearly no character-to-sound correspondence. However, Kanji words consisting of two or more characters have some subtle regularities [6] (or consistencies, according to the connectionist terminology). Therefore, strictly speaking, Kanji words are comparable to real words (regular and irregular words).

Kana nonwords   Kana words   Kanji words

letter strings   regular nonwords (pseudoword)   regular words   irregular words

---

(unpronounceable)   regular   ← Pronunciation →   irregular

absent   ← Word-form →   present

Fig. 1. Correspondence between Roman alphabet and Japanese script

II. Alexia from Focal Lesions

In the retrorolandic area, three lesions are known to give rise to reading impairment: the medial occipital gyri with the splenium, posterior inferior temporal cortex, and angular gyrus (Table 1).

Table 1. Conventional classification of alexia.

I Neurological classification of non-aphasic alexia from postrolandic lesions*
- A. Pure alexia
  - Classical type: medial occipital gyri (primary visual cortex) + splenium
  - Non-classical type:
    - Subangular alexia
    - Occipital alexia
      - Lateral and holo-occipital alexia
      - Medial occipital alexia
- B. Alexia with agraphia
  - Angular type
  - Posterior inferior temporal type

II Neuropsychological classification of reading impairments
- A. Letter-by-letter reading
- B. Surface dyslexia
- C. Deep dyslexia
- D. Phonological dyslexia

*Based on Greenblatt [11] and Kawamura. [13]

1. Pure Alexia without a Splenium Lesion

Dejerine first described alexia with agraphia due to an angular gyrus lesion and pure alexia (alexia without agraphia) due to lesions of the medial occipital gyri and the splenium. [7, 8] He thought that the visual images of letters and words are stored in the angular gyrus and that any lesion that interrupts visual input to the angular gyrus may cause alexia. [7, 9] Geschwind [10] stressed the importance of the splenium lesion in pure alexia. He argued that pure alexia results from destruction of the splenium through which visual information in written language can be transmitted from the right hemisphere to the left. However, subsequent studies [11, 12] showed that pure alexia occurs following damage to the temporo-occipital area or occipital lobe without the splenium. Greenblatt [11] called this non-classical type [13] of pure alexia "preangular alexia," and classified it into "subangular alexia" [14] and occipital alexia. [15] The anatomic substrate of pure alexia is now considered to be in the paraventricular white matter of the left occipital lobe, [12] the lingual and fusiform gyri with the white matter, [16] or the ventral occipitotemporal area. [17]

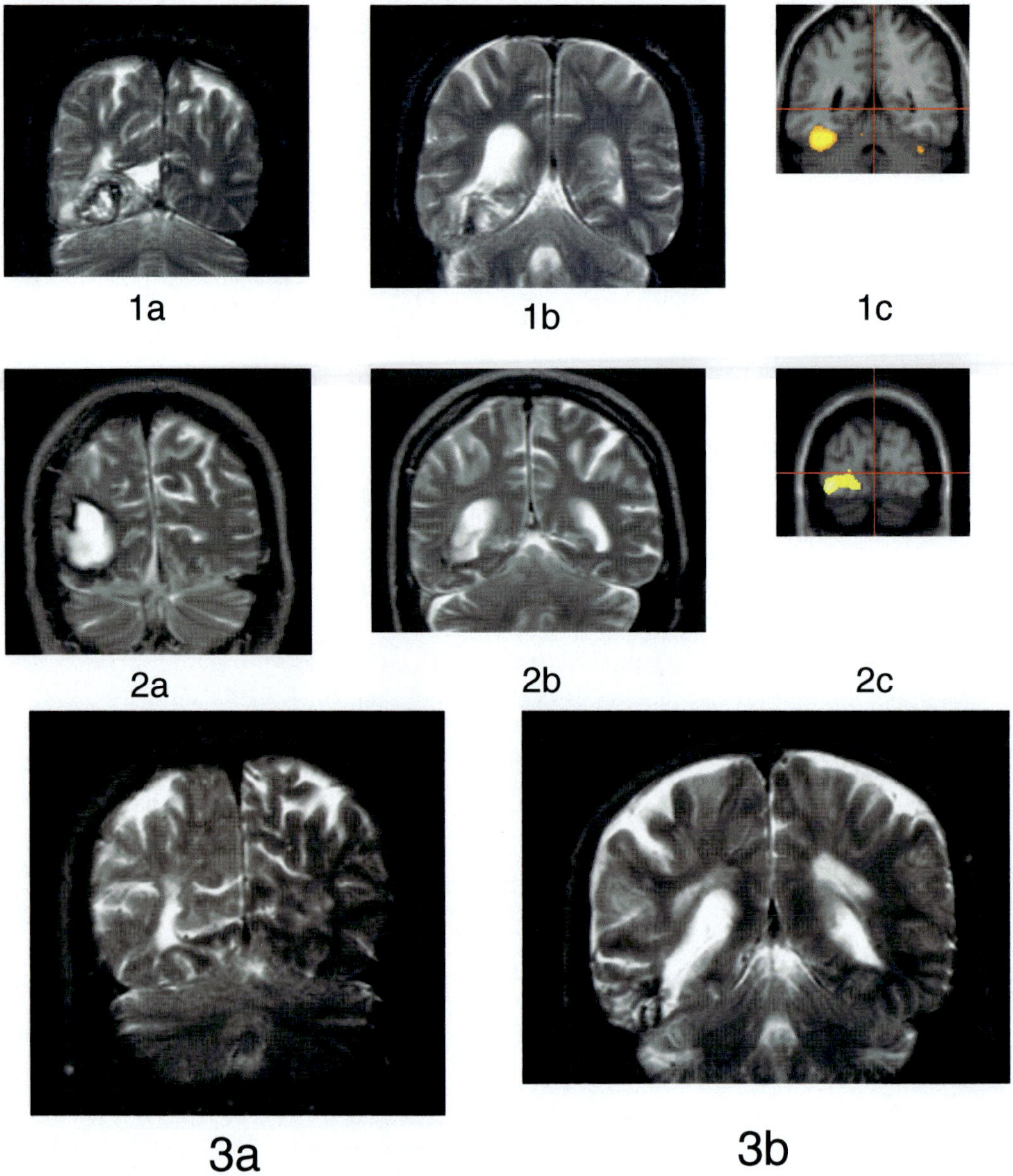

Fig. 2. MRI T2-weighted coronal images through the calcarine sulcus (a) and the posterior horn (b) in patients 1 to 3. 1a and 1b: 45 days after the second stroke in patient 1 (pure alexia for Kanji and Kana); 1c: activation of the fusiform/inferior temporal gyri in normal subjects' Kanji word reading (y=-50 mm) evaluated with Statistical Parametric Mapping Version 96 (SPM 96; uncorrected $p<0.001$); 2a and 2b: three months after onset in patient 2 (pure alexia for Kana); 2c: activation of the inferior occipital/fusiform gyri in normal subjects' Kana word reading (y=-90 mm) evaluated with SPM 96 (uncorrected $p<0.001$); 3a and 3b: six years after onset in patient 3 (alexia with agraphia for Kanji). The left side of each image is the patient's left side. Note that the lesion of patient 1 was located more medially in the fusiform gyrus than that of patient 3.

Case presentation. Patient 1 (Non-classical type pure alexia for Kanji and Kana from a lesion in the fusiform and inferior occipital gyri) [18]: a 73-year-old, right-handed man had cerebral infarction in the left lingual gyrus in May 1995, although he was not aware of any visual field defect. In April 1996 he sustained a second stroke involving the left fusiform and posterior occipital gyri, after which he could no longer read any Kana and certain Kanji symbols. He read slowly and with difficulty even words that he had just written. Neurological examination showed right upper homonymous quadrantanopsia. Quantitative evaluation with the basic 100 Kanji (one-character words) and the corresponding Kana (Kana transcription of Kanji words) [19] two months after the second stroke revealed that he read 98% of Kanji and 97% of Kana correctly, although he spent more than five times longer in reading compared with normal controls. MRI 45 days after the second attack showed an abnormal intensity lesion in the left fusiform gyrus under the posterior horn of the lateral ventricle that extended posteriorly to the ventral side of the occipital lobe (Fig. 2).

2. Pure Alexia for Kana

The posterior occipital lobe is rarely damaged in isolation in cerebrovascular disease. Information about the function of this area has been obtained solely from resection case data. [15] We reported pure alexia (letter-by-letter reading) selectively impaired for Kana after hemorrhage in the left posterior occipital lobe. Here the author summarizes the patient profile with follow-up data.

Case presentation. Patient 2 (Pure alexia for Kana from a posterior occipital gyri lesion) [20]: a 77-year-old, right-handed man became aware of a narrowed visual field in March 1998 and later noticed difficulty in reading Kana after cerebral hemorrhage under the left posterior occipital cortices, mainly affecting the lateral occipital gyri. He even had difficulty reading sentences written by himself. Neurological and neuropsychological examination showed right lower homonymous quadrantanopsia, cerebral achromatopsia, pure alexia for Kana and minor agraphia for Kanji. He read Kana words character by character, and spent more time reading five-character Kana words than three-character Kana words (word length effect). Quantitative evaluation with the 100 Kanji and Kana [19] described above two months after onset revealed that he read 99% of Kanji and 83% of Kana correctly, requiring 15 times longer than normal for Kana reading. The patient also could not recognize some single-character Kana: he misread visually similar characters, e.g. こ [ko] (incorrect) for い [i] (correct), う [u] for つ [tsu], and や [ya] for ゆ [yu]. Kinesthetic reading (tracing letters with the fingers) was mostly effective, but he sometimes traced incorrectly and wrote another Kana character. Furthermore, the patient failed to discriminate between two shapes (circles and ovals, or squares and rectangles) of a similar size (Fig. 3). He could read newspapers without difficulty after one and a half years, but letter-by-letter reading still persisted at re-examination five years after onset. MRI three months after onset disclosed a high-intensity area in the white matter of the left occipital lobe, mainly under the lateral and ventral occipital gyri (inferior occipital and fusiform gyri) (Fig. 2). Single photon emission computed tomography with ^{99m}Tc-ethylcysteinate dimer (^{99m}Tc-ECD-SPECT) two months after onset showed hypoperfusion in the overall left occipital lobe, including the angular gyrus and posterior inferior temporal cortex. But the blood flow of the posterior inferior temporal cortex recovered to within the normal range one year later (Fig. 4).

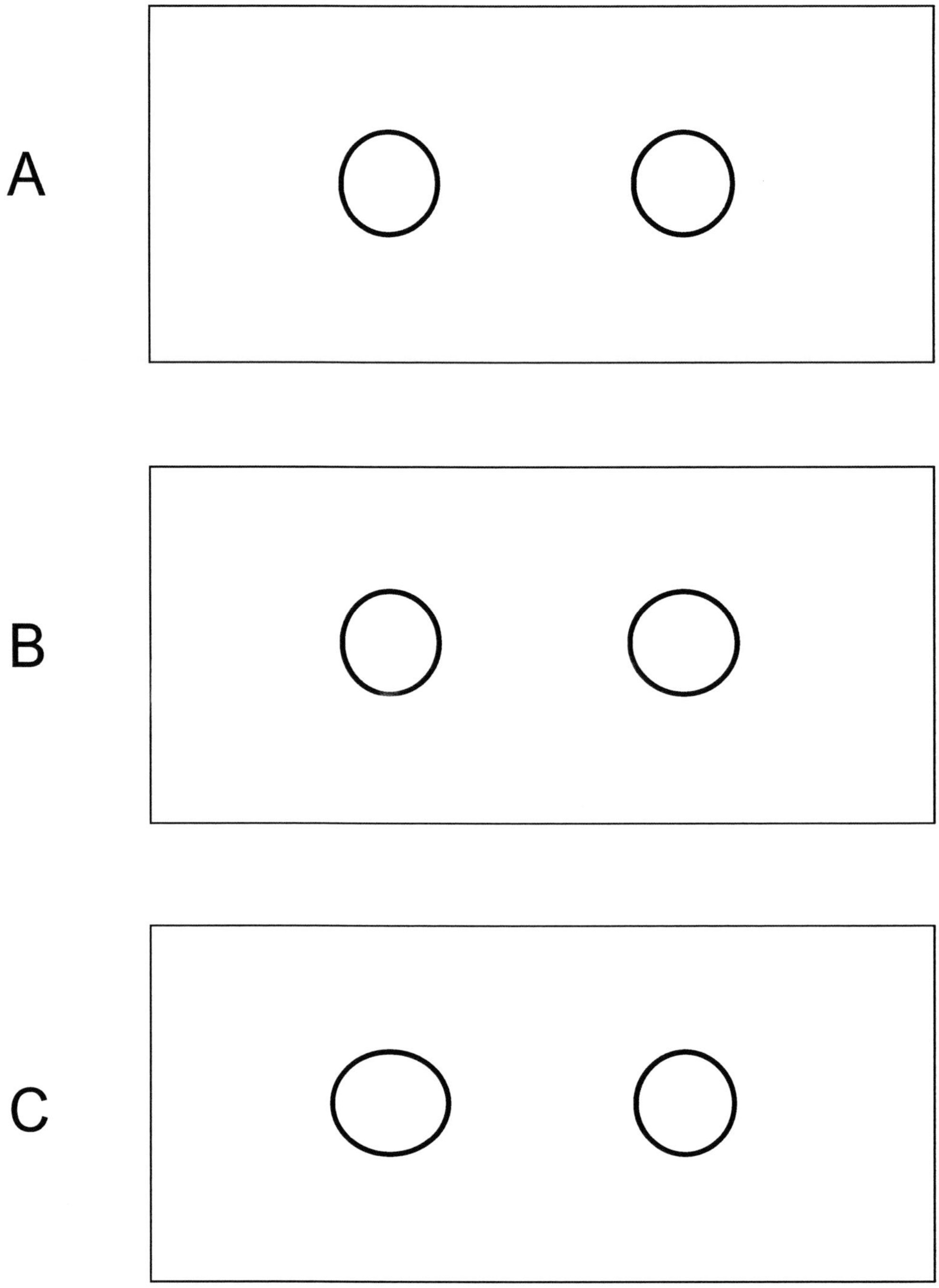

Fig. 3. Samples of the visual discrimination test (circle-oval). Two stimuli of slightly different sizes or shapes were drawn on a card. The patient was asked whether the two were the same or different and, if different, was asked to explain the difference. A. same (circle-circle), B. slightly different (circle-oval): the line of apsides of the oval is 10% longer than the diameter of the circle, C. mildly different (oval-circle): the line of apsides of the oval is 20% longer than the diameter of the circle.

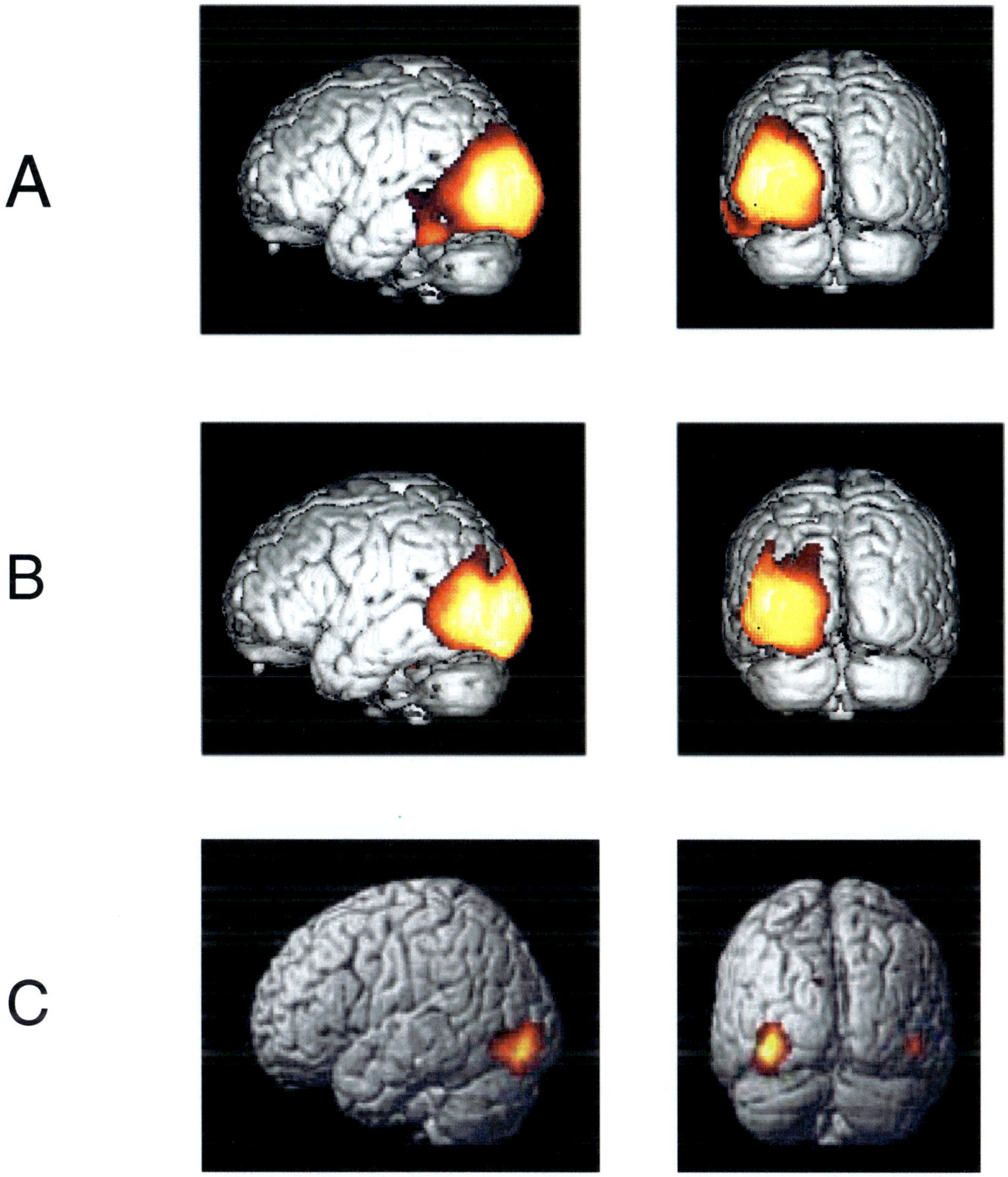

Fig. 4. Brain areas with decreased blood flow in patient 3 (pure alexia for Kana) in ^{99m}Tc-ECD-SPECT images evaluated with SPM 96 for Windows. The patient's images were compared with those of 20 normal subjects with the age of 60 or more. (corrected $p<0.01$). [21] A. two months after onset, B. one year and two months after onset, C. activation of the occipital lobe in normal subjects' Kana word covert reading evaluated with SPM 99 (uncorrected $p<0.001$). [75] An area with decreased blood flow involved the activated area in Kana word reading in the left occipital lobe.

This patient suggests that the left posterior occipital lobe, particularly the inferior lateral and ventral side (Brodmann Areas 18 and 19), is crucial for reading Kana. The fact that he misread single-characters and had minimal deficit of visual shape discrimination suggests impairment of an early stage of reading (character recognition). Also the fact that he could read Kanji without difficulty implies that there is no sequential information processing from the inferior occipital/fusiform gyri (Areas 18 and 19) to the fusiform/inferior temporal gyri (Area 37), damage to which cause Kanji alexia with agraphia (described below).

Non-classical type (without involvement of splenium) pure alexia for Kana has rarely been reported. [22] How does pure alexia for Kana present itself in Western countries? As described previously, Kana words are roughly comparable to European regular words, and Kana nonwords are comparable to regular nonwords (pseudowords) in the sense that grapheme-to-phoneme correspondence is almost complete, whereas Kanji words are comparable to regular and irregular words in the sense that a whole-word image is more involved in reading and writing. Accordingly, pure alexia for Kana parallels pure alexia for regular words and nonwords, especially for nonwords that are more difficult to read, with preserved reading of regular and irregular words. Indeed, pure alexia showing a greater impairment for nonwords was reported in Western countries in patients whose lesions involved the posterior occipital gyri. [23-25]

3. Alexia with Agraphia for Kanji from a Posterior Inferior Temporal Cortex Lesion

In 1984, Iwata [26] reported a patient with alexia with agraphia that was preferentially disturbed for Kanji, following a cerebral infarction in the posterior inferior temporal cortex. Since then, alexia with agraphia for Kanji has frequently been reported. [19, 27-30] The responsible lesion extends over the posterior middle and inferior temporal, fusiform and parahippocampal gyri, almost equivalent to Area 37. Reading and writing disturbances for Kanji are remarkable, but some patients with similar lesions showed alexia with agraphia more pronounced for Kana. [13, 31, 32] This is because the lesions extended posteriorly to the occipital gyri, [19] damage to which causes pure alexia for Kana (described above).

Case presentation. Patient 3 (Alexia with agraphia for Kanji) [19]: a 71-year-old right-handed man suddenly realized that he could not remember the names of objects and could not read newspapers or write anything but his own name, following hemorrhage under the left lateral fusiform and posterior inferior temporal gyri in June 1991. His visual field was intact. Neuropsychological examination showed alexia with agraphia preferentially disturbed for Kanji along with severe anomia. He read character-by-character sentences written in Kanji and Kana. Of note is that he could point to objects correctly, although he could not read aloud the names of the objects written in Kanji (understanding without phonology [18]). Quantitative evaluation with 100 Kanji and Kana three months after onset revealed that he read 20% of Kanji (four semantic paralexia errors were observed) and 75% of Kana correctly, and correctly wrote from dictation 4% of Kanji and 59% of Kana. Alexia with agraphia and anomia persisted at re-evaluation five years later. MRI four months after onset disclosed that the lesion involved the lateral fusiform and inferior temporal gyri (Area 37) and extended subcortically to the anterior third of the temporal lobe. Follow-up MRI six years later showed the same lesion with additional periventricular hyperintensity (Fig. 2).

There are several unsolved problems in this alexia with agraphia. First, in some patients alexia disappears in a few months, and thus some authors [29, 30] called it pure agraphia for Kanji. However, the patient described above had persistent alexia with agraphia that lasted more than five years. What caused this difference is not known. The author's view is that the most crucial region for alexia with agraphia lies in the fusiform/posterior inferior temporal gyri (see V.): if the main lesion lies upward in the posterior middle temporal gyrus [30], pure agraphia occurs, and if the lesion lies medially in the fusiform gyrus, pure alexia occurs (described below).

Second, non-classical type pure alexia occurs from nearly the same lesion. Kawamura [13] already pointed out that the lesion of pure alexia lies to some extent medially to that of alexia with agraphia for Kanji. Patient 1 with pure alexia had the same lesion. When we compared the lesion of patient 1 with that of patient 3 with alexia with agraphia, we found that the lesion of patient 1 was located more medially in the fusiform gyrus whereas the lesion of patient 3 was located more laterally in the fusiform/inferior temporal gyri (Fig. 2). We surmised that orthographic information on letters and words is stored as a neural network around the fusiform/inferior temporal gyri. Pure alexia from a fusiform gyrus lesion (patient 1) results from interrupted access to this orthography. [18]

Third, what is equivalent to alexia with agraphia for Kanji in Western countries? We assumed that reading and writing impairment for irregular words may occur from the same lesion in English-speaking countries. [19] Soma et al. [29] argued that lexical agraphia [33, 34] in Western countries parallels pure agraphia for Kanji, based on the fact that most Kanji (comparable to irregular words) agraphic errors derived from impaired character (or word) recall. Pure alexia from a lesion including the fusiform gyrus has been reported frequently in Western countries, [35, 36] although there are few cases with restricted lesion to the fusiform gyrus. [37] Conversely, alexia with agraphia from a similar lesion has rarely been reported. [38, 39] These two reports are concerned with accompanying anomia. The difference between pure alexia and alexia with agraphia depends on whether agraphia co-occurs with alexia. However, it is known that pure alexia is accompanied by minimal agraphia. [40, 41] Thus diagnosis differs according as how the authors evaluate coexisting agraphia. Moreover, letter-by-letter reading features in pure alexia, but this symptom is also observed in alexia with agraphia for Kanji, as described. Therefore, letter-by-letter reading alone does not guarantee a diagnosis of pure alexia. In this regard, it is possible that patients reported as pure alexia, particularly those with a lesion in the fusiform/inferior temporal gyri, showed in fact alexia with agraphia. The fact that regular/irregular distinction is not so evident as the Kanji/Kana difference may account for the paucity of reports on alexia with agraphia from the posterior inferior temporal cortex lesion in Western countries.

4. Angular Alexia with Agraphia

The notion of alexia with agraphia from an angular gyrus lesion seems established. [1] However, it has yet to be determined whether a restricted lesion to the angular gyrus yields alexia. Most reported patients with angular alexia with agraphia had a lesion extending from the angular gyrus forward to the supramarginal gyrus or posteriorly to the lateral occipital gyri. A lesion relatively confined to the angular gyrus produced transient alexia, whereas agraphia remained. [42, 43] It was reported that Japanese patients with angular alexia with agraphia read Kana more poorly than Kanji. [26, 44-46] Patient 2 (pure alexia for Kana) suggests that this symptom reflects the involvement of the posterior occipital gyri. Kleist [47] already attributed the alexic symptom caused by an angular gyrus lesion to damage to the middle occipital gyrus, just posterior to the angular gyrus.

III. Reading Impairments in Cognitive Neuropsychology

Since the 1970s cognitive scientists have clarified two types of reading impairment in acquired dyslexia. [48-51] One is surface dyslexia, in which reading of irregular or exceptional words (those that do not obey English spelling rules) is difficult, whereas reading of regular words remains relatively intact. It is known that this regularity effect (regular words are read more easily than irregular ones) is more evident in low-frequency words. [52] Surface dyslexics can also read regular nonwords, so long as the nonwords follow the English grapheme-to-phoneme conversion rules. The majority of the errors are regularizations (changing regular nonwords into regular real words). It is thought that surface dyslexics cannot use word-level lexical information and rely on the subword procedure for translating from orthography to phonology. [51, 53]

The other type of reading impairment in acquired dyslexia is deep (phonemic) dyslexia, in which reading of regular nonwords is difficult, whereas reading of irregular words remains relatively intact, and reading of real words, both regular and irregular, yields verbal paralexia, such as visual (e.g. "perfume" [incorrect] for "perform" [correct]), semantic (e.g. "sick" for "ill"), derivational (e.g. "strangers" for "strange") and visual-then-semantic (e.g. "orchestra" for "sympathy") errors. Characteristically, deep dyslexic patients have greater difficulties reading abstract, non-imageable words than reading concrete words (concreteness/ imageability effect), read nouns and adjectives better than verbs, and, in turn, read verbs better than function words (part-of-speech effect). It is assumed that for deep dyslexics, the direct computation of phonology from orthography is completely malfunctioning, and the computation of meaning (semantics) from orthography and/or pronunciation from meaning is partially disturbed. [54]

The pure form of deep dyslexia is called phonological dyslexia, in which regular nonword reading is selectively impaired. Phonological dyslexia differs from deep dyslexia in that real (both regular and irregular) word reading is well preserved and that the patients make few semantic errors. [55] Phonological dyslexics, like deep dyslexics, produce visual errors, but they differ from deep dyslexics in that they sometimes read nonwords as real words that have visual resemblance to the target (lexicalization error, e.g. "food" for "fod"). Furthermore, some of them make derivational/inflectional errors and show the imageability effect and the part-of-speech effect. [56, 57] Characteristically, nonword reading is subject to orthographic modulation [58]; (i) nonwords that contain two-letter graphemes (e.g. CAU) are read worse than nonwords that do not (e.g. IKO) [59]; (ii) pseudowords are read better if they are homophonous with a real word (pseudohomophony, e.g. "brane" for "brain"). This advantage is much greater when the pseudohomophone is orthographically close to the parent word. [60]

The accuracy in real word reading in phonological dyslexia is not affected by the spelling-to-sound characteristics of the words, i.e. they do not show regularity effects in reading, [61] suggesting complete damage to sublexical orthography-to-phonology transcoding procedures with an intact internal lexicon (mental dictionary).

Based on these findings, some dual-route hypotheses for reading have been proposed. [2, 48, 51, 54, 62] An early example is Coltheart's model [53] in which reading requires two distinct processing pathways, i.e. a lexical (semantic) route that depends on access to word-specific lexical information (lexicon), and a nonlexical (phonological) route that depends on general knowledge of the rules specifying the grapheme-to-phoneme correspondence. It should be noted that surface dyslexia, deep dyslexia and phonological dyslexia are neurologically aphasic alexia. Surface dyslexia arises from damage to the temporal lobe. [63] Both phonological dyslexia and deep dyslexia have damage to the territory of the left middle cerebral artery in common. In phonological dyslexia damage to the superior temporal, angular and supramarginal gyri is fairly consistent, [64] whereas in deep dyslexia the lesions are commonly extensive left-hemisphere insults. [64-66]

IV. READING PERFORMANCE OF THREE ALEXIA PATIENTS

The three patients above described underwent a reading test, [67] consisting of 100 three-character Kana words (e.g. いけん [iken], opinion), the corresponding two character Kanji words (e.g. 意見 [iken], opinion), and 100 three-character Kana nonwords (e.g. あぬめ [anume]). The Kana words were chosen from those with higher familiarity based on how often the subject had seen, heard or used the word (above 3.50, assessed with a five-point rating scale, range from 0.00 to 4.96). [68] The Kana nonwords were made by combining Kana symbols that have no association with each other. [69] All Kana word and Kana nonword materials were included among those used in our PET reading studies. [70-75] Patients' oral responses and the time spent in reading were recorded.

1. Kana Nonword Reading Impairments

Results showed that Kana nonword reading was impaired in all three patients (Table 2). Single Kana character reading was also disturbed during the course in all patients. [18, 20] These findings suggested that widespread areas in the fusiform (Areas 19 and 37), inferior temporal and posterior occipital gyri are recruited in reading Kana characters (not specific for Kana nonwords). In particular, patient 1 could read Kana words very well two months after onset, but still had difficulty with Kana nonwords. All his reading errors were phonemic paralexia (substitution of other characters), some of which were due to visual similarity. Impairment of character identification was not evident in Kana word reading, probably because the patient used lexical (orthographic, phonological or semantic) help or "lexical capture" [76, 77] in reading. In other words, even if he had difficulty identifying one character in a word, he could guess the character from the context. In fact, patient 1 reported that he used a semantic strategy while reading. Probably the same mechanism worked in patients 2 and 3, which was reflected in their performances in reading Kana words better than Kana nonwords.

Table 2. Patient profiles and reading performance. [67]

Patient	1	2	3	Controls#
Age, Sex	73M	77M	71M	
Symptom	Pure alexia (recovery phase)	Pure alexia	Alexia with agraphia	
Visual field defect	RU	RL		
Reading impairment	Kanji and Kana	Kana > Kanji	Kanji > Kana$	
Lesion	Fu, Post O	Post O	Fu/Inf T	
Time after onset (months)	2	3	61-64	
Reading test of 100 two-character Kanji words, three-character Kana words and three-character Kana nonwords				
Kanji word reading	99 (5 min; 5/5)*	96 (4 min; 1/2)	52 (8 min; 2/15)	99 (1 min)
Kana word reading	99 (4 min)	82 (16 min; 40/45)	84 (6 min)	98 (1 min)
Kana nonword reading	81 (4 min)	72 (10 min; 17/26)**	45 (6 min)	95 (2 min)

* Values are % correct (and time spent in the task; correct responses with kinesthetic reading). The fraction denotes the number of correct responses versus the total attempts at kinesthetic reading, e.g. 5/8 means that five were correct for all eight kinesthetic reading trials.

**In patient 2, Kana nonword reading was examined two weeks after the Kanji word reading and Kana word reading tests.

#Normal controls: 10 men and 1 woman, aged between 61 and 78, mean 68 years old.

$Kanji word reading was more impaired than Kana word reading.

Abbreviations. M, Man; RU, Right upper quandrantanopsia; RL, Right lower quandrantanopsia; Fu, Fusiform gyrus; Post O, Posterior occipital gyri; Inf T, Inferior temporal gyrus.

Patient 2 demonstrated more pronounced reading impairment in Kana nonwords than Kana words, though not significantly. Moreover, preserved Kanji word reading implies that whole-word reading, which is expected to be more involved in reading of graphically complex characters such as Kanji, was still possible in this patient. He had difficulty reading Kana words, suggesting that Kana word reading depends less on whole-word recognition than Kanji word reading. Prominent Kana nonword reading impairment and deficient single Kana character identification are also observed in phonological dyslexia, [57, 77] but the present case can be differentiated from phonological dyslexia in that Kana word reading was apparently disturbed, and there was only a slight difference in the reading score between Kana words and Kana nonwords. Conversely, patient 3 made far more reading errors in Kana nonwords than in Kana words. This is probably because phonological lexical help was still available, although orthographic lexical help did not work well.

The presence of pure alexia for Kanji and Kana (patient 1) and pure alexia for Kana (patient 2) suggests that pure alexia can be divided into two types; one for deficient whole-word recognition and letter or character identification due to a fusiform gyrus lesion (ventromedial type; Table 3); and the other for deficient letter or character identification solely from a posterior occipital gyri lesion (posterior type; Table 3). Patient 1 had both fusiform and posterior occipital lesions, and it thus remains unclear which lesion affected his Kana character reading. Letter-by-letter reading may be more evident in the posterior occipital gyri lesion, as in patient 2, probably because this region is more specific for letter or character identification. [20]

Table 3. A new classification of non-aphasic alexia from postrolandic lesions

A. Pure alexia
   Classical type: medial occipital gyri (primary visual cortex, lateral geniculate body, or optic radiation) + splenium (or callosal radiations)
   Non-classical type:
      Ventromedial (Fusiform, Area 37) type: Pure alexia for Kanji and Kana
      Posterior (Fusiform/Inferior occipital, Area 18/19) type: Pure alexia for Kana
B. Alexia with agraphia
   Posterior inferior temporal type

2. Semantic Errors in Patient 3

Three months after onset, patient 3 showed some semantic paralexia errors in the one-character Kanji reading test. [19] In the follow-up study five years later, he was observed to read Kana nonwords much more poorly than Kana words. In Kanji word reading, there was only one semantic error. However, in the preceding single-character Kanji reading test, [18] all circumlocution and semantic errors that amounted to 13% of total errors were associated semantically with the correct answer, e.g. "white" (incorrect) for "color" (correct), "something to eat" for "drink." He also made visual (precisely phonological and/or visual) errors in Kana word and nonword reading. These findings are characteristic of deep dyslexia, [48, 49] although most of the reading errors were non- or partial responses for Kanji words and phonological errors (literal paralexia) for Kana nonwords. In addition, the patient could not write Kanji words that he could not read, due to difficulty in recall. As his reading difficulty can be attributed to an impaired visual image of words, this type of alexia should be designated orthographic alexia.

Semiologically, orthographic alexia differs from pure alexia in that it is always accompanied by agraphia (lexical or orthographic agraphia [33]), and that kinesthetic reading is probably less helpful than in pure alexia (described later). [18]

Deep dyslexia is semiologically defined by a single feature of semantic paralexia errors that constitute at least 5% of all reading errors. [78] It is thought that this feature nearly always guarantees the presence of other alexic symptoms observed in deep dyslexia. [64] Since there were a few semantic errors in patient 3, it remains unknown whether or not this patient really had deep dyslexia. However, it is noteworthy that the patient with orthographic alexia showed features mimicking deep dyslexia. Patient 3 understood some Kanji words that he could not read (understanding without phonology [18]), probably because the deficient visual image of a word still reached semantics, or semantic lexical help compensated for insufficient visual information about word images. In this regard, visual and derivational errors in deep dyslexia have visual resemblance to the target word. Furthermore, taking it into account that semantic errors in deep dyslexia (substitution of other semantically associated words) are also observed in pure alexia [40, 79, 80] in which whole-word images are damaged, the semantic errors in patient 3 appeared to be derived from deficient whole-word images of words.

V. Kanji and Kana Reading Study with Positron Emission Tomography

We conducted PET reading studies using Kanji words, Kana words and Kana nonwords separately in different groups with region of interest (ROI)-based analysis [70-72] and later reanalyzed the data [73-75] with Statistical Parametric Mapping. [81] The main findings are summarized as follows: (i) in addition to the posterior superior temporal gyrus, the basal occipital and occipitotemporal areas (Areas 18, 19 and 37) were activated by Kanji and Kana, suggesting that these areas are crucial for real word reading; (ii) activity was more pronounced in Area 37 in Kanji, which was suggested to be concerned with the orthography of Kanji, in contrast to greater activation in Areas 18 and 19 in Kana; (iii) specific activation for a conjunction involving Kana words and nonwords was located in the middle occipital gyrus and the deep perisylvian temporoparietal cortex (Areas 22/21 and 40/22), suggesting that these areas are engaged in phonological processing of Kana character sequences; (iv) Kana nonwords activated more widespread areas in the occipital lobe and occipitotemporal cortex than Kana words; and (v) subtraction of Kana nonwords from Kana words revealed activity of the anterior part of the fusiform/inferior temporal gyri (Area 37) that was supposedly involved in semantics or Kana word-forms.

PET and functional MRI studies from Western countries also showed similar findings (for review, see Fiez et al., [82] Price, [4, 83] and Turkeltaub et al. [84]). Table 4 shows the common activated sites for the tasks. Overall, these results suggest that two distinct areas, i.e. the ventral occipitotemporal cortex (Area 37) and inferior occipital gyrus (Area 18/19), are crucial for reading. Some investigators have emphasized the importance of the ventral occipital and occipitotemporal cortices in word recognition. [36, 82, 95, 96]

VI. A Weighted Dual-Route Hypothesis for Reading

Based on the above findings, we hypothesized a weighted dual-route model of reading [73] (Fig. 5) that modifies Iwata's model about Japanese [26] to be applicable not only to Japanese but also to European languages.

Table 4. Activation of the left occipital and temporal lobes in word processing studies.

First author	Apparatus	Stimulus	Baseline	Peak activation*	Region
BA 18,19					
Sergent (1992)	PET	Letter strings	Fixation	BA19 (-38,-73,-3)	Mid/Inf O
Price (1994)	PET	Real words	False font	BA18 (-24,-90,8)	Mid/Inf O
Price (1996)	PET	Letter strings	False font	BA18 (-28,-90,4)	Inf O
				BA18 (-30,-76,-12)	Post Fu
Puce (1996)	fMRI	Letter strings	Faces	BA19 (-40,-66,-17)	Fu
		Letter strings	Textures	BA19 (-37,-71,-22)	Fu
Beauregard (1997)	PET	Concrete words	Crosshair	BA18 (-21,-102,18)	Inf O
				BA18 (-17,-85,-6)	Inf O
				BA18 (-36,-95,6)	Mid O
		Abstract words	Crosshair	BA18/19 (-29,-85,-14)	Inf O
				BA19 (-23,-85,-6)	Inf O
		Letter strings	Crosshair	BA18 (-17,-95,-2)	Inf O
				BA18 (-31,-100,14)	Mid O
				BA19 (-28,-85,-14)	Inf O
				BA19 (-46,-76,-15)	Inf O
Fiez (1999)	PET	Real words	Crosshair	BA19 (-43,-63,-4)	Fu
Hagoort (1999)	PET	Real words	Crosshair	BA18 (-4,-59,0)	Li
				BA18/19 (-19,-90,-6)	Li
		Pseudowords	Crosshair	BA18/19 (-35,-82,-6)	Li

Table 4. Continued.

First author	Apparatus	Stimulus	Baseline	Peak activation*	Region
		Real words	Pseudo-words	BA19 (-18,-48,0)	Li
		Pseudowords	Real words	BA18 (-27,-86,15)	Mid O
Tagamets (2000)	fMRI	Real Words	Shapes	BA18/19 (-38,-90,-2)	Inf O
				BA18 (-42,-74,-18)	Fu/Inf O
		Pseudowords	Shapes	BA18 (-34,-92,8)	Mid O
				BA18 (-24,-86,-16)	Li/Fu
				BA18/19 (-34,-96,0)	Inf O
				BA19 (-44,-72,-18)	Fu/Inf O
		Letter strings	Shapes	BA18 (-34,-94,12)	Mid O
				BA18 (-26,-84,-16)	Li/Fu
				BA18/19 (-38,-90,-2)	Inf O
				BA19 (-44,-66,-18)	Fu
Leff (2001)	PET	Real words	Crosshair	BA19 (-42,-72,-16)	Fu
Sakurai (2000)	PET	Kana words	Dot	BA18 (-18,-98,8)	Inf O
				BA18 (-32,-94,-8)	Inf O
				BA19 (-44,-80,-12)	Inf O
		Kana nonwords	Dot	BA18 (-46,-86,-12)	Inf O
		Words & Nonwords	Dot	BA18 (-34,-92,-6)	Inf O
				BA19 (-44,-82,-14)	Inf O

Table 4. Continued.

First author	Apparatus	Stimulus	Baseline	Peak activation*	Region
Sakurai (2001)	PET	Kana words	Kanji words	BA18 (-18,-102,10)	Mid O
Sakurai (2001)	PET	Kana words	Dot	BA18 (-38,-92,-2)	Inf O
				BA19 (-30,-72,-4)	Fu
				BA19 (-38,-84,-14)	Fu/Inf O
				BA 19 (-8,-82,28)	Cu
BA 37					
Sergent (1992)	PET	Letter-spatial	Letter-sound	BA37 (-27,-54,-9)	Fu
Bookheimer (1995)	PET	Real words	Line drawings	BA37 (-30,-48,0)	Fu
Price (1996)	PET	Letter strings	False font	BA37 (-34,-50,-12)	Mid Fu
Price (1996)	PET	Pseudowords	Letter strings	BA37 (-46,-52,-12)	Inf T
Herbster (1997)	PET	Regular words	Nonwords	BA37 (-36,-30,-24)	Fu
		Regular words	Letter strings	BA37 (-34,-38,-24)	Fu
		Irregular words	Letter strings	BA37 (-38,-40,-24)	Fu
Beauregard (1997)	PET	Concrete words	Crosshair	BA19/37 (-43,-76,-12)	Fu/Inf O
Fiez (1999)	PET	Real words	Nonwords	BA37 (-43,-45,-8)	Fu
Hagoort (1999)	PET	Pseudowords	Real words	BA37/19 (-34,-55,-11)	Mid Fu
Tagamets (2000)	fMRI	Real words	Shapes	BA37 (-46,-56,-22)	Fu
		Pseudowords	Shapes	BA37 (-46,-52,-22)	Fu
		Letter strings	Shapes	BA37 (-46,-54,-22)	Fu
Cohen (2000)	fMRI	Real words	Crosshair	BA37 (-42,-57,-6)	Fu

Table 4. Continued.

First author	Apparatus	Stimulus	Baseline	Peak activation*	Region
Sakurai (2000)	PET	Kanji words	Dot	BA37 (-42,-54,-22)	Fu/Inf T
		Kana & Kanji	Dot	BA37 (-42,-54,-22)	Fu/Inf T
Sakurai (2001)	PET	Kana words	Kana nonwords	BA37 (-52,-44,-18)	Fu/Inf T
BA 40/22					
Price (1994)	PET	Real words	False font	BA40/22 (-50,-46,20)	T-P
Bookheimer (1995)	PET	Real words	Line drawings	BA40/22 (-44,-42,20)	T-P
Price (1996)	PET	Peudowords	Letter strings	BA40/22 (-30,-40,24)	T-P
		Pseudowords	Words	BA40/22 (-24,-42,28)	T-P
		Real words	Letter strings	BA40/22 (-34,-42,20)	T-P
Sakurai (2000)	PET	Words & Nonwords	Dot	BA40/22 (-34,-40,24)	T-P
BA 22/21					
Price (1994)	PET	Real words	False font	BA22/21 (-36,-56,16)	Sup/Mid T
Price (1996)	PET	Real words	False font	BA22/21 (-48,-18,-4)	Sup/Mid T
Bookheimer (1995)	PET	Real words	Line drawings	BA22/21 (-54,-34,4)	Sup/Mid T
Beauregard (1997)	PET	Concrete words	Crosshair	BA22/21 (-58,-38,-2)	Sup/Mid T
		Letter strings	Crosshair	BA22/21 (-58,-37,-3)	Sup/Mid T
Sakurai (2000)	PET	Kana nonwords	Dot	BA22/21 (-48,-40,10)	Sup/Mid T
				BA22/21 (-72,-34,8)	Sup/Mid T
				BA22/21 (-72,-18,-2)	Sup/Mid T
		Words & Nonwords	Dot	BA22/21 (-48,-42,10)	Sup/Mid T

Table 4. Continued.

First author	Apparatus	Stimulus	Baseline	Peak activation*	Region
BA 22					
Bookheimer (1995)	PET	Real words	Line drawings	BA22 (-48,-10,4)	SupT
Price (1994)	PET	Real words	False font	BA22 (-50,-18,4)	Sup T
Herbster (1997)	PET	Regular words	Letter strings	BA22 (-52,0,0)	Sup T
		Nonwords	Letter strings	BA22 (-60,-22,4)	Sup T
Hagoort (1999)	PET	Pseudowords	Real words	BA 22 (-57,-6,-2)	Sup T
Sakurai (2000)	PET	Kanji words	Dot	BA22 (-60,-8,2)	Sup T
				BA22 (-60,-20,4)	Sup T
		Kana words	Dot	BA22 (-62,-22,6)	Sup T
		Kana nonwords	Dot	BA22 (-66,-2,2)	Sup T
		Kanji & Kana	Dot	BA22 (-60,-20,6)	Sup T

*The location coordinates for the areas of peak activity are given in Talairach [85] coordinate space [86-92, 103] or standard MNI (Montreal Neurological Institute) space. [36, 73-75, 93, 94, 104]
Abbreviations. Post, Posterior; Mid, Middle; Inf, Inferior; Fu, Fusiform; Li, Lingual, O, Occipital; Cu, Cuneus; T-P, Temporo-parietal; Sup, Superior; T, Temporal.

Iwata [26] proposed a prototype dual-route hypothesis for reading in the Japanese language. According to this model, visually perceived graphemes are recognized in the occipital lobe and then are sent to Wernicke's area along two different pathways. One is a dorsal route passing through the angular gyrus. This circuit is used mainly for the phonological reading process that is closely related to Kana reading. The other is a ventral route passing through the posterior inferior temporal cortex. This route is the semantic reading pathway indispensable for reading Kanji words.

Iwata's model is along the lines of the dual-route hypothesis for reading in Western countries (see III.). The present model also postulates two different pathways, but differs from the previous dual-route models in the following points. First, the two pathways are orthographic (conventionally termed as lexical) and phonological (conventionally termed as nonlexical or sub-lexical), but their processing is essentially visual in nature, i.e. holistic and sequential. Second, in the strict sense of the word, the two pathways are not parallel; the orthographic pathway is dominant in reading.

The orthographic pathway (ventral route) in reading proceeds from the primary visual cortex (lingual gyrus) to the posterior inferior temporal gyrus (Area 37) through the fusiform gyrus (Fig. 5). This route is used for holistic visual recognition of words. Both Kana and Kanji words (corresponding to European real words, either regular or irregular) are dominantly processed in this pathway. Visual images of Kanji characters and whole-word images of both Kanji and Kana words (corresponding to European real words), in short, the visual lexicon, are stored as a neural network around the end of this pathway (fusiform/inferior temporal gyri). A Kana character or an alphabet symbol is recognized widely in this route. In support of this view, some authors [86, 89, 94] found activation of the fusiform gyrus (Area 37) in letter processing tasks (table 4).

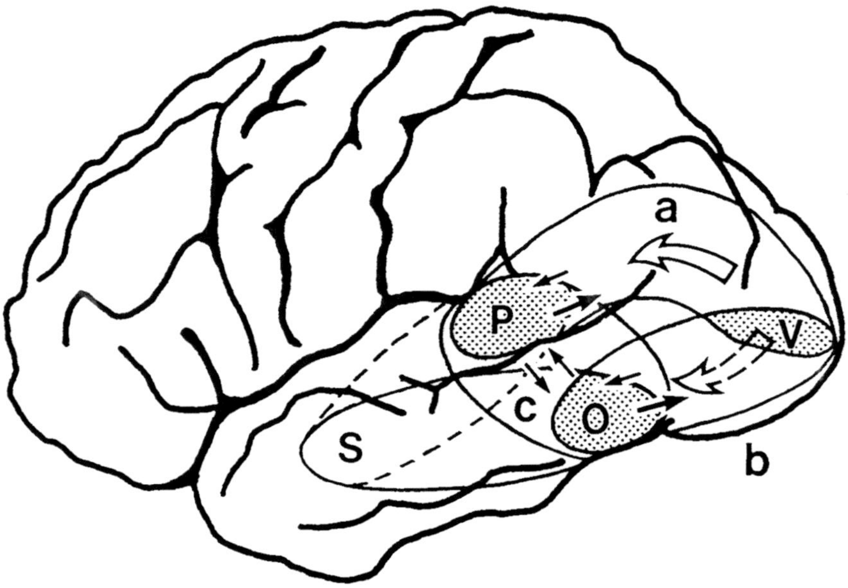

Fig. 5. Diagram of anatomically-based dual-route hypothesis for reading. Early visual analysis and the subsequent letter or character identification are performed in the primary visual cortex and the surrounding visual association cortices (V). The phonological pathway (dorsal route; a), which is used for sequential visual recognition of letter or character sequences, goes from the primary visual cortex to the posterior superior temporal gyrus via the lateral occipital gyri (middle and inferior occipital gyri) and the deep perisylvian temporo-parietal cortex. The phonological lexicon (P) is located at the end of this route. The orthographic pathway (ventral route; b), which is used for holistic visual recognition of words, proceeds from the primary visual cortex (lingual gyrus) to the posterior inferior temporal gyrus via the fusiform gyrus. The orthographic lexicon (O) is located at the lateral side of this route. The interaction between phonology and orthography (c), which connects the posterior superior temporal cortex with the fusiform/posterior inferior temporal gyri, facilitates both phonological and orthographic routes in reading (lexical help, illustrated with backward larger-black arrows). The semantic storage site (S), where lexico-semantic information is stored, extends from the fusiform/inferior temporal gyri to the anterior part of the temporal lobe. During listening, the semantic storage site connects tightly with the posterior superior temporal gyrus (illustrated with dotted lines). The semantic storage site actually includes more widespread areas in the temporal lobe (reproduced from Sakurai [97] with permission from Igaku Shoin).

The phonological pathway (dorsal route) in reading goes from the primary visual cortex to the posterior superior temporal gyrus and in part to the supramarginal gyrus through the lateral occipital (middle and inferior occipital)/fusiform gyri (Area 18/19) and deep perisylvian temporoparietal cortex (Areas 40/22 and 22/21) (Fig. 5). This route is used for sequential visual recognition of letter sequences, especially those linked to the phoneme, and thus for grapheme-to-phoneme conversion, and is recruited when a sequential analysis is necessary or when whole-word recognition is impossible, such as in reading unfamiliar real words or regular nonwords. Phonological lexical information (phonological lexicon) is stored as neural networks around the end of this pathway (posterior superior temporal gyrus). Individual Kana characters or alphabet symbols are recognized at an early processing level in this route (inferior occipital/fusiform gyri) as well as in the orthographic route. In support of this view, some authors [86, 89, 90, 94, 103] found activation of the fusiform/lateral occipital gyri (Area 18/19) in letter processing tasks (Table 4). Unfamiliar Kana words and Kana nonwords (corresponding to European regular, but unfamiliar, words and regular nonwords) are processed sequentially in this pathway. "Grapheme-to-phoneme" conversion may be performed from the lateral occipital gyri to the superior temporal gyrus, whereas "phoneme-to-grapheme" conversion may be performed mainly in the angular gyrus. Otherwise, agraphia without alexia after an angular gyrus lesion (See II. 4.) could not be explained.

The posterior superior temporal gyrus and the fusiform/inferior temporal gyri (Area 37) have a reciprocal connection, which is essentially the same as the lexico-semantic route in writing [5] and facilitates both orthographic and phonological routes in reading. That is, once a fraction of orthographic or phonological information has access to each route, then the corresponding lexico-semantic information is sent back to the orthographic or phonological route (lexical help or lexical capture [76, 77]). This feedback system makes it easier and faster to understand words and sentences. Comprehension occurs through interaction between the superior and inferior temporal gyri. Lexico-semantic information is diffusely stored in widespread areas extending from Area 37 to the anterior part of the temporal lobe. [98]

The orthographic pathway plays a dominant part in reading. This assumption is necessary to explain why words are recognized faster than letter sequences (word-superiority effect [99]) and is in accord with the findings that the ventral occipital and occipitotemporal cortices are mainly involved in word recognition. [36, 82, 95, 96]

It should be noted, however, that the dominance of the orthographic route is not inherently determined: the two routes change their weight of involvement according to the number of times the word is seen and recognized. That is, Kana nonword and unfamiliar word reading requires both routes. As the word is seen and recognized again and again, the whole-word image and meaning are stored around Area 37, thus the ventral route gains dominance in reading real words (Kanji and Kana). [73] This weighted dual-route hypothesis is mainly based on the results that Kana nonwords activated more widespread areas in the ventral and lateral occipital gyri than real words (Kanji and Kana), and that the ventral occipital and occipitotemporal gyri were predominantly activated by real words (see the results (i) and (iv) of our PET studies [V.]). The notion of graded differences between the subsystems of reading is also expressed in the connectionist model of reading. [100]

This weighted dual-route hypothesis can explain various kinds of reading impairments. Table 5 summarizes alexias and the supposed lesion sites. The author discusses the lesion-to-symptom correlations below.

Table 5. Types of alexia and lesion sites. [67]

Alexia	Ortho-graphic*	Visual-phonological*	Compli-cations	Ref.
Pure alexia: ventromedial type**	I (Fu)#		RU	37
Pure alexia for Kanji and Kana (Common type; pt 1)	I (Fu)#	I (Fu/Inf O)$	RU, RH	[1]
Pure alexia for Kana: posterior type (Pure alexia for nonwords; pt 2)		I (Fu/Inf O)$	RL	[2]
Alexia with agraphia for Kanji (Orthographic alexia with agraphia; pt 3)	I (Fu/Inf T)#		anomia	[3]

*The orthographic pathway (ventral route) proceeds from the primary visual cortex to the inferior temporal gyrus (Area 37) via the fusiform gyrus (Area 37). The phonological pathway (dorsal route) proceeds from the primary visual cortex to the superior temporal gyrus and inferior supramarginal gyrus via the inferior and middle occipital gyri (Area 18/19) and deep perisylvian temporoparietal cortex (Areas 22/21 and 40/22).

**The ventromedial type of pure alexia refers to alexia in which whole-word reading is primarily impaired, and letter-by-letter reading is not so pronounced. The posterior type of pure alexia is identical with letter-by-letter reading in a strict sense, with preserved whole-word reading. Many cases of pure alexia have both lesions, as in pure alexia for Kanji and Kana (common type).

Area 37; $ Area 18/19.

[1] [13, 22, 24, 35, 36, 105, 106].

[2] [23, 25].

[3] [26-29, 34, 38].

Abbreviations: I, Impaired; pt, patient; rt, right; Inf O, Inferior occipital gyrus; PIT, Posterior inferior temporal area; Fu, Fusiform gyrus; Inf T, Inferior temporal gyrus; Ref., References; RU, Right upper quadrantanopsia; RH, Right hemianopsia; RL, Right lower quadrantanopsia.

VII. A New Classification of Alexia

1. Pure Alexia: Ventromedial Type

Damage to the orthographic route may cause whole-word reading impairment with or without agraphia. The alexia presents as two phenotypes: pure alexia with less pronounced letter-by-letter reading and alexia with agraphia for Kanji (orthographic alexia with agraphia) or lexical agraphia in Western countries.

Pure alexia occurs when the fusiform gyrus (Area 37) is damaged and, as a result, the inferior temporal gyrus is disconnected from the fusiform gyrus. As mentioned earlier, visual images of words or orthographic lexical information is stored around the lateral fusiform/inferior temporal gyri, and widespread areas in the ventral and lateral occipital gyri are involved in letter or character recognition. Therefore, both whole-word recognition and letter identification become poor in this alexia. Eventually, impairment is evident chiefly in nonword reading, for which lexical help [76, 77] is not available, and many reading errors are visually similar to the target. Furthermore, letter-by-letter reading is not so pronounced, [37] since the posterior occipital gyri are more specialized to recognize letters or Kana characters, and thus the phonological route compensates for any reading deficit. As a result, pure alexia from this lesion is difficult to differentiate from phonological dyslexia and sometimes has been reported as isolated phonological dyslexia [101] or letter-by-letter reading with phonological dyslexia. [102] Conversely, deficient whole-word recognition in pure alexia can produce semantic paralexia that is symptomatically the same as deep dyslexia. Accordingly, letter-by-letter reading from this lesion has also been reported as being accompanied by deep dyslexia. [80]

Kawamura's patient 2, [13] reported as having pure alexia, had the same lesion. However, as in our patient 1, the lesion seemed to extend posteriorly to the lateral occipital gyri on CT. If the lesion has more occipital involvement, letter-by-letter reading with more impaired nonword reading may occur. Uchiyama and Uchiyama's patient [22] belongs to this category.

2. Orthographic Alexia with Agraphia

Another type of orthographic alexia, alexia with agraphia for Kanji, [19, 26-28] pure agraphia for Kanji [29, 30] or lexical agraphia in Western languages, [33, 34] occurs when a lesion is located more laterally in the fusiform and inferior temporal gyri in the orthographic route, where the orthographic lexical information is stored. [5, 103, 104] In this case, visual images of real words, both regular and irregular (or Kanji and Kana), are damaged. Thus, reading depends on the intact phonological pathway. As regular words and regular nonwords (or Kana words and Kana nonwords) are also read, although slowly, with the phonological pathway, reading of irregular words (or most Kanji words) is predominantly disturbed. If the damage is incomplete, verbal paralexia similar to deep dyslexia can be produced, as described above. The number of no-responses in oral reading increases, according to the severity of the damage.

Deficient orthography also affects writing; the patients cannot write, particularly not irregular words (or most Kanji words), because of impaired word recall. [18] In this sense, alexia with agraphia for Kanji should be designated "orthographic alexia with agraphia." In addition, since letters or characters are also processed in the ventral occipital gyri, a slight disturbance in letter or character identification coexists with this alexia, which is markedly observed in Kana nonword (or pseudoword) reading (patient 3).

Kinesthetic reading is unsuccessful in alexia with agraphia for Kanji caused by a posterior inferior temporal cortex lesion, probably because visual images of words per se are disrupted, and thus cannot be recalled. [18] Also, anomia accompanies this type of alexia. [19, 27, 29, 38, 39] We found in a literature review that severer anomia occurred when the lesion extended forward to the anterior third of the temporal lobe or medially to the parahippocampal gyrus. [19]

3. Pure Alexia for Kana (or Nonwords): Posterior Type

Damage to the visual analysis and the earlier stage of the phonological (dorsal) route may impair letter or Kana character identification, thus leading to letter-by-letter reading. As described earlier, letters or characters are processed widely in the ventral and posterior occipital cortices, but the posterior occipital gyri are more specialized to recognize letters or Kana characters. [20] Therefore, letter-by-letter reading is more pronounced in this lesion. Conversely, whole-word reading is possible in the intact orthographic route, thus reading of Kanji characters, which primarily depend on holistic recognition, is hardly impaired. If damage extends to the cuneus or optic radiation, right lower quadrantanopsia may occur.

As described earlier, pure alexia for Kana parallels pure alexia for regular words and nonwords, especially for nonwords that are more difficult to read, with preserved reading of real words of which whole-word images are available.

Many reported patients with letter-by-letter reading showed the involvement of both the orthographic route and the phonological route. Since recognition of both individual letters or characters and word-forms are disrupted, the patient depends on letter-by-letter reading using the deficient phonological route. Reading is thus slow and laborious. A restricted lesion of the fusiform gyrus extending posteriorly to involve the fusiform/inferior occipital gyri (Area 18/19) is sufficient to produce letter-by-letter reading, in this case, without visual field defects. [16, 35, 36, 105] If the lesion involves the lingual gyrus or optic radiation, right upper homonymous quadrantanopsia [13, 106-108] (the present patient 1) or hemianopsia [22, 44, 106, 109-111] coexists with alexia. When the lesion affects the lateral fusiform and inferior temporal gyri (Area 37), agraphia accompanies alexia (see VII. 2.).

VIII. Other Alexias

1. Phonological Dyslexia and Deep Dyslexia

The neural substrate of phonological dyslexia and deep dyslexia is not clearly defined. The following discussion concerns dyslexia from postrolandic lesions.

Damage to the phonological route may cause phonological dyslexia. [55, 112, 113] In this case, reading of regular nonwords and unfamiliar regular words is selectively impaired, because real words are usually processed in the orthographic route. Phonological dyslexia results from dysfunction of the sequential grapheme-to-phoneme conversion process from the lateral occipital gyri to the superior temporal gyrus via the deep perisylvian temporoparietal cortex (Areas 22/21 and 40/21). If the lesion involves the inferior occipital/fusiform gyri (Area 18/19) or affects the fusiform gyrus (Area 37), letter or character identification is also impaired. Conversely, if the lesion extends over the angular, supramarginal and posterior superior temporal gyrus, more general deficits in phonological processing become evident, [77, 114, 115] accompanied by agraphia. Reported cases of angular alexia or subangular alexia probably show these symptoms, [116, 117] whether letter-by-letter reading coexists or not. Phonological dyslexia occurs either without visual field defects or with right lower homonymous quadrantanopsia [55] or hemianopsia, [117] suggesting damage to the cuneate gyrus or the optic radiation within the parietal lobe.

If the lesion also affects the interaction between phonology and orthography (VI. and Fig. 5), semantic paralexia is produced. Firstly, deep dyslexia occurs, when damage to the phonological route involves the superior temporal gyrus [65, 66, 118] in which phonological lexicon is located. The disturbed phonological lexicon yields phonemic paralexia, consisting of phonological and/or visual and derivational errors, whereas disconnection between phonological lexicon and orthographic lexicon yields a mismatched phonological lexicon (verbal paralexia) consisting of semantic errors. Secondly, if the lesion involves the lateral side of the orthographic route, semantic paralexia, a symptom mimicking deep dyslexia, may occur (See VII. 1 and 2). Glosser and Friedman's patient 1 [119] seems to have had this lesion. Partial damage to the lateral side of the orthographic route (Area 37) causes deficient whole-word images, which underlies the mechanism of producing verbal paralexia. Semantic errors occur when this disrupted orthography reaches the semantic storage site, or semantic lexical help compensates for insufficient visual images of words.

Many reported cases of deep dyslexia, however, had more anterior and extensive lesions, including the periventricular white matter with the arcuate fasciculus, Broca's area, the insula and the supramarginal gyrus, [65, 120] which may have caused global, Broca's or conduction aphasia. Thus, multiple lesions are likely to contribute to the occurrence of deep dyslexia. To discuss the anatomical substrates of deep dyslexia comprehensively is beyond the scope of this article.

2. Surface Dyslexia

Surface dyslexia occurs when damage involves the fusiform/posterior inferior temporal gyri (Area 37) extending to the anterior part of the temporal lobe, which the author calls the semantic storage site (Fig. 5). Surface dyslexia is observed not only in cerebrovascular disease but also in temporal degeneration such as progressive fluent aphasia [121] called semantic dementia [122] (or semantic aphasia [123]) or Gogi (word-meaning) aphasia. [124, 125] If the semantic storage site is damaged, it will affect the information processing from the end of the orthographic route to the posterior superior temporal gyrus. Thus, whole-word reading is impaired. As regular words are not only holistically processed in the orthographic route but also sequentially processed in the phonological route, irregular word (or most Kanji word) reading is exclusively disturbed.

The lesion and symptoms of surface dyslexia or progressive fluent aphasia resemble group C alexia with agraphia [19] from a posterior inferior temporal cortex lesion; severe anomia and pronounced Kanji or orthographic alexia with agraphia. The essential difference is that anomia and paralexia in surface dyslexia result from extensive cortical damage in the temporal lobe but not the superior temporal gyrus, whereas anomia in orthographic alexia with agraphia results from a disconnection of association fibers within the temporal lobe. [19]

With respect to the difference between surface dyslexia and orthographic alexia with agraphia, it should be noted that, in the true sense of the word, a double dissociation of reading impairments exists not between surface dyslexia and phonological dyslexia, but between orthographic alexia with agraphia and phonological dyslexia. Surface dyslexia is essentially an impairment of the semantic storage site, whereas orthographic alexia with agraphia results from damage to the orthographic route. The apparent similarity of symptoms (i.e. most Kanji words or European irregular words are read or written more poorly than Kana words or regular words) is probably due to the overlap of the lesion site: the posterior inferior temporal cortex (Area 37).

IX. Similarities and Differences among Other Models of Reading

Fig. 5 illustrates the present model mapped onto a brain surface image. This model is anatomically based, thus it is easy to correlate lesions with symptoms. From a neuroanatomical point of view, the flow of information is no longer depicted with a box-and-arrow diagram. There is an overlap of localization between functional units (modules). Therefore, modules with oval-shaped areas overlapping each other were delineated. This model resembles the dual-route model of Ellis and Young [2] or Patterson and Shewell [62] in that subsequent to orthographic analysis, two routes, a direct orthographic lexical route and a sub-lexical route enabling grapheme-phoneme conversion, are postulated. According to their model, the orthographic lexical route is subdivided into a lexical (phonological) route, in which a whole-word orthographic lexicon directly accesses a phonological (output) lexicon, and a semantic route, in which the whole-word orthographic lexicon is translated to the phonological (output) lexicon via semantics. In this sense, their model has three routes. This basic architecture is also expressed in Coltheart et al.'s dual-route cascaded model. [126]

The present model is different from Ellis and Young's or Patterson and Shewell's mainly in two points. Firstly, the present model assumes direct interaction between the orthographic (input) lexicon and the phonological (input) lexicon, whereas their model has no direct connection between the two modules. Secondly, in the present model, the phonological lexical information (phonological input lexicon) is stored around the end of the phonological route (or sub-lexical route, according to Ellis and Young's or Patterson and Shewell's terminology); sub-lexical grapheme-phoneme conversion is performed in the phonological route, and access to the phonological (input) lexicon results from sequential grapheme-phoneme conversions, whereas in their model grapheme-phoneme conversion has no connection with the phonological (input or output) lexicon. In the present model, converted phonological sequences for a word may go to the superior temporal gyrus in addition to the inferior supramarginal gyrus. If there is no corresponding phonological lexicon around the superior temporal gyrus, the phonological information may be temporarily stored in the supramarginal gyrus. [43]

The present model is also different from the dual-route model of McCarthy and Warrington [127] in that two routes do not stem from what they call the whole-word system but from early visual analysis.

In these two models, letter-by-letter reading is explained either by a deficient parallel processing of letters from orthographic analysis to the orthographic input lexicon [41] or by impairment of the whole-word system. [106] However, these assumptions were suggested to be insufficient to explain sequential letter-by-letter reading. [41] Recently, Friedman and Lott [111] also claimed that letter identification is divided into an explicit serial process and an automatic parallel process, and that letter-by-letter reading is the result of disrupted parallel identification of letters. As the authors noted, this hypothesis alone cannot explain why letter-by-letter reading takes much longer than normal reading.

The author's view is that both orthographic analysis (letter identification) and access to the orthographic input lexicon (whole-word reading) are impaired in ventromedial type pure alexia (VII. 1.). As a result, the sub-word level orthographic-to-phonological conversion, the process of which is sequential in nature, compensates for reading impairment. If this process is intact, letter-by-letter reading will not be prominent. In the case of posterior type pure alexia (VII. 3.), an area specialized for letter identification is damaged, which directly affects sequential orthographic-to-phonological conversion, thus leading to pronounced letter-by-letter reading. In addition, in both types of pure alexia, the orthographic (input) lexicon itself is affected to some degree, because letter identification and whole-word reading are processed in areas anatomically close to each other.

One advantage of this model is that it can explain various degrees of letter-by-letter reading, [25] depending on the involvement of the phonological route (posterior occipital gyri). Furthermore, in the present model, the orthographic lexicon links to or overlaps with semantics at Area 37 (Fig. 5). Therefore, if this area (fusiform and inferior temporal gyri) is involved, symptoms associated with orthography or semantics may appear. This assumption probably accounts for many observations in pure alexia such as accompanying agraphia, [40, 41] semantic reading errors (described before), [40, 79, 80, 128, 129] categorization of words the patient could not read and semantic priming effects, [130] or better recognition of letters in words than in letter strings. [131] It may also explain semantic errors and comprehension of words the patient could not read (understanding without phonology) in alexia with agraphia for Kanji. [18]

The connectionist model proposed by Seidenberg and McClelland [100] consists of three functional units that interact with each other: orthographic, phonological and semantic, with additional units called hidden units, mediating between these units (triangle model). Their implemented model was simplified to contain orthographic, phonological and hidden units to simulate a reading process from detection of a letter string to pronunciation of a word. [132] They claimed that the model differed from the traditional dual-route models in that: (i) a single procedure from an orthographic unit to a phonological unit is applicable to irregular words, nonwords and regular words, and (ii) the model has no lexicon. Their implemented model probably simulates part of the process of the present phonological route. Also in the present model, the phonological route can process both words and nonwords. As described in VI, learning an unknown word, either regular or irregular, requires the phonological route, but as the word is seen and recognized again and again the orthographic route gains dominance in reading, which enables faster visual recognition of the word. This view is based on PET findings, as mentioned earlier, which showed that there was more widespread activation involving the parietal or lateral occipital areas during pseudoword or Kana nonword processing, in contrast to relatively restricted activation of the temporal areas during real word or Kanji word processing. [73, 89, 91] Thus, impairment of the phonological route (phonological dyslexia) can be simulated with the implemented model, but impairment of the orthographic route (pure alexia and orthographic alexia with agraphia) and deficits in the semantic storage site (surface dyslexia) may require other simulation models that involve semantics. [132, 133]

Whether an assumption of lexicon is necessary or not depends on what we think of "lexicon." Besner et al. [134] argued that Seidenberg and McClelland's model [100] also had a lexicon as a distributed representation of words. By "lexicon" the author means patterns of neuronal activities in a certain area of the cortex, specified for words.

A limit to Seidenberg and McClelland's triangle model is that letter identification and probably whole-word reading are not expressed, and other models are required to simulate letter-by-letter reading or word-length effect. [135, 136] In addition, trials to simulate both word-length effect and correct lexical decision have not been successful to date. [137]

Price [4] reconciled the classic neurological model [10] with cognitive models [2, 62, 111, 126, 127] using functional imaging data, and also proposed an anatomically constrained model. According to this model, Wernicke's area (Area 22/21) sustains nonsemantically mediated speech output, whereas the posterior inferior temporal cortex is involved in lexical, semantically mediated speech output. Access to semantics is made in the angular gyrus and anterior inferior and middle temporal gyri. This model differs from the present model mainly in two points: (i) the angular gyrus is engaged in semantics; and (ii) the site for the function of Wernicke's area is the upper bank of the posterior superior temporal sulcus (Area 22/21). The author's view is that: (i) the angular gyrus is less involved in reading; crucial areas for reading in this vicinity are the middle occipital gyri (posterior to the angular gyrus) continuous with the fusiform/inferior occipital gyri (Area 18/19) and the deep perisylvian temporoparietal junction (Areas 22/21 and 40/22; anterior to the angular gyrus). [73] Moreover, an essential region for lexico-semantics is the anterior part of Area 37 (x=-52, y=-44, z=-18 in MNI space), 10 mm anterior to the maximal activation locus of Area 37 for reading [74]; and (ii) the upper bank of the superior temporal sulcus (Area 22/21) is not Wernicke's area itself, but posterior to Wernicke's area which is by definition located in the posterior half or third of the superior temporal gyrus (Area 22). The supposed Wernicke's area (peak activity, x=-60, y=-20, z=6 in Kanji and Kana conjunction) and the inner temporal cortex at the superior temporal sulcus were simultaneously activated in our PET reading studies (Table 4). It is suggested that the inner temporal cortex (Area 22/21) provides access to the phonological lexicon that is distributed around the posterior superior temporal gyrus. [67]

CONCLUDING REMARKS

Pure alexia has been explained by disconnection theory, and damage to the association fibers in the occipital lobe has been regarded as critical for producing alexia. [138] It seems, however, that various clinical and experimental findings cannot be accounted for, unless we assume functional localization in the occipital cortex.

Although the present model is based on studies of Japanese alexic patients and PET activation studies, the author believes that it can also be applied to reading in general. Some of the assumptions remain untested, e.g. the mechanism of kinesthetic reading and the role of visual recognition deficits in character reading. We need further study, both clinical and experimental, to confirm the model.

REFERENCES

[1] Benson DF. Alexia. In: Frederiks JAM, ed. *Handbook of Clinical Neurology*. Vol. 45. Amsterdam: Elsevier;1985:433-455.

[2] Ellis AW, Young AW. *Human Cognitive Neuropsychology*. Augmented ed. Hove: Psychology Press; 1997.

[3] Seidenberg MS. Visual word recognition: an overview. In: Miller JL, Eimas PD, eds. *Speech, Language, and Communication*. San Diego: Academic Press;1995:137-179.

[4] Price CJ. The anatomy of language: contributions from functional neuroimaging. *J Anatomy*. 2000;197:335-359.

[5] Sakurai Y, Matsumura K, Iwatsubo T, Momose T. Frontal pure agraphia for kanji or kana: Dissociation between morphology and phonology. *Neurology*. 1997;49:946-952.

[6] Fushimi T, Ijuin M, Patterson K, Tatsumi I. Consistency, frequency, and lexicality effects in naming Japanese Kanji. *J Exp Psychol: Hum Percep Perform*. 1999; 25:382-407.

[7] Dejerine J. Sur un cas de cécité verbale avec agraphie, suivie d'autopsie. *Compt Rend Soc Biol*. 1891;3:197-201.

[8] Dejerine J. Contribution à l'étude anatomopathologique et clinique des différentes variétés de cécité verbale. *Compt Rend Soc Biol*. 1892;4:61-90.

[9] Dejerine J. *Sémiologie des affections du système nerveux*. 2nd ed. Paris: Masson et Cie; 1926.

[10] Geschwind N. Disconnexion syndromes in animals and man. *Brain*. 1965;88:237-294, 585-644.

[11] Greenblatt SH. Localization of lesions in alexia. In: Kertesz A, ed. *Localization in Neuropsychology*. New York: Academic Press; 1983:323-356.

[12] Damasio AR, Damasio H. The anatomic basis of pure alexia. *Neurology*. 1983;33:1573-1583.

[13] Kawamura M. "Non-classical type" alexia without agraphia. *Shitsugosho Kenkyu*. 1988;8:185-193 (in Japanese).

[14] Greenblatt SH. Subangular alexia without agraphia or hemianopsia. *Brain Lang*. 1976;3:229-245.

[15] Greenblatt SH. Left occipital lobectomy and the preangular anatomy of reading. *Brain Lang*. 1990;38:576-595.

[16] Isono O, Kawamura M, Hirayama K, Shiota J, Maki T. Clinico-anatomical correlations of left posterior cerebral artery occlusion: alexia without agraphia, color anomia, and memory disturbance. *Rinsho Shinkeigaku*. 1988;28:1246-1254 (in Japanese).

[17] Binder JR, Mohr JP. The topography of callosal reading pathways. A case-control analysis. *Brain*. 1992;115:1807-1826.

[18] Sakurai Y, Takeuchi S, Takada T, Horiuchi E, Nakase H, Sakuta M. Alexia caused by a fusiform or posterior inferior temporal lesion. *J Neurol Sci*. 2000;178:42-51 (published erratum appears in *J Neurol Sci*. 2001;182:173-174).

[19] Sakurai Y, Sakai K, Sakuta M, Iwata M. Naming difficulties in alexia with agraphia for kanji after a left posterior inferior temporal lesion. *J Neurol Neurosurg Psychiatry*. 1994;57:609-613.

[20] Sakurai Y, Ichikawa Y, Mannen T. Pure alexia from a posterior occipital lesion. *Neurology*. 2001; 56:778-781 (see also Reference 138).

[21] Matsuda H, Mizumura S, Soma T, Takemura N. Conversion of brain SPECT images between different collimetors and reconstruction processes for analysis using statistical parametric mapping. *Nucl Med Commun.*, 2004;25:67-74.

[22] Uchiyama S, Uchiyama C. Central visual fields in pure alexia "without hemianopsia"; Visual dysfunction in the right hemifield, and alexia for "Kana" words in the left. *Rinsho Shinkeigaku*. 1991;31:1083-1089 (in Japanese).

[23] Caffarra P. Alexia without agraphia or hemianopia. *Eur Neurol*. 1987;27:65-71.

[24] Doctor EA, Sartori G, Saling MM. A letter-by-letter reader who could not read nonwords. *Cortex* 1990;26:247-262.

[25] Behrmann M, Nelson J, Sekuler EB. Visual complexity in letter-by-letter reading: "pure" alexia is not pure. *Neuropsychologia*. 1998;36:1115-1132.

[26] Iwata M. Kanji versus kana. Neuropsychological correlates of the Japanese writing system. *Trends Neurosci*. 1984;7:290-293.

[27] Kawamura M, Hirayama K, Hasegawa K, Takahashi N, Yamaura A. Alexia with agraphia of kanji (Japanese morphograms). *J Neurol Neurosurg Psychiatry*. 1987;50:1125-1129.

[28] Kawahata N, Nagata K. Alexia with agraphia due to the left posterior inferior temporal lobe lesion -- Neuropsychological analysis and its pathogenetic mechanisms. *Brain Lang*. 1988;33:296-310.

[29] Soma Y, Sugishita M, Kitamura K, Maruyama S, Imanaga H. Lexical agraphia in the Japanese language. Pure agraphia for kanji due to left posteroinferior temporal lesions. *Brain*. 1989;112:1549-1561.

[30] Yokota T, Ishiai S, Furukawa T, Tsukagoshi H. Pure agraphia of kanji due to thrombosis of the Labbé vein. *J Neurol Neurosurg Psychiatry*. 1990;53:335-338.

[31] Mochizuki H, Ohtomo R. Pure alexia in Japanese and agraphia without alexia in kanji. The ability dissociation between reading and writing in kanji vs kana. *Arch Neurol.* 1988;45:1157-1159.

[32] Shiota J, Kawamura M, Isono O, Hirayama K. Alexia with agraphia produced by localized infarction in the inferior posterior region of the left temporal lobe. *No To Shinkei*. 1986;38:1051-1055 (in Japanese).

[33] Beauvois M-F, Dérouesné J. Lexical or orthographic agraphia. *Brain*. 1981;104:21-49.

[34] Croisile B, Trillet M, Laurent B, Latombe D, Schott B. Agraphie lexicale par hématome temporo-pariétal gauche. *Rev Neurol (Paris)*. 1989;145:287-292.

[35] Warrington EK, Langdon D. Spelling dyslexia: a deficit of the visual word-form. *J Neurol Neurosurg Psychiatry*. 1994;57:211-216.

[36] Leff AP, Crewes H, Plant GT, Scott SK, Kennard C, Wise RJS: The functional anatomy of single-word reading in patients with hemianopic and pure alexia. *Brain*. 2001;124:510-521.

[37] Verstichel P, Cambier J. Alexie lettre à lettre après lésion hémisphérique gauche sans hémianopsie ni atteinte calleuse. Deux observations. *Rev Neurol (Paris)*. 1997;153:561-568.

[38] Raymer AM, Foundas AL, Maher LM, et al. Cognitive neuropsychological analysis and neuroanatomic correlates in a case of acute anomia. *Brain Lang.* 1997;58:137-156.

[39] Foundas AL, Daniels SK, Vasterling JJ. Anomia: case studies with lesion localization. *Neurocase.* 1998;4:35-43.

[40] Torii H. Fukuta T, Koyama Y. A report of three cases of alexia without agraphia due to cerebrovascular lesion and semiological consideration. *Seishinshinkeigaku Zasshi.* 1972;74:546-576 (in Japanese).

[41] Patterson K, Kay J. Letter-by-letter reading: Psychological descriptions of a neurological syndrome. *Q J Exp Psychol.* [A] 1982;34:411-441.

[42] Ishiai S, Sugishita M, Lee E, Watabiki S, Nakayama T, Kotera M. Processes of writing in alexia with agraphia and pure agraphia. *Shitsugosho Kenkyu.* 1993;13:264-271 (in Japanese).

[43] Sakurai Y, Takeuchi S, Kojima E, et al. Mechanism of short-term memory and repetition in conduction aphasia and related cognitive disorders: a neuropsychological, audiological and neuroimaging study. *J Neurol Sci.* 1998;154:182-193.

[44] Kawamura M. Localization and symptomatology of pure alexia, pure agraphia and alexia with agraphia. *Shinkeishinrigaku.* 1990;6:16-24 (in Japanese).

[45] Yamadori A. Alexia with agraphia. *Shinkeinaika.* 1979;10:428-436 (in Japanese).

[46] Miyake H, Tanaka T. A case of alexia in Kana and agraphia in Kanji with the left temporo-parietal subcortical hematoma. *Shitsugosho Kenkyu.* 1992;12:1-9 (in Japanese).

[47] Kleist K. *Gehirnpathologie.* Leipzig: Barth; 1934.

[48] Marshall J, Newcombe F. Patterns of paralexia: A psycholinguistic approach. *J Psycholinguistic Res.* 1973;2:175-199.

[49] Newcombe F, Marshall JC. On psycholinguistic classifications of the acquired dyslexias. *Bull Ort Soc.* 1981;31:29-46.

[50] Coltheart M, Patterson K, Marshall JC. *Deep Dyslexia.* 2nd ed. London: Routledge; 1987.

[51] Patterson KE, Marshall JC, Coltheart M. *Surface Dyslexia.* London: Lawrence Erlbaum; 1985.

[52] Bub D, Cancelliere A, Kertesz A. Whole-word and analytic translation of spelling to sound in a non-semantic reader. In: Patterson KE, Marshall JC, Coltheart M, eds. *Surface Dyslexia.* London: Lawrence Erlbaum; 1985:15-34.

[53] Coltheart M. Cognitive neuropsychology and the study of reading. In: Posner MI, Marin OS, eds. *Attention and Performance XI.* Hillsdale: Lawrence Erlbaum; 1985:3-37.

[54] Morton J, Patterson K. A new attempt at an interpretation, or, an attempt at a new interpretation. In: Coltheart M, Patterson K, Marshall JC, eds. *Deep Dyslexia.* 2nd ed. London: Routledge; 1987:91-118.

[55] Beauvois MF, Dérouesné J. Phonological alexia: three dissociations. *J Neurol Neurosurg Psychiatry.* 1979;42:1115-1124.

[56] Friedman RB. Acquired alexia. In: Boller F, Grafman J, eds. *Handbook of Neuropsychology.* Vol. 1. Amsterdam: Elsevier; 1988:377-391.

[57] Sasanuma S, Ito H, Patterson K, Ito T. Phonological alexia in Japanese: A case study. *Cogn Neuropsychol.* 1996;13:823-848.

[58] Coltheart M. Phonological dyslexia: past and future issues. *Cogn Neuropsychol.* 1996;13:749-762.

[59] Dérouesné J, Beauvois MF. Phonological processing in reading: data from alexia. *J Neurol Neurosurg Psychiatry.* 1979;42:1125-1132.

[60] Derouesné J, Beauvois M-F. The "phonemic" stage in the nonlexical reading. In: Patterson KE, Marshall JC, Coltheart M, eds. *Surface Dyslexia.* London: Lawrence Erlbaum; 1985:399-457.

[61] Patterson K. Reading, writing and rehabilitation: a reckoning. In: Riddoch MJ, Humphreys GW, eds. *Cognitive Neuropsychology and Cognitive Rehabilitation.* Hove: Lawrence Erlbaum; 1994:425-447.

[62] Patterson K, Shewell C. Speak and spell: dissociations and word-class effects. In: Coltheart M, Sartori G, Job R, eds. *The Cognitive Neuropsychology of Language.* Hillsdale: Lawrence Erlbaum; 1987:273-294.

[63] Vanier M, Caplan D. CT scan correlates of surface dyslexia. In: Patterson KE, Marshall JC, Coltheart M, eds. *Surface Dyslexia.* London: Lawrence Erlbaum; 1985:511-525.

[64] Friedman RB, Ween JE, Albert ML. Alexia. In: Heilmann KM, Valenstein E, eds. *Clinical Neuropsychology.* 3rd ed. New York: Oxford University Press; 1993:37-62.

[65] Marin OSM. CAT scans of five deep dyslexic patients. In: Coltheart M, Patterson K, Marshall JC, eds. *Deep Dyslexia.* 2nd ed. London: Routledge; 1987:452-456.

[66] Price CJ, Howard D, Patterson K, Warburton EA, Friston KJ, Frackowiak RSJ. A functional neuroimaging description of two deep dyslexic patients. *J Cogn Neurosci.* 1998;10:303-315.

[67] Sakurai Y. Varieties of alexia from fusiform, posterior inferior temporal and posterior occipital gyrus lesions. *Behav Neurol.* 2004;15:35-50.

[68] Koyanagi K, Ishikawa S, Ohkubo Y, Ishii E. The familiarity values of Japanese three-letter nouns. *Shinrigaku Kenkyu.* 1959;30:357-365 (in Japanese).

[69] Akita K. Single-letter association to each letter in the Numeral, the Alphabet and the Katakana. *Shinrigaku Kenkyu.* 1967;38:215-232 (in Japanese).

[70] Sakurai Y, Momose T, Iwata M, et al. Kanji word reading process analysed by positron emission tomography. *Neuroreport.* 1992;3:445-448.

[71] Sakurai Y, Momose T, Iwata M, Watanabe T, Ishikawa T, Kanazawa I. Semantic process in kana word reading: activation studies with positron emission tomography. *Neuroreport.* 1993;4:327-330.

[72] Sakurai Y, Momose T, Iwata M, Ishikawa T, Sato T, Kanazawa I. Regional cerebral blood flow in the covert reading of kana words: A comparison with the study of reading aloud tasks. *Eur Neurol.* 1996;36:237-239.

[73] Sakurai Y, Momose T, Iwata M, Sudo Y, Ohtomo K, Kanazawa I. Different cortical activity in reading of Kanji words, Kana words and Kana nonwords. *Cogn Brain Res.* 2000;9:111-115.

[74] Sakurai Y, Momose T, Iwata M, et al. Cortical activation in reading assessed by region of interest-based analysis and statistical parametric mapping. *Brain Res Protocols.* 2001;6:167-171.

[75] Sakurai Y, Momose T, Iwata M, Sudo,Y, Ohtomo K, Kanazawa I. Cortical activity associated with vocalization and reading proper. *Cogn Brain Res.* 2001;12:161-165.

[76] Funnell E, Davison M. Lexical capture: a developmental disorder of reading and spelling. *Quart J Exp Psychol.* [A] 1989;41:471-487.

[77] Patterson K, Suzuki T, Wydell TN. Interpreting a case of Japanese phonological alexia: the key is in phonology. *Cogn Neuropsychol.* 1996;13:803-822.

[78] Coltheart M. Deep dyslexia: a review of the syndrome. In: Coltheart M, Patterson K, Marshall JC, eds. *Deep Dyslexia.* 2nd ed. London: Routledge; 1987:22-47.

[79] Beringer K, Stein J. Analyse eines Falles von "Reiner" Alexie. *Z ges Neurol Psychiat.* 1930;123:472-478.

[80] Buxbaum LJ, Coslett HB. Deep dyslexic phenomena in a letter-by-letter reader. *Brain Lang.* 1996;54:136-167.

[81] Friston KJ, Holmes AP, Worsley KJ, Poline J-P, Frith CD, Frackowiak RSJ.Statistical parametric maps in functional imaging: a general linear approach. *Hum Brain Mapp.* 1995;2:189-210.

[82] Fiez JA, Petersen SE. Neuroimaging studies of word reading. *Proc Natl Acad Sci USA.* 1998; 95:914-921.

[83] Price CJ. The functional anatomy of word comprehension and production. *Trends Cogn Sci.* 1998; 2:281-288.

[84] Turkeltaub PE, Eden GF, Jones KM, Zeffiro TA. Meta-analysis of the functional neuroanatomy of single-word reading: method and validation. *Neuroimage.* 2002;16:765-780.

[85] Talairach J, Tournoux P. Co-planar *Stereotaxic Atlas of the Human Brain.* Stuttgart: Thieme; 1988.

[86] Sergent J, Zuck E, Lévesque M, MacDonald B. Positron emission tomography study of letter and object processing: Empirical findings and methodological considerations. *Cereb Cortex.* 1992;2:68-80.

[87] Price CJ, Wise RJ, Watson JD, Patterson K, Howard D, Frackowiak RS. Brain activity during reading. The effects of exposure duration and task. *Brain.* 1994;117:1255-1269.

[88] Bookheimer SY, Zeffiro TA, Blaxton T, Gaillard W, Theodore W. Regional cerebral blood flow during object naming and word reading. *Hum Brain Mapp.*1995;3:93-106.

[89] Price CJ, Wise RJ, Frackowiak RS. Demonstrating the implicit processing of visually presented words and pseudowords. *Cereb Cortex.* 1996;6:62-70.

[90] Puce A, Allison T, Asgari M, Gore JC, McCarthy G. Differential sensitivity of human visual cortex to faces, letterstrings, and textures: a functional magnetic resonance imaging study. *J Neurosci.*1996;16:5205-5215.

[91] Herbster AN, Mintun MA, Nebes RD, Becker JT. Regional cerebral blood flow during word and nonword reading. *Hum Brain Mapp.* 1997;5:84-92.

[92] Fiez JA, Balota DA, Raichle ME, Petersen SE. Effects of lexicality, frequency, and spelling-to-sound consistency on the functional anatomy of reading. *Neuron.* 1999;24:205-218.

[93] Hagoort P, Indefrey P, Brown C, Herzog H, Steinmetz H, Seitz RJ. The neural circuitry involved in the reading of German words and pseudowords: a PET study. *J Cogn Neurosci.* 1999;11:383-398.

[94] Tagamets MA, Novick JM, Chalmers ML, Friedman RBA. Parametric approach to orthographic processing in the brain: an fMRI study. *J Cogn Neurosci*, 2000;12:281-297.

[95] Büchel C, Price C, Friston K. A multimodal language region in the ventral visual pathway. *Nature*. 1998;394:274-277.

[96] Moore C J, Price CJ. Three distinct ventral occipitotemporal regions for reading and object naming. *Neuroimage*. 1999;10:181-192.

[97] Sakurai Y. Positron emission tomography scans on kanji and kana. *Shinkeikenkyu no Shinpo* 2002;46:875-882 (in Japanese).

[98] Damasio H, Grabowski TJ, Tranel D, Hichwa RD, Damasio AR. A neural basis for lexical retrieval. *Nature*. 1996;380:499-505.

[99] Reicher GM. Perceptual recognition as a function of meaningfulness of stimulus material. *J Exp Psychol.* 1969;81:275-280.

[100] Seidenberg MS, McClelland JL. A distributed, developmental model of word recognition and naming. *Psychol Rev.* 1989;96:523-568.

[101] Rapcsak SZ, Rothi LJG, Heilman KM. Phonological alexia with optic and tactile anomia: a neuropsychological and anatomic study. *Brain Lang.* 1987;31:109-121.

[102] Caramazza A, Miceli G, Silveri MC, Laudanna A. Reading mechanisms and the organization of the lexicon: Evidence from acquired dyslexia. *Cogn Neuropsychol.* 1985;2:81-114.

[103] Beauregard M, Chertkow H, Bub D, Murtha S, Dixon R, Evans A. The neural substrates for concrete, abstract, and emotional word lexicon: a positron emission tomography study. *J Cogn Neurosci.* 1997; 9:441-461.

[104] Cohen L, Dehaene S, Naccache L, et al. The visual word form area: spatial and temporal characterization of an initial stage of reading in normal subjects and posterior split-brain patients. *Brain*. 2000;123:291-307.

[105] Henderson VW, Friedman RB, Teng EL, Weiner JM. Left hemisphere pathways in reading: Inferences from pure alexia without hemianopia. *Neurology*. 1985;35:962-968.

[106] Warrington EK, Shallice T. Word-form dyslexia. *Brain*. 1980;103:99-112.

[107] Rosati G, De Bastiani P, Aiello V, Agnetti V. Alexia without agraphia: a study of a case of verbal alexia without accompanying colour-naming defect. *J Neurol.* 1984;231:20-25.

[108] Leegaard OF, Riis JØ, Andersen G. "Pure alexia" without hemianopia or colour anomia. *Acta Neurol Scand.* 1988;78:501-505.

[109] Behrmann M, Black SE, Bub D. The evolution of pure alexia: A longitudinal study of recovery. *Brain Lang.* 1990;39:405-427.

[110] Coslett HB, Saffran EM, Greenbaum S, Schwartz H. Reading in pure alexia. The effect of strategy. *Brain*. 1993;116:21-37.

[111] Friedman RB, Lott SN. Rapid word identification in pure alexia is lexical but not semantic. *Brain Lang.* 2000;72:219-237.

[112] Bub D, Black SE, Howell J, Kertesz A. Speech output processes and reading. In: Colheart M, Sartori G, Job R, eds. *Cognitive Neuropsychology of Language*. Hilsdale: Lawrence Erlbaum; 1987:79-110.

[113] Friedman RB, Kohn SE. Impaired activation of the phonological lexicon: effects upon oral reading. *Brain Lang*. 1990;38:278-297.

[114] Patterson K, Marcel A. Phonological ALEXIA or PHONOLOGICAL Alexia ? In: Alegria J, Holender D, Junça de Morais J, Radeau M, eds. *Analytic Approaches to Human Cognition*. Amsterdam: Elsevier; 1992:259-274.

[115] Friedman RB. Two types of phonological alexia. *Cortex*. 1995;31:397-403.

[116] Yamadori A. Alexia with agraphia. *Shinkeinaika*. 1979;10:428-436 (in Japanese).

[117] Ducarne B, Bergego C, Gardeur D. Alexie "sous-angulaire" et signes neuropsychologiques associes: etude clinique et tomodensitometrique. *Cortex*. 1983;19:115-123.

[118] Schweiger A, Zaidel E. Right hemisphere contribution to lexical access in an aphasic with deep dyslexia. *Brain Lang*. 1989;37:73-89.

[119] Glosser G, Friedman RB. The continuum of deep/phonological alexia. *Cortex*. 1990;26:343-359.

[120] Hayashi MM, Ulatowska HK, Sasanuma S. Subcortical aphasia with deep dyslexia: a case study of a Japanese patient. *Brain Lang*. 1985;25:293-313.

[121] Sakurai Y, Momose T, Watanabe T, Bando M, Ishikawa T, Iwata M. Slowly progressive fluent aphasia: clinical features and an imaging study including MRI, SPECT and PET. *Rinshoshinkeigaku* 1991;31:505-511 (in Japanese).

[122] Hodges JR, Patterson K, Oxbury S, Funnell E. Semantic dementia. Progressive fluent aphasia with temporal lobe atrophy. *Brain*. 1992;115:1783-1806.

[123] Neary D, Snowden JS, Gustafson L, et al. Frontotemporal lobar degeneration: a consensus on clinical diagnostic criteria. *Neurology*. 1998;51:1546-1554.

[124] Imura T. Aphasia, its characteristics in the Japanese language. *Seishinshinkeigaku Zasshi*. 1943;47:196-218 (in Japanese).

[125] Patterson K, Suzuki T, Wydell T, Sasanuma S. Progressive aphasia and surface alexia in Japanese. *Neurocase*. 1995;1:155-165.

[126] Coltheart M, Curtis B, Atkins P, Haller M. Models of reading aloud: Dual-route and parallel-distributed-processing approaches. *Psychol Rev*. 1993;100:589-608.

[127] McCarthy RA and Warrington EK. *Cognitive neuropsychology*. San Diego: Academic Press; 1990.

[128] Iwata, M. Neuropsychological aspects of pure alexia syndrome. *Shinkei Kenkyu no Shinpo*. 1997;21:930-940 (in Japanese).

[129] Shallice T, Saffran E. Lexical processing in the absence of explicit word identification: evidence from a letter-by-letter reader. *Cogn Neuropsychol*. 1986;3: 429-458.

[130] Warrington EK, Shallice T. Semantic access dyslexia. *Brain*. 1979;102:43-63.

[131] Bub DN, Black S, Howell J. Word recognition and orthographic context effects in a letter-by-letter reader. *Brain Lang*. 1989; 6:357-376.

[132] Plaut DC, McClelland JL, Seidenberg MS, Patterson K. Understanding normal and impaired word reading: Computational principles in quasi-regular domains. *Psychol Rev*. 1996;103:56-115.

[133] Plaut DC, Shallice T. Deep dyslexia: A case study of connectionist neuropsychology. *Cogn Neuropsychol.* 1993;10:377-500.

[134] Besner D, Twilley L, McCann RS, Seergobin K. On the association between connectionism and data: Are a few words necessary? *Psychol Rev.* 1990;97:432-446.

[135] Mayall K, Humphreys G. A connectionist model of alexia: covert recognition and case mixing effects. *Br J Psychol.*1996;87:355-402.

[136] Plaut DC. A connectionist approach to word reading and acquired dyslexia: extension to sequential processing. *Cogn Sci.* 1999;23:543-568.

[137] Behrmann M, Plaut DC, Nelson J. A literature review and new data supporting an interactive account of letter-by-letter reading. *Cogn Neuropsychol.* 1998; 15:7-51.

[138] Grossman M, Nakada T. A letter is a letter is a letter. Pure alexia for kana. *Neurology.* 2001;56:699-701.

In: Trends in Dyslexia Research
Editor: Henry D. Tobias, pp. 223-244

ISBN 1-59454-219-8

Chapter IX

THE NEUROBIOLOGICAL BASIS OF DEVELOPMENTAL DYSLEXIA-CURRENT FINDINGS AND AREAS OF FUTURE RESEARCH

Wolfgang Lenhard**, *Alexandra Lenhard, and Erwin Breitenbach
University of Würzburg, Germany

ABSTRACT

A growing body of evidence suggests that developmental dyslexia might arise from impaired information processing, which is based on neural deficiencies. During the last 15 years, research on the neurobiological basis of dyslexia has dealt mainly with 3 different issues of interest: The first one concerns abnormal morphological findings like unusual asymmetries of the temporal plana and deviations of the corpus callosum and cerebellum. The second one concentrates on the analysis of abnormal activation patterns of the left hemispherical frontal and temporal lobe, namely, of the angular gyrus and the Broca's area. Researchers assume that these unusual patterns are connected with phonological deficits. The third one refers to global impairments of subcortical systems that might play a major role in the development of dyslexia. An aberration of magno-cells of the geniculate nucleus is supposed to affect rapid information processing, which results in phonemic discrimination and awareness difficulties.

In summary, the evidence for a relation between unusual asymmetries of the temporal plana and dyslexia seems to be very modest at best. A decision between the second and the third approach is beyond the scope of the available empirical data. It still remains unclear whether the information processing deficit is restricted to phonology only, or if there is a general deficit of rapid information processing.

* Correspondence concerning this article should be addressed to Wolfgang Lenhard, Institute for Special Education, Wittelsbacherplatz 1, 97072 Würzburg, Germany. Electronic mail may be sent to: wolfgang.lenhard@mail.uni-wuerzburg.de.

In the middle ages and far into modern times, literacy was regarded as an extraordinary ability. Nowadays, in western culture every adult spends about two hours per day reading - especially at work - and approximately 90 % of all jobs require literacy (Klicpera & Gasteiger-Klicpera 1995, p. 5). At the beginning of the last century, different authors— mainly physicians— independently of each other mentioned dyslexia for the first time. For example, Hinshelwood (1900) described this phenomenon as "poor reading and spelling in the absence of any other academic problems" and termed it "word blindness". At this time, the presumed causes were lesions in the field of the angular gyrus (Freund, 1889), birth traumata (Fisher, 1910), prenatal disease and deficient development during the embryonic stage (Hinshelwood, 1917). In particular, the role of the angular gyrus was discussed, since a lesion in this region results in alexia.

Medical literature of the beginning 20th century distinguished between a congenital and an acquired form of dyslexia (Pickle, 1998). Since then, the discrepancy between reading and spelling abilities on the one hand and intelligence on the other hand has served as a diagnostic criterion of developmental dyslexia. In recent times, this procedure has been subject to strong criticism because of the generally weak correlations between reading and spelling abilities and IQ ratios (Fletcher, Francis, Rourke, B. A. Shaywitz, & S. E. Shaywitz, 1992; Siegel, 1992; Stanovich, 1991). The discussion mainly concentrates on the question, whether diagnosis of dyslexia via IQ ratios is adequate or whether more reasonable classification systems should be applied. According to Zielinski (1998, p. 108), the insufficient definition represents an artificial psychometric construct of dubious utility. S. E. Shaywitz, Fletcher, and B. A. Shaywitz (1996), as well complain about the lack of empirical evidence:

> For too many years, the road to the identification of a reading disability has been littered with artificial barriers requiring children (and adults) to meet arbitrarily imposed criteria such as those requiring an ability-achievement discrepancy. Moreover, and of most concern, we now know that these definitions more often served administrative needs than reflected valid biological underpinning. (p. 213)

So far, however, it is unclear whether developmental dyslexia should be regarded as a deficit or as a developmental lag (Francis, S. E. Shaywitz, Stuebing, B. A. Shaywitz, & Fletcher, 1996). In the latter case, developmental dyslexia just represents the lower section of the normal distribution of reading ability in the total population and, therefore, does not justify a discrepancy-based diagnosis (Francis et al., 1996).

Whether there are distinguishable subgroups of children with poor reading and spelling abilities and which diagnostic criteria should be employed in this case is not yet sufficiently clarified (Fletcher et al., 1997; Francis et al., 1996; Morris et al., 1998; S. E. Shaywitz, Fletcher, et al., 1996; Stanovich, Siegel, Gottardo, Chiappe, & Sidhu, 1997). Therefore, almost all studies draw on the discrepancy-based definition. Nevertheless, a distinction between different subgroups may be crucial for the assignment of different aetiologies underlying each subgroup. Only few research groups completely refuse the distinction between "ordinary" poor readers and diagnosed dyslexics (S. E. Shaywitz et al., 1998; Nagarajan et al., 1999). Others rely, for example, on the distinction between surface- and phonological dyslexia as defined by the dual route theory (Castles & Coltheart, 1993; Coltheart, Curtis, Atkins, & Haller, 1993; Spinelli et al., 1997).

Current research on the neurobiological correlates of developmental dyslexia is dominated by three distinct approaches: First, following the work of Galaburda, Sherman, Rosen, Aboitiz, & Geschwind (1985), who observed unusual asymmetries of the temporal plana of dyslectic persons in post mortem studies, researchers have looked for relations between brain morphology and the occurrence of developmental dyslexia. Second, based on the findings of research involving imaging technologies, other scientists (e.g., S. E. Shaywitz, 1998) attribute dyslexia to the impairment of higher cognitive processes of speech processing. They assume that deficits are caused by a defective phonological module. The third approach asserts that dyslexia is due to deficits in lower sub-cortical systems involved in visual and auditory information processing which subsequently impair higher cognitive functions. This hypothesis is based on histological findings in the area of the lateral and medial geniculate nucleus, as well as on psycho-physiological observations.

Supporters of both the second and third approaches agree with the fact that developmental dyslexia is a consequence of phonological weakness. However, they localise the "true" cause of developmental dyslexia on different stages of information processing (Miles & Stelmack, 1994).

Anatomical and Histological Findings in the Region of the Plana Temporalia, the Corpus Callosum and Cerebellum

Throughout the last century, researchers reported anatomical asymmetries of the brain, but until the 1960's these insights were largely ignored. In 1968, Geschwind and Levitsky discovered an asymmetry of the temporal planum—a triangular region on the upper surface of the temporal lobe within the sylvian fissure—with the left temporal planum being larger than the right one. They interpreted this finding as the neurobiological substrate of the lateralisation of language in the brain. Geschwind and Levitsky found the asymmetry in about 65 % of the adult population (see also Morgan & Hynd, 1998; Rumsey, Donohue, et al. 1997).

In the 1980's, Galaburda and colleagues (Galaburda et al., 1985; Galaburda, 1989) examined the brains of seven young deceased developmental dyslexics. They found an unusual asymmetry of the temporal plana, specifically, an enlargement towards the right temporal lobe in all seven brains. Furthermore, abnormal cell groups (neuronal ectopias) were discovered in the left-hemispherical inferior frontal and superior temporal gyrus (Schultz et al., 1994). Whether the sample in Galaburda's studies is representative of dyslexics in general remains in doubt (Beaton, 2002).

Since an asymmetry of the temporal plana can already be observed in foetal and neonatal brains (Neuhäuser, 1994; Schultz et al., 1994), these findings led to the assumption that dyslexics show abnormal brain development during the prenatal stage (Rumsey, Donohue, et al., 1997). Furthermore, Galaburda (1989) concluded that developmental dyslexia is related to unusual morphology of the temporal plana, even if the symmetry or reversed asymmetry of the brain regions themselves is not classified as pathological. Recently, anomalies of the corpus callosum and cerebellum became a focus of research as well.

Reversed Asymetries and Unusual Symmetries of the Plana Temporalia

Recent in-vivo studies, particularly those using magnetic resonance tomography (MRI), have only partly acknowledged the findings of Galaburda (1989) or even produced contradictory results (Morgan & Hynd, 1998). Schultz et al. (1994) examined 14 dyslectic and 14 non-dyslectic, right-handed children aged between 7.5 and 9.7 years. MRI sagital images of the temporal and parietal lobes were taken. Using the MRI data, the volumes and surface areas of various brain structures were estimated. Additionally, the researchers calculated an asymmetry index of the surfaces of the temporal plana. Initially, multiple significant differences between the control and experimental group were found, but non of the effects remained significant when the statistical analysis controlled for age. An insignificant mean difference of about three months of age was thus responsible for the ostensible relations between diagnosis (dyslexic versus control) and brain morphology.

Another MRI study was carried out by Rumsey, Donohue, et al. (1997). In the same way as Schultz et al. (1994), they determined the volumes and surfaces of the temporal and parietal plana and calculated asymmetry indices for these brain regions. They could replicate the results of Geschwind and Levitsky (1968), but did not find unusual asymmetries in the brains of dyslectic persons. Eckert et al. (2003) also failed to reproduce unusual asymmetries or size for the temporal lobes, including the temporal plana and Heschl's gyri (primary auditory cortex). Measures of the temporal lobe did not differentiate between dyslexics and controls.

In contrast to the aforementioned studies, Dalby, Elbro, & Stødkilde-Jørgsen (1998) measured the length of the lateral fissura, the volume of the subcortical part of the temporal lobes and the volume of the entire temporal lobes of normally talented adolescents, dyslexics (discrepancy between IQ and reading performance) and adolescents with generally poor reading abilities (without IQ discrepancy). The group of dyslexics showed significantly more symmetry or a reversed asymmetry of the temporal lobes compared to both other groups.

In summary, the evidence for a relation between unusual asymmetries of the temporal plana and dyslexia seems to be very modest at best. The different studies have yielded contradictory findings, and most researchers were not able to reproduce the unusual asymmetries first reported by Galaburda and colleagues (Galaburda et al., 1985; Galaburda, 1989). The results of Schultz et al. (1994) indicate that morphological aberrations may be the consequence of other confounding variables like age or sex. Most likely, reversed asymmetries of the temporal lobes are neither the cause for developmental dyslexia, nor predictors of individual performance in reading and spelling.

The Corpus Callosum and Developmental Dyslexia

Due to the discussion about the symmetry or asymmetry of the temporal plana, the corpus callosum has become a focus of research (Rumsey, 1996). Since the right-hemispherical temporal lobe of dyslectic persons is presumably enlarged, some researchers assumed alterations in the size of the splenium (posterior situated fifth part of the corpus callosum), because the commisural fibers of the left and right temporal lobe cross this region (Rumsey, 1996). Contrary to these presumptions, Hynd et al. (1995) discovered in their MRI studies significant differences in the size of the genu (anterior situated fifth part of the corpus callosum), but not in the size of the splenium. The cross sectional area of the genu was on average 25% smaller in the dyslexics.

Using different methods for statistical shape analysis, von Plessen et al. (2002) reported a shorter corpus callosum in dyslectic children, which was due to a shorter posterior midbody region, whereas the genu seemed to be normal. According to the authors, dyslexics presumably fail to undergo the massive myelination in this region during reading acquisition.

The Cerebellar Defict Hypothesis

Recently, a new perspective was brought up by Nicolson, Fawcett and Dean (1995). Based on the fact that many dyslectic children exhibit problems in motor skills, automation and other tasks that include cerebellar involvement, Fawcett and Nicolson (1999) suggested that a mild cerebellar dysfunction might cause many of these problems. They have proposed a motor theory of speech perception, which views dyslexia as the result of articulatory deficits, problems in the automation of skill and knowledge and motor skill impairments (Nicolson & Fawcett, 1990; Nicolson, Fawcett, & Dean, 2001a, 2001b). According to their approach, impairments of several distinct routes accumulate to a phonological core deficit. Nicholson et al. (2001a) suggest that cerebellar deficits constitute an alternative and perhaps parallel mechanism to magnocellular abnormality, which is discussed later.

In line with this assumption, several groups of researchers observed morphological deviations within the cerebellum of dyslexics. Rae et al. (2002) reported morphometric differences in the ratios of the grey matter of the left and right cerebellar hemispheres. In contrast to the controls, who showed a larger right hemisphere, dyslexics were found to have symmetric cerebellar grey matter. Moreover, Rae et al. (1998) found significantly altered biochemical metabolite ratios within the right, but not the left, hemisphere of the cerebellum. These changes are indicative of altered patterns of cell density in the cerebellum of dyslectic individuals. Most likely this finding is due to smaller numbers of large neurons. This finding was confirmed by Eckert et al. (2003). Male dyslexics exhibited significantly smaller right cerebellar anterior lobes as well as smaller inferior temporal lobes as compared to controls. Using these distinguishing features, Eckert et al. correctly classified about 80 % of the participants.

Finch, Nicolson, and Fawcett (2002) re-examined the post-mortem tissue that was studied by Galaburda et al. (1985) years before. They investigated the morphology of the cerebellum and its connections, especially the constituents of the olivio-cerebello-dentate pathway, which they considered to be the major cerebellar-subcortical structure involved in language-related tasks. Finch et al. (2002) report fewer small cells and more large cells in the cerebellum and in the inferior olive of dyslexics compared to controls, but they did not find any significant differences in cerebellar asymmetry.

At the moment, there is a controversial debate whether a cerebellar deficit is the cause, correlate or consequence of developmental dyslexia. Moreover, it remains questionable whether this specific deficit exists at all (Beaton, 2002; Bishop, 2002). While different authors agree that many of the difficulties of developmental dyslexics are consistent with a cerebellar deficit, multiple alternative explanations stand to reason (Beaton, 2002; Bishop, 2002; Ivry & Justus, 2001; Zeffiro & Eden, 2001). Therefore, at present the cerebellar deficit hypothesis and especially the motor theory of speech perception remain speculative.

Neurophysiological und –Psychological Findings Concerning Cortical Processes of Speech Perception

In recent years, many studies have been published which used new imaging techniques, above all positron emission tomography (PET) and functional magnetic resonance tomography (fMRI). The aim of these studies was to find differences in the activation patterns of higher cortical speech processing systems in dyslectic as compared to non-dyslectic persons (e.g., Fulbright et al., 1997; Paulesu et al., 1996; Pugh et al., 1996; Pugh et al., 1997; Pugh et al., 2000; Rumsey et al., 1994; Rumsey, Nace, et al., 1997; Rumsey et al., 1999; B. A. Shaywitz et al., 1996; S. E. Shaywitz, B. A. Shaywitz, et al., 1996; S. E. Shaywitz et al., 1998; Horwitz, Rumsey, & Donohue, 1998; Ruff, Cardebat, Marie, & Démonet, 2002). The so-called subtraction paradigm was employed in all these studies. This means that activation patterns observed during a complex activity (e.g., reading) are subtracted from the activation patterns measured during a state of rest or non-specific activity, for example, during the fixation of a cross in the center of a screen. Some studies (S. E. Shaywitz et al., 1998; Pugh et al., 1996; Georgiewa et al., 1999) used more complex subtraction mechanisms, in which the activity patterns of several hierarchical tasks were subtracted from each other. By means of this procedure, researchers attempt to identify differences in the activation patterns of different cognitive subprocesses (e.g., orthographic, phonological and lexical/semantic subprocesses of reading, Pugh et al., 1996).

This procedure entails many potential difficulties. The main point of criticism is the assumption that the addition or removal of a cognitive operation from a complex task leaves the other operations unaffected. A good deal of research in cognitive neuropsychology challenges the conception of serial and unidirectional information processing in the human brain. Instead it suggests that all components of these systems are extremely interactive (Pugh et al., 1996; Rumsey, 1996). Thus, the addition or removal of a single operation can highly influence the way in which the whole neural network structure functions. By contrast, the research of activation patterns using this subtraction paradigm is based on the assumption of a strictly hierarchically organised system of information processing (see also the discussion between Poeppel 1996a, 1996b and Démonet, Fiez, Paulesu, Petersen, & Zatorre, 1996). However, despite of its methodological problems, this approach has improved our understanding of developmental dyslexia.

Phonological information processing involves a complex interaction of different brain structures (Démonet et al., 1996). PET studies found activation samples of the left hemisphere in Brodman area 21 (inferior and medial temporal gyrus), area 22/42 (Wernike's area), area 39 (angular gyrus), area 40 (supramarginal gyrus), area 44 (inferior frontal gyrus, Broca's area), and in further frontal and temporal-parietal areas (see Poeppel, 1996a). Although the results vary strongly in dependence of the experimental design, they are all consistent with traditional neurological models of speech processing. Roughly speaking, according to Geschwind's model (1972), form and pattern of visual information during reading is processed within the primary and secondary visual cortex and is then forwarded to the angular gyrus. This region is regarded as the reading center within the human brain. Subsequently, the information is passed on to Wernicke's area, the "sensory language center" and finally—via the Fasciculus arcuatus—transmitted into Broca's area, the "motor language center". From there, depending on the task setting, the information takes its way to the appropriate brain regions (Trepel, 1999, p. 222).

Activation Centers and Levels during Reading

In their fMRI studies, Pugh et al. (1996, 1997), Fullbright et al. (1997), B. A. Shaywitz et al. (1996) and S. E. Shaywitz, B. A. Shaywitz, et al. (1996) observed the reading process of normal reading persons and could thus confirm numerous results of the lesion research. In order to discover neurological correlates of different components of the reading process (visual-spatial, orthographic, phonological and lexical-semantic operations), they applied a complex system of hierarchical subtraction mechanisms. For each component, they found an involvement of various networks in left-hemispherical brain regions (Fulbright et al., 1997). During orthographic processing (e.g., detection of letters), the extra striate regions (Brodman area 18, 19) in the occipital lobe play a particularly important role (Pugh et al., 1996). Phonological recoding especially activates the inferior frontal gyrus (and to a smaller extent also the superior and medial frontal gyrus, Pugh et al., 1996). The most interesting result was observed during lexical-semantic decoding. Namely, a network of cortical structures of the temporal lobe seems to be involved in it (medial temporal gyrus, superior frontal gyrus; Pugh et al., 1996) but in addition a strong activation of the inferior frontal gyrus was also observed during this task. Seemingly, the lexical-semantic component does not function independently of the orthographic component but rather relies on it. According to Pugh et al. (1996), these insights have important implications for models of the reading process, particularly the dual route theory. There seems to be no lexical (direct) access without simultaneous activation of phonological recoding strategies (indirect route). The researchers assume that the inferior frontal gyrus operates in a multi-functional way: "[We] assume that this system is relevant to both assembling a phonological representation from print and to transferring this information into short-term store ". According to S. E. Shaywitz (1997) and Fulbright et al. (1997) these results suggest that developmental dyslexia will finally be traced to a purely phonological deficit.

In another fMRI study, S. E. Shaywitz et al. (1998) compared the activation patterns of dyslectic and non-dyslectic readers and applied the same system of subtraction mechanisms. The non-dyslectic readers showed an increase in activity with an increase in task difficulty in a large posterior area within the left hemisphere, including Wernike's area, the angular gyrus, and the extrastriate and striate cortex. There was no comparable increase in activity observable within the dyslectic readers. S. E. Shaywitz et al. (1998) interpret these findings as the neurobiological basis of an insufficiently developed phonological consciousness and the inability to segment words into their single phonemes. Instead, dyslexics showed a systematic over-activation of frontal brain structures, in particular the inferior frontal gyrus. The researchers suggested that this over-activation could be due to greater effort during reading and, therefore, be an indication of compensative efforts. The finding that the dyslectic readers showed a substantially weaker and more unsystematic increase of activity in the range of the angular gyrus confirms the results of traditional lesion research, according to which a lesion in this area usually leads to an alexia (Birbaumer & Schmidt, 1996, p. 406).

The results of Rumsey, Nace, et al. (1997) and Rumsey et al. (1999) point into a similar direction: In comparison to the control group, dyslexics showed substantially more zones of activation and deactivation, whereby the activity patterns rather differed in intensity than localisation. Rumsey, Nace, et al. (1997) likewise underline the significant roles of the inferior temporal gyrus and the entire temporal lobe of the left hemisphere in processing orthographical and phonological tasks. Besides, they found different correlations between reading ability and the intensity of the activation of the left-hemispherical angular gyrus in non-dyslectic as compared to dyslectic readers. In non-dyslectic readers, the correlation was highly positive, whereas it was highly negative in dyslexics. Therefore, a high activity within the range of the angular gyrus rather seems to disturb the reading process in dyslexics (Rumsey et al., 1999). With reference to S. E. Shaywitz et al. (1998), Rumsey and colleagues (1999) interpret their results as a confirmation of the hypothesis that a disturbance within the range of the left-hemispherical angular gyrus might cause developmental dyslexia.

Georgiewa et al. (1999) used a similar design as S.E. Shaywitz et al. (1998) and found a significantly stronger activation of the Broca's area and the left-hemispherical inferior temporal gyrus in non-dyslectic children during a phonological transformation task. However, there were no differences during reading of regular german words. Therefore, they assumed deficiencies in the processing of compound phonological units, for example, in connection with grapheme-phoneme-correspondences, but no deficits in the processing of phonologically regular words.

Developmental Dyslexia as a Phenomenon of Functional Disconnection

Some researchers view developmental dyslexia as a disconnection-syndrome and thus examined the hypothesis that, in the long run, dyslexia is due to the separation of different brain areas: Similarly to Pugh et al. (1996), Paulesu and colleagues (1996) used a system of various tasks and subtraction mechanisms in order to examine activation patterns during different phonological operations (phonological short-term memory and phonological similarity judgement) by means of PET. In contrast to normal readers, dyslexics displayed no activation of the left insula. Furthermore, the synchronization of the activated brain regions was weak as compared to the controls. On the basis of these results and other preceding studies, Paulesu et al. suggested that the inferior frontal gyrus functions as a rehearsal system whose the task is limited to the processing of individual phonemes. The supramarginal gyrus is estimated to play an important role in phonological short-term memory and sections of the superior temporal gyrus seem to process assembled phonological units on the basis of whole words. Thereby, the insula might function as a bridge between the two brain regions.

According to Paulesu et al., a lack of activation in this region leads to the separation of the anterior and posterior language regions of the temporal and frontal lobes.

Horwitz et al. (1998) pursued another approach. They used PET images to correlate the intensity of activation in different left-hemispherical areas with each other. A high correlation between the brain activity of different frontal and temporal regions and the activity of the angular gyrus was observed in normal readers. The dyslectic participants, however, showed very poor correlations. According to Horwitz and colleagues, the absence of functional connections of the angular gyrus with corresponding brain regions—in particular the inferior frontal gyrus and the superior temporal gyrus—in dyslexics is compatible with models of the reading process in acquired dyslexia.

Pugh et al. (2000) likewise analysed correlations between the activity of different brain regions and the angular gyrus. Only under conditions, which required phonological abilities, dyslexics did not show correlations between the activity of the left-hemispherical angular gyrus and other ipsilaterale posterior areas. The correlation of the right-hemispherical areas did not differ from the control group. Furthermore, the authors found no differences in tasks that did not depend on phonological abilities. Pugh et al. interpreted these results as a confirmation of their hypothesis that dyslexia is the consequence of a specific phonological deficit.

To summarize, although the observations of individual groups of researchers differ in detail, the use of imaging techniques has corroborated the results of the traditional lesion research. All quoted studies report deviated activation patterns, which can be interpreted within the context of traditional lesion research. However, these results do not necessarily permit conclusions about the cause of developmental dyslexia, nor do they lead to potential approaches for therapy.

A handicap of some of the older studies was the examination of grown-up dyslexics only, because their findings could as well be attributed to compensatory strategies. However, newer studies, for example, Corina et al. (2001), Georgiewa et al. (1999, 2002) and B. A. Shaywitz et al. (2002) focused on children and teenagers and replicated the before mentioned results. Meanwhile, there is evidence, that deficiencies of the neural system of dyslexics are already present within the first grades in elementary school. According to B. A. Shaywitz et al. (2002), developmental dyslexia in children must be seen within the same framework as developmental dyslexia and acquired dyslexia in adults.

It has to be noted, though, that findings in children at the age of 8 may not easily be transferred to pre-school-age children. After all, acquisition of reading and spelling leads to functional restructuring within neural networks (Chase, 1996; Castro-Caldas, Petersson, Reis, Stone-Elander, & Ingvar, 1998). Altered activation patterns may therefore reflect consequences of a failure in this restructuring process instead of being the true cause of developmental dyslexia.

Another point of criticism is the limited temporal and spatial resolution of imaging technologies (Poeppel, 1996a; Chase, 1996; Bookheimer & Dapretto, 1996).

DYSFUNCTIONS OF BASIC INFORMATION PROCESSING

Within the first half of the 20th century, researchers favoured the hypothesis that deficits of visual information processing lead to developmental dyslexia. Orton (1925), for example, assumed that these individuals suffered from a neuro-visual deficit based on insufficient lateralisation and hemispherical dominance in the brain. This concept was displaced by models of information processing that emphasized disturbed language processing (Näslund, 1994). In the meantime, the connection between a lack of phonological awareness and developmental dyslexia has been well estabelished (Bradley & Bryant, 1978; Liberman, Shankweiler, Fischer, & Carter, 1974; Schneider, 1997; Zielinski, 1998; Wimmer, 1996). The hypothesis of deficient processes of visual and auditory perception nevertheless has been brought up again (Eden, VanMeter, Rumsey, & Zeffiro, 1996), because the mechanisms underlying deficits in phonological awareness remain unclear.

The Transient Visual System

Since permanent use is made of the visual perception system during reading and writing, disturbed processes of perception can have a major impact on performance. Visual confusion (e.g., letter reversal, distortion, blurring and superimposition) can complicate the reading process and the visual-linguistic integration of information (Stein & Walsh, 1997; Eden, VanMeter, Rumsey, & Zeffiro, 1996).

Initially, research in this field concentrated on the observation of temporal resolution of visual stimuli, for example, via the use of flicker fusion rates (Martin & Lovegrove, 1987). By means of the method of limits, the temporal resolution capability of the visual system can be determined as a function of the spatial solution of the visual stimulus: The finer grained the visual stimulus, the lower the temporal resolution (Lovegrove, Heddle, & Slaghuis, 1980). For this purpose, researchers normally use gratings with sinusoidal varying luminescence.

Martin and Lovegrove (1987) observed a characteristic decrease of the flicker fusion frequency in dyslexic children. It was possible to differentiate between dyslexics and controls on the basis of this frequency. Moreover, approximately 75% of the dyslectic children showed a slower increase of the temporal resolution capability when stimuli with gradually reduced spatial resolution were presented (Lovegrove et al., 1980). These findings were repeatedly confirmed (Demb, Boynton, Best, & Heeger, 1998; Eden, Stein, H. M. Wood, & F. B. Wood, 1995; Lovegrove, 1993; Slaghuis & Ryan, 1998). However, other researchers failed to reproduce them (Barnard, Crewther, & Crewther, 1998; Gross-Glenn et al., 1995; Johannes, Kussmaul, Münte, & Mangun, 1996; Kronbichler, Hutzler, & Wimmer, 2002; Williams, Stuart, Castles, & McAnally, 2003). Bednarek and Grabowski (2002) found an oversensitivity to luminance contrast of low spatial gratings in developmental dyslexics. Farrag, Kehdr, and Abel-Naser (2002) reported prolonged P100 latency of visual evoked potentials in response to stimuli of low spatial frequency but not in response to stimuli of high spatial frequency.

Interestingly, Borsting et al. (1996), Slaghuis and Ryan (1998), and Spinelli et al. (1997) only observed a reduced temporal capability in dyslectic children who had problems with segmenting and analysing words (i.e., children with a phonological deficit) but not in dyslectic children without phonological problems. These findings point to a possible relationship between insufficiencies in the temporal resolution of rapid visual stimuli and phonological deficits. In contrast to these studies, Williams et al. (2003) reported different outcomes of contrast sensitivity tasks. Neither in the dyslectic group, nor in phonological subgroups of developmental dyslexics they found general deficits in magnocellular functioning.

Lovegrove (1993) interprets the results of his studies in the context of neuropsychological models of visual perception processing and stresses the role of two different subsystems, namely, the transient and sustained system. The transient visual system is characterised by high transmission rates and reacts predominantly to movements. The sustained system on the other hand is sensitive for visual stimuli of high spatial frequency.

The neuronal equivalent for these two functional subsystems can be found in the parvocellular and the magnocellular fibres (organised in six different layers) of the lateral geniculate nucleus, a thalamic body (Birbaumer & Schmidt, 1996, p. 392). The parvocells are small cells that transmit information concerning colour, shape and detail from the central fovea to the visual cortex in the occipital lobe (Wittmann & Pöppel, 1999). The magnocells have large, fast transmitting axons that convey information about brightness contrasts from the movement fields distributed across the entire retina (Kolb & Wishaw, 1993, p. 63; Birbaumer & Schmidt, 1996, p. 391).

Electrophysiological measurements have revealed that the magnocells are characterized by substantially higher transmission rates than the parvocells. Therefore, the magnocells can react much more quickly to fast moving stimuli. Altogether, the parvocellular pathways process visual stimuli of low temporal frequency and high spatial detail, whereas the magnocellular pathways process stimuli of high temporal frequency and low spatial complexity (Wittmann & Pöppel, 1999).

In post-mortem studies, Galaburda and Livingstone (1993) found characteristic differences between non-impaired and dyslectic persons within the area of the lateral geniculate nucleus: The magnocells of the dyslectic persons were on average 27% smaller and more variable in form and size. Furthermore, Galaburda, Menard and Rosen (1994) examined the medial geniculate nucleus, the thalamic body of the auditory system, and also discovered deformations of the magnocells.

By the use of fMRI, Eden, VanMeter, Rumsey, Maisog, et al. (1996) verified these phenomena in living persons as well. They examined responses to stimuli of low contrast and high temporal frequency in the V5/mt area—a part of the magnocellular pathways and the primary visual cortex. Bilateral activity in this area was observed in the normal readers but in only one of the dyslectic participants. However, both dyslectic and normal readers showed identical activation patterns in the primary and secondary visual cortex (V1 and V2) while looking at static stimuli. This points to a normal function of the parvocellular system. Demb, Boynton, & Heeger (1999) could replicate most of these findings. They also used fMRI in order to measure the activation patterns in the entire occipital lobe. In comparison to controls, dyslexics showed reduced activity within the range of MT+ and V1 on test conditions that addressed particularly the magnocellular fibres (low spatial in connection with high temporal resolution and low brightness). Those subjects who showed intense brain activity within the range of V1 and MT+ in this condition had a superior speed of reading and better temporal resolution capability. However, on test conditions that addressed the parvocellular fibres, there were no differences. Both Eden, VanMeter, Rumsey, Maisog, et al. (1996) and Demb et al. (1999) interpret their results as confirmation of the hypothesis that a magnocellular defect leads to a disturbance of the processing of rapid stimuli which in turn causes developmental dyslexia.

Possibly, a weakness of the magnocells could negatively affect the occulomotor system. The interaction of magnocellular and parvocellular pathways is fundamental for the effectiveness of the reading process. Reading is characterized by an interrelation of fixations and saccades. During a fixation, the parvocellular system can efficiently process the form and pattern of stimuli that are projected stably on the fovea. This is ensured by their functional characteristic of high spatial resolution. By contrast, the magnocells process information about the rough position of the stimuli on the entire retina. This is of crucial importance to fixate the relevant objects by means of a saccadic eye movement. Activated by a fast modificaton of the image on the retina, the magnocellular pathways suppress any activity within the parvocellular layers. Otherwise, the slow electrophysiological characteristics of the parvocellular pathways would lead to the interference of two subsequently fixated visual stimuli, for example, two sections of a text. If this tuning is not successful because of weak magnocellular fibres, the images on the retina acquired during successive saccades can no longer be separated clearly (Wittmann & Pöppel, 1999). A suboptimal position of letters on the fovea due to a lack of spatial guidance can occur as well (Stein & Walsh, 1997). The resulting visual confusions can cause letter reversal, distortion, blurring and superimposition and, therefore, complicate the reading process considerably.

It has repeatedly been shown that the saccades of dyslectic children are substantially less precise and more variable in speed compared with the saccades of children of the same age (Biscaldi, Fischer, & Aiple, 1994; Biscaldi, Gezeck, & Stuhr, 1998; Fischer, Biscaldi, & Hartnegg, 1998). Other aspects of the occulomotor system of dyslectic children as, for example, vergence and fixation control, are equally impaired (Demb et al., 1998; Eden, Stein, H. M. Wood, & F. B. Wood, 1994; Eden et al., 1995). Still further investigation is needed to corroborate the idea that these findings can be explained by a magnocellular impairment. However, it is obvious that imprecise eye movements complicate the reading process (Biscaldi et al., 1994).

Auditory Information Processing

Galaburda et al. (1994) examined the medial geniculate nucleus of five dyslectic and seven control brains. In the dyslectic sample, the neurons on the left side were significantly smaller than those on the right, whereas the controls showed no asymmetry. Moreover, the neurons were generally smaller and their size was more variable than those of the control sample. The brains had already been studied by Galaburda and Livingstone (1993) and showed aberrations in other regions as well, for example, in the lateral geniculate nucleus. However, the small size of the sample of five dyslectic and seven control brains does not permit a generalisation of the results. On the other hand, the findings are consistent with a variety of reported behavioural deficits concerning auditory information processing.

Whereas there is substantial support for a general deficit in visual perception and control of saccadic eye movements, it remains unclear whether there is a general auditory dysfunction as well. The current discussion is dominated by two different hypotheses: The first one assumes that the phonological processing of consonants and vowels at a segmental level constitutes the core deficit in developmental dyslexia. The second hypothesis focuses on deficits of discrimination abilities of rapid acoustic stimuli or even a general dysfunction of temporal information processing across modalities and argues that this can give rise to at least some subtypes of developmental dyslexia. In the light of this approach the well documented phonological processing deficits are just an epiphenomenon.

Tallal (1980) first introduced the concept of deficient processing of rapid acoustic stimuli to the field of specific language impairments (SLI) and dyslexia (Rosen & Manganari, 2001). Tallal and colleagues were convinced that it is necessary to start with the examination of basic auditory functions before higher order speech deficits are taken into consideration (Tallal, Miller, & Fitch, 1993). They analysed the performance of children with SLI and with dyslexia in a variety of tests. Children with SLI as well as those developmental dyslexics with a phonological deficit showed characteristic problems in the identification of rapidly presented sinusoidal tones of different frequency. If the interstimulus interval (ISI) of two tones was shorter than 350 ms, the performance of the impaired children dramatically decreased. They could no longer discriminate whether two sounds in rapid succession had different frequencies or not. These results were replicated by Reed (1989).

Nagarajan et al. (1999) examined the processing of rapid sequences of tones by means of magneto-encephalography (MEG) and found the same characteristic impairment. They assumed that this was due to an unusual strong and long lasting post stimulus inhibition in dyslexics, which resulted in drastically reduced discrimination ability if the ISI was 200 ms and less.

Schulte-Körne, Reimel, Bartling, & Remschmidt (1998) studied the mismatch negativity (MMN) in response to speech and tone stimuli. The MMN is a negative component of event related potentials (ERP), which is elicited automatically (i.e., without active participation of the listener) about 100 to 300 ms after the presentation of unexpected stimuli. Compared to the control sample, dyslectic children showed an attenuated MMN in response to speech, but not to tone stimuli. According to Schulte-Körne et al. (1998), these results disprove the hypothesis of general auditory deficits in dyslexics and instead indicate a pre-attentive speech perception dysfunction. Kujala et al. (2000) used the same paradigm in order to measure the neural activity in pre-attentive auditory stimulus discrimination. They presented pairs and sequences of tones with deviant stimuli differing from the standard-stimuli only in the length of the ISIs. In accordance with Schulte-Körne et al. (1998), there was no difference in the MMN in response to the pairs of tones between dyslectic and normal adults. The MMN in response to sequences, however, revealed a major difference: In the control sample, the deviant tone sequences elicited two consecutive MMN, while the dyslexic subjects totally lacked the first MMN. This finding again supports the hypothesis of a basic nonlinguistic auditory-information processing deficit in dyslexic individuals.

Other researchers (e.g., Mody, Studdert-Kennedy, & Brady, 1997; Rosen & Manganari, 2001; Share, Jorm, MacLean, & Matthews, 2002) found conflicting results. Their studies are consistent with a speech-specific but not with a general auditory deficit. Rosen and

Manganari (2001) underline "that an auditory deficit is neither necessary nor sufficient to cause dyslexia. This, of course, does not mean, that a general auditory deficit could not be a contributing factor for dyslexia in a subset of children". By contrast, Wolff (2002) observed inordinate difficulty of dyslexics in reproducing simple rhythms by finger tapping. They also showed difficulties in reproducing a rhythmic order of nonsense syllables—especially when they had to synchronize their performance to an external metronome. These results point to an even more extended deficit in temporal perception processing. An alternative explanation for the heterogeneous results may be the lack of selective attention to visual and auditory stimuli (Facoetti et al., 2003; Hari & Renvall, 2001).

Interestingly, hemispherical differences in the ERPs following linguistic and non-linguistic auditory stimuli have been found for newborns with and without risks for developmental dyslexia. For example, Molefese (2000) reported differences in the automatic processing of acoustic stimuli, which were already present at birth. In a longitudinal study, he examined the ERPs of 186 newborns evoked by linguistic and non-linguistic stimuli and repeated his investigation annually. At the age of eight, 17 children turned out to be developmental dyslexics, and 7 had a general reading disability. Using six different measures of peak latency and baseline to peak amplitudes of the ERPs recorded at birth, he was able to calculate a discriminant function that correctly predicted reading and spelling problems at the age of eight. The function identified 22 of the 24 dyslectic or poor reading children, whereas 19 of 24 randomly chosen children were rejected. If this approach turns out to be reliable in prospective studies, the risk for developmental dyslexia could be diagnosed at a very early age with a better chance of effective intervention and remediation.

In line with this study, Guttorm, Leppänen, Richardson and Lyytinen (2001) reported differences between newborns with and without familial risk for dyslexia in mean event-related brain responses to various consonant-vowel-syllables. Clear hemispherical differences were seen in responses to the syllable /ga/. The high-risk group showed stronger positivation in the right hemisphere at latencies between 50 and 170 ms, which possibly reflects diminished desynchronisation of brain activity. Rippon and Brunswick (2000) as well observed a general absence of task-related desynchronisation and a stronger right-hemispherical activation that characterised the EEG of dyslectic children at the age of ten during a phonological processing task.

The effects that a magnocellular defect may excert on auditory perception processing have not yet been clarified. This is, among other reasons, due to the fact that the auditory system has received very little investigative attention in comparison to the visual system (Kolb & Wishaw, 1993, p. 66). According to Tallal and colleagues (Tallal et al., 1993; Tallal, Miller, Jenkins, & Merzenich, 1997), deficits of the magnocells, in the end, may lead to an impaired ability to segment and discriminate speech sounds. This in turn may distort the development of phonological and orthographic representations that are essential for the acquisition of reading and spelling.

Conclusion

The majority of the mentioned studies are consistent with the hypothesis of the occurrence of developmental dyslexia in connection with a general deficit of information processing. A conceivable explanation for conflicting results could possibly lie in the confounding of different subgroups.

In summary, the evidence for a relation between unusual asymmetries of the temporal plana and dyslexia appears to be very modest. By contrast, a growing body of evidence suggests that developmental dyslexia might arise from impaired information processing that is based on neural deficiencies. However, whether the information processing deficit is restricted to phonology or a general deficit of rapid information processing, is yet to be resolved.

Author Note

Wolfgang Lenhard, Institute for Special Education, University of Würzburg, Germany; Alexandra Lenhard, Istuitute for Psychology, University of Würzburg, Germany; Erwin Breitenbach, Institute for Special Education, University of Würzburg, Germany.

Correspondence concerning this article should be addressed to Wolfgang Lenhard, Institute for Special Education, Wittelsbacherplatz 1, 97072 Würzburg, Germany. Electronic mail may be sent to: wolfgang.lenhard@mail.uni-wuerzburg.de.

References

Barnard, N., Crewther, S. G., & Crewther, D. P. (1998). Development of a magnocellular function in good and poor primary school-age readers. *Optometry and Vision Science, 75,* 62-68.

Beaton, A. (2002). Dyslexia and the cerebellar deficit hypothesis. *Cortex, 38,* 479–490.

Bednarek, D. & Grabowski, A. (2002). Luminance and chromatic contrast sensitivity in dyslexia: the magnocellular deficit hypothesis revisited. *Neuroreport, 13,* 2521–2525.

Birbaumer, N. & Schmidt, R. F. (1996). *Biopsychologie* [Biopsychology]. Berlin, Germany: Springer.

Biscaldi, M., Fischer, B., & Aiple, F. (1994). Saccadic eye movements of dyslexic and normal reading children. *Perception, 23,* 45–64.

Biscaldi, M., Gezeck, S., & Stuhr, V. (1998). Poor saccadic control correlates with dyslexia. *Neuropsychologia, 36,* 1189–1202.

Bishop, D. (2002). Cerebellar abnormalities in developmental dyslexia: cause, correlate or consequence? *Cortex, 38,* 491–498.

Bookheimer, S. Y. & Dapretto, M. (1996). Functional Neuroimaging of Language in Children: Current Directions and Future Challenges. In R. W. Thatcher, G. R. Lyon, J. Rumsey, & N. Krasnegor (Eds.), *Developmental Neuroimaging: Mapping the Development of Brain and Behavior* (pp.157–167). San Diego: Academic Press.

Borsting, E., Ridder III, W. H., Dudeck, K., Kelley, C., Matsui, L., & Motoyama, J. (1996). The Presence of a Magnocellular Defect Depends on the Type of Dyslexia. *Vision Research, 36,* 1047–1053.

Bradley, L. & Bryant, P. (1978). Difficulties in auditory organisation as a possible cause of reading backwardness. *Nature, 271,* 746-747.

Castles, A. & Coltheart, M. (1993). Varieties of developmental dyslexia. *Cognition, 47,* 149–180.

Castro-Caldas, A., Petersson, K. M., Reis, A., Stone-Elander, S., & Ingvar, M. (1998). The illiterate brain - Learning to read and write during childhood influences the functional organisation of the adult brain. *Brain, 121,* 1053–1063.

Chase, C. H. (1996). Neurobiology of Learning Disabilities. *Seminars in Speech and Language, 17,* 173–181.

Coltheart, M., Curtis, B., Atkins, P. & Haller, M. (1993). Models of reading aloud: dual-route and parallel-distributed-processing approaches. *Psychological Review, 100,* 589–608.

Corina, D. P., Richards, T. L., Serafini, S., Richards, A. L, Steury, K., Abbott, R. D., Echelard, D. R. Maravilla, K. R., & Berninger, V. W. (2001). fMRI auditory language differences between dyslexic and able reading children. *Brain Imaging, 12,* 1195-1201.

Dalby, M. A., Elbro, C., & Stødkilde-Jørgsen, H. (1998). Temporal Lobe Asymmetry and Dyslexia: An in Vivo Study Using MRI. *Brain and Language, 62,* 51–69.

Demb, J. B., Boynton, G. M., Best, M., & Heeger, D. J. (1998). Psychophyssical evidence for a magnocellular pathway deficit in dyslexia. *Vision Research, 38,* 1555–1559.

Demb, J. B., Boynton, G. M. & Heeger, D. J. (1999). Functional Magnetic Resonance Imaging of Early Visual Pathways in Dyslexia. *The Journal of Neuroscience, 18,* 6939–6951.

Démonet, J. F., Fiez, J. A., Paulesu, E., Petersen, S. E., & Zatorre, R. J. (1996). PET Studies of Phonological Processing: A Critical Reply to Poeppel. *Brain and Language, 55,* 352–379.

Eckert, M., Leonard, C., Richards, T., Aylward, E., Thomson, J., & Berninger, V. (2003). Anatomical correlates of dyslexia: frontal and cerebellar findings. *Brain, 126,* 482–494.

Eden, G. F., Stein, J. F., Wood, H. M., & Wood, F. B. (1994). Differences in Eye Movements and Reading Problems in Dyslexic and Normal Children. *Vision Research, 34,* 1345–1358.

Eden, G. F., Stein, J. F., Wood, H. M., & Wood, F. B. (1995). Verbal and Visual Problems in Reading Disability. *Journal of Learning Disabilities, 26,* 227–290.

Eden, G. F., VanMeter, J. W., Rumsey, J. M., Maisog, J. M., Woods, R. P., & Zeffiro, T. A. (1996). Abnormal processing of visual motion in dyslexia revealed by functional brain imaging. *Nature, 382,* 66–69.

Eden, G. F., VanMeter, J. W., Rumsey, J. M., & Zeffiro, T. A. (1996). The Visual Deficit Theory of Developmental Dyslexia. *Neuroimage, 4,* 108–117.

Facoetti, A., Lorusso, M., Paganoni, P., Cattaneo, C., Galli, R., Umiltà, C., & Mascetti, G. (2003). Auditory and visual automatic attention deficits in developmental dyslexia. *Cognitive Brain Research, 16,* 185–191.

Farrag, A. F., Khedr, E. M., & Abel-Naser, W. (2002). Impaired parvocellular pathway in dyslexic children. *European Journal of Neurology, 9,* 359–363.

Fawcett, A., & Nicolson, R. (1999). Performance of Dyslexic Children on Cerebellar and Cognitive Tests. *Journal of motor behavior, 31*, 68–79.

Finch, A., Nicolson, R., & Fawcett, A. (2002). Evidence for a neuroanatomical difference within the olivo-cerebellar pathway of adults with dyslexia. *Cortex, 38,* 529–539.

Fisher, J. H. (1910). Congenital word blindness. *Transactions of the ophthalmological societies of the United Kingdom, 30,* 216.

Fischer, B., Biscaldi, M., & Hartnegg, K. (1998). Die Bedeutung der Blicksteuerung bei der Lese-Rechtschreib-Schwäche [The importance of saccadic control in dyslexia]. *Sprache - Stimme – Gehör, 22,* 18–24.

Fletcher, J. M., Francis, D. J., Rourke, B. P., Shaywitz, B. A., & Shaywitz, S. E. (1992). The validity of discrepancy-based definitions of reading disabilities. *Journal of Learning Disabilities, 25,* 546 – 548.

Fletcher, M., Morris, R., Lyon, G., Stuebing, K., Shaywitz, S. E., Shankweiler, D., Katz, L., Shaywitz, B. A. (1997). Subtypes of Dyslexia: An Old Problem Revisited. In B. Blachman (Ed.), *Foundations of reading acquisition and dyslexia: implications for early intervention* (pp.115–141). New Jersey: Erlbaum.

Francis, D. J., Shaywitz, S. E., Stuebing, K. K., Shaywitz, B. A., & Fletcher, M. (1996). Developmental Lag Versus Deficit Models of Reading Disabilities: A Longitudinal, Individual Growth Curve Analysis. *Journal of Educational Psychology, 88,* 3–17.

Freund C. (1889).Über optische Aphasie und Seelenblindheit [About optical aphasia and blindness of the soul]. *Archiv von Psychiatrie und Nervenkrankheiten, 20,* 276-297.

Fullbright, R. K., Shaywitz, S. E., Shaywitz, B. A., Pugh, K. R., Skudlarski, P., Constable, T., Fletcher, J. M., Liberman, A. M., Shankweiler, D. P., Katz, L., Lacadie, C., Bronen, R. A., Marchione, K. E., & Gore, J. C. (1997). Neuroanatomy of Reading and Dyslexia. *Child and Adolescent Psychiatric Clinics of North America, 6,* 431–445.

Galaburda, A. M. (1989). Ordinary and extraordinary brain development: Anatomical variations in developmental dyslexia. *Annals of Dyslexia, 39,* 67-80.

Galaburda, A. & Livingstone, M. (1993). Evidence for a Magnocellular Defect in Developmental Dyslexia. In P. Tallal, A. M. Galaburda, R. R. Llinás, & C. von Euler (Eds.), *Temporal Information Processing in the Nervous System: Special Reference to Dyslexia and Dysphasia* (pp.70-82). New York: The New York Academy of Sciences.

Galaburda, A., Menard, M. T., & Rosen, G. D. (1994). Evidence for aberrant auditory anatomy in developmental dyslexia. *Proceedings of the National Academy of Sciences of the United States of America, 91,* 8010-8013.

Galaburda, A. M., Sherman, G. F., Rosen, G. D., Aboitiz, F., & Geschwind, N. (1985) Developmental dyslexia: Four consecutive patients with cortical anomalies. *Annals of Neurology, 18,* 222-233.

Georgiewa, P., Rzanny, R., Gaser, C., Gerhard, U-J., Vieweg, U. Freesmeyer, D., Mentzel, H-J., Kaiser, A.A., & Blanz, B. (2002). Phonological processing in dyslexic children: a study combining functional imaging and event related potentials. *Neuroscience Letters, 318,* 5-8

Georgiewa, P., Rzanny, R., Hopf, J. M., Knab, R., Glauche, V., Kaiser, W. A., & Blanz, B. (1999). fMRI during word processing in dyslexic and normal children. *Neuroreport, 10,* 3459–3465.

Geschwind, N. (1972). Language and the brain. *Scientific american, 226,* 76–83.

Geschwind, N. & Levitsky, W. (1968). Left-right asymmetries in temporal speech region. *Science, 161,* 186-187.

Gross-Glenn, K., Skottun, B. C., Glenn, W., Kushch, A., Lingua, R., Dunbar, M., Jallad, B., Lubs, H. A., Levin, B., Rabin, M., Parke, L., & Duara, R. (1995). Contrast sensitivity in dyslexia. *Visual Neuroscience, 12,* 153–163.

Guttorm, T., Leppänen, P., Richardson, U., & Lyytinen, H. (2001). Event-Related Potentials and Consonant Differentiation in Newborns with Familial Risk for Dyslexia. *Journal of Learning Disabilities, 34,* 534-544.

Hari, R. & Renvall, H. (2001). Impaired processing of rapid stimulus sequences in dyslexia. *Trends in Cognitive Sciences, 5,* 525–532.

Hinshelwood, J. (1900). Congenital word-blindness. *Lancet, 1,* 1506–1508.

Hinshelwood, J. (1917). *Congenital word blindness.* London: Lewis.

Horwitz, B., Rumsey, J. M., & Donohue, B. C. (1998). Functional connectivity of the angular gyrus in normal reading and dyslexia. *Proceedings of the National Academy of Sciences of the USA, 95,* 8939–8944.

Hynd, G. W., Hall, J., Novey, E. S., Eliopolus, D., Black, K., Gonzalez, J. J., Edmonds, J. E., Riccio, C., & Cohen, M. (1995). Dyslexia and Corpus Callosum Morphology. *Archives of Neurology, 52,* 32–38.

Ivry, R. & Justus, T. (2001). A neural instantiation of the motor theory of speech perception. *Trends in Neuroscience, 24,* 513–515.

Johannes, S., Kussmaul, C. L., Münte, T. F., & Mangun, G. R. (1996). Developmental dyslexia: Passive visual stimulation provides no evidence for a magnocellular processing defect. *Neuropsychologia, 34,* 1123–1127.

Klicpera C. & Gasteiger-Klicpera, B. (1995). *Psychologie der Lese-Rechtschreib-schwierigkeiten: Entwicklung, Ursachen, Förderung* [Psychology of dyslexia: development, causes and support]. Weinheim, Germany: Psychologie Verlags Union.

Kolb, B. & Whishaw, I. Q. (1996). *Neuropsychologie* [Neuropsychology]. Heidelberg, Germany: Spektrum Akademischer Verlag.

Kronbichler, M., Hutzler, F., & Wimmer, H. (2002). Dyslexia: Verbal impairments in the absence of magnocellular impairments. *Neuroreport, 13,* 617–620.

Kujala, T., Myllyviita, K., Tervaniemi, M., Alho, K., Kallio, J., & Näätänen, R. (2000). Basic auditory dysfunction in dyslexia as demonstrated by brain activity measurements. *Psychophysiology, 37,* 262–266.

Liberman, I. Y., Shankweiler, D., Fischer, F. W., & Carter, B. (1974). Explicit syllable and phoneme segmentation in the young child. *Experimental Child Psychology, 18,* 461–569.

Lovegrove, W. (1993). Weakness in the Transient Visual System: A causal Factor in Dyslexia? In P. Tallal, A. M. Galaburda, R. R. Llinás, & C. von Euler (Eds.), *Temporal Information Processing in the Nervous System: Special Reference to Dyslexia and Dysphasia* (pp.57–69). New York: The New York Academy of Sciences.

Lovegrove, W., Heddle, M., & Slaghuis, W. (1980). Reading diability: Spacial frequency specific deficits in visual information store. *Neuropsychologia, 18,* 111–115.

Martin, F. & Lovegrove, W (1987). Flicker contrast sensitivity in normal and specifically disabled readers. *Perception, 16*, 203–214.

Miles, J. & Stelmack, R. (1994). Learning disability subtypes and the effects of auditory and visual priming on visual event-related potentials to words. *Journal of Clinical & Experimental Neuropsychology, 16,* 43-64.

Mody, M., Studdert-Kennedy, M., & Brady, S. (1997). Speech perception deficits in poor readers: auditory processing or phonological coding? *Journal of experimental child psychology, 64,* 199–231.

Molfese, D. L. (2000). Predicting Dyslexia at 8 Years of Age Using Neonatal Brain Responses. *Brain and Language, 72,* 238–245.

Morgan, A. E. & Hynd, G. W. (1998). Dyslexia, Neurolinguistic Ability, and Anatomical Variation of thc Planum Temporale. *Neuropsychology Review, 8,* 79–93.

Morris, R. D., Stuebing, K. K., Fletcher, J. M., Shaywitz, S. E., Lyon, G. R., Shankweiler, D. P., Katz, L., Francis, D. J. & Shaywitz, B. A. (1998). Subtypes of Reading Disabillity: Variability Around a Phonological Core. *Educational Psychology, 90,* 347–373.

Näslund, J. C. (1994): Understanding literacy and cognition: Trends in psycholinguistic and neuropsychological research. *Zeitschrift für Pädagogische Psychologie, 8,* 139–151.

Nagarajan, S., Mahncke, H., Salz, T., Tallal, P., Roberts, T., & Merzenich, M. M. (1999). Cortical auditory signal processing in poor readers. *Proceedings of the National Academy of Sciences of the USA, 96,* 6483–6488.

Neuhäuser, G. (1994). Hemisphärendominanz und Entwicklungsstörungen [Hemispherical dominance and developmental disorders]. In J. Martinius & H. Amorosa (Eds.), *Teilleistungsstörungen* (pp.20-31). Berlin, Germany: Quintessenz.

Nicolson, R. & Fawcett, A. (1990). Automacity: a new framework for dyslexia research? *Cognition, 35,* 159–182.

Nicolson, R., Fawcett, A., & Dean, P. (1995). Time estimation deficits in developmental dyslexia: evidence of cerebellar involvement. *Proceedings of the Royal Society of London. Series B. Biological sciences, 259,* 43–47.

Nicolson, R., Fawcett, A., & Dean, P. (2001a). Developmental dyslexia: the cerebellar deficit hypothesis. *Trends in Neuroscience, 24,* 508–511.

Nicolson, R., Fawcett, A., & Dean, P. (2001b). Dyslexia, development and the cerebellum. *Trends in Neuroscience, 24,* 515–516.

Orton, S. T. (1925). Word-blindness in school children. *Archives of Neurology and Psychiatry, 14,* 581–615.

Paulesu, E., Frith, U., Snowling, M., Gallagher, A., Morton, J., Frackowiak, R., & Frith, C. (1996). Is developmental dyslexia a disconnection syndrome? Evidence from PET scanning. *Brain, 119,* 143-157.

Pickle, M. J. (1998). Historical Trends in Biological and Medical Investigations of Reading Disabilities: 1850 – 1915. *Journal of Learning Disabilities, 31,* 625–635.

Poeppel, D. (1996a). A Critical Review of PET Studies of Phonological Processing. *Brain and Language, 55,* 317 351.

Poeppel, D. (1996b). Some Remaining Questions about Studying Phonological Processing with PET: Response to Démonet, Fiez, Paulesu, Petersen, and Zatorre (1996). *Brain and Language, 55,* 380–385.

Pugh, K. R., Mencl, W. E., Shaywitz, B. A., Shaywitz, S. E., Fulbright, R. K., Constable, R. T., Skudlarski, P., Marchione, K. E., Jenner, A. R., Fletcher, J. M., Liberman, A. M.,

Shankweiler, D. P., Katz, L., Lacadie, C., & Gore, J. C. (2000). The Angular Gyrus in Developmental Dyslexia: Task-Specific Differences in Functional Connectivity Within Posterior Cortex. *Psychological Science, 11,* 51–56.

Pugh, K. R., Shaywitz, B. A., Shaywitz, S. E., Constable, R. T., Skudlarski, P., Fulbright, R. K., Bronen, R. A., Shankweiler, D. P., Katz, L., Fletcher, J. M., & Gore, J. C. (1996). Cerebral organisation of component processes in reading. *Brain, 119,* 1221–1238.

Pugh, K. R., Shaywitz, B. A., Shaywitz, S. E., Shankweiler, D. P., Katz, L., Fletcher, J. M., Skudlarski, P., Fulbright, R. K., Constable, R. T., Bronen, R. A., Laccadie, C., & Gore, J. C. (1997). Predicting Reading Performance From Neuro-imaging Profiles: The Cerebral Basis of Phonological Effects in Printed Word Identification. *Journal of Experimental Psychology: Human Perception and Performance, 23,* 299–318.

Rae, C., Lee, M. A., Dixon, R. M., Blamire, A. M., Thompson C. H., Styles, P., Talcott, J., Richardson, A. J., & Stein, J. F. (1998). Metabolic abnormalities in developmental dyslexia detected by Sup(1)H magnetic resonance spectroscopy. *Lancet, 351,* 1849–1853.

Rae, C., Harasty, J. A., Dzendrowskyj, T. E., Talcott, J., Simpson, J., Blamire, A., Dixon, R., Lee, M., Thompson, C., Styles, P., Richardson, A., & Stein, J. (2002). Cerebellar morphology in developmental dyslexia. *Neuropsychologia, 40,* 1285–1292.

Reed, M. A. (1989). Speech perception and the discrimination of brief auditory cues in reading disabled children. *Journal of Experimental Child Psychology, 48,* 270-292.

Rippon, G. & Brunswick, N. (2000). Trait and state EEG indices of information processing in developmental dyslexia. *International Journal of Psychophysiology, 36,* 251-265.

Rosen, S. & Manganari, E. (2001). Is There a Relationship Between Speech and Nonspeech Auditory Processing in Children With Dyslexia? *Journal of Speech, Language, and Hearing Research, 44,* 720-736.

Ruff, S., Cardebat, D., Marie, N., & Démonet, J.F. (2002). Enhanced response of left frontal cortex to slowed down speech in dyslexia: an fMRI study. *Brain Imaging, 13,* 1285–1289.

Rumsey, J. M. (1996). Neuroimaging in Developmental Dyslexia: A Review and Conceptualization. In G. R. Lyon & J. M. Rumsey (Eds.), *Neuroimaging: A Window to the Neurological Foundations of Learning and Behavior of Children* (pp.57–78). Baltimore: Paul H. Brookes Publishing Co.

Rumsey, J. M., Andreason, P., Zametkin, A. J., King, A. C., Hamburger, S. D., Aquino, T., Hanahan, A. P., Pikus, A., & Cohen, R. M. (1994). Right Frontotemporal Activation by Tonal Memory in Dyslexia: an O^{15} PET Study. *Biological Psychiatry, 36,* 153–170.

Rumsey, J. M., Donohue, B., Brady, D. R., Nace, K., Giedd, J. N., & Andreason, P. (1997). A Magnetic Resonance Imaging Study of the Planum Temporale Asymmetry in Men With Developmental Dyslexia. *Archives of Neurology, 54,* 1481–1489.

Rumsey, J. M., Horwitz, B., Donohue, B. C., Nace, K. L., Maisog, J. M., & Andreason, P. (1999). A Functional Lesion in Developmental Dyslexia: Left Angular Gyral Blood Flow Predicts Severity. *Brain and Language, 70,* 187–204.

Rumsey, J. M., Nace, K., Donohue, B., Wise, D., Maisog, J. M., & Andreason, P. (1997). A Positron Emission Tomographic Study of Impaired Word Recognition and Phonological Processing in Dyslexic Men. *Archives of Neurology, 54,* 562–573.

Schneider, W. (1997). Rechtschreiben und Rechtschreibschwierigkeiten [Spelling and spelling disabilities]. In F. Weinert (Ed.), *Psychologie des Unterrichts und der Schule* (pp.327–363). Göttingen, Germany: Hogrefe.

Schulte-Körne, G., Reimel, W., Bartling, J., & Remschmidt, H. (1998). Auditory processing and dyslexia: Evidence for a specific speech processing deficit. *Neuroreport, 9,* 337–340.

Schultz, R. T., Cho, N. K., Staib, L. H., Kier, L. E., Fletcher, J. M., Shaywitz, S. E.; Shankweiler, D. P., Katz, L., Gore, J. C., Duncan, J. S., & Shaywitz, B. A. (1994). Brain Morphology in Normal and Dyslexic Children: The Influence of Sex and Age. *Annals of Neurology, 35,* 732–742.

Share, D., Jorm, A., McLean, R., & Matthews, R. (2002). Temporal processing and reading disability. *Reading and Writing, 15,* 151-178.

Shaywitz, B. A., Shaywitz, S. E., Pugh, K. R., Skudlarski, P., Fulbright, R. K., Constable, R. T., Bronen, R. A., Fletcher, J. M., Liberman, A. M., Shankweiler, D. P., Katz, L., Lacadie, C., Marchione, K. E., & Gore, J. C. (1996). Functional Magnetic Resonance Imaging as a Tool to Understand Reading and Reading Disability. In R. W. Thatcher, G. R. Lyon, J. Rumsey & N. Krasnegor (Eds.), *Developmental Neuroimaging: Mapping the Development of Brain and Behavior* (pp.157–167). San Diego: Academic Press.Shaywitz, B. A., Shaywitz, S. E., Pugh, K. R., Mencl, E., Fulbright, R. K., Skudlarski, P., Constable, R. T., Marchione, K. E., Fletcher, J. M., Lyon, G. R., & Gore, J. C. (2002). Disruption of Posterior Brain Systems for Reading in Children with Developmental Dyslexia. *Biological Psychiatry, 52,* 101–110.

Shaywitz, S. E. (1997). Legasthenie—gestörte Lautverarbeitung [Dyslexia—impairment of phonological processing]. *Spektrum der Wissenschaft, 1,* 68–74.

Shaywitz, S. E. (1998). Dyslexia. *The New England Journal of Medicine, 338,* 307–312.

Shaywitz, S. E., Fletcher, J. M. & Shaywitz, B. A. (1996). A conceptual model and definition of dyslexia: findings emerging from the Conneticut Longitudinal Study. In J. H. Beitschman (Ed.), *Language, learning, and behavior disorders: developmental, biological and clinical perspectives* (pp.199–223). Cambridge, United Kingdom: Cambridge University Press.

Shaywitz, S. E., Shaywitz, B. A., Pugh, K. R., Fulbright, R. K., Constable, R. T., Mencl, W.E., Shankweiler, D.P., Liberman, A.M., Skudlarski, P., & Fletcher, J.M. (1998). Functional disruption in the organisation of the brain for reading in dyslexia. *Proceedings of the National Academy of Sciences of the USA, 95,* 2636–2641.

Shaywitz, S. E., Shaywitz, B. A., Pugh, K. R., Skudlarski, P., Fulbright, R. K., Constable, T., Bronen, R. A., Fletcher, J. M., Liberman, A. M., Shankweiler, D. P., Katz, L., Lacadie, C., Marchione, K. E., & Gore, J. C. (1996). The Neurobiology of Developmental Dyslexia as viewed through the Lens of Functional Magnetic Resonance Imaging Technology. In G. R. Lyon & P. Rumsey (Eds.), *Neuroimaging: A Window to the Neurological Foundations of Learning and Behavior of Children* (pp.79–94). Baltimore: Paul H. Brookes Publishing Co.

Siegel, L. S. (1992). An evaluation of the discrepancy definitions of dyslexia. *Journal of learning disabilities, 25,* 618–629.

Slaghuis, W. L. & Ryan, J. F. (1998). Spatio-temporal contrast sensitivity, coherent motion, and visible persistence in developmental dyslexia. *Vision Research, 39,* 651–668.

Spinelli, D., Angelelli, P., De Luca, M., Di Pace, E., Judica, A., & Zoccolotti, P. (1997). Developmental surface dyslexia is not associated with deficits in the transient visual system. *Neuroreport, 8,* 1807–1812.

Stanovich, K., Siegel, L., Gottardo, A., Chiappe, P., & Sidhu, R. (1997). Subtypes of Developmental Dyslexia: Differences in Phonogical and Orthographic Coding. In B. Blachman (Ed.), *Foundations of reading acquisition and dyslexia: implications for early intervention* (pp.115–141). New Jersey: Erlbaum.

Stanovich, K.E. (1991). Discrepancy definitions of reading disabilities: Has intelligence led us astray? *Reading Research Quaterly, 26,* 7–29.

Stein, J. & Walsh, V. (1997). To see, but not to read; the magnocellular theory of dyslexia. *Trends in neurosciences, 20,* 147–152.

Tallal, P. (1980). Auditory temporal perception, phonics and reading disabilities in children. *Brain and Language, 9,* 182-198.

Tallal, P., Miller, S., & Fitch, R. H. (1993). Neurobiological Basis of Speech: A Case for the Preeminence of Temporal Processing. In P. Tallal, A. M. Galaburda, R. R. Llinás, & C. von Euler (Eds.), *Temporal Information Processing in the Nervous System: Special Reference to Dyslexia and Dysphasia* (pp.27–47). New York: The New York Academy of Sciences.

Tallal, P., Miller, S. L., Jenkins, W. M., & Merzenich M. M. (1997). The Role of Temporal Processing in Developmental Language-Based Learning Disorders: Research and Clinical Implications. In B. Blachman (Ed.), *Foundations of reading acquisition and dyslexia: implications for early intervention* (pp.49–66). New Jersey: Erlbaum.

Trepel, M. (1999). *Neuroanatomie: Struktur und Funktion* [Neuroanatomy: structur and function]. München: Urban & Fischer.

Williams, M., Stuart, G. W., Castles, A., & McAnally, K. I. (2003). Contrast sensitivity in subgroups of developmental dyslexia. *Vision Research, 43,* 467-477.

Wimmer, H. (1996). Legasthenie - eine phonologische Störung? [Dyslexia—a phonological disorder?]. In C. Spiel (Ed.), *Motivation und Lernen aus der Perspektive Lebenslanger Entwicklung: Festschrift für Brigitte Rollett* (pp.75-84). Münster, Germany: Waxmann.

Wittmann, M. & Pöppel, E. (1999). Neurobiologie des Lesens [Neurobiology of reading]. In B. Franzmann & G. Jäger, (Eds.), *Handbuch Lesen* (pp.224–239). München, Germany: Saur.

Wolff, P. (2002). Timing precision and rhythm in developmental dyslexia. *Reading and Writing, 15,* 179–206.

von Plessen, K., Lundervold, A., Duta, N, Heiervang, E., Klauschen, F., Smievoll, A., Ersland, L., & Hugdahl, K. (2002). Less developed corpus callosum in dyslexic subjects – a structural MRI study. *Neuropsychologia, 40,* 1035–1044.

Zeffiro, T. & Eden, G. (2001). The cerebellum and dyslexia: perpetuator or innocent bystander? *Trends in Neuroscience, 24,* 512–513.

Zielinski, W. (1998). *Lernschwierigkeiten: Ursachen - Diagnostik – Intervention* [Learning disabilities: causes—diagnosis—intervention]. Stuttgart, Germany: Kohlhammer.

INDEX

A

B

G

H

I

J

K

L

M

N

O

P

Q

R